PATERNOSTER BIBLICAL MONOGRAPHS

Spirit and Kingdom in the Writings of Luke and Paul

An Attempt to Reconcile these Concepts

PATERNOSTER BIBLICAL MONOGRAPHS

A full list of titles in both this series and
Paternoster Theological Monographs
appears at the end of this book

PATERNOSTER BIBLICAL MONOGRAPHS

Spirit and Kingdom in the Writings of Luke and Paul

An Attempt to Reconcile these Concepts

Youngmo Cho

Foreword by Robert P. Menzies

Wipf & Stock
PUBLISHERS
Eugene, Oregon

Wipf and Stock Publishers
199 W 8th Ave, Suite 3
Eugene, OR 97401

Spirit and Kingdom in the Writings of Luke and Paul
An Attempt to Reconcile these Concepts
By Cho, Youngmo
Copyright©2005 Paternoster
ISBN: 1-59752-798-x
Publication date 6/22/2006
Previously published by Paternoster, 2005

This Edition Published by Wipf and Stock Publishers
by arrangement with Paternoster

Paternoster
9 Holdom Avenue
Bletchley
Milton Keyes, MK1 1QR
Great Britain

Unless otherwise stated, Scripture quotations are taken from the
HOLY BIBLE, NEW INTERNATIONAL VERSION
Copyright © 1973, 1978, 1984 by the International Bible Society.
Used by permission of Hodder and Stoughton Limited. All rights reserved.
'NIV' is a registered trademark of the International Bible Society UK trademark
number 1448790

PATERNOSTER BIBLICAL MONOGRAPHS

Series Preface

One of the major objectives of Paternoster is to serve biblical scholarship by providing a channel for the publication of theses and other monographs of high quality at affordable prices. Paternoster stands within the broad evangelical tradition of Christianity. Our authors would describe themselves as Christians who recognise the authority of the Bible, maintain the centrality of the gospel message and assent to the classical credal statements of Christian belief. There is diversity within this constituency; advances in scholarship are possible only if there is freedom for frank debate on controversial issues and for the publication of new and sometimes provocative proposals. What is offered in this series is the best of writing by committed Christians who are concerned to develop well-founded biblical scholarship in a spirit of loyalty to the historic faith.

Series Editors

I. Howard Marshall, Honorary Research Professor of New Testament, University of Aberdeen, Scotland, UK

Richard J. Bauckham, Professor of New Testament Studies and Bishop Wardlaw Professor, University of St Andrews, Scotland, UK

Craig Blomberg, Distinguished Professor of New Testament, Denver Seminary, Colorado, USA

Robert P. Gordon, Regius Professor of Hebrew, University of Cambridge, UK

Tremper Longman III, Robert H. Gundry Professor and Chair of the Department of Biblical Studies, Westmont College, Santa Barbara, California, USA

*To Naan and Hajune for making life a joy
and particularly
to Grace for keeping life meaningful*

Contents

Foreword by Robert P. Menzies		xiii
Acknowledgements		xv
Abbreviations		xvii

Chapter 1
Introduction 1
1.1 A Review of Recent Scholarship 1
1.1.1 *R.P. Menzies* 2
1.1.2 *J.D.G. Dunn* 5
1.1.3 *M.M.B. Turner* 8
1.2 The Thesis 11
1.2.1 *Outline of Study* 12

Chapter 2
The Spirit and Life-Giving Wisdom in Intertestamental Literature 14
2.1 Introduction 14
2.2 The Spirit in the Messianic Traditions 16
2.2.1 *The Nature of the Characteristics of Messianic Figures* 16
2.2.2. The Spirit and Wisdom in the Messianic Tradition in 1 Enoch and the Psalms of Solomon 17
2.3 The Spirit and the 'Life-Giving Wisdom' in Qumran and the Wisdom of Solomon and the Spirit and Extraordinary Wisdom in other Intertestamental Literature 20

2.3.1	*The Spirit and the Life-Giving Wisdom in 1 QH and the Wisdom of Solomon*	21
2.3.2	*The Spirit and Extraordinary Wisdom in Intertestamental Literature*	23
2.3.3	*The Sprit and Extraordinary Wisdom*	28
2.3.4	*The Sprit and Extraordinary Wisdom in Hellenistic Literature*	32
2.3.5	*Summary*	38
2.4	The Spirit in Rabbinic Literature	39
2.4.1	*A Consideration of Anachronism*	40
2.4.2	*The Spirit and Extraordinary Wisdom*	40
2.4.3	*Midr Ps 14:6 and Deut R 6:14: The Removal of Evil Impulse and the Eschatological Outpouring of the Spirit*	43
2.4.4	*Summary*	48
2.5	The Spirit and the Resurrection of the Dead in Jewish Apocalyptic Perspective	48
2.6	Conclusion	51

Chapter 3
The Relationship between the Spirit in Paul and the Kingdom of God in the Synoptics — **52**

3.1	Introduction	52
3.2	Kingdom Terminology in Paul	53
3.2.1	*The Scarcity of References to the Kingdom of God in Paul*	53
3.2.2	*Kingdom of God Sayings in Paul*	55
3.3	Paul's Choice of Spirit Language for the Kingdom of God	61
3.3.1	*Statistical Analysis*	61
3.3.2	*The Eschatological Framework in Paul and the Synoptics*	62
3.3.3	*The Similarity between Life in the Spirit in Paul and Life in the Kingdom in the Synoptics*	68
3.3.4	*Righteousness in Paul and the Synoptics*	90
3.3.5	*Ethics in Paul and the Synoptics*	99
3.3.6	*Summary*	107
3.4	Conclusion	107

Chapter 4
The Spirit and the Blessings of the Kingdom of God in Luke-Acts — 110

4.1	Introduction	110
4.2	The Spirit and Sonship (The Sense of Abba): The Experience of Jesus' Pneumatic Anointing (Lk. 3:21-22; cf. Lk. 11:2; 22:42): A Spirit-given Sonship?	111
4.2.1	*Lukan Redactional Features*	112
4.2.2	*The Messianic Figure of the Heavenly Proclamation and Its Pneumatological Concern*	112
4.2.3	*The Spirit: The Inauguration of Jesus' Sense of Sonship or of the Messianic Task?*	113
4.3	The Spirit and Ethics	116
4.3.1	*The Role of the Spirit-endowed Mighty One: John the Baptist's Prophecy (Lk. 3:16-17)*	117
4.3.2	*The Temptations of Jesus (Lk. 4:1-13)*	122
4.3.3	*Summaries of Community Life (Acts 2:42-47; 4:32-37; cf. 5:12-16)*	128
4.3.4	*Summary*	133
4.4	The Spirit and Resurrection	133
4.4.1	*The Spirit and the Proclamation of the Resurrection*	135
4.5	Salvific or Conversional Experience and the Gift of the Spirit	136
4.5.1	*The Spirit in Luke-Acts (Infancy Narratives): Prophetic or Soteriological?*	136
4.5.2	*Conversion and the Reception of the Spirit*	140
4.5.3	*Summary*	159
4.6	Conclusion	160

Chapter 5
The Primary Role of the Spirit in Relation to the Kingdom of God in Luke-Acts: Proclamation — 162

5.1	Introduction	162
5.2	The Spirit as the Presence of the Kingdom of God?	163
5.2.1	*Luke 11:2*	163
5.2.2	*Luke 12:31-32 (cf. Luke 11:13)*	164
5.2.3	*Luke 11:20*	168

5.2.4	*Summary*	171
5.3	The Spirit and the Proclamation of the Kingdom of God	171
5.3.1	*The Spirit and Jesus' Proclamation of the Kingdom of God (Lk. 4:16-30, 42-44)*	171
5.3.2	*The Spirit and the Church's Proclamation of the Kingdom of God*	178
5.4	Conclusion	194

Chapter 6
Conclusion 196

Bibliography 199

Index of References 213

Index of Authors 224

FOREWORD

It is with a great deal of satisfaction that I commend to the reader this book penned by Youngmo Cho. I have known Youngmo since his student days at Asia Pacific Theological Seminary in Baguio City of The Philippines. Youngmo was a very fine and dedicated student. So, in spite of the challenges of operating in a new culture and a second language, I was not surprised to learn that Youngmo produced this very fine work while pursuing Ph.D. studies at the University of Aberdeen. I congratulate Youngmo on this outstanding achievement. I do believe that his book is important for several reasons.

First, Youngmo has developed an important line of inquiry into the nature of the relationship between the teaching of Jesus, as recorded by Luke, and Paul's theology. His suggestion that Paul's Spirit language conveys much of the import of what Jesus says about life in the Kingdom of God is persuasive in my opinion. In this way, Youngmo highlights a significant thread of continuity that binds together the message of the New Testament.

Secondly, Youngmo's work addresses, in a fresh way, the question of the nature of the development of early Christian pneumatology, a special interest of mine. I believe that Youngmo's thesis challenges us to critically reassess traditional approaches to the early church's understanding of the work of the Spirit - approaches that have largely disregarded its diversity and power. As such, Youngmo's thesis has relevance for the life of the church today as well.

Finally, I believe that Youngmo represents a growing and significant group of emerging Asian New Testament scholars. I am convinced that the next decade will witness a burst of creative theological contributions from this region. Contributions like this will undoubtedly serve to strengthen the church universal. They will help us all understand the biblical text and ourselves better.

Robert P. Menzies
Kunming, China, 2005

ACKNOWLEDGEMENTS

I would like to express my gratitude to several individuals who, in a variety of ways, enabled me to write this book, originally written as a PhD thesis at the University of Aberdeen. I thank my supervisor, Dr. Andrew Clarke. His careful reading and criticism have helped me more than anything. But also his concern and encouragement when faced with difficult times in our family was one of the main reasons for continuing to write this work and finally to complete it. I also wish to express my appreciation to Prof. I. Howard Marshall, who guided me in the early stages of my study. I will treasure his careful and sharp insights for the rest of my scholarly life. I am also deeply grateful to Dr. Robert Menzies who first encouraged me to study in Aberdeen. His teaching combined with the sacrificial lifestyle in APTS has been a great source of inspiration for this work and my Christian life.

I would like to express my gratitude to the publishers for accepting this work in Paternoster Biblical Monographs. I would also like to thank my colleague and PhD student Bhojraj Bhatta for his kind and helpful assistance in revising this work

Finally, and most of all, I would like to thank my wife, Grace (Gyunhee). She has carried the major burden during the long process of this study. In spite of difficult circumstances in many occasions, her encouragement and support have made this study possible. I gratefully dedicate this book to her. I also wish to show my gratitude to my lovely daughter, Naan and my son, Hajune. They have been not only the source of my joy, but have also always reminded me of the father's role in making them good Christians.

Youngmo Cho

ABBREVIATIONS

AB	Anchor Bible
ABD	*Anchor Bible Dictionary*
ANTC	Abingdon New Testament Commentaries
ATR	*Anglican Theological Review*
BCENT	Baker Exegetical Commentary on the New Testament
BibSac	*Bibliotheca Sacra*
BNTC	Black's New Testament Commentaries
BS	The Bible Seminar
CBQ	*Catholic Biblical Quarterly*
CTJ	*Canadian Journal of Theology*
CV	*Communio Viatorum*
DJG	*Dictionary of Jesus and the Gospels*
DLNTD	*Dictionary of the Later New Testament and Its Developments*
DPL	*Dictionary of Paul and His Letters*
EBC	Expositor's Bible Commentary
ExpT	*Expository Times*
EvQ	*Evangelical Quarterly*
EvTh	*Evangelical Theologie*
FRLANT	Forschungen zur Religion und Literatur des Alten und Neuen Testaments
GNS	Good News Studies
HNTC	Harper's New Testament Commentaries
HTR	*Harvard Theological Review*
HTS	*Harvard Theological Studies*
IBS	*Irish Biblical Studies*
ICC	International Critical Commentary
Int	*Interpretation*
JBL	*Journal of Biblical Literature*
JJS	*Journal of Jewish Studies*
JPT	*Journal of Pentecostal Theology*
JPTS	*Journal of Pentecostal Theology* Supplement Series
JSJ	*Journal for the Study of Judaism in the Persian, Hellenistic and Roman Period*
JSNT	*Journal for the Study of the New Testament*

JSNTS	*Journal for the Study of the New Testament* Supplement Series
JSOTS	*Journal for the Study of the Old Testament* Supplement Series
JSPS	*Journal for the Study of the Pseudepigrapha* Supplement Series
LCL	Loeb Classical Library
NAC	The New American Commentary
NCB	New Century Bible
NIBC	New International Biblical Commentary
NICNT	The New International Commentary on the New Testament
NIGTC	The New International Greek Testament Commentary
NovT	*Novum Testamentum*
NovTS	*Novum Testamentum Supplements*
NTS	New Testament Studies
NTT	New Testament Theology
OTP	*Old Testament Pseudepigrapha*
RevQ	*Revue de Qumran*
RQ	*Restoration Quarterly*
SBL	Society of Biblical Literature
SBS	Stuttgarter Bibel-Studien
SBT	Studies in Biblical Theology
SJT	*Scottish Journal of Theology*
SJTOP	*SJT* Occasional Papers
SNTSMS	Society for New Testament Studies Monograph Series
TDNT	*Theological Dictionary of the New Testament*
TJ	*Trinity Journal*
TNTC	Tyndale New Testament Commentaries
TynB	*Tyndale Bulletin*
VoxEv	*Vox Evangelica*
VT	*Vetus Testamentum*
WBC	Word Biblical Commentary
WEC	Wycliffe Exegetical Commentary
WTJ	*Westminster Theological Journal*
WUNT	Wissenschaftliche Untersuchungen zum Neuen Testament
WW	*Word and World*
ZNW	*Zeitschrift für die neutestamentliche Wissenschaft*
ZTK	*Zeitschrift für Theologie und Kirche*

CHAPTER 1

Introduction

The aim of this study is to shed light on the differences between Luke and Paul with regard to their understanding of the Spirit. This will be achieved by examining the specific question of the relationship of the concept of the Spirit to the concept of the kingdom of God in each writer.[1] I will begin this study by reviewing recent scholarship with regard to the quest for the relationship between Lukan and Pauline pneumatologies. I will then elucidate the thesis, which will contribute to the discussion concerning the nature of the relationship between the two pneumatologies. Then I will briefly state the outline of this study.

1.1. A Review of Recent Scholarship

This review will show the three main positions with regard to the relationship between Luke and Paul's pneumatologies. Since a survey of contemporary scholarship before the 90s on this issue has already been summarized comprehensively by others,[2] there is no need to repeat it here. The review rather will focus on the very recent significant contributions of scholarship based on the works of three key scholars, who will be the main dialogue partners in this study: R.P. Menzies (discontinuity); J.D.G. Dunn (continuity); M.M.B. Turner (mediating position).[3]

---

[1] This study builds upon the premise that 'Luke' is the author of Luke-Acts and the latter are two parts of one work from the same author. This is the majority view in discussing Lukan pneumatology. For the Pauline authorship, see n. 2 in chapter 3.

[2] For a comprehensive classification of the three groups over a century of scholarship, see R.P. Menzies, *The Development of Early Christian Pneumatology with Special Reference to Luke-Acts*, JSNTS 54 (Sheffield: JSOT Press, 1991), 18-47; M. Turner, *Power from on High: The Spirit in Israel's Restoration and Witness in Luke-Acts*, JPTS 9 (Sheffield: SAP, 1996), 20-79; cf. F. Bovon, *Luke the Theologian: Thirty Years of Research (1950 - 1983)* (Allison Park: Pickwick, 1987), 202-38.

[3] Apart from these three scholars, there seem to be no major works in recent times which specifically deal with the relationship between Luke and Paul's pneumatologies. However, some notable studies in each writer's pneumatology are

1.1.1. R.P. Menzies

Menzies, whose fundamental framework of contention can be traced back to Gunkel[4] and Schweizer,[5] is a prominent and recent representative of those who hold the discontinuity perspective.[6] While he has recently published several books and articles, a particularly influential work, which contains his original pneumatological discussion, is *The Development of Early Christian Pneumatology with Special Reference to Luke-Acts*.[7] In this

---

worthy of reference here: for the study of Pauline pneumatology, see F.W. Horn, *Das Angeld des Geistes: Studien zur paulinischen Pneumatologie* (Göttingen: Vandenhoeck & Ruprecht, 1992); G. Fee, *God's Empowering Presence: The Holy Spirit in the Letters of Paul* (Peabody: Hendrickson, 1994); for the study of Lukan pneumatology, see J.B. Shelton, *Mighty in Word and Deed: The Role of the Holy Spirit in Luke-Acts* (Peabody: Hendrickson, 1992); H.S. Kim, *Die Geisttaufe des Messias: Eine kompositionsgeschichtliche Untersuchung zu einem Leitmotiv des lukanischen Doppelwerks. Ein Beitrag zur Theologie und Intention des Lukas* (Bern: Peter Lang, 1993); W.H. Shepherd Jr., *The Narrative Function of the Holy Spirit as a Character in Luke-Acts* (Atlanta: Scholars Press, 1994); J.M. Penney, *The Missionary Emphasis of Lukan Pneumatology*, JPTS 12 (Sheffield: SAP, 1997); M. Wenk, *Community-Forming Power: The Socio-Ethical Role of the Spirit in Luke-Acts*, JPTS 19 (Sheffield: SAP, 2000); E.J. Woods, *The 'Finger of God' and Pneumatology in Luke-Acts*, JSNTS 205 (Sheffield: SAP, 2001); J. Hur, *A Dynamic Reading of the Holy Spirit in Luke-Acts*, JSNTS 211 (Sheffield: SAP, 2001).

[4] Gunkel may anticipate the Pentecostal view by taking the reception of the Spirit in the primitive community as essentially an experience of supernatural power in glossolalia which was the most striking gift of the Spirit in early Christianity. H. Gunkel, *Die Wirkungen des heiligen Geistes nach der populären Anschauung der apostolischen Zeit und nach der Lehre des Apostels Paulus* (Göttingen: Vandenhoeck & Ruprecht, 1888), ET, *The Influence of the Holy Spirit: The Popular View of the Apostolic Age and the Teaching of the Apostle Paul* (Philadelphia: Fortress Press, 1979), 31-33.

[5] Following E. Schweizer, 'πνεῦμα', *TDNT*, VI, 407-09, Menzies maintains that neither intertestamental literature nor Luke attribute miracles to the Spirit; there is a distinction between 'δύναμις', and 'πνεῦμα'.

[6] Prior to Menzies, those who have argued for discontinuity are mainly as follows: Gunkel, *Influence*; Schweizer, 'πνεῦμα', 389-455; D. Hill, *Greek Words and Hebrew Meanings: Studies in the Semantics of Soteriological Terms*, SNTSMS 5 (Cambridge: CUP, 1967).

[7] See n. 2 above for a full reference of this volume. See also his *Empowered for Witness: The Spirit in Luke-Acts*, JPTS 6 (Sheffield: SAP, 1994): this volume is a revised form of his earlier work in 1991 for a wider audience; *Spirit and Power: Foundations of Pentecostal Experience* (Grand Rapids: Zondervan, 2000): this volume contains several articles, which were previously published elsewhere. I will refer to this volume title in quoting references, unless otherwise indicated; 'The Distinctive Character of Luke's Pneumatology', *Paraclete* 25 (1991), 17-30; 'Spirit and Power in Luke-Acts: A Response to Max Turner', *JSNT* 49 (1993), 11-20; 'Luke and the Spirit: A Reply to James Dunn', *JPT* 4 (1994), 115-38; 'The Spirit of

volume, as the title indicates, Menzies reconstructs the development of the concept of the Spirit from Jewish intertestamental literature to early Christianity, particularly focusing on Luke-Acts and some Pauline material. The main contribution of Menzies lies in his extensive study of the Jewish concept of the Spirit outlined in the intertestamental literature in connection with the concept of the Spirit in Luke-Acts. Menzies argues that the typical Jewish understanding of the Spirit is as the Spirit of prophecy who is almost always portrayed as the source of prophetic activity in intertestamental literature. The crucial issue that Menzies raises is whether this pneumatological concept of the Spirit simultaneously functions as the dispenser of life-giving wisdom. Menzies concludes that the literature rarely indicates the Spirit as the source of life-giving wisdom. This fundamental level of wisdom, i.e., 'wisdom necessary for authentic existence before God', is rather associated with a rational study of the law. In other words, the source of a fundamental level of life-giving wisdom is the instruction of the law, independent of the aid of the Spirit.[8] The only exceptions to this perspective appear in a few texts such as the Wisdom of Solomon and 1 QH, where the gift of the Spirit is given soteriological significance.[9] Menzies claims that 'In these texts, the gift of the Spirit, previously viewed as the source of esoteric wisdom and inspired speech, is presented as the source of sapiential achievement at every level'.[10] This indicates that 'the developments within the sapiential tradition culminate in the attribution of soteriological significance to the gift of the Spirit'.[11]

Menzies then examines the Lukan pneumatological perspective. According to him, Luke in his two works retains the traditional Jewish understanding of the Spirit. Thus the Spirit in Luke-Acts is not represented as a soteriological necessity, but as the source of special insight and inspired speech. Against Dunn, who argues that Jesus' reception of the Spirit and the heavenly declaration at Jordan marked the beginning of his experience of sonship and the new age, Menzies asserts that the Jordan event (Lk. 3:21-22) does not designate his sonship or messiahship but rather it represents the inauguration of Jesus' messianic task.[12] Likewise, the endowment of the Spirit upon the disciples at Pentecost (Acts 2) illustrates the equipment of the disciples for their prophetic vocation, granting special insight and inspiring speech rather than mediating the new covenant or

---

Prophecy, Luke-Acts and Pentecostal Theology: A Response to Max Turner', *JPT* 15 (1999), 49-74.

[8] *Development*, 56-57, 68-70.
[9] *Development*, 61-63, 77-90. A further detailed discussion of these texts will be offered in chapter 2.
[10] *Development*, 112.
[11] *Development*, 112.
[12] *Development*, 146-54.

providing a new heart. This gift of the Spirit is principally for the benefit of others.[13]

Menzies then moves on to the Pauline material. He argues that Paul was the first Christian to attribute soteriological functions to the Spirit. This understanding discovered by Paul arises from Ezekiel 36 and other OT passages, but is strongly influenced by the Wisdom of Solomon 9:9-18, which is demonstrated by the unique parallels with 1 Corinthians 2:6-16 and Galatians 4:4-6.[14] However, according to Menzies, Paul's view was not widely influential on the writer of Luke-Acts. Luke, who adopted the early non-Pauline notion of the Spirit, was not familiar with Paul's epistles and Luke's exposure to Paul's theology was confined to personal dialogue or secondary sources.[15] Furthermore, Luke's summaries of Paul's preaching, which Luke argues are to be regarded as representations of Paul's gospel – 'do not contain any traces of Paul's soteriological pneumatology'.[16]

Above all, Menzies concludes that 'Luke's "prophetic" pneumatology must be distinguished from the "soteriological" pneumatology of Paul', as the former mainly functions as the source of power for effective witness.[17] Paul's pneumatology is broader than that of Luke. Whereas Paul's pneumatology contains both soteriological and charismatic dimensions, Luke's view is less developed and more limited to the charismatic dimension of the work of the Spirit in bearing witness.[18] In short, Luke's pneumatology is different from that of Paul and his distinctive characteristic centres in empowering the church for witness.

Much of what Menzies concludes about pneumatology in Luke and intertestamental literature and its relationship with that of Paul is similar to the arguments which I will set out. In particular, his conclusion that Paul was the first innovator to associate the Spirit with soteriological functions has significant implications for the present study. However, while the basic argument of the present study at this point is analogous with that of Menzies, there is a considerable difference in methodology. This study will approach the subject from a new angle by focusing on the relationship between the Spirit and the kingdom in the writings of Luke and Paul. Furthermore, Menzies' primary concern is not specifically with the unique nature of the relationship between Paul's concept of the Spirit and the concept of the kingdom of God in the early church (Synoptics).[19]

---

[13] *Development*, 205-44, 279.
[14] *Development*, 282-315.
[15] *Development*, 317.
[16] *Development*, 317.
[17] *Development*, 316-17.
[18] *Development*, 317.
[19] See §1.2. below.

1.1.2. J.D.G. Dunn

Dunn is, without any doubt, a significant contributor to the current discussion concerning the continuity of NT pneumatology, especially the pneumatologies of Luke and Paul.[20] While Dunn's views are predominantly represented in *Baptism in the Holy Spirit*, *Jesus and the Spirit* and his various essays, his article in 1993 (re-appearing in *Pneumatology* in 1998) further clarifies his earlier position.[21] However, since Dunn's position on pneumatology has not substantially changed since 1970, I will begin by reviewing his earlier works and then will outline his recent position.

Following von Baer's scheme of salvation-history in Luke-Acts, Dunn weighs the events of Jordan and Pentecost in Luke-Acts in the light of the salvation-historical scheme divided into three periods: the period of Israel before Jordan, the period of Jesus from the Jordan experience, and the period of the Church from Pentecost to Jesus' parousia.[22] So, Jesus' experience at Jordan is not simply personal, it is rather 'a unique moment of history: the beginning of a new epoch in salvation-history - the beginning... of the messianic age, the new covenant'.[23] As the beginning of a new stage in salvation-history, the descent of the Spirit upon Jesus at the Jordan is characterized as his sense of divine sonship. Dunn asserts that its primary purpose should not be in 'empowering for service' but rather 'it is only a corollary to it... its function is to initiate the individual into the new age and covenant'.[24] Jesus initially experiences the kingdom of God in his own

---

[20] Prior to Dunn, those scholars who have emphasized the continuity are as follows: F. Büchsel, *Der Geist Gottes im Neuen Testament* (Gütersloh: C. Bertelsmann, 1926); J.H.E. Hull, *The Holy Spirit in the Acts of the Apostles* (London: Lutterworth, 1967); F. Bruner, *A Theology of the Holy Spirit: The Pentecostal Experience and the New Testament Witness* (Grand Rapids: Eerdmans, 1970), 155-224; J. Vos, *Traditionsgeschichtliche Untersuchungen zur paulinischen Pneumatologie* (Assen: Van Gorcum, 1973).

[21] See J.D.G. Dunn, *Baptism in the Holy Spirit: A Re-examination of the NewTestament Teaching on the Gift of the Spirit in Relation to Pentecostalism Today* (London: SCM Press, 1970); *Jesus and the Spirit* (Philadelphia: Westminster, 1975); 'Spirit and Kingdom', *ExpT* 82 (1970), 36-40; 'Baptism in the Spirit: A Response to Pentecostal Scholarship on Luke-Acts', *JPT* 3 (1993), 3-27; and more recently, *The Christ and the Spirit: Pneumatology*, vol. 2, (Grand Rapids: Eerdmans, 1998). This volume constitutes the various essays on pneumatology, which were previously published elsewhere. I will refer to this volume title in quoting references, unless otherwise indicated.

[22] Dunn, *Baptism*, 40-43. Cf. Von Baer's three fold division of salvation-history in Luke-Acts: 1) before Jesus' birth; 2) beginning from Jesus' birth to Pentecost; 3) beginning with Pentecost. H. von Baer, *Der Heilige Geist in den Lukasschriften* (Stuttgart: Kohlhammer, 1926), 45-50.

[23] *Baptism*, 24, 99.

[24] *Baptism*, 32. Before Dunn, Büschel regarded the pneumatic experience of Jesus at the Jordan as the sense of sonship: 'Jesu Geistbesitz ist Gottessohnschaft'. *Geist Gottes*,

life through his reception of the Spirit. In short, the bestowal of the Spirit makes an individual a believer. But this is not dissimilar to the Pauline concept of sonship in Romans 8:15-16 and Galatians 4:6. There is thus a link between the Spirit and divine sonship in both Luke and Paul.[25] Similarly, the outpouring of the Spirit at Pentecost is also the decisive transition as the beginning of the new covenant for the disciples in the fulfillment of the promises of the new covenant (Ezek. 36:27; Jer. 31:33). Hence, for Luke, the Spirit is to be seen as the essence and embodiment of the new covenant. These promises are not distinct from Paul's understanding of them: 'Paul is simply drawing out the logical corollary to Pentecost'.[26] Therefore, for Dunn, there is a continuity between Luke and Paul in terms of the understanding of the covenantal promises.

Dunn, who offers his argument almost two decades later in responding to his critics,[27] reasserts his previous position by raising the question, 'Does Luke separate the outpouring of the Spirit on individuals from conversion-initiation and see it as an empowering gift rather than a soteriological gift?'[28] As he argued before in 1970, Dunn rejects this assertion in his remaining argument in the article in 1993 and the book in 1998. In 1970, Dunn remarked that 'the baptism in or gift of the Spirit was part of the event (or process) of becoming a Christian', and 'the beginning of the Christian life is to be reckoned from the experience of Spirit-baptism' in all NT writers.[29] Then later, Dunn concludes that there is no difference between Luke and Paul in the definition that the gift of the Spirit is the essence and embodiment of the new covenant: 'the pneumatology of Luke is essentially one with the pneumatology of Paul'.[30] Although, recently, Dunn admits to a distinctive Lukan pneumatology as the Spirit of prophecy by saying 'The Spirit for Luke is indeed preeminently the "Spirit of prophecy", the Spirit that inspires speech and witness',[31] he still tends to read Pauline pneumatology into that of Luke.

Dunn's argument on the continuity between Luke and Paul also appears in his crucial article, 'Spirit and Kingdom'.[32] Dunn, in this article, basically argues that the Spirit is the manifestation of the kingdom in both Luke (and

---

165.

[25] *Baptism*, 24; *Jesus and Spirit*, 22; *Pneumatology*, 138 (cf. 136).

[26] *Baptism*, 48.

[27] Dunn's article (1993) is re-published in his latest volume (*Pneumatology*) in 1998 without any amendment. This means that his view is consistent even over three decades.

[28] 'Baptism in the Spirit', 6-7; *Pneumatology*, 225.

[29] *Baptism*, 4.

[30] 'Baptism in the Spirit', 27; *Pneumatology*, 242.

[31] 'Baptism in the Spirit', 8; *Pneumatology*, 226.

[32] This article was originally published in *ExpT* 82 (1970-71), 36-40, but since his recent volume, *Pneumatology*, contains the article (133-41), I will refer to *Pneumatology* for the article in what follows when quotations are needed.

the other Synoptics) and Paul. For Paul, the Spirit is closely related to the kingdom of God: 'the Spirit not only prepares a person for the future kingdom, the Spirit also enables the Christian to experience the future kingdom in the present'.[33] The condition for future inheritance of the kingdom is the experience of the work of the Spirit in the present (1 Cor. 6:9-11; Gal. 5:16-23). This is the reason why the kingdom is described as the believer's present experience of the Spirit (Rom. 14:17; 1 Cor. 4:20; 1 Thess. 2:12-13). The Spirit, as the presentness of the coming kingdom, entirely functions in conveying the blessings of the new covenant in the present. So, for Paul, 'Where he (the Spirit) is the kingdom is, so that to have the Spirit is to have part and lot in the kingdom here and now'.[34]

Likewise, in Luke (and the other Synoptics), the kingdom is being realized in and through Jesus by the Spirit who functions as the catalyst for the kingdom.[35] According to Dunn, the Spirit is the dominant partner of Jesus during his earthly life and hence 'the manifestation of the Spirit is the manifestation of the kingdom'.[36] This equation between the Spirit and the kingdom is shown in Lukan passages such as Luke 11:2; 11:13; 12:31; and Acts 1:3-8. For the disciples, this kingdom was still a future experience which would be tasted at Pentecost since they would only experience the gift of the Spirit at that time. Therefore, as in the case of Paul, Dunn concludes that, for Luke (and his Jesus), the Spirit is the presence of the kingdom: 'Where the Spirit is there is the kingdom'.[37] In this way, Dunn finds an apparent continuity between Paul and Luke.

While a detailed criticism of Dunn's argument will be offered in the major part of this study, some questions can be raised from the outset. Does the descent of the Spirit at the Jordan really function as a matrix for Jesus' sense of sonship? Is it true that the bestowal of the Spirit makes an individual a believer according to Luke? How far does such a notion differ from Paul's perspective? Most significantly, I will raise the question: does Dunn's thesis that the Spirit is the presence of the kingdom accurately reflect Luke's interpretation?

---

[33] *Pneumatology*, 134.
[34] *Pneumatology*, 136.
[35] 'Jesus' proclamation of the imminence of the kingdom was balanced by his consciousness that in his possession of the Spirit the presence of the kingdom had been realized'. *Pneumatology*, 140.
[36] *Pneumatology*, 138.
[37] *Pneumatology*, 138; *Jesus and Spirit*, 49; cf. Dunn, *The Theology of Paul the Apostle* (Grand Rapids: Eerdmans, 1998), 191.

1.1.3. M.M.B. Turner[38]

Turner, who has been considerably influenced by H. von Baer, continues to make a substantial contribution to the current discussion of Lukan and NT pneumatology. Turner's interest in pneumatology may be divided into two stages over the last two decades: the first stage is the 80s with his PhD thesis in Cambridge and a series of articles which complement his main argument as delineated in his doctoral work.[39] His main dialogue partners at this stage are mainly Dunn and Schweizer. The second stage is the 90s with two notable works and a series of articles,[40] where Turner still maintains his main thesis, but further focuses his investigation on the Jewish concept of the Spirit in intertestamental literature. At this stage, his new stimulating dialogue partner is Menzies.

In the first stage,[41] Turner disagrees with Dunn's claim that the gift of the Spirit initiates Jesus into the new age or new covenant. According to Turner, Luke presents that Jesus' reception of the Spirit at the Jordan is not fundamentally attributed to Jesus' own existential life before God, but it is for the exercise of his messianic role as herald or servant. Turner comments that 'Luke identifies the Spirit received there primarily, if not exclusively, as a power enabling Jesus to effect the unique task of the prophet-like-Moses'.[42] This conclusion concurs with the view of Menzies. However,

---

[38] Scholars who have taken a mediating position before Turner are as follows: von Baer, *Heilige Geist*; G. Haya-Prats, *L'Esprit force de l'e'glise: Sa nature et son activite'd'après les Actes des Apôtres* (Paris: Cerf, 1975); G.W.H. Lampe, *The Bampton Lectures, 1976* (Oxford: Clarendon, 1977).

[39] M. Turner, 'Luke and the Spirit: Studies in the Significance of Receiving the Spirit in Luke-Acts', (PhD Dissertation; Cambridge University, 1980); 'The Significance of Receiving the Spirit in Luke-Acts: A Survey of Modern Scholarship', *TJ* 2 (1981), 131-58; 'Jesus and the Spirit in Lucan Perspective', *TynB* 32 (1981), 3-42; 'Spiritual Gifts: Then and Now', *VoxEv* 15 (1985), 7-64.

[40] M. Turner, 'The Spirit and the Power of Jesus' Miracles in the Lucan Conception', *NovT* 33 (1991), 124-52; 'The Spirit of Prophecy and the Power of Authoritative Preaching in Luke-Acts: A Question of Origin', *NTS* 38 (1992), 66-88; 'The Spirit of Prophecy and the Ethical/Religious Life of the Christian Community', in M.W. Wilson (ed.), *Spirit and Renewal: Essays in Honour of J. Rodman Williams*, JPTS 5 (Sheffield: SAP, 1994), 166-90; *Power; The Holy Spirit and Spiritual Gifts: Then and Now* (Carlisle: Paternoster, 1996); 'The "Spirit of Prophecy" as the Power of Israel's Restoration and Witness', in I.H. Marshall and D. Peterson (eds.), *Witness to the Gospel: The Theology of Acts* (Grand Rapids: Eerdmans, 1998), 327-48.

[41] Although I distinguish two stages in the discussion of Turner's argument, the following points he made at the earlier stage are mostly identical with his later arguments indicated in his monograph, *Power*. The intention of this division is to emphasize Turner's extensive interest in the concept of the Spirit in Jewish literature in his second stage.

[42] 'Luke and the Spirit', 95. Turner maintains this claim in his later writing by saying that Jesus' reception of the Spirit 'must be understood as bringing Jesus a new nexus

although the Spirit is related to a charismatic power in his words and acts, the power can also draw his people to the kingdom, granting forgiveness and salvation.[43]

With regard to the disciples' experience of the Spirit, Turner argues that although there is no indication that the disciples 'received the Spirit' in Luke's gospel, it would be reasonable to contend that they had already begun to experience the gift of the Spirit before Pentecost through Jesus' ministry and proclamation (Lk. 9:1-10:22; 11:9-13).[44] The significance of the disciples' experience of the Spirit at Pentecost involves a new sphere of the activity of the Spirit in the lives of the apostles. It should not be a matrix of new covenant life for the disciples (contra Dunn), nor should it be confined to empowering witness (contra Menzies), but it is to be understood as both prophetic empowering for witness and a soteriological gift.[45] Above all, Turner's understanding of the nature of Lukan pneumatology is related to Luke's use of Isaiah 61 and Joel 3 rather than Ezekiel 36 as the programmatic passages, but nonetheless, he closely associates the gift of the Spirit in Luke-Acts with conversion and initiation motifs (e.g., Acts 2:38-39 as 'a paradigm').

In the second stage, while Turner continues to develop his earlier claims, he turns his interest to the concept of the Spirit in Judaism. Like Menzies, Turner argues that the intertestamental literature generally presents the Spirit as the source of prophetic inspiration, the Spirit of prophecy. However, Turner's understanding of the Spirit of prophecy goes much further. If Menzies understands the Spirit of prophecy as mainly prophetic inspiration based on special divine wisdom and revelation, Turner apprehends the same term more broadly; namely as the source of 'charismatic revelation and guidance', 'charismatic wisdom', 'invasive prophetic speech', and 'invasive charismatic praise and worship'.[46] According to Turner, these are called prototypical gifts attributed to the Spirit of prophecy. Furthermore, as in the case of Luke-Acts, Turner sees that the Spirit is the source of miraculous power in the wide influential literature of Judaism.[47] The same Spirit of prophecy is simultaneously apprehended as 'a fundamental power of ethical renewal'.[48]

---

of activities – not (contra Dunn) 'eschatological sonship', . . . but empowering for the messianic task'. *Power*, 428-29. Moreover, Turner develops a Lukan portrait of Jesus as the Isaianic soteriological prophet by elaborating on the passage Lk. 4:16-30 (cf. Isa. 61). *Power*, 206, 213-66.

[43] 'Luke and the Spirit', 53, 95; 'Jesus and the Spirit', 29-31; *Power*, 199, 211-12, 266.

[44] 'Luke and the Spirit', 86-88, 96-115; *Power*, 333-47.

[45] 'Luke and the Spirit', 148-76; *Power*, 267-315. There is a distinction between the two receptions of the Spirit: while Jesus received the gift of the Spirit for others, the disciples received it for themselves.

[46] *Holy Spirit*, 5-12; *Power*, 92-101.

[47] *Power*, ch. 4. '. . . the two conceptions do not appear to have seemed as foreign to

With particular regard to the present study, Turner maintains that the Spirit in intertestamental literature grants life-giving wisdom so that he mediates the wisdom of God at a fundamental level as necessary for true life (or fellowship) with God in the covenant community. This wisdom granted by the Spirit thus becomes central for authentic faith, Christian life, and transformation. Turner argues that 'even in Judaism these gifts of the "Spirit of prophecy" could be anticipated not as empowering alone, but also as the very "life" of the restored community, and the power of its holiness'.[49] This understanding which appeared in Judaism is, according to Turner, essentially reflected in the various NT writers, namely Luke, John and Paul, who attribute the gift of the Spirit as a soteriological necessity. In Luke-Acts, the Spirit functions in the same way as in intertestamental Jewish literature, i.e., as the giver of life-giving wisdom. Thus, since this concept is undoubtedly found in Paul (and John), there is a certain unity between Luke's (and the early church) and Paul's pneumatology: 'Luke's understanding of the Spirit is not so distant from that of either Paul or John as is regularly assumed'.[50]

While there can be no doubt that Turner's study of NT pneumatology, particularly Luke's pneumatology as well as that of Judaism, has widely contributed to modern scholarship on pneumatology, questions still remain. Is the Spirit in both Luke and the literature of intertestamental Judaism

---

each other. . .' 114. Thus, unlike Schweizer and Menzies, Turner argues that the Spirit is the source of miracles of healing and exorcism.

[48] *Power*, ch. 5 (121).

[49] *Holy Spirit*, xii; see also 'Authoritative Preaching', 86-88; 'Ethical/Religious Life', 186-90; *Power*, 90, 114-18, 132-37, 348-52. A more detailed discussion concerning Turner's overall understanding of the Spirit as the giver of life-giving wisdom in Judaism and its criticism will be offered in the next chapter.

[50] 'Spirit of Prophecy', 347; *Holy Spirit*, 55, 150-59. For this reason, it should be noted that while Turner's argument can be regarded as the mediating position when he regards the Spirit in Luke-Acts as the source of ethical power or community life (as in the case of Paul) as well as empowering for mission, nonetheless, his latest argument makes him a strong advocate of the position which holds to the unity between Luke and Paul. 'Paul's conception of the gift of the Spirit is simply *broader* than Luke's *while nevertheless containing everything that Luke implies*. . . Paul's comprehensive understanding of the gift of the Spirit granted to Christians at conversion does not leave anything for Luke's to "add"'. *Holy Spirit*, 150-68 (154-55. Emphasis is original). Furthermore, this position appears more clearly in his slightly developed statement on the issue of receiving the Spirit. For instance, in his earlier work (over against Dunn), he states that Luke 'did not identify receiving the Spirit as the gift of messianic salvation itself, but as one particular nexus within it: the christian version of judaism's hope for the Spirit of prophecy'. Turner, 'Luke and the Spirit', 170; in his latest work, he argues that 'Luke sees the Spirit as the principal means of God's salvation/transforming presence for Israel. . . and that receiving the gift of the Spirit enables participation in this'. *Power*, 402. Therefore, his position may be best classified as a mediating position *close* to continuity.

really portrayed as the giver of 'life-giving wisdom' as Turner argues? Can one safely assume that since the Spirit of prophecy in intertestamental Jewish literature grants 'life-giving wisdom', that Luke understands the Spirit in a similar way?

1.2. The Thesis

This brief survey has demonstrated that with the exception of Menzies, the recent major studies of the pneumatologies of Luke and Paul presented by Dunn and Turner indicate a correspondent agreement of the early church's pneumatology. Indeed, this perspective was not first introduced by Dunn and Turner. It has been generally argued that Paul's pneumatology, which is widely characterized as having a soteriological dimension, is very similar to that of the early (non-Pauline) church, particularly that of Luke.[51] This notion is affirmed by the following statements by some scholars prior to Dunn and Turner: 'The author of Acts (in understanding his pneumatology) seems to be in wholehearted agreement with Paul'[52]; or more indirectly, the Spirit in Luke-Acts is represented as 'Zeichen und Mittel der Errettung und des Lebens'.[53]

In the following study I will argue that, contrary to this general perspective that Paul's pneumatology simply reflects what already existed, Paul as an innovator adds something new and important to the theology of the early church. Paul reformulates the Christian message, which centres on the kingdom of God, in new terms, primarily by speaking of the Spirit in a new and more comprehensive way. In other words, Paul communicates the essence of Jesus' teaching about the kingdom in a different way, focusing on the work of the Spirit; consequently, what Jesus sees as the blessings brought about when God's kingdom is inaugurated, Paul describes as the effects of the working of the Spirit in Paul (e.g., Rom. 14:17).[54] Here we may explore the unique nature of the relationship between Paul's concept of the Spirit and the concept of the kingdom of God in the Synoptics.

In relation to this thesis, I will specifically ask how the Spirit is related to the kingdom of God in the works of Luke and Paul. Indeed, it has been generally assumed that both Luke and Paul regard the presence of the Spirit as essentially the same as the presence of the kingdom of God by

---

[51] E.g., Büchsel's argument that the Spirit is the Spirit of sonship in both Jesus and Paul, *Geist Gottes*; Von Baer, *Heilige Geist*; Lampe, *God as Spirit*, 64-73: For Luke, the Spirit brings 'men to repentance and faith so that they can enter into communion with himself, glorifying Jesus by creating in them the sonship which was perfectly exhibited in Jesus and refashioning them according to the pattern of Jesus' (73).

[52] Hull, *Holy Spirit*, 164.

[53] J. Kremer, *Pfingstbericht und Pfingstgeschehen: Eine exegetische Untersuchung zu Apg 2,1-13*, SBS 63-64 (Stuttgart: KBW, 1973), 197.

[54] This matter will be discussed in detail in chapter 3.

concluding that Paul's pneumatology is similar to that of the early church. For instance, Dunn, as seen above, has seen the Spirit as mediating the blessings of the kingdom (or the means by which the disciples experience the kingdom) in both Luke and Paul.[55] However, while this may be the case for Paul, can it be maintained that this is Luke's perspective as well? I will argue that Dunn's thesis is not precise enough at this important point. I will maintain that Paul develops the role of the Spirit more fully than Luke, understanding the Spirit as the means by which all may participate in the blessings of the kingdom in the present. Ultimately, for Paul, life in the Spirit becomes his way of speaking about the blessings of life in the kingdom in the early church (Synoptics). Luke, however, presents the Spirit in a more limited way in relation to the concept of the kingdom of God. For instance, the Spirit inspires the proclamation of the kingdom of God and in this way, the Spirit makes it possible for people to enter the kingdom of God. A question can be asked: is it true that for Luke (Jesus) the Spirit inspires the proclamation of the kingdom of God, enabling others to enter into it while for Paul the Spirit becomes the source of the life of the kingdom in its entirety, mediating all of the blessings of life in the kingdom? Discussion of this distinction will elucidate the difference between Luke's and Paul's understanding of the Spirit in connection with the concept of the kingdom.

1.2.1. Outline of Study

This study will be undertaken in the following manner: in Chapter 2, the intertestamental Jewish literature will be investigated concerning the role of the Spirit, particularly focusing on the question whether the Spirit of prophecy in this literature is associated with life-giving wisdom. Is the Spirit of prophecy, the generally accepted concept of the Spirit, to be reasonably understood in the literature as the dispenser of life-giving wisdom? How does one compare the pneumatological perspective appearing in this literature to Luke's and Paul's understanding of the Spirit? Is it fair to argue that because the Spirit of prophecy in the literature grants life-giving wisdom that Luke understood the Spirit as the source of prophecy in a similar way? If not, can we say that Paul presents that life in the Spirit is equivalent to the present life of the kingdom in the Synoptics?

In Chapter 3, I will discuss the relationship between the Spirit in Paul and the kingdom of God in the Synoptics. The lack of frequency of the phrase 'kingdom of God' in Paul raises the question as to why it is used so rarely and this makes it highly possible that Paul uses an alternative concept for it. I will argue that Paul's concept of the Spirit is substituted for that of the presentness of the kingdom by showing how life in the Spirit in Paul is

---

[55] See §1.1.2. above. Similarly, Turner argues that the Spirit is the source of the kingdom blessings in Luke-Acts. I will discuss this in detail in chapter 4.

virtually synonymous with the present life of the kingdom of God in the Synoptics. From this discussion, can we say that Paul presents that the Spirit is the totality of the present blessings of the kingdom? This chapter is compared with the subsequent chapter (ch. 4) clarifying certain Lukan and Pauline distinctives regarding the way in which the Spirit functions in the blessings of the kingdom.

So, in Chapter 4, an assessment will be made of the characteristics of the kingdom, to ascertain how far the functions of the Spirit according to Paul are or are not attributed to the Spirit by Luke. Whereas it is clear that the Spirit functions as the source of the blessings of the kingdom according to Paul, is it true that Luke also links the Spirit to these blessings? If Luke does not associate the Spirit with them, is it fair to assume that Luke's pneumatological perspective is less developed in comparison with the pneumatology of Paul?

In Chapter 5, remembering that the role of the Spirit is limited to the kingdom blessings in Luke established in chapter 4, I will seek to elucidate the role of the Spirit in connection with the kingdom in Luke-Acts. What is the nature of the relationship between the Spirit and the kingdom according to Luke? Is it true that the Spirit is the presence of the kingdom in Luke (as in Paul) as is generally recognized? I will investigate whether this thesis accurately reflects Luke's perspective. I will examine whether for Luke the role of the Spirit is related in a narrower and more restricted way to the kingdom.

Finally, in conclusion (Chapter 6), I will draw together the threads of the discussion with some crucial implications from this study.

CHAPTER 2

The Spirit and Life-Giving Wisdom in Intertestamental Literature

2.1. Introduction

It is generally recognized that Lukan pneumatology is an extension of the intertestamental Jewish concept of the Spirit.[1] There is also considerable agreement among scholars that the intertestamental literature presents the Spirit as the source of prophetic inspiration, i.e., the Spirit of prophecy.[2] However, it is debatable whether this general concept of the Spirit in the literature (and that of Luke) is to be understood as the giver of 'life-giving wisdom' as well.

Recently, as observed in the previous scholarly review, Turner has argued that the Spirit in intertestamental Jewish literature is linked to other related concepts.[3] In particular, Turner maintains that one of the main features of the Spirit in this literature is a 'life-giving function' as a soteriological agent. He claims that the charismatic wisdom afforded by the Spirit is essentially understood as 'life-giving'. The role of the Spirit in various pieces of Jewish literature is almost inevitably regarded 'as *virtually essential* for fully authentic human existence before God, and so also for that future state

---

[1] See n. 3 in chapter 4.
[2] E.g., Schweizer, 'πνεῦμα', G.W.H. Lampe, 'The Holy Spirit in the Writings of St. Luke', in D.E. Nineham (ed.), *Studies in the Gospels* (Oxford: Blackwell, 1957); Hill, *Greek Words*; Turner, *Power*; Menzies, *Development*.
[3] As seen above, Turner subdivides the prophetic role of the Spirit into four gifts which include; 1) charismatic revelation and guidance; 2) charismatic wisdom; 3) invasive inspired prophetic speech; and 4) invasive inspired charismatic praise or worship. Turner explains that these four gifts are prototypically associated with the Spirit of prophecy. In addition, this Spirit of prophecy is connected with different acts of power, i.e., miracles and healing. Turner, *Holy Spirit*, 5-12; for related references to this in the intertestamental and rabbinic literature, see esp. *Power*, 92-118.

of it which writers mean by salvation'.[4] Then Turner further asserts that this pneumatological perspective found in intertestamental Jewish literature is essentially reflected in the pneumatologies of Luke and Paul. Consequently, since the Spirit functions as the giver of 'life-giving wisdom' in the literature, we would expect the Spirit to function in the same way in both Luke and Paul. I will challenge this position argued by Turner in this chapter. In particular, the aim of this chapter is to consider whether the Spirit of prophecy in the pre-Christian era is associated with this 'life-giving wisdom', a wisdom that mediates the wisdom of God at a fundamental level as Turner maintains.[5] The overall discussion of this chapter will help us understand the thesis that Paul is an innovator in that he presents the Spirit as the life of the kingdom of God as portrayed in the Synoptics.

Turner builds his case on three primary Jewish sources: messianic traditions, giving the Jewish understanding of the Spirit on the Messiah; Qumran literature (and Wisdom of Solomon); and rabbinic traditions echoing Ezekiel 36.[6] In addition to material from these three sources, I will add the relationship between the Spirit and the resurrection of the dead from a Jewish perspective, which is an unavoidable issue in this thesis. I will investigate each of them in turn together with other relevant literature in order to establish whether Turner has made a convincing case.[7]

---

[4] *Holy Spirit*, 15 (Emphasis is original); see also *Power*, 119-38.

[5] In other words, the scope of the study in this chapter is not the broad understanding of the Spirit in intertestamental Judaism such as the discussion of miraculous power in relation to the Spirit, but rather whether the generally accepted concept of the Spirit, i.e., the Spirit of prophecy, in the period, is reasonably understood as the dispenser of 'life-giving wisdom'.

[6] Menzies has briefly responded to Turner in his recent book, *Spirit and Power*, 91-93, in responding to Turner's *Holy Spirit and Spiritual Gifts: Then and Now*. This study will focus on and extend Menzies' challenge to Turner's conclusion. However, my argument over against Turner extends to his crucial monograph, *Power* under these three main categories.

[7] In the following discussion, the sources examined disregard the division of time and space in intertestamental literature, unless otherwise indicated. However, the works which are possibly late such as *2 Baruch* and *Joseph and Aseneth*, and possible Christian origins or elements such as the *Testaments of the Twelve Patriarchs* and the *Martyrdom of Isaiah*, where the reference to the Spirit is contained directly or indirectly, will be excluded from this analysis, unless otherwise noted. Rabbinic material, which Turner brings in his argument, will however be considered in this discussion. For a general methodological reflection on the literature, see R. Kraft, 'The Pseudepigrapha in Christianity', in J.C. Reeves (ed.), *Tracing the Threads: Studies in the Vitality of Jewish Pseudepigrapha* (Atlanta: Scholars Press, 1994), 55-86 (60-63, 71-86). In this article, Kraft points out that it is problematic to presuppose a work in OT Pseudepigrapha as having a purely Jewish rather than a Christian context, because the Pseudepigrapha have had a long association with

2.2. The Spirit in the Messianic Traditions

The first example that Turner brings is that of the Spirit on the Messiah. Turner argues that the role of the Spirit in the messianic passages associated with Isaiah 11:1-4 is closely connected not only to power and ethical vitality, but to the source of life-giving wisdom. Turner renders the *Targum of Isaiah* 11:1-2[8] and claims that the role of the Spirit on the messianic figures is understood as the source of 'wisdom', 'understanding', 'counsel', 'might', 'knowledge', and 'the fear of the Lord'. In these figurations, the gift of the Spirit is basically regarded not only as the source of power and ethical influence,[9] but also as a soteriological agent.[10]

So Turner says that 'the Spirit on the messiah would inevitably be the *major* force in Zion's renewal – and in that sense "soteriologically necessary". And as the salvation concerned means the transformation of Zion, and the new order which results, the gift of the Spirit is as necessary to the messiah's experience of this "salvation"'.[11]

However, is it really credible to argue that the Spirit grants the Messiah life-giving wisdom as a soteriological agent? To answer this, two questions should be asked: 1) Are these qualities of the messianic figures related to the Spirit essentially associated with soteriological necessity? 2) What does other intertestamental Jewish literature which refers to the messianic traditions (such as *1 Enoch* and the *Psalms of Solomon*) say about the messianic role?

2.2.1. The Nature of the Characteristics of Messianic Figures

Isaiah 11:1-4 illustrates that the righteous ruler of the future will reign with six different traits as the messianic king, anointed and equipped by the Spirit for his task. The king's duties on right decisions will be performed through his inspired 'wisdom' and 'understanding', and 'knowledge'. His inspired 'counsel' and 'might' will transfer his decisions into action on

---

Christianity and most of them were transmitted by Christians for long periods.

[8] Turner cites C.A. Evans's translation of Isa.11:1-2 in the Targum: 'And a *king* shall come forth from the *sons* of Jesse, and *the Messiah* shall *be exalted* from *the sons* of his *sons*. And upon him shall rest the spirit of *prophecy*, a spirit of wisdom and understanding, a spirit of counsel and might. A spirit of knowledge and fear of the Lord'. Turner, *Holy Spirit*, 17. See also C.A. Evans, 'From Anointed Prophet to Anointed King: Probing Aspects of Jesus' Self-Understanding', in *Jesus and His Contemporaries* (Leiden: Brill, 1995), 449.

[9] *Power*, 114-18, 132-33; *Holy Spirit*, 17-18. As implied in the words, 'the fear of the Lord' in messianic passages and 'the Spirit of righteousness', in *1 En.* 62:1-2.

[10] *Power*, 133; *Holy Spirit*, 18 where Turner says that 'The Spirit's revelatory and wisdom-granting roles were understood (in many quarters) as transformative, and thus as potentially soteriological'.

[11] *Power*, 136. Emphasis is original.

behalf of his people.[12] He will have the right attitude to his people with the mind of 'the fear of the Lord'.[13] These traits are granted to the Spirit-endowed messianic king 'to assure his inspired rule over the people of God'.[14]

Here, as will be seen in what follows, the wisdom granted by the Spirit is closely related to the Messiah's task rather than 'life-giving wisdom' as Turner asserts. Turner rightly argues that the Spirit here in this text is the source of ethical insight. However, it is not the sort of insight which is necessary for one (the Messiah) *to know the will of God* or *to live in right relationship with God*. But the wisdom granted to the Messiah in these traditions is charismatic or extraordinary wisdom to rule effectively over his people. This extraordinary wisdom may have an ethical significance, but it is not necessary for spiritual life.

2.2.2. The Spirit and Wisdom in the Messianic Tradition in 1 Enoch and the Psalms of Solomon

How did the Jewish readers then in the intertestamental period precisely understand this biblical text in messianic contexts? Two Jewish books of the period contain the messianic tradition related to the Spirit: *1 Enoch* and the *Psalms of Solomon*.

2.2.2.1. 1 ENOCH

The author of the book of the *Parables*[15] describes the eschatological leader by four epithets: the Righteous One, the Elect One (the Chosen One), the Anointed One (Messiah), and the Son of Man. These all refer to one individual, an eschatological leader, not four (cf. *1 En.* 53:6; 52:4, 6; 48:6; 62:1, 5, 7).[16] One of the crucial messianic pictures of the eschatological leader, who is anointed with the Spirit is 'the Elect One'. The picture of 'the Elect One' is described in *1 Enoch* 49:2-4;

> For his might is in all the mysteries of righteousness, and oppression will vanish like a shadow having no foundation. The Elect One stands before the Lord of the

---

[12] R. Koch, *Geist und Messias* (Wien: Herder, 1950), 81f.
[13] O. Kaiser, *Isaiah 1-12* (Philadelphia: Westminster Press, 1974), 158.
[14] G. Montague, *The Holy Spirit: Growth of a Biblical Tradition* (New York: Paulist Press, 976), 41.
[15] The *Book of Parables* (37-71) is the second section out of five sections. On the other hand, it is generally assumed that *1 En.* was written between the 2nd century BC and the 1st century AD. E.g., E. Isaac, '1 Enoch', *OTP*, 1, 5-7.
[16] J.C. Vanderkam, 'Biblical Interpretation in *1 Enoch* and *Jubilees*', in J.H. Charlesworth and C.A. Evans (eds.), *The Pseudepigrapha and Early Biblical Interpretation*, JSPS 14 (Sheffield: JSOP Press, 1993), 98-117 (116).

Spirits; his glory is forever and ever and his power is unto all generations. In him dwells the spirit of wisdom, the spirit which gives thoughtfulness, the spirit of knowledge and strength, and the spirit of those who have fallen asleep in righteousness. He shall judge the secret things. And no one will be able to utter vain words in his presence. For he is the Elect One before the Lord of the Spirits according to his good pleasure.[17]

The author shows a biblical figure in biblical interpretation. There is little doubt that this text is reminiscent of Isaiah 11:2 and the figure (the Elect One) is the Messiah.[18] Here the Messiah is endowed with the Spirit and described as the judge of the world and ruler of the righteous. The indwelling Spirit of wisdom equips him for the task of rule and judgement with thoughtfulness, knowledge and strength so that no one is able to utter vain words before him.[19] The Spirit of wisdom according to *1 Enoch* is clearly related to the Messiah's *reigning power* rather than life-giving wisdom.

2.2.2.2. THE PSALMS OF SOLOMON

Another description of the coming of the messianic deliverance related to the role of the Spirit is given in the *Psalms of Solomon* 17:37: 'And he will not weaken in his days, (relying) upon his God, for God made him powerful in the holy spirit and wise in the counsel of understanding, with strength and righteousness'.[20] This text is also reminiscent of Isaiah 11:2.[21] This messianic passage proclaims that the Messiah does not weaken since the power of the Spirit abides in him so that the blessing of the Lord is with him (v. 38) and he is mighty in actions (v. 40a), faithful and righteous (40c).[22] As in *1 Enoch* 49:2-4 and 62:2, the role of the Spirit in the *Psalms of Solomon* is mainly associated with the ruling power of the Messiah so that he will reign over his people with understanding, strength, and

---

[17] Cf. also 62:2. Isaac, '1 Enoch', 36.

[18] I.F. Wood, *The Spirit of God in Biblical Literature* (London: Hodder and Stoughton, 1904), 64f.; M. Black, *The Book of Enoch* (Leiden: Brill, 1985), 212; J.R. Levison, *The Spirit in First Century Judaism* (Leiden: Brill, 1997), 181.

[19] R.H. Charles, *The Book of Enoch or 1 Enoch* (Oxford: Clarendon, 1912), 217. This role of the Spirit is described in another chapter: 'The Lord of the Spirit has sat down on the throne of his glory, and the spirit of righteousness has been poured out upon him (the elect one). The word of his mouth will do the sinners in; and all the oppressors shall be eliminated from before his face' (62.2). Isaac, '1 Enoch', 43.

[20] R.B. Wright, 'Psalms of Solomon', *OTP*, 2, 668. The expression, holy spirit denotes a description of God's spirit in this passage. See Levison, *Spirit*, 105, n. 13.

[21] Levison, *Spirit*, 143, 182.

[22] Furthermore, the additional crucial instrument of the ruler is the power of his inspired word marked by the wisdom as in 17:43. K.E. Pomykala, *The Davidic Dynasty Tradition in Early Judaism: Its History and Significance for Messianism*, SBL 7 (Atlanta: Scholars Press, 1995), 168.

righteousness. This notion is also clearly depicted in the subsequent chapter of the work. The eschatological figure will reign over his people 'under the rod of discipline of the Lord Messiah, in the fear of his God, in wisdom of the spirit, and of righteousness and of strength, to direct people in righteous acts, in the fear of the Lord, to set them all in the fear of the Lord' (18:7-8).[23]

Turner is probably right to connect the Spirit with power and might in these texts, particularly in the *Psalms of Solomon* 17:37, but it is inappropriate to associate this mighty power derived from the Spirit with life-giving wisdom.[24] It is rather, as the texts indicate, extraordinary wisdom which helps the Messiah to efficiently rule and judge his people. In short, messianic portraits in the intertestamental Jewish literature such as *1 Enoch* and the *Psalms of Solomon* do not attribute life-giving wisdom to the Spirit on the Messiah. Rather, the Spirit is usually described as the source of the ruling power of the Messiah.

On the other hand, beyond these messianic traditions, the fact that the Jewish texts (e.g., *MHG* Gen. 135, 139-140; cf. *t. Soṭ.* 6:2; *2 Bar.* 85:3; 1 Macc. 4:46; 14:44) speak of the withdrawal of the Spirit from Israel due to her sin also makes weak Turner's association of the Spirit upon the Messiah with life-giving wisdom. It is legitimate to think that the Spirit does not grant Israel a heart for God, but it is rather given to the righteous, the people of God who already have a heart for God to enable them to fulfill a specific task or calling. The Jewish texts which speak of the withdrawal of the Spirit from Israel because of her sin affirm this fact. So, when Israel falls into sin and rebels against God, the Spirit departs. With this fact in mind, the Spirit on the Messiah should be seen as an empowering presence; not that which enables the Messiah to live in right relationship with God. The Messiah is already righteous and the Spirit comes upon him and empowers him because he is worthy of the Spirit.[25] This is true of Jewish texts which speak of the Spirit in relationship to the Messiah and also the texts in Luke, as will be seen, which relate the Spirit to Jesus. The Spirit

---

[23] Wright, 'Psalms of Solomon', 669.

[24] Turner may also be right to attribute the gift of the Spirit to power in Qumran messianic material such as 1 QSb 5:24-25, 11QMelchizedek, but it is not accurate to apply it to life-giving wisdom. 1 QSb 5:24-25 states that 'May you be [...] with the power of your [mouth.] With your sceptre may you lay waste the earth. With the breath of your lips may you kill the wicked. May he give [you a spirit of counsel] and of everlasting fortitude, a spirit of knowledge and of fear of God'. F.G. Martínez and E.J.C. Tigchelaar, *The Dead Sea Scrolls* (Grand Rapids: Eerdmans, 2000).

[25] Menzies asks a question that if some Jewish traditions indicate that the Spirit is removed from Israel because of her sin, 'is it really credible to think of the Spirit as granting to the Messiah the righteousness and wisdom "necessary for authentic existence before God"'? *Spirit and Power*, 92. This is clearly not the case in the Jewish texts.

comes on the Messiah to empower him for his ministry, not to enable him to relate to God as Father or to give him a new heart for God.

It is notable that Turner, disagreeing with Dunn, argues that Jesus' Jordan endowment by the Spirit is almost exclusively understood as empowering for mission, rather than new covenant life or eschatological sonship.[26] If Turner is right when he says that Luke 'takes up' these Jewish messianic traditions associated with life-giving wisdom reflecting on Isaiah 11:1-4,[27] how does he reconcile the difference between the strands of Jewish thinking and Luke which he interprets? If there is no difference, any endeavour to associate the messianic traditions with "life-giving wisdom" needs to be modified.

To sum up, the first-century Jewish readers such as the authors of *1 Enoch* and the *Psalms of Solomon* understand that the role of the Spirit indwelling the Messiah is to give him special wisdom and power to rule effectively over his people (*Amtscharisma*).[28] The wisdom upon the Messiah derived from the Spirit is not a fundamental level of wisdom, 'life-giving wisdom' as Turner argues, but is a distinct and elevated form of wisdom.

2.3. The Spirit and the 'Life-Giving Wisdom' in Qumran and the Wisdom of Solomon and the Spirit and Extraordinary Wisdom in other Intertestamental Literature

The next body of literature from which Turner argues his case is Qumran literature and Wisdom. Indeed, as has been generally agreed, Turner is undoubtedly correct when he argues that the Spirit in 1 QH and Wisdom (9:17-18) is understood as the source of life-giving wisdom.[29] However, while there is soteriological pneumatology in the literature, is this notion found in many other pieces of Jewish literature as well? On the basis of this crucial question, in this section, I will first briefly examine the soteriological elements of the pneumatologies of 1 QH and Wisdom.[30] I

---

[26] Turner says that 'but it will be apparent that the gospels were more interested in assuring their readers *that* Jesus was the expected Messiah of the Spirit and *that* he was so empowered for his mission, than they were in explaining what Jesus' endowment at the Jordan contributed to his own life before God'. *Holy Spirit*, 34. Emphasis is original.

[27] Turner, *Power*, 138; *Holy Spirit*, 37

[28] Menzies, *Development*, 71-73.

[29] This is persuasively argued by Menzies; 'In these texts (Wisdom and 1 QH), the gift of the Spirit. . . is presented as the source of sapiential achievement at every level'. *Development*, 112. See also 62-63, 84-87.

[30] Since, although the identity of the two spirits is still controversial, the reference to the Spirit in 1 QS, particularly 1 QS 3-4 can possibly be interpreted as an inclination in human beings and not with reference to the Spirit of God, I will only discuss 1 QH in

will then examine whether the majority of the literature in the period maintains the same view.

2.3.1. *The Spirit and the Life-Giving Wisdom in 1 QH and the Wisdom of Solomon*

2.3.1.1. 1 QH

The texts Turner cites in Qumran literature derive mostly from 1 QH (7:6-7; 9:32; 12:11-13; 13:18-19; 14:12b-13; 14:25; 16:6-7; 16:9; 16:11b-12; 17:25-26). As noted, the Spirit in these texts of 1 QH is presented as a soteriological necessity. The following are some of the examples of this notion.[31]

The cleansing role of the Spirit is exhibited as the means for entering into the community. In other words, the gift of the Spirit enables the constituents of the community to be the 'true Israel' or 'House of Holiness'.

> And I know that man is not righteous except through Thee, and therefore I implore Thee by the Spirit which Thou has given [me] to perfect Thy [favours] to Thy servant [for ever], purifying me by Thy Holy Spirit, and drawing me near to Thee by Thy grace according to the abundance of Thy mercies (1 QH 16:11b-12).

The Spirit enables the author to possess wisdom to attain knowledge of God and the mystery of God.

> I, the Master, know Thee, O my God, by the Spirit which Thou hast given to me, and by Thy Holy Spirit I have faithfully hearkened to Thy marvelous counsel. In the mystery of Thy wisdom Thou hast opened knowledge to me, and in Thy mercies [Thou hast unlocked for me] the fountain of Thy might (1 QH 12:11-13, cf. 13:18-19).

The Spirit makes the author rejoice with 'certain truth'.

> Thou hast upheld me with certain truth; Thou hast delighted me with Thy Holy Spirit and [hast opened my heart] till this day (1 QH 9:32).

Through these passages, the author thanks God for providing the gift of the

---

which a soteriological pneumatology is clearly revealed and Turner convincingly cites major texts from it to establish his case. See M. Treves, 'The Two Spirits of the Rule of the Community', *RevQ* 3 (1961), 449-52; Menzies, *Development*, 78-83. Menzies, following Wernberg-Møller and Treves, argues that the two spirits in 1 QS are the spirits in human dispositions which are implanted in all men so that the Spirit in 1 QH is basically different from that of 1 QS.

[31] All translations are from G. Vermes, *The Complete Dead Sea Scrolls in English* (Allen Lane: Penguin, 1997), unless otherwise indicated.

Spirit whose role lies in cleansing and imparting wisdom. In this way, the gift of the Spirit is given soteriological functions in the community. This makes it reasonable enough for some, such as Turner, to be able to claim that 'The revelatory Spirit has thus itself become simultaneously the soteriological Spirit, the very basis of the transformed "life" and sustained righteousness of the restored community'.[32]

2.3.1.2. THE WISDOM OF SOLOMON

Another case in which the Spirit is depicted as life-giving wisdom is in the Wisdom of Solomon. The most explicit reference that salvation is brought by the divine wisdom is Wisdom 9:13-18, particularly verses 17-18: 'Who was privy to your design, unless you gave him wisdom, and sent your holy spirit from on high (ἔπεμψας τὸ ἅγιόν σου πνεῦμα ἀπὸ ὑψίστων]? Thus it was that the paths of earthlings were set aright, and men were taught what pleases you, and were saved by Wisdom (τῇ σοφίᾳ ἐσώθησαν)'.[33] In the literature, the 'Spirit' is generally interchangeably used with 'wisdom' (1:6; 7:7, 22; 8:21; 9:4, 10) so that here the reference 'wisdom' also means the 'Spirit'.[34] The word, ἐσώθησαν is used for the first time in this book and announces the theme of the book.[35]

It is often argued that the word σώζω in Wisdom 9:18 should be understood in the sense of physical preservation rather than having salvific significance. This is indeed the primary sense if one sees the following texts of the work in which the author retells the stories of the history of Israel (cf. 10:4; 14:4, 5; 16:7, 11; 18:5).[36] However, what is to be particularly considered in these stories is that the author never mentions one person's name in the biblical narratives where this word is used. In these depersonalized accounts, the author plausibly intends to illustrate the ultimate redemptive power of wisdom, not only in the history of Israel, but in a universal and eschatological sense (Wis. 3:1-9; 6:18; 8:17; 15:3).[37]

---

[32] Turner, *Holy Spirit*, 16; cf. 'What is envisaged is not primarily esoteric knowledge, but *the sort of understanding of God and of his word that elicits righteous living*'. *Power*, 128. Emphasis is original.

[33] D. Winston, *The Wisdom of Solomon*, AB 43 (Garden: Doubleday & Company, 1979), 206. GT is from A. Rahlfs, *Septuaginta* (Stuttgart: Deutsche Bibelgesellschaft, 1979).

[34] Cf. Reider's statement: 'That Wisdom is a πνεῦμα is stated expressly in 1:6, and 9:17 σοφία is parallel to πνεῦμα ἅγιον'. J. Reider, *The Book of Wisdom* (New York: Harper & Row, 1957), 36.

[35] Winston, *Wisdom*, 209.

[36] E.g., R. Scroggs, 'Paul: ΣΟΦΟΣ and ΠΝΕΥΜΑΤΙΚΟΣ', *NTS* 14 (1967), 33-55 (50).

[37] Menzies, *Development*, 309-10. Note also Kee's statement: 'It is significant that personal names are not used in these summaries of the biblical narratives, since what is essential for the writer is the operation of the wisdom principle rather than the specifics of historical individuals and experience'. H.C. Kee, 'Approaching the

Thus, like 1 QH, the standpoint of pneumatology in Wisdom 9:17-18 is soteriological. The achievement of a right relationship with God depends on the gift of the Spirit. This indicates that unlike other intertestamental Jewish literature the gift of the Spirit in this work is not only the source of morality (6:12-13; 8:2, 18), but also the essential element of salvation (9:17-18). In short, the pneumatology of both 1 QH and Wisdom 9:17 is soteriological.

At this point, Turner is undoubtedly right in his understanding that the soteriological pneumatology is prevalent in 1 QH and Wisdom. However, it should be remembered that these are only minor sapiential traditional sectarian groups in the midst of much larger Jewish groups.[38] The majority of the Jewish intertestamental literature indicates that this life-giving function is foreign to the Jewish concept of the Spirit. With regard to this, two critical questions are to be asked: 1) How can life-giving wisdom be attained, according to the Jewish conception in this period? 2) How do most Jewish authors of this period understand the Spirit - do they understand the Spirit as the source of life-giving wisdom like Qumran? These questions will help in elucidating how the pneumatology of one small Jewish group, the group which settled at Qumran (also Wis. 9:17), compares with that of the much larger, dominant groups within Judaism.

2.3.2. The Spirit and Extraordinary Wisdom in Intertestamental Literature

2.3.2.1. THE LAW AND LIFE-GIVING WISDOM[39]

It is argued that sapiential achievement at a more fundamental level is closely associated with the study of the law in intertestamental literature.

History of God's People: A Survey of Interpretations of the History of Israel in the Pseudepigrapha, Apocrypha and the New Testament', in *The Pseudepigrapha and Early Biblical Interpretation*, 52.

[38] Menzies, *Spirit and Power*, 93.

[39] For the detailed discussion of the relationship between the law and wisdom in various intertestamental literature such as *Baruch* (3:9-14; 4:1-4), *Enoch* (5:8-9; 42:1-3; 48:1; 49:1-3; 61:1-13; 91:10 etc.), the *Letter of Aristeas* (31, 127, 139, 144, 161, 168, 169), *Sibylline Oracle* (3:219-220, 573-600, 669-697), *4 Maccabees* (1:17; 5:35), *4 Ezra* (5:9-11; 7:88-99; 7:70-74; 8:7-13 etc.), the *Apocalypse of Baruch* (15:5; 38:1-2; 44:14 etc.), the *Psalms of Solomon* (4:8-13; 14:1-12; 16:7-8), and the *Wisdom of Solomon* (2:12; 7:26-27; 18:4), see E. Schnabel, *Law and Wisdom from Ben Sira to Paul: A Tradition Historical Enquiry into the Relation of Law, Wisdom, and Ethics*, WUNT 2.16 (Tübingen: Mohr, 1985), 93-165. As Schnabel argues, granted that the association of law and wisdom widely appears in the intertestamental literature, the sapiential achievement at a more fundamental level most explicitly emerges in relation to the law in the two writings such as Ben Sira and *4 Maccabees* in comparison to the Spirit. So in the following section, I will be discussing only the two pieces of literature. More concern for the present study lies in the relationship between the Spirit and extraordinary wisdom.

However, the fundamental wisdom is not associated with the divine Spirit. This perspective is clearly announced in two pieces of Jewish literature, namely *4 Maccabees* and Ben Sira.

2.3.2.1.1. 4 Maccabees

The author of *4 Maccabees* delineates his treatise as a 'highly philosophical exposition' and depicts its subject as 'devout reason is absolute master of the passions' (1:1).[40] Nevertheless, the author, who lived in a Hellenized environment, remained within his Jewish heritage by keeping his ancestral law and defending his Jewish way of life of obedience to the law (5:16; 9:2, 16; 17:19; 18:1).[41] Thus, for the author of the book, the law was a greater guide for virtue than the Hellenistic way of life and those who sacrifice for the sake of the law are highly vindicated.

The way of true religious life in Judaism is based on reason choosing wisdom acquired through maintenance of the law. This is well illustrated in the story of the honourable victory of Eleazar, who died in disgrace, but finally achieved the honour of a noble soul through devout reason (9:6-9; 17:18; 18:18, 23). Eleazar's heroic example of keeping firmly to the law (6:17-19) empowers the seven brothers (9:5-7) and all the Jewish people to resist the Greek cultural rule over the whole nation.[42] Hence, the author is able to praise Eleazar as 'O mind in perfect unison with the Law, and philosopher of the divine life' (7:7) and appeals to his readers to hold firm to the law by saying that 'So must all those be who are skilled in the craft of keeping the Law and who defend it with their own blood and noble sweat even in the face of sufferings unto death' (7:8).[43] The victory of reason over the passions, i.e., the victory of true religious life over the Greek cultural imperialism, is possible through steadfast commitment to God's law. In his final exhortation, the author says 'O offspring of the seed of Abraham, children of Israel, obey this Law and be altogether true to your religion' (18:1).[44]

---

[40] H. Anderson, '4 Maccabees', *OTP*, 2, 544.

[41] '. . . we must lead our lives in accordance with the divine Law, consider that no compulsion laid on us is mighty enough to overcome our own willing obedience to the Law' (5:16). Anderson, '4 Maccabees', 550. The term law appears in *4 Maccabees* forty times and it designates the Jewish law as shown in the book itself, e.g., 9:2 and 18:10. Cf. P.L. Redditt, 'The Concept of *Nomos* in Fourth Maccabees', *CBQ* 45 (1983), 249-70 (250-51).

[42] Cf. The nation's overall victory over Antiochus in 18:5.

[43] Anderson, '4 Maccabees', 552.

[44] Anderson, '4 Maccabees', 563. It is conceivable that in the beginning the author of *4 Maccabees* invites a Greek-sounding exhortation in 1:2 (pay earnest attention to philosophy) but in the end he draws 'the very Jewish exhortation to "obey this law and exercise piety in every way"' in 18:1. D.A. de Silva, *4 Maccabees* (Sheffield: SAP, 1998), 44. This simply indicates how the author has been steeped in the Greek

According to the author, this reason is 'the mind making a deliberate choice of the life of wisdom' (1:15). So, like Ben Sira's assertion, 'in all wisdom there is the fulfilment of the Law' (19:20), the author of *4 Maccabees* defines wisdom as 'education in the Law'.[45] The definition is well presented in the author's own words;

> Wisdom, I submit, is knowledge of things divine and human, and of their causes. And this wisdom, I assume, is the culture we acquire from the Law, through which we learn the things of God reverently and the things of men to our worldly advantage. The forms of wisdom consist of prudence, justice, courage, and temperance (φρόνησις καὶ δικαιοσύνη καὶ ἀνδρεία καὶ σωφροσύνη). Of all these prudence is the most authoritative, for it is through it that reason controls the passion (1:16-19).[46]

This passage shows that the Jewish law is depicted as the source of wisdom. The association between the two is also made in 5:35 where '"wisdom-loving reason" (φιλόσοφος λόγος) is closely linked with the venerated priesthood and with "the knowledge of the law" (νομοθεσίας ἐπιστήμη)'.[47] Before the author shows the different sorts of passion (1:20-29), the forms of wisdom are then listed under four main virtues: prudence, justice, courage, and temperance (1:18). It is notable that the author regards prudence as the best fountainhead among the four virtues. This is because virtue forces reason to control the passions (1:19). The law clearly stands as the instructor in the components of wisdom.

In short, for *4 Maccabees*, wisdom at a more fundamental level is not associated with the divine gift, but rather the instruction of the law. The example of Eleazar shows that adherence to the law is primarily the source of true piety and religion. A further instance of this phenomenon is seen in the Wisdom of Sirach.

2.3.2.1.2. Ben Sira

Like *4 Maccabees*, in the Wisdom of Sirach, wisdom at a more fundamental level is closely associated with the law. For Sirach, the acquisition of the divine wisdom is dependent upon the study of the law: 'if you desire wisdom, keep the commandments' (1:26);[48] 'Reflect on the statutes of the Lord, and meditate at all times on his commandments. It is he who will give

---

thought and language but at the same time how he has been faithful to his Jewish heritage and the law.

[45] de Silva, *4 Maccabees*, 56. de Silva further points out that, for the author of *4 Maccabees*, 'the two curriculum of "wisdom", namely divine and human matters, is fully covered by the Torah's instruction'.

[46] Anderson, '4 Maccabees', 545. GT is from Rahlfs, *Septuaginta*.

[47] Schnabel, *Law and Wisdom*, 137.

[48] All ET of Ben Sira is from RSV and GT is from Rahlfs, *Septuaginta*.

insight to your mind, and our desire for wisdom will be granted' (6:37); Or, 'Whoever keeps the law controls his thoughts, and the fulfillment of the fear of the Lord is wisdom' (21:11);

> On the other hand he who devotes himself to the study of the law of the Most High will seek out the wisdom of all the ancients, and will be concerned with prophecies; he will preserve the discourse of notable men and penetrate the subtleties of parables; he will seek out the hidden meanings of proverbs and be at home with the obscurities of parables. He will serve among great men and appear before rulers; he will travel through the lands of foreign nations, for he tests the good and the evil among men. He will set his heart to rise early to seek the Lord who made him, and will make supplication before the Most High; he will open his mouth in prayer and make supplication for his sins (39:1-5).

Thus, 'To define the one who is wise, Sirach asserts, "whoever holds to the law will obtain wisdom" (14:20-27)'.[49]

In addition, beyond the relationship between wisdom and the law, Sirach goes further when he links wisdom to the gift of the Spirit. This motif is clearly indicated in the description of 39:6-11, esp. 39:6-8;

> If the great Lord is willing, he will be filled with the spirit of understanding (πνεύματι συνέσεως ἐμπλησθήσεται); he will pour forth words of wisdom of his own and give thanks to the Lord in prayer. The Lord will direct his counsel and knowledge, as he meditates on his mysteries (ἐν τοῖς ἀποκρύφοις). He will show the wisdom of what he has learned, and will glory in the law of the Lord's covenant.

The key verse in this passage is verse 6 where the conception of the scribe's prophetic inspiration is clear. When he is filled with the Spirit, the scribe pours forth wisdom. The description of the 'spirit of understanding' is significant and indicates nothing other than wisdom bestowed by the Spirit of God.[50] While the wise man devotes himself to the study of the law in order to seek out wisdom (39:1), i.e., the acquisition of the fundamental level of wisdom through human effort, the Spirit fills the scribe with

---

[49] Kee, 'Approaching the History of God's People', 46.

[50] Menzies, *Development*, 69. This judgment is reasonably explained by Menzies, who follows Davis: first, in the case of Sirach 48:24, where Isaiah's prophetic spirit, which enables him to see the future, is described as a πνεύματι μεγάλω, the anarthrous use of πνεῦμα (a circumlocution for the Spirit of God) accords with the assertion; second, the collocation of πνεῦμα and σύνεσις is often found in the LXX with reference to wisdom granted by the Spirit of God (Exod. 31:3; Deut. 34:9; Isa. 11:2); third, the context, where 'the Spirit of understanding is given in accordance with the will of the Lord (39:6a)', supports the judgment. Cf. J.A. Davis, *Wisdom and Spirit: An Investigation of 1 Corinthians 1.18-3.20 against the Background of Jewish Sapiential Tradition in the Greco-Roman Period* (Lanham: University Press of America, 1984), 21, 164, n. 53; Montague, *Holy Spirit*, 99.

wisdom and inspires him to fulfill *his vocation* by proclaiming sapiential words and to give thanks to the Lord in prayer (39:6), i.e., the acquisition of the higher level of wisdom through the divine Spirit.

With regard to this, Orton's argument is persuasive when he distinguishes the way of achieving wisdom in 39:1-5 from that of 39:6. In the former, the achievement of wisdom is associated with the study or interpretation of the secrets of the scriptures while, in the latter, it is related to 'special insight, a "spirit of understanding"' based on the understanding already achieved.[51] Davis also claims that there are three different levels or stages of sapiential acquisition in Sirach 38:24-39:11, calling the former (39:1-5) the second or higher level and the latter as the highest level (39:6).[52] Thus, for Ben Sira, it seems clear that the highest level of wisdom is attained through the prophetic inspiration of the Spirit whereas a more fundamental level of wisdom is achieved through the study of the law. This understanding is further supported by the following. The scribe whom Ben Sira is talking of is not an ordinary person, but the exceptional one or the ideal one, and his endowment is 'special insight that is given to the eminent, righteous scribe... (and) for the benefits of others'.[53] Furthermore, the clause 'if the great Lord is willing' in 39:6 indicates that not all scribes could obtain the special gift or the inspired wisdom, but it is given only to some who are chosen and elevated by the divine initiative. So, the experience described in 39:6 is extraordinary and exceptional in comparison with that of verses 39:1-5.

In short, for Ben Sira, a fundamental level of wisdom, life-giving wisdom, is acquired by human effort through the study of the scriptures, but the ultimate plateau of sapiential achievement is closely associated with the divine Spirit as the source of extraordinary wisdom.

2.3.2.1.3. Summary

According to the perspectives of *4 Maccabees* (Hellenistic) and Ben Sira (Palestinian), life-giving wisdom is not connected to the prophetic activity of the Spirit, but rather can be achieved by studying and keeping the law. Along with this notion, the activity of the Spirit is rather associated with extraordinary wisdom according to Ben Sira. The latter perspective is further supported by many other intertestamental documents both in

---

[51] D.E. Orton, *The Understanding Scribe: Matthew and the Apocalyptic Ideal*, JSNT 25 (Sheffield: JSOP Press, 1989), 75.

[52] Davis, *Wisdom and Spirit*, 16-21 (21).

[53] Orton, *Understanding*, 70; cf. Schnabel's statement on this issue: '. . . whereas the "normal" scribe was engaged in the reproducing investigation of the Torah and tradition, in political service and in personal piety, the inspired scribe is involved, on top of that, (1) in the production of wisdom material. . . (2) in "speculative" thinking. . . and (3) in the pedagogical communication of his wisdom'. *Law and Wisdom*, 53-54.

Palestinian and Hellenistic writings as will be shown in what follows.

2.3.3. The Spirit and Extraordinary Wisdom[54]

The purpose of this section is to examine how the authors of the vast body of other intertestamental Jewish literature usually understand the role of the Spirit in a manner different from the sectarian viewpoints of Qumran and Wisdom. We begin this discussion with the Spirit and the extraordinary wisdom in Palestinian literature.[55]

---

[54] In the following discussion, the term 'extraordinary wisdom' contains the meaning of special wisdom, insight, vision, dream, revelation etc., in which the Spirit functions as the source in the unaided human ability. Although Turner attempts to distinguish charismatic revelation from charismatic wisdom in the concept of the Spirit of prophecy, the distinction is not so sharp, as Turner himself admits, and should not be heeded in the definition of extraordinary wisdom in this study.

[55] It has been debated whether the references to the Spirit in the *Testaments of the Twelve Patriarchs* (e.g., *T. Sim.* 4:4; *T. Lev.* 2:3; 18:7, 11; *T. Ben.* 8:3; 9:3; *T. Jud.* 20:1f.; 24:2) should be classified as the prophetic characteristic of the Spirit in Palestinian interpretation of Jewish literature. This is because, particularly in the area of discussion on pneumatology, some references to the Spirit are found to be characterized by a Christian origin. The reason why this document is also controversial is because some Spirit references depict the prophetic activity of the Spirit as the source of sanctification and moral effectiveness. So, viewing the texts like *T. Sim.* 4:4, *T. Ben.* 8:1-3, and *T. Lev.* 2:3 as the editor's own hand and the texts like *T. Ben.* 9:3 and *T. Jud.* 24:2-3 as a Christian interpolation, Turner supports his case that the activity of the Spirit in the intertestamental period is associated with a life-giving function. Menzies, on the other hand, argues that since four texts are of Christian origin (*T. Lev.* 18:7, 11; *T. Ben.* 9:3; *T. Jud.* 24:2) and the remaining passages are uncertain (except *T. Jud.* 20:1f., which is parallel with 1QS 3:13-4:26), he does not include the literature in his analysis. However, beyond the discussion of the origin of the Spirit references, the major debate in the literature remains whether it is an originally Jewish document with light or heavy Christian interpolation or a Christian work originally in Greek that has mainly re-worked some Jewish materials. Those who support the former include R.H. Charles and H.C. Kee while those who assert the latter include H.W. Hollander and M. de Jonge. Indeed this debate is going on, and does not seem yet to be satisfactorily resolved. However, in particular, de Jonge's thorough analysis and consideration over almost a half-century (from *The Testaments of the Twelve Patriarchs: A Study of their Text, Composition and Origin* [Manchester: Assen, 1953] to 'Levi in Aramaic Levi and in the Testament of Levi', in E.G. Chazon and M.E. Stone (eds.), *Pseudepigraphic Perspectives: the Apocrypha and Pseudepigrapha in light of the Dead Sea Scrolls. Proceedings of the International Symposium of the Orion Center for the Study of the Dead Sea Scrolls and Associated Literature, 12-14 January, 1997* [Leiden/ Boston/ Köln: Brill, 1999], 71-89) in concluding that 'The Testament must be studied as a Christian composition' (and) 'were fitted into a specific Christian framework' ('Levi', 71, 89) should never be neglected in any discussion of the literature. See de Jonge's

2.3.3.1. THE SPIRIT AND EXTRAORDINARY WISDOM IN PALESTINIAN LITERATURE

2.3.3.1.1. 1 Enoch

In the earlier section, we have observed that the wisdom of the Messiah endowed by the Spirit in *1 Enoch* (e.g., 49:3; 62:2) is to rule over his people effectively and not for life-giving wisdom. Beyond these two messianic texts, the same tendency to identify the Spirit with extraordinary wisdom is also shown in a different context (*1 En.* 91:1),[56] where Enoch begins to admonish his children:

> Now, my son Methuselah, (please) summon all your brothers on my behalf, and gather together to me all the sons of your mother; for a voice calls me, and the spirit is poured over me so that I may show you everything that shall happen to you forever.[57]

Enoch in this text is moved by the Spirit to have extraordinary vision and insight into the future in his final testament so that he will see everything that is to happen. Thus, this example, along with the messianic passages (49:3; 62:2), indicates that the purpose of pneumatology in the work is to attribute extraordinary insight and wisdom to the Spirit.[58]

2.3.3.1.2. 4 Ezra

This apocryphal composition also does not fail to connect the Spirit to special insight, particularly in the form of inspiration. *4 Ezra* 14:19f. describes Ezra's inspired scribal experience. For this experience, Ezra begins to make request of the Holy Spirit:

> For your Law has been burned, and so no one knows the things which have been done or will be done by you. If then I have found favour before you, send the

---

thoroughgoing articles for further discussion on the issue: 'The Main Issues in the Study of the Testaments of the Twelve Patriarchs', in *Jewish Eschatology, Early Christian Christology and the Testaments of the Twelve Patriarchs* (Leiden: Brill, 1991), 147-63 and in the same book 'The Testaments of the Twelve Patriarchs: Christian and Jewish', 233-43. Therefore, due to this unsolved major problem, in the light of the high possibility of Christian composition of the literature, I will exclude the *Testaments of the Twelve Patriarchs* in this analysis. Likewise, although the association between the Spirit and prophetic activity is indicated in the *Martyrdom of Isaiah* 1:7 and 5:15, the work will also be omitted in our discussion due to a possibility of Christian editorial addition on the term 'the Beloved'. Cf. M.A. Knibb, 'Martyrdom and Ascension of Isaiah', *OTP*, 2, 157, n. t.

[56] In *1 Enoch*, the reference to the divine Spirit emerges only three times (49:3; 62:2; 91:1; cf. 67:10; 99:16).

[57] Isaac, '1 Enoch', 72.

[58] Cf. Levison, *Spirit*, 179.

Holy Spirit to me. . . , and I will write everything that has happened in the world from the beginning, the things which were written in your Law, that men may be able to find the path, and that those who wish to love in the last days may live (14:21-22).[59]

The result of Ezra's inspiration is that he is able to receive special insight to write what happened in the world from the beginning. God immediately replies, 'I will light in your heart the lamp of understanding, which shall not be put out until what you are about to write is finished' (14:25).[60] The promise of the lamp of understanding connotes the Spirit's continuing inspiration upon Ezra's heart until his task is finished.[61] Furthermore, the giving of the Spirit, which is depicted as a divine cup filled with water like fire, empowers Ezra in understanding and wisdom and memory retention when he drinks (14:40).[62] Consequently, the outcome of this inspired experience for forty days is the writing of ninety-four books (14:45). In short, the role of the Spirit described in *4 Ezra* is not life-giving wisdom, but extraordinary wisdom.

2.3.3.1.3. Jubilees

The author of *Jubilees* also attributes the Spirit with special inspiration and wisdom. In *Jubilees* 25:14, when a divine gift descends upon Rebekah's mouth, she is able to bless her son, Jacob: 'And at that time, when a spirit of truth[63] descended upon her mouth, she placed her two hands upon the head of Jacob and said. . .'.[64] In *Jubilees* 31:12, the special blessing that Isaac gives to his grandchildren, Levi and Judah is caused by the inspiration of the Spirit: 'And a spirit of prophecy came down upon his mouth. And he took Levi in his right hand and Judah in his left hand'.[65] Thus, in these blessing modes, the blessings of Rebecca and Isaac to their children are caused by the advent of the Spirit.

On the other hand, in *Jubilees* 40:5, the fact that the gift of the divine Spirit is essential to understand and interpret dreams and visions is indicated in the statement of Pharaoh, who praises Joseph on the extraordinary interpretation of his dreams: 'And the LORD gave Joseph

---

[59] B.M. Metzger, 'The Fourth Book of Ezra', *OTP*, 1, 554.
[60] Metzger, 'The Fourth Book of Ezra', 554.
[61] Levison, *Spirit*, 205.
[62] 'And I took it and drank; and when I had drunk it, my heart poured forth understanding, and wisdom increased in my breast, for my spirit retained its memory' (14:40).
[63] The Ethiopic manuscript C reads 'a holy spirit', rather than 'a spirit of truth'. Cf. O.S. Wintermute 'Jubilees', *OTP*, 2, 105. n. b. 'Either reading would be appropriate in this context'.
[64] Wintermute 'Jubilees', 105.
[65] Wintermute 'Jubilees', 115.

favour and mercy in the sight of the Pharaoh. And the Pharaoh said to his servants, "We will not find a man wise and knowledgeable as this man because the spirit of the LORD is with him"'.[66] Here again, the Spirit is depicted as the source of extraordinary wisdom.

2.3.3.1.4. Pseudo-Philo (Liber Antiquitatum Biblicarum)

In a similar form to *Jubilees* in terms of retelling the biblical story, the author of Pseudo-Philo apparently connects the activity of the Spirit to special insight (in dreams), prophetic inspiration and praise in numerous cases. According to 9:10, when the Spirit of God comes upon Miriam, she experiences the extraordinary dream in which she predicted the birth of Moses. In the description of Kenaz's final experience of the Spirit, the author connects the Spirit to an extraordinary vision: 'And they (the prophets and elders of Israel) had sat down, a holy spirit came upon Kenaz and dwelled in him and put him in ecstasy, and he began to prophesy, saying. . .' (28:6).[67] Here the Holy Spirit that inspires Kenaz is a divine force to see a prophetic vision of the future. A similar prophetic experience to that of Kenaz is depicted in Saul's final experience of the Spirit: 'And a spirit abided in Saul, and he prophesied, saying. . .' (62:2).[68] Like that of Kenaz, the Spirit, who indwells Saul, becomes the source of Saul's ability to prophesy.[69] The inspiration of the Spirit is also depicted as the ability to predict the death of an enemy, Sisera, in Barak's statement when he (Barak) found Sisera dead: 'Blessed be the Lord, who sent his spirit and said, "Into the hand of a woman Sisera will be handed over"' (31:9).[70]

The activity of the Spirit is also described in the form of inspiration for praise: 'But you, Deborah, sing praises, and the grace of the holy spirit awaken in you, and begin to praise the works of the LORD. . .' (32:14).[71] Here Deborah's potential to praise the Lord's works which bring about the victory of Israel is attributed to the endowment of the Spirit. In short, the Spirit in Pseudo-Philo is a special endowment which inspires people to see the future in a dream, or a vision, to praise and to prophesy.[72]

---

[66] Wintermute 'Jubilees', 130.
[67] D.J. Harrington, 'Pseudo-Philo', *OTP*, 2, 341. Although Harrington translates *spiritus* in Latin as 'a holy spirit', it is not difficult to assume it to be 'the Spirit of God' if one sees other references of prophetic inspiration in this work (cf. 9:10; 18:10; 27:9-10; 31:9; 32:14; 60:1; 62:2 etc.). See further Levison, *Spirit*, 104, n. 10.
[68] Harrington, 'Pseudo-Philo', 374.
[69] Both accounts are also comparable in their inability to recollect what was seen or said under the effect of the Spirit. Of Kenaz, 'But he (Kenaz) did not know what he had said or what he had seen' (28:10). Of Saul, 'And Saul went away and did not know what he had prophesied' (62:2).
[70] Harrington, 'Pseudo-Philo', 345.
[71] Harrington, 'Pseudo-Philo', 347.
[72] In addition to this prophetic insight in Pseudo-Philo, the Spirit is also associated with

2.3.3.1.5. Summary

The general perspective of pneumatology in Palestinian literature such as Ben Sira, *1 Enoch*, *4 Ezra*, *Jubilees*, and Pseudo-Philo is that the Spirit as the source of prophecy undoubtedly functions as extraordinary insight and wisdom rather than life-giving wisdom. The Spirit is depicted as a key source of the wisdom which is otherwise incomprehensible to the people of God. This notion is also consistent with that of Hellenistic literature.

2.3.4. The Spirit and Extraordinary Wisdom in Hellenistic Literature[73]

2.3.4.1. JOSEPHUS

There can be little doubt that in his writings Josephus preserves significant information about prophecy and this is closely associated with the activity of the Spirit. The biblical references to the Spirit which Josephus records are almost always related to prophetic activity (e.g., *Ant*. 4:118; *Ant*. 6:222; *Ant*. 6:223; *Ant*. 10:239; cf. *Ant*. 1:27, which is the only exception). This idea is also evident by Josephus' redaction of the biblical texts. Josephus adds the reference to πνεῦμα in his writings which does not appear in the LXX or the MT (e.g., *Ant*. 4:108; *Ant*. 4:119-120; *Ant*. 6:166; *Ant*. 8:408) and depicts it as the source of prophetic inspiration. Josephus also omits πνεῦμα which clearly emerges in the LXX to highlight the prophetic role of the Spirit (e.g., *Ant*. 4:165; *Ant*. 5:285; *Ant*. 8:295; *Ant*. 9:10; *Ant*. 9:168).[74] Thus, in various ways, Josephus emphasizes the attribution of prophecy to the Spirit. This attribution, according to Josephus, is also closely depicted as an extraordinary wisdom and insight.

In the *Antiquities*, Daniel was viewed in the highest regard by Josephus. Of particular significance for the present study is a Danielic figuration which is inspired by the Spirit and accordingly shows extraordinary wisdom. A clear instance is in *Antiquities* 10:239. Josephus, citing Daniel 5:14, associates the activity of the Spirit with this extraordinary wisdom after

---

the military success of Gideon in 36:2 and similarly with the great deed of Kenaz in 27:9-10. Levison argues that Pseudo-Philo 20:2-3, where the reference to the Spirit is omitted, but which is clearly reminiscent of Deut. 34:9a (Joshua son of Nun was full of the spirit of wisdom, because Moses had laid his hands on him. . .), further indicates the role of the Spirit as the power of transformation in becoming a new person and the source of wisdom and understanding. *Spirit*, 99-101.

[73] Although the neat distinction between Palestinian and Hellenistic Judaism is an arbitrary issue, maintaining it here is simply for a structural reason. Cf. M. Hengel, *Judaism and Hellenism: Studies in their Encounter in Palestine during the Early Hellenistic Period*, vol. 1 (Minneapolis: Fortress Press, 1981), 251.

[74] Menzies, *Development*, 58-60; M.E. Isaacs, *The Concept of the Spirit: A Study of Pneuma in Hellenistic Judaism and its Bearing on the New Testament* (London: Heythrop College, 1976), 47-48; Levison, *Spirit*, 244-45.

Daniel's remarkable interpretation of the handwriting on the wall: 'On hearing this, Baltasar (Belshazzar in Hebrew text) called Daniel and, after telling him that he had learned of him and his wisdom and of the divine spirit (τὸ Θεῖον πνεῦμα) that attended him and how he alone (μόνος) was fully able to discover things which were not within the understanding of others...' (*Ant.* 10:239).[75]

Several observations are notable in this passage and its context. First, the strength of Josephus' praise of Daniel's marvelous wisdom may be compared with the original text. In the previous lines (*Ant.* 10:235-236), according to Josephus, the magicians called by the king failed twice to interpret the handwriting on the wall in spite of their more earnest and ambitious manners and efforts in their second attempt. But in Daniel 5:8, it is recorded that they failed to do it just once. This enhances the concept of Daniel's extraordinary ability, inspired by the Spirit, which it was impossible for others to have. This is why Josephus adds the simple and important word, 'only' (μόνος) in the text. Only Daniel, who is accompanied by the Spirit, is capable of finding out what others cannot.

Secondly, Josephus more clearly relates the extraordinary wisdom of Daniel to the Spirit by adding the article τό, and the adjective θεῖον. The LXX reading of Daniel 5:14 is '... ὅτι πνεῦμα Θεοῦ ...' As shown in the LXX, the article before πνεῦμα is omitted so that the designation of the word does not make it clear whether it is a spirit or the Spirit of God in Daniel. However, Josephus' text makes it clear that the Spirit that inspired Daniel was the divine initiative.[76]

In short, Josephus' presentation of Daniel in *Antiquities* 10:239 suggests that the source of extraordinary wisdom emerging in Daniel is the Spirit. This simply indicates that the prophetic activity of the Spirit is not associated with life-giving wisdom, but it is related to extraordinary insight and wisdom in Josephus.

2.3.4.2. PHILO

Philo's language and understanding of the Spirit seems quite elusive. Thus, Philo describes the concept of the Spirit in a variety of expressions depending on the context of his argument.[77] Particularly, in the concept of the rational aspect of the soul, Philo often associates the gift of the Spirit with an animating life principle as the source for knowing the will of God. But, at the same time, the gift of the Spirit is also generally described as a

---

[75] All Greek and English Translations are from R. Marcus, *Josephus* (LCL, 1937).

[76] Levison, *Spirit*, 169.

[77] E.g., an angel (e.g., *Vit. Mos.* 1:274; *Vit. Mos.* 2:264-265), wind (e.g., *Plant.* 23-24; *Spec. Leg.* 3:1-6), air (e.g., *Gig.* 22), wisdom (e.g., *Gig.* 27), the rational aspect of the Soul (e.g., *Leg. All.* 4:123; *Op. Mund.* 134-135, 144; *Plant.* 18; *Der. Pot. Ins.* 83). Isaacs, *Spirit*, 42; Menzies, *Development*, 63-65; cf. W. Bieder, 'πνεῦμα', *TDNT*, VI, 372-75; Levison, *Spirit*, 238-39.

specific gift, a prophetic endowment according to him (*Vit. Mos.* 1:277: 'There fell upon him (Balaam) the truly prophetic spirit which banished utterly from his soul his art of wizardry': see also *Mig.* 34-35; *Rev. Div. Her.* 249, 265; *Spec. Leg.* 1:65; 4:49; *Quaest. In Gen.* 3:9; *Vit. Mos.* 2:188, 191; *Som.* 2:252; *Cher.* 27-29; *Jos.* 110-116).[78] However, the difference between these two concepts is that the latter is granted to only the few, with temporary possession, while the former is given to all men at creation with permanent possession.[79] This distinctive of Philo's pneumatology thus gives ground for caution in ascertaining what Philo means by the term, the divine Spirit.

In spite of the different nature of Philo's pneumatology, Turner attempts to link it together to build his argument for the Spirit as the source of the ethical and spiritual life in Philo. Turner argues that: 'both gifts (the rational aspect of the soul and the specific prophetic gift) share the important characteristic that they enable the (ethically and spiritually oriented) wisdom which facilitates knowledge of – and fellowship with – God'.[80] Turner lists *Quis Rerum Divinarum Heres* 57 and *De Opificio Mundi* 144, and *De Gigantibus* 55 as examples. However, with the uniqueness of Philo's pneumatology in mind, the nature of the Spirit in the first two passages (*Rev. Div. Her.* 57 and *Op. Mund.* 144) belongs to the rational aspect rather than to the specific prophetic gift, but not both. The text *De Gigantibus* 55[81] seems at first sight to suggest that Moses has a permanent endowment of the Spirit and one which is positively associated with righteousness. However, what is to be understood in the text is the nature of the relationship, i.e., *does the Spirit inspire prophetic words which reveal God's righteous will* or *does the Spirit actually impart righteousness to Moses so transforming his heart*? In the light of the traditional Jewish portraits of Moses as the supreme prophet (e.g., *Vit. Mos.* 2:187), the accentuation of the text about Moses as having a permanent gift of the Spirit and in view of Philo's broader understanding of pneumatology, it is highly probable that the Spirit here is the Spirit of prophecy which reveals God's will to *others through* Moses.[82] For Philo, this prophetic nature of the divine Spirit is more prevalent in his extensive writings than any other concept and is closely associated with extraordinary wisdom and vision like the analogous case of Josephus.

As Josephus associates the Spirit with extraordinary wisdom in the story

---

[78] All quotations of Philonic texts in English and Greek are from F.H. Colson and G.H. Whitaker, *Philo* (LCL, 1929-1962).

[79] Isaacs, *Spirit*, 42; Menzies, *Development*, 64-65.

[80] Turner, *Power*, 124-25 (125).

[81] 'He (Moses) then has ever the divine spirit at his side, taking the lead in every journey of righteousness, but from those others, as I have said, it quickly separates itself...'

[82] See below in this section.

of Daniel, so Philo links it to Moses and Joseph. In *De Vita Mosis*, Philo expresses the highest regard for Moses, '. . . Moses was a most excellent king, and lawgiver, and high priest. . .' and particularly describes him as 'a prophet of the highest quality' (*Vit. Mos.* 2:187). In the subsequent verse, Philo depicts three kinds of oracles,

> Of the divine utterances, some are spoken by God in His own Person with His prophet for interpreter, in some the revelation comes through question and answer, and others are spoken by Moses in his own person, when possessed by God and carried away out of himself (*Vit. Mos.* 2:188).

In particular, the third oracle requires attention because it includes two irreconcilable divisions. Moses' utterance derives from his own person in the former, while Moses is carried away out of himself by divine inspiration. This clear definition of a prophet in the second part of the third kind of oracle presents Moses as a prophet 'par excellence'.[83]

In various instances, Philo supports the notion that Moses is given extraordinary insight and wisdom by inspired possession. For example, the Spirit, as the source of extraordinary wisdom, is imparted to the seventy elders by Moses to be Israel's leaders (*Gig.* 24). In particular, Philo, in his *De Vita Mosis*, gives five further examples with some redactional alteration of the biblical texts.[84]

1) When the Israelites faced a desperate moment and were trapped between their enemies and the sea, the prophet Moses was no longer master of himself, but rather became inspired (οὐκέτ' ὢν ἐν ἑαυτῷ θεοφορεῖται καὶ θεσπίζει τάδε) and gave a message of assurance to his people (2:246-257 [250]). According to Exodus 14:13 (LXX), Moses simply spoke (εἶπεν) to the people. However, Philo's Moses became inspired by divine possession.

2) According to Philo, Moses, who was 'under inspiration' (ἐπιθειάσας), commanded the Israelites to collect manna only for each day (2:259). But, according to Exodus 16:15 (LXX), Moses simply said (εἶπεν) to them that the manna is the bread which is given from God.

3) Philo records Moses' prophecy of the sabbath as of divine inspiration by saying that

> Moses, when he heard of this and also actually saw it, was awestruck and, guided by what was not so much surmise as God-sent inspiration, made announcement (θεοφορηθεὶς ἐθέσπισε) of the sabbath. I need hardly say that conjectures of this

---

[83] So, Philo further ensures the latter of the third kind by saying that 'the speaker appears under that divine possession in virtue of which he is chiefly and in the strict sense considered a prophet' (*Vit. Mos.* 2:191).

[84] J.R. Levison, 'Inspiration and the Divine Spirit in the Writings of Philo Judaeus', *JSJ* 25 (1995), 271-323 (310-12).

kind are closely akin to prophecies. For the mind could not have made so straight an aim if there was not also the divine spirit (θεῖον πνεῦμα) guiding it to the truth itself (2:264-265).

This text indicates that the guidance of Moses' mind and the announcement of the prediction of the sabbath is by the divine Spirit. However, Moses in Exodus 16:23 (LXX) just 'said (εἶπεν) to them' that they have to take rest on the seventh day.[85]

4) In 2:272, Philo's Moses retells what Moses said (εἶπεν) in Exodus 32:36 (LXX), 'who is on the Lord's side?' after he was 'filled with the Spirit' (ἐπιφημίσας) in the context of the creation of the golden calf.

5) Philo depicts Moses who was God's agent in the story of Korah's rebellion (2:275-287) attributing divine inspiration so: 'This again came from his own mouth when again under possession (πάλιν χατασχεθεὶς ἀνεφθέγξατο). . .' (2:275). However, according to Numbers 16:28 (LXX), Moses simply said (εἶπεν) that '. . . the Lord has sent me to perform all these works. . .'

Two observations are to be noted in these instances. First, Philo substitutes the word (εἶπεν) in the LXX with the words associated with prophetic inspiration. This transformation of language possibly enables Philo to attribute to Moses the description 'the prophet as a true seer, an interpreter of God, and alone gifted with foreknowledge of the hidden future' (*Vit. Mos.* 2:269). Secondly, in relation to the first observation, as shown above, the effect of Moses' inspiration lies in his extraordinary insight and wisdom in each context by encouragement of his people, right guidance, prediction or decision. This indicates that Philo, who reconsiders Moses and underscores his inspired experiences, links the prophetic activity of the Spirit with this extraordinary wisdom and insight. This opinion also emerges in Philo's recapitulation of Joseph.

In *De Iosepho* 110-116 Philo summarizes Joseph's interpretation of Pharaoh's dream in Genesis 41:14-45 (LXX). Here, before he illustrates the account, Philo attributes the source of Joseph's successful interpretation of the dream to the divine voice: 'Such are the facts which appear from the interpretation, but I also hear the promptings of the divine voice, devising safeguards for the disease, as we may call it. . .' (*Jos.* 110). It seems unclear whether or not the divine voice is the Spirit in this text. However, in the concluding part of the account and following Genesis 41:38 (LXX), Philo clearly employs it once again depicting Joseph as the one 'who has in him the Spirit of God' (ὅς ἔχει πνεῦμα θεῖον ἐν ἑαυτῷ) (*Jos.* 116). This parallelism between the introduction and conclusion to Joseph's interpretation indicates a unity between 'the promptings of the divine voice

---

[85] Furthermore, Philo, who goes on to speak of the sabbath, replaces the word 'εἶπεν' in Exod. 16:25 (LXX) with 'prophesied' (θεσπίζει) in 269.

and the presence of the divine spirit in Joseph'.[86] With this in mind, Philo recapitulates the story of Joseph's interpretation of the king's dreams. The source of Joseph's extraordinary insight, wisdom and ability to interpret unknowable facts is the Spirit.

In short, Philo's portraits of Moses and Joseph show that they are prominent and extraordinary figures in whom the Spirit functions as the cause of their extraordinary insight and wisdom.[87]

2.3.4.3. SUSANNA (THEODOTION)

This short book of Theodotion's version is the story about the persecution and restoration of Susanna based on chapters 3 and 6 of Daniel. Susanna, daughter of Hilkiand and wife of Joakim, was sentenced to death by the false accusation of two Jewish elders. While on their way to carry out the sentence, young Daniel appeared and stopped the procession to ask the elders a question. He, inspired with extraordinary knowledge and wisdom, separated them and asked them the same question which resulted in finding that their testimony was different and false. Finally, Susanna was released, her life saved and the elders received the death sentence instead. The reputation of Daniel was thus brought to the attention of his people.

The particular concern in this story lies with how Daniel was provided with such special wisdom. Verse 45 illustrates this: 'And as she (Susanna) was being led away to be put to death, God aroused the holy spirit (τὸ πνεῦμα τὸ ἅγιον) of a young lad named Daniel'.[88] There is no possibility here of reading the holy spirit of a young boy as any other than the Holy Spirit since 'The occurrence of this modified idiom in Susanna 45 provides a certain reference to the human spirit as the holy spirit during the Greco-Roman era'.[89] Furthermore, from the text, there appears to be a clear association of the Spirit with the extraordinary wisdom and knowledge found in Daniel. This link is supported by Theodotion's alteration of Susanna in LXX. The Susanna passage of LXX (vv. 44-45) reads as follows: 'An angel of the Lord appeared just as she was being led away to be put death. And the angel gave, as he was ordered, a spirit of understanding (πνεῦμα συνέσεως) to a youth named Daniel'. As clearly indicated, the source of Daniel's extraordinary knowledge and wisdom is

---

[86] Levison, *Spirit*, 176.
[87] On Philo's autobiographical experience of prophetic inspiration, see *Abr.* 35; *Mig.* 34-35; *Cher.* 27-29; and *Som.* 2:252; on Abraham's ability of persuasiveness as a public orator as the result of divine inspiration, see *Virt.* 217-218; for further examples of an analogous manner, see *Spec. Leg.* 4:49; *Gig.* 23-27, where it is said that the Spirit is the source of knowledge and wisdom.
[88] RSV. GT is from Rahlfs, *Septuaginta*.
[89] Levison, *Spirit*, 72. Levison further points out that in the Greco-Roman era when the text was written the human spirit is identified with the holy spirit, 73.

distinguished in the Theodotion and the LXX.[90] While the latter attributes it to an angel, who imparted a 'spirit of understanding', the holy spirit is directly associated with the special wisdom in the former. Theodotion's alteration of the LXX emphasizes the connection between the Spirit and extraordinary wisdom. In short, the Spirit in Theodotion's Susanna is not associated with life-giving wisdom, but rather extraordinary wisdom.

2.3.4.4. ARISTOBULUS

The relationship between extraordinary wisdom and the Spirit appears in the second fragment of Aristobulus quoted by Eusebius, *Praeparatio Evangelica*.[91] Eusebius says that 'Therefore (οὖν), those who are able to think well marvel at his (Moses) wisdom and at the divine spirit (τὸ θεῖον πνεῦμα) in accordance with which he has been proclaimed as a prophet also' (*Pr. Ev.* 8.10.4).[92] The conjunction, 'therefore or consequently' (οὖν), concludes what is said about Moses' extraordinary wisdom by which he proclaims 'arrangements of nature and preparations for great events' in the previous verse (8.10.3). Aristobulus associates this special wisdom of Moses with the divine spirit in the subsequent verse. Aristobulus then claims that Moses has been proclaimed as a prophet due to the vivid activities of the Spirit in his life. So, the mode of existence of Moses as a prophet results from the Spirit, who is at the same time the source of his marvelous wisdom.

2.3.4.5. SUMMARY

In Hellenistic literature the prominent role of the Spirit is to inspire prophetic activity. The authors of this literature portray several biblical heroes such as Moses, Joseph and Daniel and depict them as prophetic figures who are inspired by the divine Spirit. However, as in the Palestinian literature, this prophetic experience is not associated with life-giving wisdom. It is rather closely related to extraordinary wisdom and insight.

2.3.5. Summary

The outcome of the examination of pieces of other Jewish literature (both Palestinian and Hellenistic) indicates that the soteriological pneumatology presented at Qumran (particularly in 1 QH) and Wisdom by which Turner considerably supports his argument, is not a major or dominant strand

---

[90] H. Engel, *Die Susanna-Erzählung: Einleitung, Übersetzung und Kommentar zum Septuaginta-Text und zur Theodotion-Bearbeitung* (Göttingen: Vandenhoeck & Ruprecht, 1985), 165.

[91] It is well known that the second fragment of Aristobulus furnishes an allegorical illustration for biblical anthropomorphisms.

[92] A.Y. Collins, 'Aristobulus', *OTP*, 2, 838. The GT is from C.R. Holladay, *Fragments from Hellenistic Jewish Authors: Aristobulus* (Atlanta: Scholars Press, 1995), 136.

within Judaism. A much larger and more prevalent perspective presents the Spirit of prophecy as the source of extraordinary, not life-giving, wisdom.

2.4. The Spirit in Rabbinic Literature

It is generally recognized that the rabbinic writings do not substantially present the concept of the Spirit of prophecy as life-giving wisdom. Rather, the role of the Spirit is seen as the Spirit of prophecy who can be recognized in charismatic inspiration and wisdom.[93] Nevertheless, Turner maintains his case supporting rabbinic traditions on Ezekiel 36 as an example, although he admits the paucity of the aspect of life-giving wisdom in the general rabbinic literature.[94] Turner argues that the gift of the Spirit cited in several references to Ezekiel 36:25-27 refers to '. . . the means of Israel's renewed existential knowledge of God's will. . .'.[95] The promise of this gift is to be closely related to that of Joel 3:1-5 rather than a subsequent gift: 'Joel's promise of the Spirit of prophecy is itself understood as the means of fulfilling Ezekiel 36:26-27 (rather than something additional to it)'.[96] They are not different events but rather two sides of one coin.

On the basis of Turner's thesis, I will mainly discuss the rabbinic traditions pertaining to Ezekiel 36:26-27 and Joel 3:1 (MT) in this section. Important questions should be asked: 'is it correct that one should interpret the gift of the Spirit prophesied by Joel in the light of the promise of Ezekiel?' And 'how does one understand the rabbinic texts quoted together

---

[93] For this reason, Turner shows many exemplary rabbinic references to charismatic revelation and wisdom in his illustration of the prototypical charismatic functions of the Spirit of prophecy. See *Power*, 92-111. On the other hand, numerous rabbinic texts identify the Spirit (or Holy Spirit) with prophecy: *t. Soṭ.* 13.2; *ARN* A.34; *MHG* Gen. 242; cf. *ARN* B.37; *Gen. R.* 44:6; *Cant. R.* 3:4. For example, *ARN* A.34 reads: 'By ten names was the Holy Spirit called, to wit: parable, metaphor, riddle, speech, saying, glory, command, burden, prophecy, vision'. This close connection between the Spirit and prophecy is also evident in the Mekilta, one of the oldest of the Tannaitic Midrashim: *Mek. Shir.* 10 on Exod. 2:4, where, like *LAB* 9:10 in which Miriam experiences a prophetic dream by the Spirit, Miriam's prophetic role is also related to the Spirit. See also *Mek. Pisha* 1 on Exod. 12:1. Schäfer, in his study of the terminology of the Holy Spirit and the Spirit of prophecy in the Targumic literature, finds that the phrase the 'Spirit of prophecy' is regularly used in *Targum Onqelos*. Similarly, in *Targum Pseudo-Jonathan*, the phrase is used eleven times while the expression Holy Spirit occurs fifteen times. P. Schäfer, 'Die termini "Heiliger Geist" und "Geist der Prophetie" in den Targumim und das Verhältnis der Targumim zueinander', *VT* 20 (1970), 304-14 (307-08). The Spirit of prophecy used in the targums is widely characterized as the source of extraordinary revelation and wisdom. See below (§2.4.2.) for a detailed explanation.
[94] Turner, *Power*, 129-31.
[95] Turner, *Power*, 131.
[96] Turner, *Power*, 131.

of Ezekiel 36:26 (and 27) and Joel 3:1 (and 1f.)?' Prior to answering them, I will briefly notice a methodological consideration in discussing rabbinic material and then discuss the general notion of the Spirit of prophecy attributed to extraordinary wisdom in the rabbinic literature.

2.4.1. A Consideration of Anachronism

As noted above, one of the main elements of evidence that Turner gives for his case comes from the rabbinic literature. However, it is generally recognized that in any discussion of rabbinic literature in connection with early Jewish literature, the danger of anachronism should be taken into account. This notion is well illustrated by Alexander: 'Many New Testament scholars are still guilty of massive and sustained anachronism in their use of rabbinic sources. Time and again we find them quoting *texts from the 3rd, 4th, or 5th centuries AD, or even later, to illustrate Jewish teaching in the 1st century*'.[97]

The dating of the rabbinic texts (*Midr. Ps.* 14:6 and *Deut. R.* 6:14), on which Turner rests some of his argument, is certainly categorized after the 2nd century AD.[98] This suggests that Turner's evidence from rabbinic literature contains a danger of anachronism and requires a degree of critical prudence in terms of the dating issue.

But some, including Turner, might say that although the rabbinic material was compiled after the 2nd century AD, it still contains traditions from the pre-Christian era[99] so that they have a similar pneumatological perspective to that of early Judaism. However, even, if they reflect the early Jewish pneumatological perspective, it is rather of a prophetic character than life-giving wisdom. The following section will confirm this claim.

2.4.2. The Spirit and Extraordinary Wisdom

The concept of extraordinary wisdom attributed to the Spirit of prophecy is most widely represented in the Targumic material with redactional additions from the Hebrew Bible.[100] For example, in the marginal reading of *Targum*

---

[97] P.S. Alexander, 'Rabbinic Judaism and the New Testament', *ZNW* 74 (1983), 237-46 (244). Emphasis is original.

[98] E. Schürer, *The History of the Jewish People in the Age of Jesus Christ*, vol. 1, rev. and ed. G. Vermes, F. Millar, and M. Black (Edinburgh: T. & T. Clark, 1973), 90.

[99] E.g., M. McNamara, *Palestinian Judaism and the New Testament*, GNS 4 (Wilmington: Michael Glazier, 1983), 174-77.

[100] Since it is generally accepted that the Spirit in the rabbinic literature (whether it is the Spirit of prophecy or the Holy Spirit) is understood as the source of extraordinary wisdom or insight, it is not necessary to repeat the notion here. I will just discuss, as an example, the view of the targumists which is most common in the rabbinic literature. For other rabbinic examples, see *Midr. R. Gen.* 75:8 (Isaac); 91:6

Neofiti 1 Exodus 2:12, Moses experiences extraordinary revelation by the Spirit: 'Moses looked in a spirit of prophecy in this world and in the world to come and he saw and behold, there was no innocent man to go forth with him and he smote the Egyptian and buried him in the sand'.[101] In *Targum Onqelos* Genesis 41:38, Joseph's extraordinary wisdom in interpreting Pharaoh's dream is clearly associated with the Spirit of prophecy: 'Thereupon the Pharaoh said to his servants, "Can we find a man like this in whom there is *the spirit of prophecy from before the Lord*?"'[102] An almost identical parallel to this wording appears in *Targum Pseudo-Jonathan* Genesis 41:38 where the Spirit of prophecy is identified with extraordinary wisdom in Joseph.[103] Jacob's special insight to see what is happening with his son is associated with the presence of the Spirit:

> And he (Jacob) recognised it and said: 'It is my son's garment; a wild beast has not devoured him nor has my son been killed at all; however, I see through the

---

(Jacob), 7 (Joseph's brothers); 93:12 (Joseph); cf. 37:7; 84:12, 19 (Jacob); 97; *Midr. R.* Exod. 1:28 (Moses); *Midr. R.* Lev. 1:3; 21:8 (R. Akiba); 32:4 (Moses); cf. 15:2; *Midr. R.* Num. 9:20 (R. Meir); 14:5 (Jacob); 19:3 (Solomon); cf. 21:9 (Eleazar); *Midr. R.* Ruth 2:1 (Rahab); *Midr. R.* Ecc. 3.21.1 (Abigail); *Midr. R.* Cant. 1.1.8-9 (Solomon); *Midr. Ps.* 10:6 (Isaac); 105:5 (Rebecca); *Per. R.* 3:4 (Joseph). For example *Midr. Ps.* 105:5 reads: 'For R. Yudan in the name of R. Isaac, in interpreting *And what Esau her elder son said in his heart was told to Rebekah* (Gen. 27:42), observed: Who could possibly have told Rebekah, if not the Holy Spirit?' See also *t. Pes.* 2:15 (R. Gamaliel); *y. Sot.* 1:4; *y. Šeb.* 9:1; *b. Sot.* 11b (Miriam); *b. Meg.* 14a (Sarah); *Mek. Pisha* 13 (the people of Israel); *Mek. Shir.* 7 (the people of Israel); cf. *b. Yom.* 73b etc.

[101] M. McNamara, *Targum Neofiti 1: Exodus* (Edinburgh: T. & T. Clark, 1994). See also *Targ. Neof.* Gen. 31:21 (the reading of margin); Gen. 42:1; Num. 11:28; Exod. 2:12 (M2). These references of *Targ. Neof.* except the reading of M1 of Exod. 2:12 cited above contain references to the Holy Spirit (רוח קודשה) with whom the extraordinary wisdom is associated.

[102] B. Grossfeld, *The Targum Onqelos to Genesis* (1988). Note Onqelos's rendering of the רוח נבואה from the Hebrew text in which 'the spirit of God' (רוּחַ אֱלֹהִים) is read. This alteration from the spirit of God to the spirit of prophecy, which is described as the source of extraordinary wisdom, also occurs in numerous references in the targum. See *Targ. Onq.* Exod. 31:3; 35:31; Num. 11:25, 26, 29; 24:2; 27:18.

[103] Rebecca's prophetic wisdom is derived from the Holy Spirit in *Targ. Ps.-J.* Gen. 7:5, 42. See also *Targ. Ps.-J.* Gen. 30:25; 31:25; 35:22; 37:33; 43:14; 45:27; Exod. 31:3; 33:16; 35:31; Deut. 5:21; 18:15, 18; 28:59; 32:26; Num. 11:17, 25, 26, 28, 29; 24:2; 27:18. In these references, the extraordinary vision or wisdom is connected to either the spirit of prophecy or the Holy Spirit. This can be compared with *Targ. Onq.*, where the 'Spirit of prophecy' consistently occurs, and *Targ. Neof.* in which the 'Holy Spirit' mainly occurs. Cf. n. 93 above. It is notable that, as discussed earlier, Philo also attributes Joseph's special insight for interpreting the king's dream to the influence of the Spirit in *Jos.* 116: 'who has in him the Spirit of God' (ὃς ἔχει πνεῦμα θεῖον ἐν ἑαυτῷ).

holy spirit that an evil woman stands opposite him, the wife of Potiphar, Pharaoh's official, chief executioner, and she is compared to a beast'.[104]

Job attributes to the spirit of inspiration the unique understanding that a human being normally could not have: 'In truth, it is the spirit of inspiration in a human being, and the *Memra* of the Almighty, (which) makes them (his friends) understand' (*Targ. Job* 32:8).[105]

The notion is also clear in *Targum Jonathan to the Prophets*. For instance, the source of David's prophetic insight about the end of the world is a spirit of prophecy in *Targum of the Prophets* 2 Samuel 23:1-2.[106] According to *Targum of the Prophets* 2 Kings 5:26, Elisha's ability to know of Gehazi's deceitful actions was by a spirit of prophecy

> And he (Elisha) said him (Gehazi): '*In a spirit of prophecy it was revealed to me* when the man turned around from upon his chariot to meet you. Is this the time for you that *you should take* silver and *you should take* clothing? *And you planned in your heart to buy* olives and vineyards and sheep and oxen slaves and handmaidens...'.[107]

Ezekiel's extraordinary prophetic vision before the elders of Judah is directly related to the spirit of prophecy from before the Lord in *Targum Ezekiel* 8:1-3.[108]

It is notable that extraordinary wisdom or insight in the examples cited in the targum is mostly attributed to the רוח נבואה while *Targum Neofiti* attributes it to the holy spirit. This is particularly prevalent in *Targum Onqelos*, *Targum of the Prophets* and *Targum Pseudo-Jonathan* although the latter attributes it also to the Spirit of God.[109] This reflects that the targumists usually understand the role of the Spirit as being of a prophetic character.

To sum up, it is apparent that the Spirit, as the Spirit of prophecy, is generally depicted within rabbinic literature as the source of extraordinary

---

[104] M.L. Klein, *The Fragment-Targums of the Pentateuch according to their Extant Sources* (Rome: Biblical Institute, 1980). In this passage, the biblical sense is changed. See also *Frag. Targ.* Gen. 27:1; 42:1; 2:12; Num. 11:26.

[105] C. Mangan, *The Targum of Job* (1991).

[106] Cf. MT reads a spirit of the Lord instead of the spirit of prophecy.

[107] D.J. Harrington and A.J. Saldarini, *Targum Jonathan of the Former Prophets* (1987). See also *Targ. Neb.* 2 Kings 2:9.

[108] The Hebrew text reads the 'hand of the Lord God' (יד אֲדֹנָי יהוה) for the 'spirit of prophecy'. This alteration is also indicated in other references: *Targ.* Ezek. 1:3; 3:14, 22; 37:1; 40:1. Note particularly *Targ.* Ezek. 37:1 where two linguistic alterations of the biblical texts occur: the 'spirit of prophecy' (v. 1a) from the 'hand of the Lord' (יד־יהוה); the 'spirit of prophecy' (v. 1b) from the 'spirit of the Lord' (ברוּחַ יהוה).

[109] See the relevant references above.

wisdom and insight rather than life-giving wisdom as seen in the above discussion. This notion is particularly prevalent in the targumic tradition which has a rich source of references to the Spirit. Turner builds his case upon the texts related to Ezekiel 36 in the rabbinic literature. The next section will speak to this matter.

2.4.3. Midrash Psalms 14:6 and Deuteronomy Rabbah 6:14: The Removal of Evil Impulse and the Eschatological Outpouring of the Spirit

The most debatable texts on the reference to the eschatological endowment of the Spirit are *Midrash Psalms* 14:6 and *Deuteronomy Rabbah* 6:14 in which citations of both Ezekiel 36:26 and Joel 3:1 (MT) are presented.

> Another comment: David spoke the first time in behalf of the Master, the Holy One, blessed be He, who said: *Oh that they had such a heart as this always, to fear Me, and keep My commandments* (Deut. 5:26); and he spoke the second time in behalf of the disciple Moses who said: *Would that all the Lord's people were prophets* (Num. 11:29). Neither the words of the Master nor the words of the disciple are to be fulfilled in this world, but the words of both will be fulfilled in the world-to-come: The words of the Master, *A new heart also will I give you and ye shall keep Mine ordinances* (Ezek. 36:26), will be fulfilled; and the words of the disciple, *I will pour out My spirit upon all flesh; and your sons and your daughters shall prophesy* (Joel 3:1), will also be fulfilled (*Midr. Ps.* 14:6).[110]

> God said: 'In this world, because there are amongst you slanderers, I have withdrawn My Divine Presence from amongst you', as it is said, *Be Thou exalted, O God, above the heavens* (Ps. 57:12). 'But in the time to come, when I will uproot the Evil Inclination from amongst you', as it is said, *And I will take away the stony heart out of your flesh* (Ezek. 36:26), 'I will restore My Divine Presence amongst you'. Whence this? For it is said, *And it shall come to pass afterward, that I will pour out My spirit upon all flesh*, etc. (Joel 3:1); 'and because I will cause My Divine Presence to rest upon you, all of you will merit the Torah, and you will dwell in peace in the world', as it is said, *And all thy children shall be taught of the Lord; and great shall be the peace of thy children* (Isa. 54:13) (*Deut. R.* 6:14).[111]

These rabbinic texts show that the reference to Ezekiel 36:26 was understood as being the future removal of the evil *yatsar* (inclination or impulse) of the human heart (*Deut. R.* 6:14) and as the transformation of Israel's heart of stone (*Midr. Ps.* 14:6). Joel 3:1 was interpreted by the rabbis as being the eschatological outpouring of the Spirit of prophecy.

---

[110] All references in English translation from the midrash on Psalms are from W.G. Braude, *The Midrash on Psalms*, 2 vols (New Haven: Yale University, 1959).
[111] J. Rabinowitz, 'Deuteronomy', in *The Midrash Rabbah* (London/Jerusalem/New York: Soncino, 1977).

However, as indicated in the texts, the involvement of the Spirit in the subject of the heart of stone and the heart of flesh is surprisingly absent in Ezekiel 36:26, while it is clearly indicated in Joel 3:1 in terms of a restoration of prophecy.

With this basic exegesis, both of these texts have been variously interpreted among scholars, particularly by Turner and Menzies, with no agreement. Turner, as mentioned above, understands the two citations as a simultaneous event, i.e., the restoration of the Spirit of prophecy in Joel 3:1 is to be interpreted in the light of Ezekiel 36:26, while Menzies reads them as chronologically different events, i.e., the event occurring in Ezekiel 36:26 is a prerequisite for that of Joel 3:1 so that the former text is to be understood in terms of the latter. Each interpretation is possible but it is difficult to draw an adequate conclusion about the intrinsic relationship between the two citations in the texts themselves. This is probably because rabbinic texts are a 'literature of quotation'[112] in which readers look at each pertinent quotation as it occurs, and as a result, may read it differently. Nevertheless, seeking certain assertions or purposes in the quotations by the respective rabbis should not be underestimated.[113] It is often suggested that the purpose can be known by the study of uniform redaction in other texts of a contemporary period.[114] Therefore, the critical requirement to be examined lies in how the other uniform texts are understood in different places. This will help us to understand the two scriptural quotations (Ezek. 36:26 and Joel 3:1) in both midrashic texts.

2.4.3.1. THE RABBINIC TRADITION ON EZEKIEL 36:26

References to Ezekiel 36:26 are plentifully recorded in the rabbinic traditions in terms of the end-time to come. Along with *Midrahs Psalms* 14:6 and *Deuteronomy Rabbah* 6:14, there are copious data on the traditions:

> ... So also Israel is sunk in iniquity on account of the evil impulse which is within them, but they do penitence, and God each year pardons their iniquities and renews their heart to fear Him; for it says: *A new heart also will I give you* (Ezek. 36:26). Hence it says: *'Terrible as an army with banners'* (*Exod. R.* 15:6).

> ... God then said to Moses: In this world they made idols because of the Evil Inclination in them, but in the millennium I will uproot from them the Evil Inclination and give them a heart of flesh, as it says, *And I will take away the stony heart from out of your flesh, and I will give you a heart of flesh* (Ezek.

---

[112] H.L. Strack and G. Stemberger, *Introduction to the Talmud and Midrash* (Edinburgh: T. & T. Clark, 1991), 53.

[113] Strack and Stemberger, *Introduction*, 61; A. Goldberg, 'Form-Analysis of Midrashic Literature as a Method of Description', *JJS* 36 (1985), 171.

[114] Cf. Strack and Stemberger, *Introduction*, 61.

36:26) (*Exod. R.* 41:7).[115]

... In the same way the Holy One, blessed be He, said: 'The Torah is called a stone and the Evil Inclination is called a stone'- that the Torah is called a stone is proved by the text, *The tables of* stone, *and the law and the commandment* (Exod. 24:12); that the Evil Inclination is called a stone is proved by the text, *I will take away the heart of stone out of your flesh* (Ezek. 36:26).-Thus the Torah is a stone and the Evil Inclination is a stone. The stone shall watch the stone! (*Lev. R.* 35:5).[116]

... If you have laboured much in the study of their words, the Holy one, blessed be He, will remove your evil passions. This is borne out by the expression '*flesh*', as is confirmed by the quotation, *And I will give you a heart of flesh* (Ezek. 36:26) (*Num. R.* 14:4).[117]

Another interpretation of NOW THERE WAS A LITTLE CITY: i.e., the body, AND FEW MEN WITHIN IT: i.e., the limbs. AND THERE CAME A GREAT KING AGAINST IT: i.e., the Evil Inclination. . . David said: Happy is he who obeys it, as it is written, *Happy is he that considereth the poor* (Ps. 41:2). YET NO MAN REMEMBERED THAT SAME POOR: the Holy One, blessed be He, said: 'You have not remembered it, but I will remember it', as it is written, *I will take away the stony heart out of your flesh, and I will give you a heart of flesh* (Ezek. 36:26) (*Eccl. R.* 9.15.8).[118]

... R. Nehemiah said: When Israel heard the command '*Thou shalt not have*', the Evil Inclination was plucked from their heart. . . They returned to Moses and said to him, 'Moses, would that God would reveal Himself to us a second time. Would that God would kiss us WITH THE KISSES OF HIS MOUTH!' He replied to them: 'This cannot be now, but in time to come it will be, as it says, *And I will take away the stony heart out of your flesh*' (Ezek. 36:26) (*Cant. R.* 1.2.4).[119]

... The evil inclination is called a stone, as it says, *And I will take away the stony heart out of your flesh* (Ezek. 36:26) (*Cant. R.* 6.11.1).

... In the future too it will be thus: *And I will take away the stony heart out of your flesh, and I will give you a heart of flesh*-leb basar (Ezek. 36:26), i.e., a heart which has no desire of (boser) his neighbour's portion (*Gen. R.* 34:15).[120]

... Ezekiel called it Stone, as it is said, *And I will take away the heart of stone out of your flesh and I will give you a heart of flesh* (Ezek. 36:26) (*b. Suk.* 52a).[121]

---

[115] S.M. Lehrman, 'Exodus', in *The Midrash Rabbah*.
[116] J.J. Slotki, 'Leviticus', in *The Midrash Rabbah*.
[117] J.J. Slotki, 'Numbers', in *The Midrash Rabbah*.
[118] A. Cohen, 'Ecclesiastes', in *The Midrash Rabbah*.
[119] M. Simon, 'Song of Songs', in *The Midrash Rabbah*.
[120] H. Freedman, 'Genesis', in *The Midrash Rabbah*.
[121] W. Slotki, 'Sukah', in *The Babylonian Talmud* (London: The Soncino, 1938).

> ... 'But in the world to Come I shall pull it out of you by the roots'; as it says, *And I will give you way the stony heart out of your flesh, and I will give you a heart of flesh* (Ezek. 36:26) (*Num. R.* 15:16).

> ... It is like a stone, as it is said, *I will take away the stony heart out of thy flesh* (Ezek. 36:26) (*Eccl. R.* 1:16).

Some important observations should be noted regarding these citations about Ezekiel 36:26. First, the promise of a new heart in the age to come is closely related to the withdrawal of the evil impulse in the first seven citations while the corresponding promise is also referred to in the rest of the citations without the reference to the evil impulse.[122] Second, in the texts cited above, whether citations contained the phrase 'evil impulse or inclination' or not, they are silent about the activity of the Spirit.[123] Third, in this regard, the fact that they are almost all conveyed in an abbreviated form with omission of the reference to the Spirit possibly means that there is a general purpose of the rabbis in their re-wording of the original reference in quoting Ezekiel 36:26.

From these points, possible corollaries can be deduced: 1) The promise of a new heart for God in Ezekiel 36:26 is not generally associated with the eschatological gift of the Spirit since the reference to the Spirit in relation to the transformation of the heart is strikingly lacking in most citations. 2) The general purpose of the rabbis' citations on Ezekiel 36:26, as they appear in the literature, is closely associated with the end-time removal of the evil inclination. These assumptions reasonably suggest that any connection of Ezekiel 36:26 with the eschatological bestowal of the Spirit should be reconsidered.

2.4.3.2. THE RABBINIC TRADITION ON JOEL 3:1

Joel 3:1f. is also cited by the rabbis with reference to the end-time. There are numerous examples in the rabbinic literature outside *Midrash Psalms* 14:6 and *Deuteronomy Rabbah* 6:14:

> The Holy Spirit, as in Scripture: 'I will raise up prophets from your sons' (Amos 2:11). But because they sinned, he departed from them, as it is written: 'Also, her

---

[122] Menzies, *Development*, 105-06. In addition to the list that Menzies has given, I find one additional reference to Ezek. 36:26 in *Lev. R.* 35:5, where the reference to the Spirit is clearly absent. This text is also used in terms of the end-time removal of the evil impulse.

[123] Menzies, *Development*, 105-06; Turner, *Power*, 130. On the other hand, some texts cited on Ezek. 36:26 are also lacking in reference to the Spirit while the following verse (Ezek. 36:27) refers to it. See *b. Ber.* 31b; *b. Suk.* 52b; *Num. R.* 9:49. *Midr. Ps.* 73:4 does not refer to Ezek. 36:26, but only to Ezek. 36:27 with reference to the Spirit. The only reference to Ezek. 36:26 with the activity of the Spirit in found in *Tan. add*.

prophets find no vision from the Lord' (Lam. 2:9). But one day the Holy One will bring him back to Israel, as it is written: *And afterward, I will pour out my Spirit on all flesh, and your sons and daughters will prophesy* (Joel 3:1) (*MHG* Gen. 140).

... The Holy One, blessed be He, said: 'In this world only a few individuals have prophesied, but in the World to Come all Israel will be made prophets'; as it says, *And it shall come to pass afterward, that I will pour out my spirit upon all flesh; and your sons and your daughters shall prophesy, your old men,* etc. (Joel 3:1). Such is the exposition given by R. Tahuma, son of R. Abba (*Num. R.* 15:25).

... IN THE TENT OF THE DAUGHTER OF ZION HE HATH POURED OUT HIS FURY LIKE FIRE. There are four pourings (recorded) for good and four for evil. . . *And it shall come to pass afterward, that I will pour out My spirit upon all flesh* (Joel 3:1) (*Lam. R.* 2:8).

... Raai (Judah ha-Nasi) said: There are four pourings (recorded) for good and four for evil. There are four pourings (recorded) for good, as it is said,. . . *And it shall come to pass afterward, that I will pour out My spirit upon all flesh,* etc. (Joel 3.1) (*Lam. R.* 4:14).[124]

... That is, the children of Israel will say to the Holy One, blessed be He: Thou hast made Thy name and Thy word greater than all the things which Thou didst promise us through the Prophets. And what didst Thou promise? Not merely *And it shall come to pass afterward, that I will pour out My spirit upon all flesh* (Joel 3:1); but also, *It shall come to pass in that day, that the mountains shall drop down sweet wine* (ibid. 4:18) (*Midr. Ps.* 138:2).

A notable observation derived from the citations above[125] is that the concept of the eschatological endowment of the gift of the Spirit identically relies on Joel 3:1f. in terms of a restoration of the Spirit of prophecy in the age to come.

Thus, one clear indication from the study of the uniform texts of Ezekiel 36:26 and Joel 3:1 cited in *Midrash Psalms* 14:6 and *Deuteronomy Rabbah* 6:14 is that there appear to be two eschatological promises of the age to come. At the same time, the different character of the promises is also apparent. If the reference to Ezekiel 36:26 is not generally read in the light of an eschatological endowment of the Spirit, but rather as a promise of end-time withdrawal of the evil impulse, and if Joel 3:1 is usually understood as a restoration of the Spirit of prophecy, a reasonable conclusion can be arrived at: the promise of the transformation of the heart (Ezek. 36:26) is to be understood as a prerequisite for the other promise, the eschatological bestowal of the Spirit, a restoration of the Spirit of prophecy (Joel 3:1). That is, the promise of Ezekiel is to be understood in the light of

---

[124] A. Cohen, 'Lamentaions', in *The Midrash Rabbah*.

[125] In addition to the references offered by Menzies, I find one additional reference to Joel 3:1 in *Lam. R.* 2:8.

that of Joel.

2.4.4. Summary

The general activity of the Spirit discussed in the rabbinic texts is not primarily a life-giving function but one which is prophetic in nature, i.e., of charismatic inspiration and wisdom. Ezekiel 36, on which Turner's interpretation mainly depends, should be understood in the light of Joel 3:1. Furthermore, it should be remembered that the evidence that Turner gives from the rabbinic material is relatively late for use in construing the Jewish pneumatological perspectives in the intertestamental period.

2.5. The Spirit and the Resurrection of the Dead in Jewish Apocalyptic Perspective

Menzies argues that there are some rabbinic texts which contain the 'chain' saying of R. Phineas b. Jair (*m. Soṭ.* 9:15; b. *'Abod. Zar.* 20b; *Yalq. Isa.* §503; *j. Sheq.* 3:4; *Cant. R.* 1:1:9) and texts which cite Ezekiel 37:14 (*Gen. R.* 14:8; 96:5 (*MSV*); *Exod. R.* 48:4; *Cant. R.* 1:1:9; *Midr. Ps.* 85:3; *Pes. R.* 1:6) in connecting the Spirit to the resurrection in the age to come. In this argument, Menzies asserts that although there appears to be an association of the Spirit with resurrection in the 'chain' saying, the texts referring to Ezekiel 37:14 are considered to be 'few and relatively late', and function as ancillary to Ezekiel 37:12f. where the resurrection is associated with the land of Israel. At the same time, the early rabbinic material such as R. Phineas b. Jair (*m. Soṭ.* 9:15) which associates the Spirit with resurrection should be viewed in the light of intertestamental literature in which we see how the Spirit is related to the resurrection.[126] If there is no particular reason to object to Menzies' view, it would be more judicious to look at the view of intertestamental literature than the rabbinic sources in order to understand the general Jewish view on this matter. This is also the safeguard of avoiding the danger of anachronism.

Although apocalyptic belief in the doctrine of resurrection was not generally agreed among the Jews, it was probably more widespread than was its denial.[127] This is indicated by the numerous intertestamental Jewish apocryphal and pseudepigraphical texts in which a reference to resurrection from the dead is recorded, including 2 Maccabees (7:8, 13, 14, 23, 29; 14:46), *4 Ezra* (4:41-43; 7:32-38), the *Psalms of Solomon* (3:11-16; 13:9-11; 14:10; 15:12-15), *LAB* (3:10; 19:12; 25:7; 51:5; 64:7), *Sibylline Oracles*

---

[126] Menzies, *Development*, 108-10.

[127] For example, the Sadducees (Josephus, *Ant.* 18:14; Acts 23:8; 26:8) denied any form of afterlife, immortality or resurrection while the Pharisees (Acts 23:6-8, and possibly the Essenes) accepted the resurrection from the dead. Cf. G.E. Ladd, *I Believe in the Resurrection of Jesus* (Grand Rapids: Eerdmans, 1975), 52.

(4:176-182),[128] and *1 Enoch*.[129] The variety of these references clearly suggests that the subject of resurrection in intertestamental Judaism is much more prevalent than it is in the Hebrew Bible.[130] However, in spite of the great interest, it is surprising to discover in these texts the paucity of references which associate the Spirit explicitly with resurrection. Nonetheless, some scholars endeavour to link the resurrection of the dead with the gift of the Spirit in this period.

Horn, for example, is one of them and the texts which he suggests, particularly on the non-rabbinic side, are 2 Maccabees 7:23 and *Joseph and Aseneth* 8:9.[131] But the correct nature of the Spirit of the former is the breath of life rather than the gift of the divine Spirit.[132] The latter is somewhat concerned with internal renewal, but not the eschatological renewal in terms of physical resurrection from the dead. Moreover, as noted earlier, the overall discussion of *Joseph and Aseneth* has been excluded from this analysis because of a possible late ancient composition(s), perhaps from a Christian author(s).[133] Turner, on the other hand, proposes *2 Baruch* 21:4; 23:5; and *4 Ezra* 6:39-41 as examples.[134] However, both of

---

[128] *4 Maccabees* also contains the notion of afterlife in terms of immortality but without the reference to a physical resurrection (see 7:3; 9:22; 14:5f.; 16:13; 17:12; cf. Wisdom of Solomon 3:1-4; 2:23-24).

[129] Although the five books contain the various views on the subject, the last book of Enoch (91-104) contains several references to afterlife with a physical life. For instance, that a resurrection for the righteous is to be conceived is indicated in 91:10; 92:3-5; 104:2, 4 etc. For a detailed discussion on the topic in *1 Enoch* 91-104, see G.W.E. Nickelsburg, *Resurrection, Immortality, and Eternal Life in Intertestamental Judaism*, HTS 26 (Cambridge: Harvard University, 1972), 112-30.

[130] This eschatological development on the question of resurrection possibly stems from Dan. 12:1-3, Isa. 24-27, and Ezek. 37. D.S. Russell, *The Method and Message of Jewish Apocalyptic* (London: SCM Press, 1964), 367-68.

[131] F. W. Horn, 'Holy Spirit', *ABD*, 3, 267.

[132] 'Therefore the Creator of the world, who shaped the beginning of humankind and devised the origin of all things, will in his mercy give life and breath back to you again (τὴν ζωὴν ὑμῖν πάλιν ἀποδίδωσιν μετ' ἐλέους), since you now forget yourselves for the sake of his laws' (RSV and GT is from Rahlfs, *Septuaginta*).

[133] See R. Kraemer's recent monograph, *When Aseneth Met Joseph: A Late Antique Tale of the Biblical Patriarch and His Egyptian Wife, Reconsidered* (New York/Oxford: OUP, 1998) where she pushes the dating back towards late stage (after 2nd century). Kraemer's conclusion is that 'the cumulative evidence overwhelmingly places our Aseneth (and Joseph) no earlier than the third or fourth century CE, on both negative and positive criteria' (237). According to Kraemer, the 'negative' evidence means both the absence of any reference to the literature *Joseph and Aseneth* in Jewish material and the exclusive Christian transference of the work, while the 'positive' means the abundant analogies found with late ancient literature. See particularly chapters 1 and 8 of the work.

[134] *Power*, 106.

the texts that Turner suggests also have some flaws. For example, Menzies, following Müller, argues that only *2 Baruch* 23:5 genuinely refers to the Spirit as the divine agent of resurrection, but doubts it owing to the insecure dating problem of *2 Baruch*, i.e., the period after the New Testament (2nd century AD origin).[135] The concept of the Spirit in relation to the story of creation in *4 Ezra* 6:39 derived from Genesis 1:1-4 presumably needs to be understood as the source of life for all people (i.e., the Spirit as a life principle which is at work in every man) rather than a special endowment granting spiritual life or power to human beings after birth.[136] The eschatological concept of the resurrection from the dead is rather viewed by the author of *4 Ezra* in other references. For instance, *4 Ezra* 6:26 states that one of the signs of the end of the age is the eschatological renewal based on Ezekiel 36:26. However, this text is silent with reference to the Spirit. Similarly, *4 Ezra* 7, particularly verse 32, clearly speaks of the eschatological resurrection but without the reference to the Spirit.[137] In this view, it seems a general notion that the eschatological renewal or resurrection clearly appears in the work but is not linked to the agency of the Spirit.

To sum up, the texts which Turner and Horn cite are not clear in their illustration of the connection between the Spirit and the eschatological resurrection and not as significant as the many other Jewish texts which maintain the eschatological resurrection from the dead without reference to the activity of the Spirit.[138]

---

[135] Menzies, *Development*, 73. Cf. Müller's argument that *2 Bar.* 23:5 is the only reference which links the Spirit with resurrection in the OT Pseudepigrapha. D. Müller, 'Geisterfahrung und Totenauferweckung: Untersuchungen zur Totenauferweckung bei Paulus und in den ihm vorgegebenen Überlieferungen' (PhD Dissertation; Christian-Albrecht-Universität, Kiel, 1980), 111-32. Although it is debatable whether or not there was a shift in the pneumatological perspectives between the NT and the date of *2 Bar.* (e.g., Turner, *Power*, 84, 106; Menzies, *Development*, 73), one apparent point is that there was no clear Jewish antecedent in the intertestamental period before *2 Bar.* in associating the Spirit with the authorship of resurrection. For the hypothesis of the second century AD origin of the work, see A.F.J. Klijn, '2 Baruch', *OTP*, 1, 616-17.

[136] We know this fact from some of the authors of intertestamental literature such as Philo, but the concept of the Spirit as the source of life stemming from Gen. is relatively rare in the period.

[137] *4 Ezra* 7:32 reads 'And the earth shall give up those who are asleep in it; and the chambers shall give up the souls which have been committed to them.' Cf. *4 Ezra* 4:41-42.

[138] It seems clear that the later works after Paul such as *2 Bar.* tend to connect the gift of the Spirit to the eschatological resurrection from the dead. But before him, it is extremely rare to associate the Spirit to resurrection. We will discuss how Paul closely links the activity of the Spirit to the resurrection in the subsequent chapter.

2.6. Conclusion

The intertestamental Jewish literature generally understands the Spirit as the source of prophetic inspiration, but the Spirit is not generally understood as the giver of life-giving wisdom. The examples that Turner suggests are insufficient as evidence that the Spirit is the source of life-giving wisdom. Several messianic traditions relating to Isaiah 11:1-4 in the period indicate that the presence of the Spirit upon the Messiah equips him with special wisdom and power to rule effectively over his people. Although soteriological pneumatology is presented in 1QH and Wisdom 9:17, this notion should be seen as one minor strand among a much larger and more dominant tradition which presents the Spirit in a non-soteriological way, i.e., as the source of extraordinary and charismatic wisdom of prophetic nature. The general purpose of the rabbis' citations of Ezekiel 36:26 without reference to the Spirit, as they appear in the literature, is closely associated with the end-time removal of the evil inclination. This transformation of the heart is understood as a pre-condition for the eschatological endowment of the gift of the Spirit in terms of Joel 3:1 (MT). The notion that the connection between the gift of the Spirit and the eschatological resurrection is extremely rare further ensures that the Spirit is not widely understood as the source of life-giving wisdom in the period. All the strands of evidence lead us to conclude that in intertestamental literature the life-giving function of the Spirit is reasonably limited.

If this is right, Turner's understanding that the Jewish perspective on the Spirit as the giver of 'life-giving wisdom' is the conceptual framework for the pneumatological reflection of both Luke and Paul needs to be reconsidered. In chapter 3, when we examine Paul's writings, we will explore the effect of the intertestamental pneumatological perspective on Paul, i.e., whether or not for him the Spirit is the source of life-giving wisdom. We will also consider in chapter 4 whether Luke understands the gift of the Spirit as being the source of life-giving wisdom. Therefore, we will seek to demonstrate that Paul is an innovator who conceives the Spirit as being identical to life in the kingdom of God. This claim will be elucidated in the following chapters.

CHAPTER 3

The Relationship between the Spirit in Paul and the Kingdom of God in the Synoptics

3.1. Introduction

It is curious that while the central message of Jesus, the kingdom of God, is only sporadically used by Paul, he uses the Spirit-language so often. Some pertinent questions arise from this. If the concept of the kingdom nonetheless remains an important element in Paul, in what sense does Paul convey it in his letters? Is it conceivable that Paul has expressed the concept of the kingdom so central in Jesus' teaching in terms of the Spirit? If so, does a relationship exist between the Pauline emphasis upon the Spirit and the kingdom of God phraseology in the Synoptics?

In this chapter, I will explore these questions. First of all, I will examine Paul's kingdom of God language in order to show how infrequent its use is in his writings and ask the reasons why. If Paul expresses the essence of Jesus' teaching about the kingdom in a different way, might a similar concept apply in regard to the category of the 'kingdom of God'. For this, I will particularly focus on Paul's concept of the Spirit. It is possible that Paul uses the Spirit to speak about the blessings or life of the kingdom. Should it be tenable to establish a correlation between these two, the attempt will be made to find an association between 'life in the Spirit' as Paul's way of speaking about 'life in the kingdom' in the Synoptics. Above all, it is the aim of this chapter to investigate whether Paul's understanding of salvation, which is shaped by the Spirit, parallels the blessings of life in the kingdom of God in the Synoptics.[1]

---

[1] In this regard, it should be noted that the key to this discussion is not to focus exclusively on the kingdom of God language in Paul, but rather to show the unique nature of the relationship between Paul's concept of the Spirit and the concept of the kingdom of God in the Synoptics.

3.2. Kingdom Terminology in Paul

3.2.1. The Scarcity of References to the Kingdom of God in Paul

In the Synoptics, the concept of the kingdom of God permeates the message of Jesus. However, in the Pauline corpus,[2] one finds only limited references to the kingdom of God.[3] This phenomenon has led scholars to reach two possible interpretations. One is that the phrase kingdom of God as used by Paul is not a central concept in his theology.[4] The other is that although the phrase is sparse in Paul's letters, it is to be regarded as one of the principal concepts in his proclamation.[5] While there is a possible supportive argument for each case,[6] one clear thing is that Paul uses the phrase to a lesser degree than the Synoptics in terms of its frequency and the substance of its content.

This raises the question: why is Paul cautious in using the term if the concept of the kingdom of God is nonetheless important to him? Recent scholarly discussion on this question has not reached a definitive consensus of opinion. Not many experts have in fact addressed the issue. However,

---

[2] In this thesis, only seven universally accepted letters will be regarded as Pauline (Romans, 1 and 2 Corinthians, Galatians, Philippians, 1 Thessalonians, Philemon).

[3] As will be noted in detail, the phrase βασιλεία τοῦ Θεοῦ occurs seven times in the Pauline corpus (Rom. 14:17; 1 Cor. 4:20; 6:9, 10; 15:50; Gal. 5:21; 1 Thess. 2:12 (ἑαυτοῦ βασιλείαν); cf. 1 Cor. 15:24 [τὴν βασιλείαν]; Col. 4:11; 2 Thess. 1:5). On the other hand, the noun form βασιλεία (kingdom or reign) appears eight times (Rom. 14:17; 1 Cor. 4:20; 6:9, 10; 15:24, 50; Gal. 5:21; 1 Thess. 2:12; cf. Eph. 5:5; Col. 1:13; 4:11; 2 Thess. 1:5; 2 Tim. 4:1, 14, 18) whereas the verb form βασιλεύω (to reign) occurs nine times (Rom. 5:14, 17 [2 times], 21 [2 times]; 6:12; 1 Cor. 4:8 [2 times]; 15:25; cf. the verb συμβασιλεύω [to reign with] appears in 1 Tim. 2:12). Cf. L.J. Kreitzer, *Jesus and God in Paul's Eschatology*, JSNTS 19 (Sheffield: JSOT Press, 1987), 132.

[4] E.g., H.A.A. Kennedy, *Paul's Conception of the Last Things* (London: Hodder and Stoughton, 1904), 290; N. Walter, 'Paul and the Early Christian Jesus-Tradition', in A.J.M. Wedderburn (ed.), *Paul and Jesus: Collected Essays*, JSNTS 37 (Sheffield: JSOT Press, 1989), 63.

[5] E.g., D. Wenham, *Paul: Follower of Jesus or Founder of Christianity?* (Grand Rapids: Eerdmans, 1995), 71-80; G. Haufe, 'Reich Gottes bei Paulus und in der Jesustradition', *NTS* 31 (1985), 467-72.

[6] For instance, for the former, it has been argued that the methodology of Paul tends to carry his favourite conceptions to the foreground of his teaching. But Paul fails to do so with the concept, 'kingdom of God'. Furthermore, in terms of the usage of the phrase, it functions in a much reduced way in Paul. For the latter, it has been noted that it is impossible for the post-Easter members in general and Paul in particular to refrain from Jesus' kingdom preaching, the good news of salvation assured by the death and resurrection of Jesus (cf. 1 Cor. 15:3-11).

recently, Wenham has suggested three possibilities regarding this point.[7]

Firstly, it is possible that 'the "kingdom of God" language that would have been familiar and intelligible to Jews in Palestine would have been much less intelligible to Paul's Greek-speaking readers'.[8] The proclamation of the kingdom of God would mean little to Paul's Greek-speaking readers who would have been steeped in individualism and humanism.[9]

Secondly, it is conceivable that '"king/kingdom" language, which was sensitive enough in Jesus' rural Jewish context, would have been even more sensitive in Paul's urban Greco-Roman context'.[10] In other words, Paul wanted to be wary of possible political overtones in the use of kingdom language.[11] Paul may also have restricted his use of kingdom language in order not to be misunderstood by both the authorities and his Gentile readers.

A third possibility is that 'Jesus' "kingdom" language had been – in Paul's perception at least – hijacked by some of his opponents and that he was therefore wary of such language'.[12] The Corinthians regarded themselves as having entered into the life of the kingdom and even in some cases as having been resurrected in the Spirit (e.g., 1 Cor. 4:8; 15:12).[13]

---

[7] Wenham, *Paul*, 78-80.

[8] Wenham, *Paul*, 78. Cf. Mark reports Jesus' saying to his readers who are familiar with the phrase, 'the kingdom of God'. 'The time is fulfilled, and the kingdom of God is at hand' (Mk. 1:15).

[9] Similarly, F.W. Beare has made an important statement which is cited by Johnston in this regard: 'Naturally, he [Paul] sought for ways of making his gospel intelligible to Greeks; he makes no bones about borrowing words and phrases and good ideas from the religions and philosophies of the Greek world, if only he could bring them into the service of the gospel. The kingdom of God, of which Jesus spoke so often, meant nothing to a Greek; and so Paul hardly ever makes use of the phrase when he is writing to Greeks... the transposing of the gospel into the language and the thought-forms of another people, the kind of adjustment that was needed if the gospel of Jesus was to be brought effectively into the Greek world'. G. Johnston, '"Kingdom of God" Sayings in Paul's Letters', in P. Richardson and J.C. Hurd (eds.), *From Jesus to Paul* (Ontario: Wilfred Laurier University, 1984), 143. Wenham points out that a possible parallel appears in John's gospel in which the term kingdom of God is little used (Jn. 3:3, 5; cf. 18:36) and might be replaced by the concept of 'eternal life'.

[10] Wenham, *Paul*, 78.

[11] Similarly, Wedderburn argues that 'Paul may have found it safer politically to avoid references to God's kingdom in his preaching'. A.J.M. Wedderburn, 'Paul and Jesus: The Problem of Continuity', in *Paul and Jesus*, 112; see also Dunn, *Theology*, 190, n. 37.

[12] Wenham, *Paul*, 79.

[13] While some scholars question an over-realized eschatology in Corinth, others argue that the phenomenon seems to appear on the part of Corinthians (e.g., 1 Cor. 4:8; 15). An example of the former position is E. Ellis, 'Christ Crucified', in R. Banks (ed.), *Reconciliation and Hope* (Grand Rapids: Eerdmans, 1974), 69-75. For the latter

This led to an arrogant attitude about their position in Christ which prevented Paul from using the language.

While these possibilities are noteworthy, some flaws can be found in these proposals. For instance, the danger of mirror-reading should be remembered, particularly in relation to the third possibility.[14] Furthermore, if the term kingdom of God used by Jesus was hijacked by Paul's antagonists, it is strange that Paul used it more frequently in 1 Corinthians than in other letters.[15] In addition, caution is required in Wenham's use of the word 'avoid'[16] because Paul is still using the term kingdom of God. Despite these weak points, Wenham's general illustrations give an indication that Paul in any event would tend to be cautious in his use of the term. Before we observe Paul's choice of Spirit language for the kingdom of God, it is appropriate to look at how the term kingdom of God is used in his writings.

3.2.2. *Kingdom of God Sayings in Paul*[17]

a. 1 Thessalonians 2:12 ('urging [παρακαλοῦντες] and encouraging [παραμυθούμενοι] you and pleading [μαρτυρόμενοι] that you lead a life worthy of God, who calls [καλοῦντος] you into his own kingdom and glory [ἑαυτοῦ βασιλείαν[18] καὶ δόξαν]' [NRSV]).

The immediate context of the present verse describes Paul's faithful ministry among his readers in Thessalonica. Paul encourages them that God is the one who calls them into his kingdom and glory and reminds them that God is concerned with their growth in likeness to his glory.

Paul does not develop the meaning of the kingdom of God in 1 Thessalonians 2:12. Furthermore, the time of the kingdom is not explicitly indicated. Three participles in the present verse do not help to identify the

---

position, see F.F. Bruce, *I & II Corinthians*, NCB (Grand Rapids: Eerdmans, 1982), 49-50; G. Fee, *The First Epistle to the Corinthians*, NICNT (Grand Rapids: Eerdmans, 1987), 171-73; A. Thiselton, 'Realized Eschatology at Corinth', *NTS* 24 (1976/77), 510-26.

[14] Cf. M.D. Hooker's review of Wenham (*JBL* 115 [1996], 756-58 [757]).
[15] Cf. n. 3 above: 1 Cor. 4:20; 6:9-10; 15:50; cf. 15:24; Rom. 14:17; 1 Thess. 2:12; Gal. 5:21.
[16] Wenham, *Paul*, 79.
[17] For a fuller discussion of Paul's kingdom of God sayings, see G.R. Shogren, 'The Pauline Proclamation of the Kingdom of God and the Kingdom of Christ within Its New Testament Setting' (PhD Dissertation; Aberdeen University, 1986); Johnston, 'Kingdom of God'; Haufe, 'Reich Gottes'.
[18] Although a qualifying genitive τοῦ θεοῦ is not used with βασιλείαν, ἑαυτοῦ implies τοῦ θεοῦ so that ἑαυτοῦ βασιλείαν is comparable with βασιλεία τοῦ θεοῦ. The author of 2 Thess., who apparently adopts the phrase in 1 Thess. 2:12, clearly uses the traditional phrase, βασιλεία τοῦ θεοῦ. Shogren, 'Kingdom of God', 41.

time of the kingdom. The aspect of the participle of καλέω also depends on whether the reading is the present participle (καλοῦντος) or the less well attested aorist participle (καλέσαντος).[19] Some may deduce the present aspect of the kingdom here since the purpose of God's calling (καλέω) the Thessalonians is to walk in a way worthy of God.[20] However, although the syntactical difficulty remains in the text, the overall eschatological context in the letter rather supports its future sense (1:10; 3:13; 4:6; 5:1-11; 5:23-24). For example, Paul, in 1 Thessalonians 5:23-24, presents almost the same saying as 1 Thessalonians 2:12 in a clear eschatological sense. God, who is faithful and calls the Thessalonians, will keep them until the parousia. This eschatological meaning is closely associated with the kingdom and the glory of God in 1 Thessalonians 2:12.[21] Here the terms 'glory' and 'kingdom' indicate the true future goal of God's calling of his people.[22] Paul, in 1 Thessalonians 2:19-20, further connects 'the glory' with the consummation of Jesus. Thus, the Thessalonians should have a relationship with God who has called them in the present time, but their final goal is to participate in 'the kingdom' and 'the glory of God' at the parousia.[23]

In short, the sense of the kingdom in the text is futuristic and this does not conflict with Jesus' traditional kingdom teaching, which is also futuristic (as well as present). But beyond this, Paul does not specify the meaning of the phrase.

b. Galatians 5:21 ('envy, drunkenness, carousing, and the like. I warn you, as I warned you before, that those who do such things shall not inherit the kingdom of God [βασιλείαν θεοῦ οὐ κληρονομήσουσιν]' [RSV]).

c. 1 Corinthians 6:9-10 ('Do you not know that the unrighteous will not inherit the kingdom of God [θεοῦ βασιλείαν οὐ κληρονομήσουσιν]; Do not be deceived; neither the immoral, nor idolaters, nor adulterers, nor sexual perverts, nor thieves, nor the greedy, nor drunkards, nor revilers, nor robbers will inherit the kingdom of God [βασιλείαν θεοῦ κληρονομήσουσιν]' [RSV]).

d. 1 Corinthians 15:50 ('I tell you this, brethren: flesh and blood cannot inherit the kingdom of God [βασιλείαν θεοῦ κληρονομῆσαι οὐ δύναται], nor

---

[19] Shogren, 'Kingdom of God', 42. The aorist tense καλέσαντος is read by ℵ A 104 326 606 1611 1831 1906 1912 2005 but the present tense καλοῦντος is strongly supported by B D F G H K L P and most minuscules. B.M. Metzger, *A Textual Commentary of the Greek New Testament* (London: UBS, 1975), 630.

[20] E.g., F.F. Bruce, *1&2 Thessalonians*, WBC 45 (Waco: Word, 1982), 37-38; cf. Johnston, 'Kingdom of God', 145-47.

[21] Shogren, 'Kingdom of God', 42.

[22] I.H. Marshall, *1 and 2 Thessalonians*, NCB (Grand Rapids: Eerdmans, 1983), 75; G. Kittel, 'δόξα', *TDNT*, II, 247-51 (250). Kittel further argues that the authors of the NT mostly use the term in an eschatological sense in comparison with present suffering.

[23] Marshall, *1 and 2 Thessalonians*, 75.

does the perishable inherit the imperishable' [RSV]).

These kingdom references deal with the idea of eschatological exclusion referring to 'inheriting the kingdom'. The basic argument of Paul in both 1 Corinthians 6:9-10 and Galatians 5:21 is that those who practise fleshly conduct will not inherit the kingdom of God. In both cases, the catalogues of vices and virtues are used by Paul: those characterized by vices will not inherit the kingdom of God while the righteous, portrayed by virtues, will.

In 1 Corinthians 15:50, Paul uses a similar formula to those in 1 Corinthians 6:9-10 and Galatians 5:21, but there are some differences. The primary distinction appears in terms of syntax. Paul in 1 Corinthians 15:50 employs a present form of δύναται with the aorist infinitive of κληρονομέω while the other two references have a clear future sense, κληρονομήσουσιν.[24] Furthermore, while the latter concerns the formula in terms of exclusion from the kingdom in relation to present moral unfaithfulness, the former concerns it in terms of the mode of existence: the future dimension of the kingdom of God is a completely different mode from the present.[25] The present mode (flesh and blood) cannot simply be ushered in to the final kingdom of God. It requires a radical change by transforming the physical corruption to a heavenly state.[26] Nonetheless, the fundamental concept of the kingdom in 1 Corinthians 15:50 is almost identical to the other two inheritance texts.

Thus, there is little doubt that the time element in these references is the future sense since the kingdom of God simply indicates a final judgment in the form of a threat and connotes, ultimately, the future reign of God. At the same time, this eschatological inheritance clearly depicts a spatial dimension since the idea of entry suggests the eschatological realm, the kingdom of God.

It is often argued that Paul's exclusion formula (esp. 1 Cor. 6:9-10 and Gal. 5:21) can be traced from a pre-Pauline Christian tradition since the Synoptic writers also contain a few similar expressions in Jesus' teaching;[27] e.g., 'inherit the earth' (Mt. 5:5), 'to enter the kingdom of God' (Mk. 10:23, 24, 25/Mt. 19:23, 24/Lk. 18:24, 25), and 'shall enter the kingdom of heaven' (Mt. 7:21/Lk. 6:46).[28] While this point may be acceptable in light of the 'inheriting/entering description', it should not be overlooked that

---

[24] Shogren, 'Kingdom of God', 79.
[25] Cf. Haufe, 'Reich Gottes', 468-69.
[26] Most scholars reject Jeremias' interpretation of 1 Cor. 15:50 that there is a difference between 1 Cor. 15:50b and 1 Cor. 15:50c rather than a synonymous parallelism. According to Jeremias, the former refers to the metamorphosis of the living believer before the parousia while the latter refers to presently decomposed corpses of dead believers. J. Jeremias, 'Flesh and Blood cannot Inherit the Kingdom of God', *NTS* 2 (1955-56), 151-59.
[27] E.g., Wenham, *Paul*, 76; Johnston, 'Kingdom of God', 147.
[28] See also Mt. 5:20; 18:3; 25:34; Mk. 9:43-48/Mt. 18:8f.; Lk. 10:25; 13:24-30.

there are some major distinctions between the two. The Synoptic texts do not include the 'catalogues of vices and virtues' in references to inheriting the kingdom of God as Paul does.[29] Indeed, only the Pauline corpus connects the kingdom of God to the catalogues in the NT.[30] Furthermore, and more importantly, the kingdom of God in relation to the catalogues is not linked to the Spirit in the Synoptics while Paul clearly associates it with the work of the Spirit in each case (Gal. 5:16f.; 1 Cor. 6:9-11; cf. 1 Cor. 15:42f.). Thus, there is difficulty in making precise parallels between the two exclusion formulas in Paul and the Synoptics. For Paul, the language of inheritance rather appears in his pneumatological perspective in relation to the kingdom of God while the Synoptics do not connect them in this way.

This suggests that the contention that Paul's formulation of the inheritance of the kingdom of God has been derived from an early Christian tradition should be treated with caution. Perhaps Paul, who may possibly have used the early Christian source, has not wholeheartedly adopted the formula from it. In view of his unique employment of a reference to the Spirit in his exclusion formula, Paul rather seems to have developed the traditional exclusion formula with a special connection to the Spirit.

e. 1 Corinthians 4:20 ('For the kingdom of God does not consist in talk but in power' [οὐ γὰρ ἐν λόγῳ ἡ βασιλεία τοῦ θεοῦ ἀλλ' ἐν δυνάμει] [RSV]).

This short aphoristic text, which is closely parallel with Romans 14:17, associates the kingdom with power.

There can be no doubt that the time element of the kingdom of God in 1 Corinthians 4:20 lies in the present time.[31] As a present reality, the kingdom of God for Paul is not simply attained by talk or ideological dispute, but demonstrated by powerful deeds and preaching. This demonstrative character is clearly represented by the use of δυνάμις in 2 Corinthians 12:12: 'The things that mark an apostle -- signs, wonders and miracles -- were done among you with great perseverance' (cf. 1 Cor. 2:4; Rom. 15:19). When the Corinthians were expressing excessive spiritual arrogance, Paul points out that the kingdom of God does not consist of boastful talk but powerful deeds and words.

On the other hand, there is little question that the saying here is Paul's

---

[29] Menzies, *Development*, 298. Catalogues in the Synoptics appear only in Mt. 15:19/Mk. 7:21f. H. Conzelmann, *1 Corinthians*, Hermeneia (Philadelphia: Fortress Press, 1975), 101, n. 69. See above for the Synoptic references to 'inheriting/entering the kingdom'.

[30] Cf. Eph. 5:5. On the other hand, Conzelmann argues that the language style of 1 Cor. 15:50b (flesh and blood) has been influenced by traditional material. *1 Corinthians*, 289. However, Fee argues that along with the expression 'inherit the kingdom of God', the phrase 'σὰρξ καὶ αἷμα' in 1 Cor. 15:50 is Pauline idiom and found in Gal. 1:16 (cf. the reversed form as 'blood and flesh' in Eph. 6:12). Fee, *1 Corinthians*, 798, n. 12.

[31] Johnston, 'Kingdom of God', 151; Fee, *1 Corinthians*, 192.

own expression since it is difficult to find a parallel kingdom formula in Jewish literature.[32] Haufe seeks the origin of Paul's speech form, particularly in the couplet form of οὐ γάρ and ἀλλά, in Hellenistic philosophical language.[33] However, this is not convincing since 1 Maccabees 3:19 is similarly structured with the form οὐ γάρ and ἀλλα: 'It is not on the size of the army that victory in battle depends, but strength comes from heaven' (ὅτι οὐκ ἐν πλήθει δυνάμεως νίκη πολέμου ἐστίν, ἀλλ' ἐκ τοῦ οὐρανοῦ ἡ ἰσχύς).[34]

f. Romans 14:17 ('For the kingdom of God is not food and drink but righteousness and peace and joy in the Holy Spirit' [οὐ γάρ ἐστιν ἡ βασιλεία τοῦ θεοῦ βρῶσις καὶ πόσις ἀλλὰ δικαιοσύνη καὶ εἰρήνη καὶ χαρὰ ἐν πνεύματι ἁγίῳ·] [RSV]).

Another present aspect of the kingdom in the Pauline corpus appears in Romans 14:17 which is the only reference to the kingdom in the letter. As in 1 Corinthians 4:20, in the couplet form of οὐ γάρ and ἀλλά, Paul gives two alternatives: one is to be rejected and the other is to be accepted.[35] So, 'The kingdom of God is not (οὐ) eating and drinking but (ἀλλά) righteousness, peace, and joy in the Holy Spirit'.

As Paul rebuked the talkative believers in Corinth (1 Cor. 4:20), he reminds his Gentile readers in Rome what it means to live under the rule of the Spirit, invalidating their fascination with diet. The passage addresses personal relationships which have become strained because of the reproving attitude of the Jewish brethren who had their own understanding of what constituted 'acceptable' (Rom. 14:16).

It has been generally argued that the statement in Romans 14:17 stemmed from Jesus' teaching in the Synoptics. This is shown through, for instance, 1) Thematic resemblance: 'Do not worry about what you will eat or drink. . . But seek first his kingdom' (Lk. 12:22-31/Mt. 6:25-33; Mt. 5); 2) Righteousness is seen as keeping God's commandments (Mk. 10:19; Mt. 7:12a/Lk. 6:31; Mt. 12:35/Lk. 6:45a). The righteous will inherit eternal life, the kingdom being one of its aspects (Mt. 25:46); 3) Jesus calls his disciples to offer 'peace' ('Peace to this house') in God's name as they minister on the mission field, the context being that the 'kingdom of God is at hand' to the hearers (Lk. 10:5-6f./Mt. 10:7, 13); 4). Joy is a recurring and significant theme in the parables about finding the lost (Lk. 15:6, 9, 24, 32; cf. Mt. 18:13): 'Rejoice in that day and leap for joy, because great is your reward in heaven (Lk. 6:23)'. God's ultimate reward for his people becomes obvious (Lk. 6:20-23; cf. Mt. 13:44).[36] According to this assertion, it is probable that

---

[32] Haufe, 'Reich Gottes', 469. Cf. Rom. 14:17; Gal. 6:15.
[33] Haufe, 'Reich Gottes', 469.
[34] Shogren, 'Kingdom of God', 58.
[35] Cf. J.P. Lewis, 'The Kingdom of God. . . is Righteousness Peace and Joy in the Holy Spirit (Rom 14:17): A Survey of Interpretation', *RQ* 40 (1998), 54.
[36] Johnston, 'Kingdom of God', 153-55; Wenham, *Paul*, 73; Dunn, *Theology*, 191.

Paul's use of traditional language here betrays the influence of the Jesus tradition upon his teaching. However, although some verbal similarities can be found that may indicate Paul's knowledge of that tradition, the force of this argument is mitigated by the fact that the Synoptic writers barely attribute these blessings to the Spirit.[37] They never connect all three blessings to the Spirit in a verse or a passage as Paul clearly does in Romans 14:17. A careful examination of Romans 14:17 clarifies this.

Romans 14:17 is the most explicit example of Paul referring to the kingdom of God in relation to the Spirit. The verse conveys the idea that the Spirit is the vigorous source of the kingdom which 'produces the effects in the present human life that are appropriate to future life in the kingdom'.[38] The Spirit is integrated into human life and a life yielded to his workings clearly produces the blessings of the kingdom. According to Paul, 'life in the Spirit' is a life which produces the 'kingdom blessings' of 'righteousness, peace and joy'. Romans 14:17 clearly indicates this idea and gives an indication that Paul's connection of the Spirit to the blessings of kingdom life is more obvious than in the Synoptics.[39] As will be shown in detail, Paul extensively relates the qualities of kingdom life to the role of the Spirit: for him, life in the kingdom is life in the Spirit. Thus, one should be cautious in attempting to connect the sayings of Romans 14:17 with the early tradition, particularly in light of Paul's pneumatological concern.

In summary, Jesus' two-fold delineation of the kingdom is mirrored in Paul's kingdom of God sayings and some verbal similarities can be found in the kingdom of God sayings of Jesus and Paul. However, at the same time, there are some notable dissimilarities between the two. Paul's kingdom of God sayings are relatively sparse compared with the number in the Synoptics. Furthermore, they are not clearly depicted as pivotal messages about salvation as are those in the Synoptics.[40] From the pneumatological point of view, while Paul's exclusion formula (1 Cor. 6:9f.; Gal. 5:16f.; cf. 1 Cor. 15:42f.) is conceptually synonymous with that of the Synoptics, the insertion of the Spirit in the references is Paul's unique expression. The close association of the Spirit with the blessings of the kingdom life (Rom. 14:17; cf. 1 Cor. 4:20) is Paul's own concept. So Paul associates the present kingdom with the presence of the Spirit. Therefore, it is important to remember that while the kingdom of God is still a part of Paul's language, it is clear that Paul does not use it to the same extent or in the same way as the Synoptists.

---

[37] Cf. Lk. 10:21; Acts 13:52.
[38] N.Q. Hamilton, *The Holy Spirit and Eschatology in Paul*, SJTOP 6 (Edinburgh: Oliver & Boyd, 1957), 22.
[39] A further discussion of Rom. 14:17 will be offered in a later section (§3.3.4.1).
[40] R. Bultmann, *Theology of the New Testament*, vol. 1 (London: SCM Press, 1952), 189; see also J.M.G. Barclay, 'Jesus and Paul', *DPL*, 500. The phrase 'kingdom of God' appears 'never in the central statements about salvation'.

3.3. Paul's Choice of Spirit Language for the Kingdom of God

The above discussion (§3.2) leads one to wonder whether Paul intended to express kingdom language using other concepts which are thematically akin to Jesus' proclamation of the kingdom. In other words, Paul may have chosen various alternative terms to depict kingdom language in order to preserve its fundamental concept in his theology.[41] While other terms have been suggested by others, Paul's use of Spirit-language warrants special attention for the present study.[42]

3.3.1. Statistical Analysis

On a superficial level, it is striking to note the inverse ratio between the term kingdom in the Synoptics and the Spirit in Pauline corpus. While the term 'kingdom of God' is referred to 92 times in the Synoptics[43] and only 7 times in the Pauline corpus, the word 'Spirit' occurs only 13 times in the

---

[41] Jüngel offers two methods of addressing the issue of Paul's treatment of Jesus' teaching: one way is to focus on the unlikeness of their language; the other pertains to assessing the language dissimilarities on the basis of their common theological factors. That is, the latter indicates that the difference in language highlights one perspective of their theology. The latter methodology will be employed in this discussion. E. Jüngel, *Paulus und Jesus: eine Untersuchung zur Präzisierung der Frage nach dem Ursprung der Christologie* (Tübingen: Mohr, 1964), 263.

[42] For example, it is generally suggested that Paul has chosen the concept righteousness/justification' for the kingdom of God. This theory explains that Paul places salvation in Christ within the context of the eschatological fulfillment of OT promises, focusing instead upon important concepts of 'righteousness/justification' rather than utilizing the particular phrase of the kingdom of God. On the other hand, it should be noted that although Paul uses different concepts such as 'righteousness' or 'Spirit' to explain the concept of the kingdom, it does not mean that the two concepts are in conflict but rather that they are compatible. Both concepts (righteousness and Spirit) are habitually used by Paul in salvific dimensions which present the saving activity of God. On the relationship between the kingdom (Jesus) and righteousness (Paul), See Jüngel, *Paulus und Jesus*, 263-67; R. Bultmann, 'The Significance of the Historical Jesus for the Theology of Paul', in *Faith and Understanding: Collected Essays* (London: SCM Press, 1969), 232; Wedderburn, 'Paul and Jesus', 99-115; Wenham, *Paul*, 54; Dunn, *Theology*, 190. On the other hand, although Dunn points out a close relationship between the Spirit in Paul and the kingdom in Jesus, he does not fully develop their relationship. See his *Theology*, 191. Elsewhere, Dunn also discusses the relationship between the Spirit and the kingdom in both Paul and the Synoptics. *Pneumatology*, 133-41. But the point that he argues is not in accord with our present discussion that Paul's Spirit language overlaps the Synoptics' kingdom language, but rather claims that the Spirit is the presence of the kingdom of God in both Jesus (Luke) and Paul. A criticism of this latter thesis will be offered in chapter 5.

[43] This includes references to 'Kingdom of heaven', 'His Kingdom' and the like.

former and 110+ times in the latter.⁴⁴ This proportionate distribution of data warrants investigation whether it may be inferred that Jesus' emphasis on the kingdom may have been expressed by Paul's doctrine of the Spirit.⁴⁵

However, beyond the statistical analysis, can this orientation be demonstrated more convincingly? A question arises as to what extent Paul relates the Spirit in his letters to the kingdom of God in the Synoptics. In this question, two considerations must be taken into account: 1) The similarity of the eschatological framework of the two concepts; 2) The viability of a synonymous relationship between the present life in the Spirit for Paul and the present life in the kingdom in the Synoptics. The latter is crucial since the result of its examination has the important implication that, for Paul, the Spirit is portrayed as the life of the kingdom in its totality.

3.3.2. *The Eschatological Framework in Paul and the Synoptics*

The following examination shows the similarity between the Spirit in Paul and the kingdom of God in the Synoptics in terms of their eschatological function: while the future kingdom breaks into the present in the ministry of Jesus in the Synoptics, the Spirit in Paul is described as the first ἀρραβών of what is to come, having been manifested in the present life of believers.

3.3.2.1. THE SPIRIT IN PAUL

It is argued that Paul's eschatological framework mainly concentrates on a future-orientation because of the influence of Jewish eschatology. Simultaneously, Paul's eschatological concept is found as a present dimension in his letters. What influences Paul's shift of focus from the Jewish concentration on the future to this present dimension? The answer can be found in Paul's doctrine of the Spirit.⁴⁶ Paul views the role of the

---

[44] Cf. Dunn, *Theology*, 191, n. 38; I.H. Marshall, *Luke: Historian and Theologian* (Grand Rapids: Zondervan, 1970), 89.

[45] From these statistics, one might ask the question why Paul spoke so much about the Spirit. However, this question is somewhat subjective. The basic fact is that we do not have access to Paul himself, so the best we can do is speculate on this matter based on the evidence from his writing and the historical background. A more persuasive factor is that Paul associates kingdom-related concepts to the Spirit in a manner unlike other Christian writers of his time as will be seen in what follows. Nevertheless, what led Paul to use the term Spirit more frequently is perhaps closely related to the early Christian communities' experience of the Spirit in their midst and indeed Paul's own experience. On the other hand, Wenham gives Paul's own contextual reasons for the alteration of his kingdom language to other concepts: '(1) after the resurrection, (2) after his own conversion experience, (3) in the arena of the Roman Empire, not in Palestine, and (4) to Christian communities with particular problems'. *Paul*, 70.

[46] E.g., Dunn, *Theology*, 413-41, 466-72 (469-70), 477-82; Hamilton, *Holy Spirit*, 3-38; G. Vos, 'The Eschatological Aspect of the Pauline Conception of the Spirit', in R.B.

Spirit as one of preparation for the future, enabling believers to experience a foretaste of the future kingdom in the present because the Spirit is the ἀρραβών of the coming age.[47] While this notion is well known, a condensed review of the present aspect of the Spirit in Paul will be helpful for the present purpose.

It is notable that the references to the present aspect of the Spirit in the Pauline letters exceed those of the future.[48] According to Paul, the Spirit is given to believers in the present as an eschatological sign which becomes their 'hallmark' and a representation of the power of the age to come. This concept is clear in a number of Pauline letters.

In Galatians 4:4-5, Paul declares that when the time had fully come, God sent forth his Son to save people under the law and has made them his sons. Then, in the following verse (v. 6), Paul says 'God has sent the Spirit of his Son into our hearts' (ἐξαπέστειλεν ὁ θεὸς τὸ πνεῦμα τοῦ υἱοῦ αὐτοῦ). In this passage (Gal. 4:4-6), using the same sentence pattern,[49] Paul relates the coming of the Spirit and the coming of Jesus to the 'fullness of the time', that is, an eschatological event.[50] The Spirit is understood as the one who intervenes in the fullness of time that Jesus has brought. As 'τὴν ἐπαγγελίαν τοῦ πνεύματος' (Gal. 3:14) and 'τὴν ἀπαρχήν' (Rom. 8:23) of the eschaton,

---

Gaffin (ed.), *Redemptive History and Biblical Interpretation* (New Jersey: Presbyterian and Reformed, 1980), 91-125; Fee, *Empowering*, 803-26.

[47] The eschatological aspect of the Spirit is further founded in Pauline metaphors such as ἀρραβών (2 Cor. 1:22; 5:5; cf. Eph. 1:14) and ἀπαρχή (Rom. 8:23). Cf. σφραγίζω (2 Cor. 1:22). The metaphors point to the Spirit himself as ἀρραβών or ἀπαρχή and final 'harvest' or 'payment' is the completion of redemption initiated by the Spirit. So the Spirit is the beginning of the redemptive process. In these metaphors, Paul explains the role of the Spirit in the believer's present existence in terms of 'already' and 'not yet'.

[48] For instance, the present aspect of the Spirit pertains to Rom. 1:4, 11; 2:29; 5:5; 7:6; 8:1-17, 23-27; 14:17; 15:13, 16, 19, 27, 30; 1 Cor. 2:4-26; 3:16; 6:11, 17, 19; 7:40; 9:11; 12-14; 2 Cor. 1:22; 3:1-18; 4:13; 5:5; 13:13; Gal. 3:1-5, 14; 4:6, 29; 5:5, 13-26; 6:1, 8; Phil. 1:19; 2:1; 3:3 etc. Cf. The possible future references to the Spirit: Rom. 8:11, 23; 1 Cor. 15:44-46; 2 Cor. 1:22; 5:5; Gal. 5:5; 6:8. However, except for the reference to the Spirit in 1 Cor. 15:44-46, the rest of them contain both the present and future aspects of the Spirit.

[49] Fee, *Empowering*, 405. Cf. Dunn who claims that 'the variant formulation in Gal 4:4-6 is probably determined by Paul's decision to put the two sending formulae in parallel'. *Theology*, 436.

[50] It should be noted that the events, the coming of Jesus and the Spirit, brought the time of fulfillment rather than the former being subordinated to the latter. Because Jesus and the Spirit have come, the time is fulfilled and history is turned to the eschaton. Cf. G. Bornkamm, *Paul* (New York: Harper and Row, 1971), 196-200. However, as Fee claims, the locus of the sending is not the same: 'Within the context of human history and among the Jews, in the case of Jesus; within the hearts of believers, in the case of the Spirit'. Fee, *Empowering*, 405, n. 133.

the Spirit has come into the world and has been dispensed as promised, and so the future breaks into the present, bringing a new age. So the coming of the Spirit makes real to believers that they are God's children (Gal. 4:6) whose status will ultimately be completed in the future (e.g., Rom. 8:23).

The present reality of the Spirit is also manifested in Galatians 3:1-14 where Paul argues that the Spirit is the promised blessing of God. Here Paul likens the promise of the Spirit to the blessing of Abraham.[51] He closely associates the Galatians' reception of the Spirit (Gal. 3:3) with God's transaction with Abraham, whom God justified by his faith. In this analogy, Paul views the Spirit as part of God's promised blessing and inheritance for his people just as the blessing of Abraham (righteousness) was promised by God (Gal. 3:1-14, esp. v. 14). However, Paul's argument is more extensive than this in Galatians. Paul maintains that if they do not continue to live and walk in the promised Spirit, the eschatological inheritance will become futile in the end (Gal. 6:8). Thus, the way to inherit the final blessing as promised by God is 'to live and walk in the Spirit' in their present life (Gal. 5:16, 25). For this reason, although Paul connects the Spirit with both tensions of eschatology (Gal. 5:5; 6:8), the present working of the Spirit is given more emphasis than the future dimension in the letter (Gal. 3:1-4:6; 5:13-26).

A further clear presentation of Paul's concept of the Spirit as a present reality lies in the notion of the Spirit indwelling believers (Rom. 8, esp. 8:9f.).[52] The indwelling of the Spirit is a cause of believers' life and action (Rom. 8:9, 'in the Spirit') and provides them with power to please God (Rom. 8:5-8; 12:1; 1 Thess. 4:1f.). For Paul, the 'life of the believer' is described as 'life according to the Spirit' (Rom. 8:4-5) and this is well exhibited by his sayings 'led by the Spirit' (Rom. 8:14) and 'walking in the Spirit' (Rom. 8:4; Gal. 5:16, 25). This characteristic of the indwelling of the Spirit is also represented by Paul from an eschatological point of view. The Spirit, who dwells in believers, will raise the dead in Christ Jesus (Rom. 8:11), give sonship which guarantees the future inheritance (Rom. 8:15-17) and help them wait for the redemption of the body at the new creation (Rom. 8:23).

In short, for Paul the present time is a transitory period between Jesus' death and resurrection and his glorious parousia. This transitory period has the essential feature of the believer's current experience of the Spirit.[53] The Spirit is presented as evidence and a foretaste of the believer's experience of the fullness of the eschaton in the present time. Paul therefore understands the Spirit as an eschatological realization and regards this

---

[51] For a fuller discussion of the relationship between righteousness/justification and the Spirit, see §3.3.4.1 below.
[52] Hamilton, *Holy Spirit*, 29.
[53] Rom. 8:8-11; 1 Cor. 6:19; 12:4-11; 1 Thess. 4:8.

recognition as the starting point of his pneumatology.

3.3.2.2. THE KINGDOM IN THE SYNOPTICS

It is generally agreed among New Testament scholars that the kingdom of God in the Synoptics conveys a future aspect as well as a present one. Although the future references to the kingdom of God[54] dominate the present ones, the latter still appear, particularly in the person of Jesus and his ministry.[55]

This is most clearly indicated in his ministry of exorcism in Matthew 12:28/Luke 11:20, which shows that the kingdom of God as the inbreaking of God's reign into the believer's present life has come upon his people. Although a lack of consensus on the interpretation of ἔφθασεν persists, the significance of ἔφθασεν, particularly in connection with the prepositional reference to 'upon you' (ἐφ' ὑμᾶς), points to the arrival of the kingdom of God among believers.[56] The sovereignty of the Almighty has been made evident among his people through Jesus' ministry of exorcism, a representative taste of the presence of his kingdom in the here and now. The miracles and exorcisms of Jesus demonstrate the kingdom of God in action.

A further significant passage which provides evidence of the present character of the kingdom of God is found in Luke 17:21, which is more controversial than Matthew 12:28/Luke 11:20. Here the Pharisees pose a question concerning the time of the kingdom of God. Jesus answers 'the kingdom of God does not come with your careful observation, nor will people say, "Here it is", or "There it is", because ἡ βασιλεία τοῦ θεοῦ ἐντὸς ὑμῶν ἐστιν'. The answer of Jesus implies not only the time of the kingdom, but also the way in which it will come to people. There are two questions which call for further discussion in the present verse: what is the best way to interpret the word ἐντός with ὑμῶν and how can the tense of ἐστιν be rendered in the text?

---

[54] Mk. 14:25; Mt. 6:10; 8:11-12; 13:47-50; 16:28; 18:3; 20:21; 26:29; Lk. 13:29; 18:17 etc.

[55] Mk. 1:15; Mt. 11:12; 12:28; Lk. 10:9; 11:20; 17:21. See G.R. Beasley-Murray, *Jesus and the Kingdom of God* (Grand Rapids: Eerdmans, 1986), 71-143.

[56] For those who interpret the word ἔφθασεν as 'has come/has drawn near', see R.H. Fuller, *The Mission and Achievement of Jesus*, SBT 12 (Naperville: Allemson, 1954), 25-27; I.H. Marshall, *The Gospel of Luke*, NIGTC (Grand Rapids: Eerdmans, 1978), 476; Beasley-Murray, *Kingdom of God*, 75-76; D.C. Allison, *The End of the Ages Has Come: An Early Interpretation of the Passion and Resurrection of Jesus* (Philadelphia: Fortress Press, 1987), 105-06; C.L. Blomberg, *Matthew*, NAC 22 (Nashville: Broadman, 1992), 202; D.L. Bock, *Luke 9:51-24:53*, BECNT 3 (Grand Rapids: Baker, 1996), 1080. By contrast, for those who emphasize the word as 'the imminence of the event', see C.C. Caragounis, 'Kingdom of God, Son of Man and Jesus' Self-Understanding', *TynB* 40 (1989), 3-23, 223-38; J.C. O' Neill, 'The Kingdom of God', *NovT* 35 (1992), 139-41.

Concerning the first issue, one consideration is that it may mean 'within you'.[57] This sense is supported by some texts of the LXX such as Psalms 39:3; 103:1; 109:22 and Isaiah 16:11. The *Gospel of Thomas* also utilizes the word 'within' in a similar sense to Luke's text. The third logion reads:

> Jesus said, 'If those who draw you on say to you, Look, the kingdom of heaven', then the birds of heaven will be there before you. If they say to you, 'It is in the sea,' then the fish will be there before you. But the kingdom is within you and outside you.

However, although a similar expression is found in the text, it is often argued that caution is required in using the data from the *Gospel of Thomas* since 'the Gnostic agenda has affected how these sayings have been rendered in this source'.[58] Furthermore, if one applies this translation (within you) to Luke's gospel itself (or the Synoptics), the kingdom of God comes to mean an inward spiritual entity. If the object ὑμῶν is taken to refer to the Pharisees, the kingdom would be within them. Such a rendering would be unnatural, fails to fit with the context, and must be evaluated as not certain. On the other hand, Caragounis similarly argues that the meaning of ἐντὸς ὑμῶν ἐστιν should be interpreted in terms of its contradistinctive expression μετὰ παρατηρήσεως, which has to do with observable signs. So it becomes preferable to interpret it as referring to the inward nature of the kingdom of God.[59] However, the difficulty remains that such an internal view of the kingdom is not found elsewhere in Jesus' kingdom sayings. Here Jesus speaks of 'men entering the kingdom, not of the kingdom entering men'.[60]

With regard to the tense of the verb, some scholars argue that although ἐστιν is present in form, it should be taken as an imminent future in view of Luke 17:24 where Jesus' saying refers to a sudden, future event.[61] However, Jesus' saying may possibly address two different hearers in v. 21 and v. 24 and therefore it should not be assumed that he makes the same point.[62] Caution should be exercised before assuming that Jesus is making the same point here.

With the difficulties observed above in mind, a preferable solution can be

---

[57] G. Dalman, *The Words of Jesus* (Edinburgh: T. & T. Clark, 1902), 145-47; R.J. Sneed, 'The Kingdom of God within You (Lk 17:21)', *CBQ* 24 (1962), 363-82; and more recently, C.C. Caragounis, 'Kingdom of God/Heaven', *DJG*, 423-24.

[58] B. Witherington, *Jesus, Paul and the End of the World: A Comparative Study in New Testament Eschatology* (Downers Grove: Westminster Press, 1988), 53.

[59] Caragounis, 'Kingdom of God', 423.

[60] Marshall, *Luke*, 655.

[61] So the translation must be taken as 'will be suddenly among you'. Cf. J. Nolland, *Luke 9:21-18:34*, WBC 35b (Dallas: Word, 1993), 853-54.

[62] R. Tannehill, *Luke*, ANTC (Nashville: Abingdon, 1996), 259.

found if one takes the words, ἐντὸς ὑμῶν as 'among you', or 'in the midst of you'. This rendering finds support in some Hellenistic literary texts (Xenophon *Anab*. 1.10.3; *Hell*. 2.3, 19; Herodotus *Hist*. 7.100.3). The text of Herodotus (*Hist*. 7.100.3) provides a particularly collaborative example of ἐντός with a plural object with this meaning.[63] Moreover, this translation indicates that the kingdom of God might lie within the scope of the experience of the audience of Jesus regardless of whether ὑμῶν refers to the Pharisees or the eventual followers of Jesus in Luke 17:21. The kingdom of God, which is manifested in the person of Jesus, *is* present and active among people (so the tense of ἐστιν is to be rendered as present). This does not conflict with other references that represent God's dynamic saving activity on behalf of his people - the present kingdom of God - demonstrated in Jesus' powerful ministry (e.g., Mt. 12:28/Lk. 11:20).[64] The overall characteristic of the present aspect of the kingdom is well summarized by Kümmel:

> Jesus gives its full meaning to this eschatological character of the present primarily through the numerous statements in which he declares the coming kingdom of God to be realizing itself already in his person, his actions, and his message . . . he who will bring in the kingdom of God in the future has appeared in the present in Jesus himself.[65]

3.3.2.3. SUMMARY

For Paul, the Spirit manifests himself by breaking into the present as an eschatological instrument of eternal inheritance. This presentness of the Spirit represented in Paul is similar to the portrayal of the kingdom in the Synoptics which is also manifested as a present reality in believers through Jesus and his ministry. Thus, there are common features in the eschatological tension of the breaking of the future into the present in the kingdom in the Synoptics and the Spirit in Paul.[66] This is a possible indication of Paul's use of the Spirit for what is the kingdom in the Synoptics.

---

[63] Cf. Kümmel's analysis of the text of Herodotus (*Hist*. 7.100.3), 'ὁ δ' ἐντὸς τῶν πρωρέων πλέων ἐθηεῖτο καὶ τοῦ αἰγιαλοῦ = "as he drove between the ships" prows and the shore'. *Promise and Fulfillment* (London: SCM Press, 1957), 33, n. 50.

[64] Marshall, *Luke*, 655; Witherington, *Jesus*, 72; Kümmel, *Promise*, 34.

[65] Kümmel, *Promise*, 153.

[66] Hamilton correctly notes this concept: 'Just as in the Synoptics the future kingdom breaks into the present in the action of Jesus, so in Paul the future age has broken into the present in the action of the Spirit. The role of the Spirit in Paul's teaching is similar to that of the kingdom in the Synoptics. In the Synoptics, "kingdom" denotes the situation in which God rules; in Paul, "the Spirit" defines the same situation in terms of the inner dynamic which implements God's rule'. *Holy Spirit*, 23-24.

3.3.3. *The Similarity between Life in the Spirit in Paul and Life in the Kingdom in the Synoptics*

A more plausible explanation of Paul's use of the Spirit for the concept of the kingdom becomes evident when similarities commonly occur between life in the Spirit in Paul and life in the kingdom in the Synoptics. An important question arises: what are the various key aspects of the presentness of the kingdom (salvation) which are linked to the Spirit in Paul and how do we know that these overlap conceptually with the kingdom of God in the Synoptics? This ultimately shows how the Spirit in Paul functions as the mediator of the blessings and life of the kingdom in their entirety.

In order to find the similarities that occur in the two, I will list the key aspects of the presentness of the kingdom, particularly focusing on new life, sonship, resurrection, righteousness/justification, and ethics.[67]

3.3.3.1. NEW LIFE IN PAUL AND THE SYNOPTICS

New life as the beginning of salvation is an essential theme common to Paul and the Synoptics. While Paul attributes new life to the Spirit, the Synoptics' Jesus connects it to the arrival of (and life in) the kingdom of God.

3.3.3.1.1. The Spirit and New Life (Rom. 8:2; 2 Cor. 3:3-6)

Paul more than any other New Testament writer closely connects the concept of new life with his pneumatology.[68] The eschatological nature of the believer's present life is widely indicated in his writings as observed above: new life in the new age stands between the 'already', and the 'not yet'. Paul presents new life as a new creation (2 Cor. 5:17) and attributes it to the Spirit (Rom. 7:6). For Paul, the new life in the Spirit is the beginning of salvation and is characterized as a blessing of a new age. This idea is well articulated in several Pauline texts, notably, Romans 8:2 and 2 Corinthians 3:3-6.

---

[67] Although the present purpose is to find the similarity between 'life in the Spirit' (Paul) and 'life in the kingdom' (Synoptics) in each of these aspects, the 'mode of role' between the Spirit and the kingdom is different. For instance, as will be seen, the key aspects listed above are integral to 'life in the kingdom' according to Jesus in a more indirect way, i.e., the presence of the kingdom can be attributed to new life, sonship etc. However, in Paul, although they are mediated by the Spirit, the Spirit enables believers to experience them subjectively and directly. Nonetheless, this difference in view of the 'mode of role' does not influence the present purpose, i.e., 'life in the Spirit' is synonymous with 'life in the kingdom'.

[68] Although the new life of believers originates from the death and resurrection of Christ Jesus in God's redemptive plan according to Paul (e.g., 1 Cor. 15:3-4; cf. 2 Cor. 3:17; 1 Cor. 12:4, 5), the link of the Spirit with the concept of the new life is peculiar to Paul.

Paul in Romans 8:2 states 'ὁ γὰρ νόμος τοῦ πνεύματος τῆς ζωῆς ἐν Χριστῷ Ἰησοῦ ἠλευθέρωσέν σε ἀπὸ τοῦ νόμου τῆς ἁμαρτίας καὶ τοῦ θανάτου'. In verse 1, the word νῦν is introduced by ushering in an eschatological sense[69] inaugurated by Christ's death and resurrection (ἐν Χριστῷ Ἰησοῦ). Paul then connects God's eschatological redemptive plan in Christ to the work of the Spirit (νόμος τοῦ πνεύματος τῆς ζωῆς). Thus in verses 1-2, Paul exhibits his eschatology, soteriology, and pneumatology all together.[70]

What is crucial in the present verse for the purpose of this section is the phrase, ὁ νόμος τοῦ πνεύματος τῆς ζωῆς ἐν Χριστῷ. Some assert that ὁ νόμος in the phrase refers to the Mosaic law.[71] However, this is highly improbable because if the Mosaic law 'set you free from the law of sin and death', it is difficult to make good sense of the following verse since there Paul proclaims the law's inability (Rom. 8:3, 'ἀδύνατον τοῦ νόμου') to bring freedom from sin and death (Rom. 8:2). Indeed, Paul never attributes this freedom to the law whilst elsewhere he connects it with Christ and the Spirit (Gal. 5:1; 2 Cor. 3:17-18).[72] The commonly accepted view is that the 'law' in Romans 8:2a is a rhetorical emphasis without a substantial connection with the 'law of sin and death' in verse 2b. So it is used in a

---

[69] Although the word νῦν elsewhere in the Pauline letters is used in a non-temporal sense (e.g., 1 Cor. 12:18, 20; 14:6; Rom. 7:17 etc.) its meaning here is clearly temporal, the time between the manifestation of Jesus and the full consummation of the world. This temporal sense of 'now' is also connected to the new life as the work of the Spirit in Rom. 8:1-2. In Rom. 7:6, Paul clearly links the renewing power of the Spirit to the 'now' in the temporal sense. G. Stählin, 'νῦν, *TDNT*, IV, 1117-18. In the letter of Romans, Paul particularly maintains the word in the eschatological sense (3:26; 5:9, 11; 6:19, 21; 8:18, 22; 11:5, 30, 31; 13:11; 16:26). J.A. Bertone, 'The Function of the Spirit in the Dialectic between God's Soteriological Plan Enacted but Not Yet Culminated: Rom 8:1-27', *JPT* 15 (1999), 77.

[70] Bertone, 'Function', 77.

[71] E.g., E. Lohse, 'ὁ νόμος τοῦ πνεύματος τῆς ζωῆς: Exegetische Anmerkungen zu Röm 8:2', in H.D. Betz and L. Schotroff (eds.), *Neues Testament und christliche Existenz* (Tübingen: Mohr, 1973), 279-87 ('eindeutig das alttestamentliche Gesetz', 284); H. Hübner, *Law in Paul's Thought* (Edinburgh: T. & T. Clark, 1984), 144-48; P. Stuhlmacher, *Paul's Letter to the Romans: A Commentary* (Louisville: Westminster Press, 1994), 119; J. Dunn, *Romans 1-8*, WBC 38a (Dallas: Word, 1988), 416-17. These scholars also believe that the 'law' in Rom. 8:2b is the Mosaic law. But, an alternative interpretation is asserted in the figurative meaning, 'principle' or 'power' as in Rom. 3:27: 'Then what becomes of our boasting? It is excluded. On what principle? On the principle of works? No, but on the principle of faith'. C.E.B. Cranfield, *A Critical and Exegetical Commentary on the Epistle to the Romans*, 1, (ICC; Edinburgh: T. & T. Clark, 1975), 376; W. Gutbrod, 'νόμος', *TDNT*, IV, 1071.

[72] Cf. E. Käsemann, *Commentary on Romans* (Grand Rapids: Eerdmans, 1980), 216.

figurative sense, meaning 'principle', 'rule', or 'power'.[73] Therefore, Paul's main point in the phrase ὁ νόμος τοῦ πνεύματος τῆς ζωῆς in Romans 8:2a should be 'πνεῦμα' rather than 'νόμος' and the phrase emphasizes the life-giving function of the Spirit. The focus of the rest of the context of Romans 8, which extensively deals with the Spirit, particularly his various life-giving functions, agrees with this deduction (see vv. 5, 6, 9, 10, 11, 13, 14, 15, 16, 23, 26, 27).[74]

For Paul, the Spirit is the source of life in God's soteriological operation through the work of Christ. This appears in verse 2 where there is a close connection between the life-giving Spirit and Christ in the phrase, ὁ νόμος τοῦ πνεύματος τῆς ζωῆς ἐν Χριστῷ. The fact that the genitive τῆς ζωῆς in the phrase modifies τοῦ πνεύματος makes it clearer that the Spirit is the life-giver.[75] The prepositional phrase ἐν Χριστῷ, which is used as an instrumental meaning (cf. Rom. 3:24), indicates that God's saving activity through Christ is the foundation of the life-giving work of the Spirit.[76] This fact becomes clear in the following text: God condemned sin in the flesh through his own Son, Christ (Rom. 8:3). Consequently, for Paul, the soteriological function is apparently shown in his pneumatological concern. Presenting the direct antithesis in one phrase ὁ νόμος τῆς ἁμαρτίας καὶ τοῦ θανάτου, Paul in the other phrase ὁ νόμος τοῦ πνεύματος τῆς ζωῆς claims that the eschatological new life is from the Spirit. The Spirit, as a sign of a new eschatological age, has set believers free from the tyranny of sin and death by giving the new life. Paul maintains this idea in his other earlier letter, 2 Corinthians.

Paul's main argument in 2 Corinthians 3 defends his personal integrity and apostleship. His defence is that his apostolic ministry is qualified not by the letter of the old covenant which his opponents practise but the Spirit of the new covenant, who gives new life.[77] This appears particularly in 2 Corinthians 3:6. Paul says in the passage that God has made himself (Paul) and his readers His ministers in a new covenant, 'οὐ γράμματος ἀλλὰ πνεύματος· τὸ γὰρ γράμμα ἀποκτέννει, τὸ δὲ πνεῦμα ζωοποιεῖ'.

Although some interpret the letter and the Spirit antithesis in the light of the literal and spiritual sense of the scripture based on the hermeneutical principle,[78] scholarly consensus has it as an eschatological point of view of

---

[73] Cranfield, *Romans*, 1, 326; L. Morris, *The Epistle to the Romans* (Grand Rapids: Eerdmans, 1988), 300-01; H. Räisänen, *Jesus, Paul and Torah*, JSNTS 43 (Sheffield: SAP, 1992), 48-68 (68); Fee, *Empowering*, 522; C.K. Barrett, *The Epistle to the Romans*, HNTC (Peabody: Hendrickson, 1987), 155.

[74] Fee, *Empowering*, 527-91.

[75] Fee, *Empowering*, 525, n. 156; D. Moo, *Romans 1-8*, WEC (Chicago: Moody, 1991), 530.

[76] Fee, *Empowering*, 524.

[77] V.P. Furnish, *II Corinthians* (New York: Doubleday, 1984), 185-86.

[78] That is, the Spirit is understood as interpreter for the letter rather than that the former

the contrast based on the old and new epoch.⁷⁹ The overall context of 2 Corinthians 3 draws a contrast between the old covenant and the new covenant (vv. 6, 14): the former is identified with the tablets of stone (v. 3) while the latter is energized by the Spirit (v. 6). In contrast to both the 'tablets of stone', in verse 3 and 'the letter' in verse 6, which represent the ministry of the old covenant characterized as the medium of the death and condemnation, Paul and his readers now experience the new way of existence under the new covenant, the life-giving Spirit.⁸⁰

This clearly shows the eschatological life-giving function of the Spirit. Hence, whatever is meant by the term γράμμα in the present text,⁸¹ Paul's emphasis is rather the Spirit and his life-giving function. The phrase τὸ γράμμα ἀποκτέννει, τὸ δὲ πνεῦμα ζῳοποιεῖ in 2 Corinthians 3:6 makes the fact clear. The phrase τὸ πνεῦμα ζῳοποιεῖ is antithetical to τὸ γράμμα ἀποκτέννει.⁸² Just as the letter kills, so the Spirit makes alive: the eschatological Spirit brings new life. This contrast is indeed not different from that already introduced in verse 3, 'written not with ink but with the Spirit of the living God'. The immediate context develops this role of the Spirit outlined in verse 6 in contrast with the γράμμα: the διακονία of death and διακονία of the Spirit. Unlike the ministry of Moses, one of death and condemnation, Paul declares the greater glory of the διακονία of the Spirit as a ministry of life and righteousness (vv. 7-11, cf. vv. 17-18). The Spirit becomes the life-giving Spirit, providing the internal motivation to fulfill what the written law required externally. Like Romans 8:2, the phrase τὸ γράμμα ἀποκτέννει, τὸ δὲ πνεῦμα ζῳοποιεῖ serves as a thesis statement to

---

is antithetically related to the latter. E.g., P. Richardson, 'Spirit and Letter: A Foundation for Hermeneutics', *EvQ* 45 (1973), 214-18. However, this seems a difficult interpretation because of its failure to illustrate the extreme contrast between the two: τὸ γράμμα ἀποκτέννει, τὸ δὲ πνεῦμα ζῳοποιει.

⁷⁹ Fee, *Empowering*, 304; Dunn, *Theology*, 149; Furnish, *II Corinthians*, 200.

⁸⁰ Dunn, *Theology*, 147-48; Furnish, *II Corinthians*, 199.

⁸¹ Some interpret the word letter as the Mosaic law itself while others render it not simply as the law itself, but rather as the law which makes concrete demands for obedience. Those who favour the former include T.R. Schreiner, *The Law and its Fulfillment: A Pauline Theology of Law* (Grand Rapids: Baker, 1993), 81-83. Those who like the latter include Fee, *Empowering*, 305-06; S. Westerholm, *Israel's Law and the Church's Faith: Paul and His Recent Interpreters* (Grand Rapids: Eerdmans, 1988), 213. On the other hand, an alternative view is suggested by Cranfield, who takes it as a law which is misused in Corinth. Based on Rom. 7:6, Cranfield remarks that the letter is not simply, 'equivalent of the "law". "Letter" is rather what the legalist is left with as a result of his misunderstanding and misuse of the law. It is the letter in separation from the Spirit'. *Romans*, 1, 339f. But in any case, one thing is clear that the connotation of the term in the context is antithetically portrayed by the Spirit. See the following discussion.

⁸² Cf. Rom. 2:28-29; 7:6, where the oldness of the letter and newness of the Spirit is antithetically described.

the whole of 2 Corinthians 3.[83] Hence, Paul's depiction of the Spirit as the source of life is particularly important: τὸ πνεῦμα ζῳοποιεῖ. Indeed, the main point of 2 Corinthians 3:6 is almost identical with that of Romans 8:2, which was discussed above.[84]

In short, for Paul, the intimate connection between the Spirit and new life is clear. The Spirit plays the decisive role in conferring the power which brings new life to believers. So new life is realized in the presence of the Spirit. In this manner, Paul attributes the new life to the work of the Spirit as a blessing in the new age.

3.3.3.1.2. The Kingdom and New Life (Mk. 1:15; Lk. 15:11-32; cf. Lk. 7:48-50; Lk. 18:18-30; Mk. 10:17-31; Mt. 19:16-28 etc.)

If Paul closely connects the concept of new life with the Spirit, then the Synoptic writers fundamentally attribute it to the kingdom of God.[85]

A present experience of the cosmic dimension of new life (salvation) related to the kingdom is well summarized in Mark 1:15 (Mt. 4:17) where Jesus declares that 'The time is fulfilled, and the kingdom of God is at hand (ἤγγικεν[86] ἡ βασιλεία τοῦ θεοῦ); repent, and believe in the gospel'. The announcement of the fulfilled time and the coming of the kingdom is synthetically paralleled indicating that the day of salvation has arrived.[87] Jesus unites the arrival of the kingdom with his call for repentance and belief in the good news of God's sovereignty. The two imperatives 'believing' and 'repenting' are characterized as the way to experience the kingdom of God so that those who respond to the kingdom of God will experience a new life with God.[88] An offer of salvation is now available with the coming of the kingdom. Hence, Jesus' message of the kingdom here refers to 'the decisive beginning of the promised coming of God to

---

[83] S. Hafemann, *Paul, Moses, and the History of Israel: The Letter/Spirit Contrast and the Argument from Scripture in 2 Corinthians 3*, WUNT 81 (Tübingen: Mohr, 1995), 1. Hafemann in this book extensively argues the issue of the letter and Spirit antithesis, though the main focus seems to be on the law rather than the Spirit.

[84] Fee, *Empowering*, 306.

[85] As Beasley-Murray notes, 'The general thrust of his (Jesus') teaching on the kingdom of God. . . implies that in his word and work there is an *initiation* of the sovereign action of God that brings salvation'. Beasley-Murray, *Kingdom of God*, 74. On the other hand, the discussion of the limited relationship between the Spirit and the concept of new life in the Synoptics, particularly in Luke, will be seen in the following chapter.

[86] For the various interpretations of the word ἤγγικεν, see Beasley-Murray, *Kingdom of God*, 72-74; R.A. Guelich, *Mark 1-8:26*, WBC 34a (Dallas: Word, 1989), 44. But note Guelich's conclusion: 'the thrust of 1:1-15, the context of 1:14-15, and the synthetic parallelism of 1:15 underscore the presence of the Kingdom as the theme of Jesus' message'.

[87] Guelich, *Mark 1-8:26*, 43.

[88] J. Becker, *Jesus of Nazareth* (Berlin: Walter De Gruyter, 1998), 236.

bring the saving sovereignty'.[89]

Furthermore, the fact that the saving activities of Jesus presently reveal the realization of the kingdom shows a close relation between new life (or salvation) and kingdom.[90] For instance, Jesus' healing ministry in the Synoptics not only indicates physical healing (Lk. 6:9/Mk. 3:4; Lk. 8:36, 48/Mk. 5:34; Lk. 8:50; 17:19; 18:42/Mk. 10:52; cf. Acts 4:9; 14:9), but also shows spiritual salvation, i.e., a blessing of the new life (Lk. 7:50; 8:12; 19:10; cf. 13:23).[91] In particular, Luke, in 7:48-50, indicates a spiritual sense of salvation, presenting 'forgiveness of sin' as the content of salvation. The woman's new life is realized in believing in Jesus, who is God's sovereign agent and who inaugurates the kingdom (Lk. 2:11; 4:43; 8:1; 9:11; 10:9-11; 11:20; 17:21). So Jesus' familiar announcement, 'Your faith has saved you'[92] denotes that the reception of new life is derived from a commitment to Jesus by faith.

The new life in relation to the kingdom of God is also found in the teaching of Jesus, particularly in his parables.[93] No text better indicates the relationship than do the three parables presented in Luke 15, particularly the third parable. The parable of the prodigal son (Lk. 15:11-32) gives a similar message to the first two parables,[94] but shows a detailed form.[95] The main figure of the parable is the father: the conversation and the interaction between the father and the younger son in Luke 15:20-24 represents the deeper level of the father's merciful forgiveness.[96] The central event of the parable is the re-gaining of a new life by the younger son: here the dispenser of a new life is the father, the only one who can restore the broken

---

[89] Beasley-Murray, *Kingdom of God*, 74.

[90] M.A. Powell, 'Salvation in Luke-Acts', *WW* 12:1 (1992), 8.

[91] In comparison to the other gospels, a spiritual sense of salvation is mentioned more in Luke. Marshall, *Historian*, 92.

[92] Lk. 8:48; 17:19; 18:42; cf. 8:50.

[93] It is generally recognized that Jesus' purpose in teaching the parables (except the parables of judgement) is to make the saving nearness of the kingdom of God real. See Becker, *Jesus*, 141-55. Becker further comments that 'With his (Jesus') parables he (Jesus) established the reality of the Kingdom of God in the reality of the world of human experience in the narrative. Thus parabolic speech became a formative way of speaking that... made the Kingdom of God happen as a saving experience'. 143.

[94] The general focus of the first two parables is on the activities of the finders, seeking and finding the lost objects, and rejoicing as a result of regaining what they had lost. The primary message of the parables is that God offers a hope for the lost and it is *the joy of God* to find what has been lost (cf. v. 7: 'joy in heaven', and v. 10: 'joy before the angels of God'). Jeremias, following Gulin, argues that this joy is the 'redemptive joy' of God. J. Jeremias, *The Parables of Jesus* (London: SCM Press, 1963), 136.

[95] Marshall, *Luke*, 597.

[96] According to Lk. 15:20-24, the father's action appears prior to the confession of the son's sin.

relationship (Lk. 15:24, 'my son was dead and is alive again').[97] The parable then points to the father's joyous celebration because of his son's restoration to a new life in spite of his elder son's protest.

What is Jesus' central message in the parable to his present hearers? According to the context of this parable, Jesus is criticized by the Pharisees and scribes when he welcomes sinners and eats with them, and then presents this parable (and the previous two parables) to justify his action. Jesus' action toward the sinners can be justified by the mercy of the father in the parable. The hearers are invited to identify what Jesus has done with God's conduct. So when the hearers understand what Jesus presents, 'they are not simply reminded in general about what God does; Jesus' activity is revealed to them as the turning-point in which God offers them salvation'.[98] In this way, they are also required to 'understand the special recognition that *it is Jesus who makes the kingdom of God happen*'.[99] Thus, the primary message of the parable is an announcement of the offer of the kingdom of God and an invitation to the hearers to enter the kingdom and to taste the present beginning of salvation. This is certainly a new reality of salvation in the new world of the kingdom in contrast to the hearers' existing reality.[100]

The purpose of Jesus' coming is to seek and to save the lost (Lk. 19:10). The lost is found, therefore it is time to celebrate together here and now in the kingdom of God. Thus, when the sovereignty of God (the kingdom of God) in Jesus' saving ministry and teaching breaks into human life, the sinners are forgiven, the lost are found and the dead are brought back to life again.[101] Whoever participates in the present blessings of the kingdom in Jesus' saving ministry is being saved (cf. Lk. 19:10). In essence, 'To enter the kingdom means to allow one's life to be brought under the ruling power of God'.[102]

In a number of passages in the Synoptics, the eschatological characteristic of new life (in the concept of eternal life) is associated with the kingdom of God. In the story of a rich ruler (Lk. 18:18-30/Mk. 10:17-31/Mt. 19:16-28), Jesus links the cosmic new life (eternal life) in the future with the kingdom of God. The reference to 'eternal life' (Lk. 18:18, 30) is another way of expressing 'being saved' (Lk. 18:26) and these expressions

---

[97] Becker, *Jesus*, 154.
[98] Becker, *Jesus*, 140. Similarly, note Jeremias' claim, 'The parable (of the prodigal son), without making any kind of christological statement, reveals itself as a veiled assertion of authority: Jesus makes the claim for himself that he is acting in God's stead, that is he God's representative'. Jeremias, *Parables*, 132.
[99] Becker, *Jesus*, 140. Emphasis is added.
[100] Becker, *Jesus*, 155; Beasley-Murray argues that 'the parable of the Prodigal Son is indeed a parable of the kingdom'. *Kingdom of God*, 114.
[101] Cf. Powell, 'Salvation', 6. Powell comments that 'Defined as a "participation in the reign of God", salvation means living life, even now, as God intends it to be lived'.
[102] C. Mitton, *Your Kingdom Come* (London and Oxford: Mowbrays, 1978), 53.

are parallel with the phrase 'entering the kingdom of God' (Lk. 18:24, 25, 29).[103] The equation between the kingdom and being saved is also presented in Luke 13:23-29 (cf. Mt. 8:11-12). In Luke 13:23, the question is raised whether 'few will be saved'. Jesus' answer to this question is that whatever their number, participating in the kingdom of God needs an observant alertness. Jesus then depicts those who are saved as ones who will participate in the feast of the kingdom of God in verse 29. Jesus further connects the kingdom of God to the promise of the full realization of redemption in Luke 21:28, 31 (cf. Mt. 24:31-33; Mk. 13:27-29).[104] The term ἀπολύτρωσις (redemption) connotes the eschatological sense referring to consummated eternal life (final salvation).[105] There is a parallel between verses 28 and 31 where the coming of the kingdom of God indicated in the latter is associated with the promise of the coming of final salvation in the former. Finally, in the passion narrative, Luke links Jesus' kingdom to the criminal's gain of new life (Lk. 23:42-43).

In short, according to the Synoptics, new life means the experience of believers in personal encounter with Jesus and a participation in the realization of the kingdom of God. In this way, the concept is closely linked to the kingdom of God.

3.3.3.1.3. Summary

For the Synoptic writers, (esp. for Luke), the beginning of new life means participating in the kingdom of God in Jesus. This is comparable with Paul's way of speaking about new life in the Spirit: the Spirit is the source of new life. So, experiencing a new life in the Spirit according to Paul conceptually overlaps with experiencing a new life in the kingdom according to the Synoptics. This recognition reflects Paul's use of his Spirit language for kingdom language.

3.3.3.2. SONSHIP IN PAUL AND THE SYNOPTICS

The conceptual similarity between the Spirit (Paul) and the kingdom (Synoptics) is also found in terms of sonship. In both of them the concept of sonship is portrayed as the primary evidence that believers are saved. While Paul undoubtedly links the concept to the Spirit, the Synoptic writers associate it with the kingdom. The following discussion will elucidate this

---

[103] R. O'Toole, 'The Kingdom of God in Luke-Acts', in W. Willis (ed.) *The Kingdom of God in Twentieth-Century Interpretation* (Peabody: Hendrickson, 1987), 155-56; Powell, 'Salvation', 8; G. Schneider, 'ἔρχομαι', *TDNT*, II, 670. A fuller discussion of the story of the rich ruler and the concept 'eternal life' as resurrection will be discussed in what follows.

[104] In comparison with the other Synoptic writers, only Luke inserts the phrase the kingdom of God in the parable of the fig tree. Marshall, *Luke*, 779.

[105] F. Büchsel, 'ἀπολύτρωσις', *TDNT*, IV, 352. There is an identification of redemption as salvation according to Luke (e.g., Lk. 1:68; 2:38; cf. 24:21).

idea.

3.3.3.2.1. The Spirit and Sense of Sonship (Rom. 8:14-15, 23; Gal. 4:6)[106]

The role of the Spirit in salvation is clearly elucidated in the concept of the sense of sonship in Paul. The Spirit forms a new existential relationship between God and his children in the present. Further, the eschatological characteristic of the sense of sonship is also Paul's concept. Believers experience being sons of God in the present, but the fullness of their inheritance will be accomplished in the future. Paul links this sense of sonship to the Spirit.

Two substantial passages are notable: Galatians 4:6 and Romans 8:14-15. As in Galalatians 3:13-14, the core of Paul's argument in Galatians 4:4-5, based on his christological-soteriological point of view, is that the promised blessing of inheritance has been effected by Christ.[107] The coming of Christ, which is set by God, gives believers a new status in which they are to live freely as sons of God. Hence, the life of believers, including Gentiles, is to be lived not under the law but in Christ. However, although Christ has an undeniable efficacy in the believer's adoption as sons, Paul continues to present his argument in the light of his pneumatology. In the following verse (v. 6), Paul clarifies the evidence of such adoption in the gift of the Spirit.[108] The evidence of such shared adoption is the presence of the Spirit of the Son whom God sent forth (υἱοῦ αὐτοῦ). The Spirit brings the 'adoption of sons' to believers and bears witness to the presence of the Son who made them sons. The evidence of this adoption is further confirmed by the Spirit crying out 'Abba' within the believer.[109] So Paul in the present passage connects the work of Christ and his Spirit to the full freedom of mature sonship in a thoroughly christological-soteriological manner.[110]

The sense of sonship also appears plainly in Romans 8. However, unlike Galatians 4:4-6, Paul's focus in Romans 8 is far more on the Spirit than christocentric (Gal. 4:5) and he develops the eschatological aspects of the sense of sonship based on his pneumatology, especially in verses 14-15, and 23.[111] In Romans 8:14 Paul links being 'led by the Spirit of God' to 'being

---

[106] For a general discussion on sonship, see J.M. Scott, *Adoption as Sons of God: An Exegetical Investigation into the Background of ΥΙΟΘΕΣΙΑ in the Corpus Paulinum*, WUNT 2.48 (Tübingen: Mohr, 1992).

[107] Fee, *Empowering*, 402.

[108] Fee, *Empowering*, 404.

[109] See below in this section for further discussion on the 'Abba cry'. For a discussion of the relationship between the term 'Abba Father' used by Paul and that used by Jesus (and his disciples) in the Synoptics, particularly in Luke, see §4.2 in chapter 4.

[110] Cf. Fee's claim: the work of Christ is 'an objective, historical, once-for-all reality' while the work of the Spirit is experienced and realized in the believer. *Empowering*, 407.

[111] Therefore, the focus of the adoption of sons in Galatians and Romans is more or less

the sons of God'. Paul in verse 13b says '. . . if by the Spirit you put to death the deeds of the body you will live'. He then subsequently says 'For all who are led by the Spirit of God are sons of God'. The conjunction, γάρ in verse 14 is an explanatory word to verse 13b, 'you will live'. The status of the sons of God referred to in verse 14 is related to the statement of verse 13b, 'you will live' under the effect of the Spirit. There is thus a close correlation between the two verses, designating that those who put to death the practices of the flesh by the indwelling Spirit will live and those led by him are God's adopted sons. Paul's emphasis here is that the true evidence of sonship is being dependent on the leading of the Spirit ('all who are *led* by the Spirit *are* sons of God'). Paul's declaration in verse 14 is clearly substantiated in the following firm statements in verses 15-17b where the eschatological Spirit presently bears witness to the believer's status as God's adopted sons. So the believer's status is identified by the role of the Spirit.[112] Paul therefore calls the Spirit 'the Spirit of sonship' in verse 15 since those who are led by the Spirit of God are the sons of God (v. 14).[113] The present reality of sonship caused by the Spirit appears in Romans 8:15 at several points.

First of all, Paul draws the image of slavery in contrast with that of sonship resulting from the work of the Spirit.[114] For Paul, the image of slavery simply pictures the old life of both Jews, who were under 'the tyranny of sin awakened by Torah', and Gentiles, who were under 'the tyranny of sin without God', both of which are characterized by fear.[115] However, believers, whether Jews or Gentiles, have been set free from the lowest level of slavery (Rom. 8:2) and are heirs to the promised redemption by Christ (Gal. 4:6), effected by receiving the Spirit of sonship (Rom. 8:15). The new status of believers is now set as sonship which is effected by the Spirit in contra-distinction to their old status, slavery. It is the sign of the Spirit of sonship that he puts the stamp of his witness on them as sons of God, delivering them from the bondage of fear.

---

distinguishable although the Spirit is evidence of sonship in both of them. The adoption of sons is effected by Christ in the former while there is no close connection between sonship and Christ as the sons of God but rather sonship is referred to 'as the Spirit's thing: he is "the Spirit of adoption as sons"'. Fee, *Empowering*, 562; see also Hamilton, *Holy Spirit*, 31; Dunn, *Theology*, 469.

[112] Fee, *Empowering*, 563-64.

[113] Barrett doubts the present aspect of sonship in this verse and argues it as the reality of the future as in Rom. 8:23. Barrett, *Romans*, 163. However, this view has been rejected by most commentators (e.g., Cranfield, Dunn, Fee etc.). See below.

[114] However, Paul, in the present verse, does not mean the existence of two kinds of spirit, but rather the phrase is Paul's rhetorical style to emphasize the work of the Spirit, here the Spirit of sonship. So most commentators, Barrett, *Romans*, 163; Cranfield, *Romans*, 1, 396; Fee, *Empowering*, 565; Dunn, *Romans 1-8*, 451.

[115] Fee, *Empowering*, 565-66.

Furthermore, Paul's alteration of the tense in the following sentence and verse clarifies the realization of sonship in the present life of believers. While Paul uses a past tense ἐλάβετε πνεῦμα υἱοθεσίας in verse 15b, he applies the present tense κράζομεν in 15c. The focus on the present tense is more clearly seen in verse 16: 'The Spirit himself testifies (συμμαρτυρεῖ) with our spirit that we are (ἐσμέν) God's children'. Paul's reason for this shift is to emphasize the present aspect of sonship as evident and effective in believers.[116]

A further observation of this present reality of sonship is apparently described by the 'Abba' cry. Compared with Galatians 4:6, where the Spirit himself cries 'Abba Father', Romans 8:15 expresses it in a more precise way, 'you have received the Spirit of sonship by whom *we* cry (ἐν ᾧ κράζομεν)'.[117] In other words, believers presently receive the Spirit of sonship and cry out *by means of* the Spirit in Romans 8:15 whereas the 'ἀββά', cry is attributed directly to the Spirit in Galatians 4:6. Nonetheless, it is obvious that the two instances intrinsically mean the same by emphasizing the work and witness of the Spirit in the 'ἀββά', cry in believers.[118] The inspirational expression of the cry 'ἀββά', evidences the presence of the Spirit, who dwells in believers and enables them to call God, 'Father'. The cry 'ἀββά', thus becomes for believers a point of new entry into the spiritual experience of a filial intimacy with God which leads to eschatological newness by the Spirit. In short, since believers receive the Spirit and have the privilege and right to cry out 'Abba Father', the status of sonship in believers exists as a present entity. In this way, the Spirit makes the status of God's children into a subjective reality from the objective possibility.

However, Paul does not conclude his teaching on this point of sonship with the dimension of present experience but moves on to an eschatological climax in verse 23.[119] After Paul encourages his readers regarding the believers' present status as sons, he turns to the issue of the present suffering of believers in relation to the future glory in an eschatological perspective in verses 17b-18. The glory in the future (full inheritance) will be given to believers who share Christ's suffering.[120] Paul then argues the cosmic perspective in the light of the present and the future by using the term, κτίσις (vv. 19-22).[121] The final redemption is not simply applicable to

---

[116] Fee, *Empowering*, 567; Cranfield, *Romans*, 1, 397.

[117] Fee, *Empowering*, 567. As most writers concede, here the antecedent of ἐν ᾧ is 'πνεῦμα' rather than 'in that'.

[118] Dunn, *Romans 1-8*, 453; Fee, *Empowering*, 406.

[119] Hamilton, *Holy Spirit*, 32; Berton argues that v. 23 'is pivotal in understanding Paul's line of thought from vv. 17b-27'. 'Function', 86.

[120] Cf. Rom. 7:24; 8:13 where Paul speaks of the body of death and the putting to death of sinful deeds.

[121] 'For the creation waits with eager longing for the revealing of the sons of God' (v.

humans, but also pertinent to the whole creation in God's purpose. Using the term sonship, Paul again in verse 23 encourages his readers by giving assurance of their future destiny as God's adopted sons. In this argument, Paul indicates the critical role of the Spirit in both the present and future and continually employs the Spirit as the dominant theme in his argument until verse 27. The leading and witness of the Spirit in the present are simply the first-fruits, especially regarding sonship. Although believers are already adopted, they nevertheless should eagerly await full sonship ('the redemption of our bodies') on the basis of hope assured by the Spirit of the future completion of God's redemption.[122] The believers' present possession of sonship (Gal. 4:6 and Rom. 8:15) will be certain in the light of anticipation of the future possession of the Spirit (Rom. 8:23). For the former, the Spirit becomes the effective cause of the experiential reality while he acts for the latter as the surety for full reception of the status of sonship in the future.

In summary, for Paul, salvation is realized in the life of believers through the presence of the Spirit who imparts the assurance of sonship and confirms them in their new status as God's children. The sense of sonship, which is presently experienced by believers and will be confirmed at the eschaton, is certainly related to the Spirit as an eschatological reality. Again, the life-giving work of the Spirit causes the sense of sonship in the light of Pauline pneumatology.

3.3.3.2.2. The Kingdom and Sense of Sonship (Mt. 5:45/Lk. 6:35; Mt. 6:9-10/Lk. 11:2; cf. Mt. 5:9; Mt. 17:25)

If the idea of sonship is related to the Spirit in Paul as seen above, in the Synoptics it is integral to the kingdom of God rather than to the role of the Spirit.[123] Furthermore, if eschatological sonship is realized in the present because of the presence of the Spirit according to Paul, then, in the Synoptics, its realization is also related to the presence of the kingdom of God. A number of passages link the concept of sonship to the kingdom in the Synoptics, notably Matthew 5:45/Luke 6:35 (cf. Mt. 5:9; 17:25); Matthew 6:9-10/Luke 11:2.

According to the Matthean beatitudes, the eschatological sonship (to be sons of God in Mt. 5:9) is described as one of the blessings in the promised kingdom (Mt. 5:3, 10). This eschatological blessing is also depicted in Matthew 5:45: 'so that (ὅπως) you may be sons of your Father (γένησθε υἱοὶ τοῦ πατρὸς ὑμῶν) in heaven'. This is clearer in Luke's saying, 'you

---

19); 'the creation will be set free from its bondage to decay and obtain the glorious liberty of the children of God' (v. 21).

[122] Fee, *Empowering*, 574.

[123] While it is clear that there is no connection between the Spirit and believers' sonship in the Synoptics, it has been debated whether Jesus' sonship is associated with the Spirit. I will discuss this matter in chapter 4.

will be sons of the Most High (καὶ ἔσεσθε υἱοὶ ὑψίστου)' (6:35).

On the basis of Matthew 5:43-48/Luke 6:27-36, Piper argues that to 'become a son of God' is equivalent to 'enter into the kingdom of God'.[124] The overall picture of Matthew 5:43-48/par. indicates that the fulfillment of Jesus' love command is a condition for entering into the kingdom of God. In particular, the reward spoken of in Jesus' rhetorical questions (Mt. 5:46f.) makes this clearer. Piper then concludes that sonship in this context can be understood as the reward in the eschatological kingdom: 'to love enemies is to receive the reward of sonship'.[125] While Piper rightly connects the concept of son with the kingdom and there are no specific reasons to disagree with his overall exposition, an important aspect, which Piper does not seem to develop, needs to be added to his argument. That is, if Piper understands the concept sonship as 'reward' (i.e., the eschatological goal) as a result of loving enemies, the idea of sonship should be understood only as a future reality in the eschatological kingdom of God. As a matter of fact, this is undoubtedly right in light of God's ultimate recognition or confirmation of sonship at the final judgment, but the present text surely implies the present aspect of sonship in addition to the promise of sonship in the future.

The section on 'love your enemy' in Matthew (and Luke) is related to two aspects: one is 'how to become a son of God at eschaton'; the other is 'how to act as a son in the present'.[126] As seen above, the reward of eschatological sonship is closely connected to loving enemies so that the notion, 'how to become a son of God' particularly in an *eschatological sense* clearly appears. However, the present aspect of sonship is also implicitly presented in the concept of love for enemies (or peacemaking in Mt. 5:9).[127] For love for enemies, as an expression of God's love, is conduct

---

[124] J. Piper, *Love your Enemies: Jesus' Love Command in the Synoptic Gospels and in the Early Christian Paranesis*, SNTSMS 38 (Cambridge: CUP, 1979), 76-77. Piper cites Bayer's comments 'Aus Teilhabern jener Welt, die als Bruderliebe durch Feindeshass besteht, sollen sie zu "Söhnen des himmlischen Vaters" werden, dh. zur nahen und Vertrauen schaffenden Herrschaft Gottes gehören'. For the whole argument of Bayer, see O. Bayer, 'Sprachbewegung und Weltveränderung, Ein systematischer Versuch als Auslegung von Mt 5:43-48', *EvTh* 35 (1975), 309-21 (above quotation is from p. 313).

[125] *Love your Enemies*, 76-77 (76).

[126] Cf. R.A. Guelich, *The Sermon on the Mount: A Foundation for Understanding* (Waco: Word, 1982), 230.

[127] It is generally admitted that the section on 'love your enemies' is identical with the beatitude of Mt. 5:9. The promise of sonship commonly appears in both texts: peacemakers are those who demonstrate love for their enemies so that peace-making and loving enemies express God's love and are identically represented as conditions to being sons of God in both texts. E.g., D. Lührmann, 'Liebet eure Feinde (Lk 6, 27-36/Mt 5, 39-48)', *ZTK* 69 (1972), 412-38 (414-15); Guelich, *Sermon*, 92.

typical of sonship and is 'indicative of sonship'.[128] So as sons of God, they represent the work of the Father. They must show mercy and love, which the Father demonstrated, to all including their enemies (cf. Mt. 5:48/Lk. 6:36) and in this way they reveal themselves to be the sons of God. At this point, the implication of the word, γένησθε (becoming) in Matthew 5:45a is not an alteration of the nature of sonship, but its complete realization in the future which is already realized.[129] Guelich concludes this matter clearly: 'The future promise pertains to the ultimate recognition of sonship at the final judgment, but sonship is already a present reality in view of God's redemptive activity (the kingdom of God) through Christ in the present'.[130]

This present aspect of sonship in relation to the kingdom becomes even clearer in the Lord's prayer (Mt. 6:9-10/Lk. 11:2). In his teaching on prayer, Jesus encourages the disciples to call God Father (Πάτερ) (Mt. 6:9-10/Lk. 11:2).[131] It has been frequently noted that the word 'Father' used by Jesus reflects an underlying Aramaic word 'abba', which exhibits an intimate relationship with God.[132] The use of the word 'Father' shows the key relationship between God as Father and the disciples as sons. It is surprising that Jesus encourages his disciples to use such an intimate expression when addressing God. Elsewhere in the Synoptics, notably in Matthew, Jesus frequently uses the personal pronoun 'your Father' to the disciples and this further confirms the disciples' status of sonship in a most intimate relationship with God (Mt. 5:16, 45, 48; 6:1, 4, 14, 15, 26, 32; 7:11; 10:20, 29; Mk. 11:25; Lk. 6:36; 12:30, 32).

However, in Matthew 6:9, the evangelist's Jesus speaks of 'Our Father in heaven' and this pronoun undoubtedly includes Jesus himself. Elsewhere in Matthew (and other Synoptics), Jesus frequently calls God 'my Father' which demonstrates his unique relationship with God (Mt. 7:21; 11:27; 15:13; 16:17; 18:10, 19; 19:35; 20:23; 25:34; 26:29, 53; Mk. 8:38; Lk. 2:49; 10:22; 22:29; 24:49). God is the Father who reveals Himself in the Son (Mt. 16:17, cf. 15:13; Lk. 10:22, particularly 11:27). The suffering death of Jesus as an obedient Son is the fulfillment of the will of Father (Mt. 26:42; Mk. 14:36, cf. 23:34, 46). On the basis of this unique relationship between Jesus and God, those who are in Jesus become the sons of God. So the foundation of the disciples' sonship in Jesus' saying 'your Father' is derived from his unique relationship with God as 'my Father'.[133] The nature of the disciples'

---

[128] Guelich, *Sermon*, 230-31.

[129] H.D. Betz, *The Sermon on the Mount*, Hermeneia (Minneapolis: Fortress Press, 1995), 315.

[130] Guelich, *Sermon*, 231.

[131] Matthew has 'Our Father in heaven', which reflects ordinary Jewish usage, while Luke has the unqualified form 'Father'. Schrenk argues that this is 'a deeper form of personal designation'. G. Schrenk, 'πατήρ', *TDNT*, V, 986.

[132] E.g., J. Jeremias, *The Prayers of Jesus* (Naperville: Allenson, 1967), 54-57, 89-98.

[133] Schrenk, 'πατήρ', 988-89. But cf. Schrenk's claim: 'In sayings which have "your

sonship is in this sense closely linked to the revelation of the Son by whom the kingdom is manifested.[134] Jesus is therefore able to encourage his disciples to call God 'our Father' in this relationship.

Furthermore, this sense of sonship in the phrase 'our Father' is also closely related to the kingdom. The second and third petitions, particularly in the Matthean form (Mt. 6:10) include 'Thy kingdom come', and 'Thy will be done'.[135] The coming of the kingdom is connected with accomplishing the will of God.[136] The establishment of God's reign over his people means to accomplish the will of God on earth.[137] When God's reign is recognized through Jesus, the blessing of sonship (cf. our 'Father') is also realized in the very reign of God (the kingdom of God). Therefore, the disciples, who are taught to pray for the kingdom, 'already participate in the reign of God brought by Jesus and are therefore representatives of that reign in the present'.[138]

However, once God's will has been established in the present, the petitioners (the disciples) should accept what God's will has declared and obey it.[139] At this point, God's will is also done *partly* through the disciples in the present.[140] So the sonship of the disciples connotes a strong sense of their task of manifesting the reality of the presence of the reign of God (God's will).[141] Elsewhere in Matthew, Jesus instructs his disciples that entering the kingdom is doing the 'will of my Father' (Mt. 7:21) as Jesus himself is fully obedient in accomplishing God's redemptive rule (Mt. 26:42; cf. Mk. 14:36). In this sense, as seen above, love for one's enemies is a present conduct which keeps the will of the Father as is the nature of sonship. Therefore, the accomplishment of the will of the Father (God's sovereign rule) is intrinsically related to the disciples' relationship with the Father and with conduct characteristic of their sonship, namely obedience

---

Father"' the thesis cannot be sustained that the content is the same as that in sayings with "my Father'". 987.

[134] Schrenk, 'πατήρ', 988-89. See also Guelich, *Sermon*, 288, 308-09.

[135] Luke does not have the phrase 'thy will be done' (Lk. 11:2).

[136] So most, e.g., D.A. Hagner, *Matthew 1-13*, WBC 33a (Dallas: Word, 1993), 148; Betz, *Sermon*, 392; Guelich, *Sermon*, 310-11; D.C. Allison and W.D. Davies, *The Gospel according to Saint Matthew*, 1, ICC (Edinburgh: T. & T. Clark, 1988), 603; Beasley-Murray, *Kingdom of God*, 151.

[137] For the kingdom here as the God's reign, see §3.3.5.2 below.

[138] Hagner, *Matthew 1-13*, 148.

[139] Betz, *Sermon*, 392.

[140] As Hagner points out, 'Although they (the disciples) cannot bring that kingdom into existence by their own efforts, yet they are to reflect the good news of its inauguration in and through Jesus'. *Matthew 1-13*, 148-49. The form of the third person imperatives ('let' ἐλθέτω, γενηθήτω) points to the involvement of those who pray. *Matthew 1-13*, 148.

[141] Hagner, *Matthew 1-13*, 148-49.

to the will of the Father.[142] Life in the kingdom as sons of the Father is none other than doing His will.

To sum up, the sonship of believers in the Synoptics is represented as an ultimate promise in the eschatological kingdom, but it is also characterized as a present reality in God's sovereign rule through Jesus Christ. In this way, sonship is integral to the kingdom and described as a kingdom blessing in the Synoptics.

3.3.3.2.3. Summary

The concept of sonship as a new status is certainly delineated as a blessing in this age and the age to come. Paul relates this blessing to the work of the Spirit while the Synoptic writers link it to the kingdom of God. Although the word "Father" seems to be commonly used in the early church, it is only Paul who attributes it to the work of the Spirit (Rom. 8:15; Gal. 4:6). By way of contrast, the word in the Synoptics is generally used in the context of the kingdom (Mt. 6:9-10; Lk. 11:2). This concept of a sense of sonship can illustrate the fact that Paul expresses his Spirit language in place of kingdom language. This also shows that the Spirit in Paul functions as the mediator of kingdom life.

3.3.3.3. RESURRECTION: THE BELIEVERS' HOPE IN THE SPIRIT IN PAUL AND IN THE KINGDOM OF GOD IN THE SYNOPTICS

Another similarity between life in the Spirit and life in the kingdom is found in the concept of the resurrection. The resurrection is central to the believers' hope and would appear to be pivotal to the life of the kingdom in the New Testament. However, while the Synoptic writers (and Johannine) attribute this to the kingdom, Paul specifically links it to the Spirit.

3.3.3.3.1. Hope of Resurrection in the Spirit (Rom. 8:11, 23; 1 Cor. 15:44-46; cf. 1 Cor. 6:14; Rom. 6:4)

The resurrection of Jesus is the main event in Paul's eschatological framework which guarantees that the new age has arrived (1 Cor. 15:20-28). Also, for him, the resurrection of Jesus is a sign of the resurrection of believers in the future.[143] Furthermore, Paul, more than any other New Testament writer, attributes the resurrection of both Jesus and believers (in future) to the work of the Spirit.[144]

---

[142] Guelich, *Sermon*, 290, 310-11.

[143] Cf. 1 Cor. 15:20, 23. Fee notes that the resurrection of Jesus makes the believer's resurrection both inevitable and necessary: 'inevitable, because his (Jesus') is the first-fruits which sets the whole process in motion; necessary, because death is God's enemy as well as ours, and our resurrection spells the end to the final enemy of the living God who gives life to all who live (1 Cor. 15:20-28)'. *Empowering*, 805.

[144] Indeed, the Spirit's association with resurrection is primarily restricted to Paul's letters. Horn argues that the idea of the resurrection of Jesus as the work of the Spirit

According to Paul, the resurrection in the future prompts believers to have a hope of a new world to be determined by God. The foundation of this hope is the Spirit who furnishes a provisional ground for it in the present so that the present incomplete status of believers in the midst of suffering is not in vain (Rom. 5:1-5; 8; 15:13). That is, the presence of the Spirit indicates the believers' hope for the complete manifestation of God's reign through resurrection. This hope, however, has already been anticipated in the present by the power of the Spirit: Paul says that in the Spirit believers are set free from the power of death in this age (Rom. 8:2, 6). At the same time, the future hope of resurrection still lies at the centre of the believer's life in the Spirit. Paul's various writings support this concept.

In contrast with the view of some of the Corinthians in 1 Corinthians 15:12, Paul's main argument in the chapter is the hope of the future resurrection from the dead on the basis of the certainty of the resurrection of the body. Paul draws on the Adam and Christ typology (cf. Rom. 5) and then brings out the first-fruits analogy to describe the hope of the future resurrection of believers. In the Adam and Christ typology in 1 Corinthians 15, Paul says

---

is derived from the claim of the early church. Horn supports his arguments with a number of Pauline texts (Rom. 1:3f.; 6:4; 8:11; 1 Cor. 6:14; 15:45; 2 Cor. 13:4 etc.) along with two particular texts outside the Pauline letters such as 1 Pet. 3:18-22 (18), and 1 Tim. 3:16 and argues that they 'zeigen, daß in der frühen Gemeindetheologie der Geist Gottes als Mittel verstanden wurde, durch dessen Kraft Jesus auferweckt wurde'. Horn, *Das Angeld des Geistes*, 90-115 (106); cf. 'Holy Spirit', 267. However, while Horn is undoubtedly right when he understands Jesus' resurrection as the work of the Spirit in these texts (contra Dunn and Fee, see below in this section), it is difficult to concur with his assertion that the connection originates in the early tradition. There are two primary reasons to disagree with him. First of all, the Spirit's relation to the resurrection is remarkably confined to the Pauline epistles as Horn himself shows. In particular, as will be seen, the fact that the Synoptics and Acts are entirely silent regarding Jesus' resurrection as the work of the Spirit prevents Horn from quickly concluding his case. Secondly, although similar statements are found outside the Pauline epistles, i.e., 1 Tim. 3:16 and 1 Pet. 3:18, they are virtually derived 'from a milieu influenced by Paul. This is undoubtedly the case for 1 Tim. 3:16 and, in view of the affinities between 1 Peter and Pauline theology, most likely the case for 1 Pet. 3:18 as well'. Menzies, *Development*, 294-95. Although Paul is not regarded as the author of 1 Peter and the pastoral epistles, it is generally accepted among the NT scholars that they are deeply influenced by Pauline theology. E.g., W.G. Kümmel, *Introduction to the New Testament* (Nashville: Abingdon, 1975), 384 (on the pastoral epistles), 423 (on 1 Peter). The validity of Horn's argument is alleviated by these two points. Furthermore, as already noted, we disagreed with Horn's allegation that it was the general idea to attribute resurrection to the work of the Spirit in intertestamental literature. But, we noted that although the idea of the eschatological resurrection is prevalent in the literature, texts which associate the resurrection with the activity of the Spirit are exceedingly rare before Paul. Cf. Müller's statement, 'der heilige Geist bei der Totenauferstehung vor Paulus keine quantitative bedeutende Rolle spielt'. 'Geisterfahrung', 131. See §2.5.

that in the former all die while in the latter all will be made alive (v. 22).[145] Paul then compares the relationship between the two by relating that the first man Adam became a living being while the last Adam became a life-giving spirit (v. 45). Paul's emphasis might be on the fact that although believers inherit life of a physical nature from the first Adam, they receive 'life in Spirit, and eventually resurrection of the body from the one who became a "life-giving Spirit" by means of the resurrection'.[146] So, Paul is able to say to his readers that their hope in a future resurrection is based on the resurrection of Christ Jesus who became a life-giving Spirit and the first-fruits of the resurrection (vv. 19, 20, 23). Here the life-giving Spirit, whose role is to make believers alive, is not to be understood as being different from the first-fruits.[147] The concept of the first-fruits of the resurrection is closely connected with the image of the first-fruits of the Spirit in Romans 8.[148]

There is a clear connection between the resurrection of Christ and that of believers related to the Spirit in Romans 8:11 and 23. On the basis of Romans 8:11, Dunn asserts that Paul seems to be reluctant to associate the resurrection of Jesus with the Spirit. He states that while Paul 'has no qualms in attributing the future resurrection of the body to the Spirit' (Rom. 8:11), he nonetheless 'almost seems to fall over backwards in the same text to avoid saying that God raised Jesus from the dead through the Spirit'.[149] However, Romans 8:11, which Dunn regards as a great cumbersome sentence, is a clear presupposition of Paul's association of the two.

Paul, in Romans 8:11b, says the indwelling Spirit is the mediator of resurrection-life: 'διὰ τοῦ ἐνοικοῦντος αὐτοῦ πνεύματος ἐν ὑμῖν'. Paul's primary argument in the passage is that God will make the mortal bodies of believers alive through His Spirit, who dwells in them. Indeed, as seen above, this indwelling Spirit in believers is implied in an earlier verse, 8:9a ('... you are in the Spirit, if in fact the Spirit of God dwells in you'). This assumption could be a foundation for the deduction in the following sentences. Paul depicts this indwelling Spirit as 'τὸ πνεῦμα τοῦ ἐγείραντος τὸν Ἰησοῦν ἐκ νεκρῶν οἰκεῖ ἐν ὑμῖν' (v. 11a). Paul subsequently indicates that God is the one who raised Christ from the dead and will give life to

---

[145] Cf. Rom. 6:8, '... we believe that we shall also live with him'.

[146] Witherington, *Jesus*, 192.

[147] Dunn, *Theology*, 261.

[148] Witherington aptly points out a twofold proleptic realization of the final consummation in Pauline theology as follows: 'Christ's resurrection and believers having the Spirit are both pledges and pointers that the resurrection of believers will yet happen. Thus Paul can speak not only of the first-fruits of the resurrection (1 Cor. 15:20, 22) but also of the first-fruits of the Spirit (Rom. 8:23). In both cases Paul uses the term ἀπαρχή'. *Jesus*, 194.

[149] Dunn, *Theology*, 262. Cf. J. Dunn, *Christology in the Making* (Philadelphia: Westminster Press, 1980), 144.

believers through (διά)¹⁵⁰ the indwelling Spirit. Furthermore, the references to the indwelling Spirit in verse 11 reinforce the fundamental line of deduction by analogy. This point continues to be made in verse 23 in which Paul says that the work of the Spirit in believers is the first-fruits of final redemption. The first-fruits of the Spirit function as the first harvest in the present as a basis of hope for the eventual harvest (the final redemption of the body). Since believers possess the first-fruits of the Spirit, they might eagerly expect the full benefits of adoption through resurrection. So Paul's emphasis is that the instrument through whom God operated in Christ's resurrection is already at work in believers. God's salvific work is accomplished by means of Christ's resurrection (cf. Rom. 1:3-4) and the future resurrection of believers will be given through the Spirit who indwells them.¹⁵¹ There is thus a certain link between the two. So, while there is little reason for Paul in Romans 8:11 to 'fall over backwards' to avoid referring to the Spirit's role in Jesus' resurrection, he rather emphasizes the instrumental role of the Spirit in resurrection using the analogy between the resurrection of Christ and that of the believer. As the agency of the future resurrection, the Spirit functions as the pledge of the

---

¹⁵⁰ A notable discussion in Rom. 8:11 affects the way of reading the word, διά. Some scholars read this as the accusative translating 'because' whereas others interpret it as the genitive, rendering 'through', or 'by means of'. Those who assert the former include Fee, *Empowering*, 543, n. 205; Schweizer, 'πνεῦμα', 422. Those who take the latter are Cranfield, *Romans*, 1, 391-92; G. Vos, *The Pauline Eschatology* (Grand Rapids: Baker, 1979), 163-64; Dunn, *Theology*, 262, n. 149; M.J. Harris, *Raised Immortal: The Relation between Resurrection and Immortality in New Testament Teaching* (London: Marshall, Morgan & Scott, 1983), 145. Some difficulties remain in making a conclusive reading because both readings have strong and early reliable attestation (For διὰ τοῦ: ℵ A C 81 104 256 263 436 1319 1506; for διὰ τὸ: B D F G ψ 6 33 424 459). Fee, who denies the Spirit as an agency in resurrection and takes God as a subject of resurrection, renders it as the accusative, 'because' and views the Spirit as a guarantor of resurrection. *Empowering*, 808-09. But, 'the logic of guarantee is much more transparent if it is assumed that it is precisely *through* the Spirit that God accomplishes the act of resurrection' (Emphasis is original). Turner, *Holy Spirit*, 125, n. 20. In addition, Paul indicates that the Spirit who dwells in believers gives life to them as the agency (Rom. 8:2, 6, 10, 13). The Spirit, who bears life in them at present, will function to the full in their life in the future. Paul also connects the resurrection references to concepts similar to the Spirit such as 'power' (1 Cor. 6:14) and 'glory' (Rom. 6:4). Nonetheless, whichever option is taken, the most important thing in this reading is that the vital activity of the Spirit is still implied as the resurrecting force. The thought of the activity of the Spirit is 'present entirely apart from the question of the textual variant'. R.B. Gaffin, Jr., *The Centrality of the Resurrection* (Grand Rapids: Baker, 1978), 67, n. 99. See also Harris, *Raised*, 145-46.

¹⁵¹ Vos, *Pauline Eschatology*, 163; Gaffin, *Centrality*, 67; Harris, *Raised*, 143-49.

future resurrection of believers in the present.[152] Only those who live in the Spirit have a guaranteed hope of the coming resurrection. Paul in Galatians says that in contrast to the way of life in the flesh, life in the Spirit will result in eternal life (resurrection life) in the future (Gal. 6:8).[153] The eschatological role of the Spirit in the present and the future is clear and his function is to bestow eternal life on those who live in him.

In short, for Paul, the event of Christ's resurrection has already signaled the process of God's final redemption which will guarantee the believer's ultimate resurrection in the future. The certainty of this ultimate resurrection is on the basis of the believer's experience of the Spirit in the present life. In this way, the believer's life is a life of hope in the resurrection in the ultimate consummation of the new age. This hope of resurrection is deeply rooted in the life in the Spirit according to Paul.

3.3.3.3.2. Hope of Resurrection in the Kingdom (Lk. 18:18-30, pars.; Lk. 20:27-40, pars.; cf. Lk. 14:14; Lk. 16:17-31)

Although resurrection references are mentioned with less frequency in the Synoptics than in Paul's writings, the idea of resurrection is widespread in each of the gospel writers in the words of Jesus: Jesus not only believes in resurrection (Lk. 20:27-40; Mk. 12:18-27; Mt. 22:23-33), but also performs miracles of resuscitation (Lk. 7:11-17; 8:40-42, 49-56 and pars.; cf. Jn. 11:1-46).[154] Furthermore, Jesus teaches that believers are heirs of eternal life in the kingdom of God and in this belief he exhorts his audience to have a resurrection hope.[155] In particular, Jesus teaches that the believer's hope of resurrection is grounded on the condition of present life in the kingdom of God.

This notion is well depicted in the story of the rich ruler in Luke 18:18-30 (cf. Mt. 19:16-30; Mk. 10:7-31). The passage contains Jesus' conversation with the rich ruler in verses 18-23 and the statement about him in verses 24-27, and then the encouragement to his disciples in verses 28-30.

---

[152] Note Paul's argument in the expression of the protasis and apodosis in Rom. 8:11, 'And if the Spirit of him who raised Jesus from the dead is living in you, he who raised Christ from the dead will also give life to your mortal bodies through his Spirit, who lives in you'.

[153] D.J. Lull, *The Spirit in Galatia: Paul's Interpretation of Pneuma as Divine Power*, SBL 49 (Chico: Scholars Press, 1980), 175. Note Perkins's statement: 'The language of eternal life occurs as frequently as that about resurrection in the Jewish writings of this period (first century)'. P. Perkins, *Resurrection: New Testament Witness and Contemporary Reflection* (London: Geoffrey Chapman, 1985), 309.

[154] Perkins, *Resurrection*, 75-78. It is not difficult to assume that Jesus' performance in resuscitating Jairus's daughter and a widow's son in Nain was a forerunner of the resurrection of Jesus himself. This shows Jesus' (and God's) control over the power of death.

[155] Perkins, *Resurrection*, 309. Cf. Harris, *Raised*, 173.

The question of the rich ruler appears in verse 18: 'what shall I do to inherit eternal life?' Jesus answers him by giving him conditions that include not only selling his possessions to distribute to the poor, but also involve a total commitment to discipleship (v. 22). After the rich ruler refuses the conditions, Jesus pityingly says, 'How hard it is for the rich to enter the kingdom of God' (v. 24). In the following context, responding to Peter's saying, Jesus then turns the issue to his disciples by laying out the promise about a far greater recompense in this life and 'eternal life' in the age to come (v. 30).

Whereas it seems certain that Luke's (and the other Synoptic writers') concern here is to warn of the dangers of riches, the theme of the future hope of eternal life in the kingdom of God should also be remembered.[156] The first question given by the rich ruler is closely related to the topic of eternal life and the final saying of Jesus in verse 30, which functions as an inclusio with the ruler's prior question, is certainly connected to the afterlife.[157] Here the phrase 'inherit eternal life' reflects 'the new life through resurrection' in the eternal new age[158] and it possibly alludes to the image of resurrection indicated in Daniel 12:2.[159] However, this eternal life at the future resurrection is promised by present conduct in the sovereignty of God.[160] Jesus says to his disciples that everyone who leaves their earthly possessions and family behind will receive eternal life in the age to come. This concluding saying of Jesus derives from the failure of the rich ruler to accede to Jesus' demand, i.e., giving up his earthly treasures and following Jesus.[161] One thing that he lacks is living according to the standards of the kingdom of God so that he is disqualified as a candidate for the resurrection that brings eternal life in the coming age. So it can be said that the hope of

---

[156] Beasley-Murray points out that '. . . the subject of the narrative is the attainment of *eternal life* in *the kingdom of God*, which is final salvation in *the age to come*'. *Kingdom of God*, 177. Emphasis is original.

[157] Jesus' prior preaching of the kingdom of God in Lk. 18:15-17 evokes the ruler's question (v. 18) about his desire to enter the kingdom, which implies its realized presence. At the same time, as indicated in verse 30, the eternal life, which is already inaugurated in the present age through Christ Jesus, is fully realized only in the future. There is thus both a present and future implication in eternal life in Lk. 18:18, 30. Cf. Nolland, *Luke 9:21-18:34*, 887; Beasley-Murray, *Kingdom of God*, 177.

[158] Beasley-Murray, *Kingdom of God*, 176.

[159] Bock, *Luke 9:51-24:53*, 1476. Bock links the rich ruler's question in Lk. 18:18 ('what shall I do to inherit eternal life?') to the lawyer's question in Lk. 10:25 ('what shall I do to inherit eternal life?') and identifies the concept 'eternal life' with the future 'resurrection' by rewording the questions as follows, 'How can I be sure I'll be saved in the final resurrection?' 1023. See also Perkins' claim in n. 153 above.

[160] R. Bultmann, 'ζάω', *TDNT*, II, 864.

[161] So, as Bock points out, 'In a crucial contrast to the rich ruler, the disciples are used as a counterexample to show that Jesus' request is possible'. Bock, *Luke 9:51-24:53*, 1473.

resurrection to eternal life is rooted in the condition of life in the kingdom at the present in this story.[162]

Elsewhere in Luke, resurrection to eternal life is described as the reward of the righteous. Those who faithfully practise the life of servanthood in the present life in the kingdom of God 'will be repaid at the resurrection of the just' (Lk. 14:14).[163] The reversal of the roles of the two men at the future resurrection in the parable of the rich man shows the significance of present life in the kingdom (Lk. 16:17-31). The life-style of the rich man is counter to the model of the present kingdom life and does not carry the promise of future resurrection.

In Luke 20:27-40 (cf. Mt. 22:23-33; Mk. 12:18-27), there is a dispute over resurrection between Jesus and the Sadducces. The Sadducees ask whose wife the woman will be in the afterlife since seven husbands on earth had her as wife (v. 33). There is an implication of the futility of 'a resurrection hope' behind this question because of the absurdity of the woman's dilemma. Jesus, while avoiding direct mention of the reality of resurrection, makes the point that the future resurrection will be experienced only by those who are accounted worthy (v. 35). He then explains that the resurrection of the righteous brings immortality through divine sonship (v. 36). Jesus' final response is that the foundation of all life, whether the present life or the life to come, is the sovereign living God (v. 38). The point that Jesus makes from these answers is that he endorses the reality of resurrection which sets up the hope that is central to faith in the living God. Further, its presence will be affected by present life in the reign of God.[164] In short, Luke's (and the Synoptics') description of resurrection is that it is the believer's central hope and it would appear to be integral to life in the kingdom of God.

3.3.3.3.3. Summary

Both the Synoptic writers and Paul regard an eschatological resurrection as the believer's central hope. While the former attribute it to life based on the kingdom, the latter ascribes it to life in the Spirit. So there is a similarity between the two concepts in light of the believer's hope in the future resurrection. This reflects Paul's shift in terminology from kingdom to the Spirit.

---

[162] Cf. Harris, *Raised*, 172-73.

[163] Here, resurrection in the story belongs to the context of reward for the just at the time of final divine judgement. Perkins, *Resurrection*, 73.

[164] Bock, *Luke 9:51-24:53*, 1627.

3.3.4. Righteousness in Paul and the Synoptics

3.3.4.1. THE SPIRIT AND RIGHTEOUSNESS/JUSTIFICATION (1 Cor. 6:11; Rom. 8:10; 14:17; Gal. 3:14; Gal. 5:5; cf. 2 Cor. 3:8-9)

For Paul, δικαιοσύνη is understood as God's fundamental salvific act of eschatological blessing since it has already been realized in Christ (Rom. 1:17; 3:21-26; 5:1; 8:10; 1 Cor. 6:11 etc.) and will be consummated in the future (Gal. 2:13; 5:5).[165] For him, δικαιοσύνη is thus the blessing of the new age to those who believe, who are justified by initiating the life of faith.[166] For Paul, this faith, upon which δικαιοσύνη is made dependent, is also produced by the function of the Spirit as a subjective essential of God's justifying performance. Of more significance for our present concern, the soteriological dimension of justification in connection with the Spirit will be discussed.[167]

The relationship between the Spirit and justification/righteousness is evident in Paul's various writings, notably in 1 Corinthians 6:11, Romans 8:10, Galatians 3:1-14, and Galatians 5:5.

According to the context of 1 Corinthians 6:11, Paul reproached the Corinthian believers who were involved in serious immorality (1 Cor. 5:1-8; 6:1-6). Although the Corinthian believers had been converted, some of them were still involved in practices which were incompatible with inheritance of the kingdom of God. Thus, after Paul describes the kinds of wrong-doings (1 Cor. 6:9-10), he reassures them that they are redeemed, saying that, '. . . But you were washed, you were sanctified, you were justified in the name of the Lord Jesus Christ and in the Spirit of our God' (1 Cor. 6:11). Certainly, Paul has the Corinthians' past sinful life in mind when he reminds them that they have been redeemed through the salvific work of God, being washed, being sanctified, and being justified.[168] The

---

[165] Paul uses the verb 'justify' twenty-nine times in his corpus out of the thirty-nine times in the NT and uses two cases of the cognate noun (Rom. 4:25, 18).

[166] Rom. 5:1; cf. Rom. 4:2; 5:9.

[167] Unfortunately, this concept has not been emphasized among commentators, although some (e.g., Fee, Dunn, Turner, Hamilton in the discussion of their Pauline pneumatology) have briefly treated the relationship. However, note S.K. Williams, 'Justification and the Spirit in Galatians', *JSNT* 29 (1987), 91-100, though he only deals with the relationship in the letter of Galatians.

[168] Elsewhere in the letter, Paul often uses a similar pattern of argument, concluding with a positive note after a warning: e.g., 1 Cor. 3:22-23; 4:14-17 (as a conclusion to all of 1:18-4:21); 5:7; 6:20; 10:13; 11:32. Fee, *1 Corinthians*, 245, n. 29. On the other hand, Bultmann (*Theology*, vol. 1, 136) argued that the theme of righteousness in this passage is not meant in the specific sense of Paul's doctrine of justification. However, this view is widely rejected by others. See Conzelmann, *1 Corinthians*, 107; Fee, *Empowering*, 127-32 (131); esp. R.Y. Fung, 'Justification by Faith in 1&2 Corinthians', in D.A. Hagner & M.J. Harris (eds.), *Pauline Studies: Essays Presented*

intention is that this threefold assurance should also function as a reminder that from this transforming experience the community should retain a transformed moral life.[169]

The sentence consists of three verbs, ἀπελούσασθε,[170] ἡγιάσθητε, ἐδικαιώθητε, the adversative ἀλλά, which is posed before each of the three verbs, and two prepositional phrases, ἐν τῷ ὀνόματι τοῦ κυρίου Ἰησοῦ Χριστοῦ καὶ ἐν τῷ πνεύματι τοῦ θεοῦ ἡμῶν. With this text, Vos favours distributing the two prepositional phrases chiastically and thus construes the former phrase (ἐν τῷ ὀνόματι τοῦ κυρίου Ἰησοῦ Χριστοῦ) with the last verb (ἐδικαιώθητε), the latter phrase (ἐν τῷ πνεύματι τοῦ θεοῦ ἡμῶν) with the prior two verbs (ἀπελούσασθε, ἡγιάσθητε).[171]

However, the soteriological locus of the text does not necessarily seem to connect the phrases to the specific verbs. Rather, the three verbs, in which there is a conceptual overlap, are placed in juxtaposition in order to signify being made clean: 1) ἀπελούσασθε, the Corinthians had washed away their old lifestyles; 2) ἡγιάσθητε, they had been sanctified; and 3) ἐδικαιώθητε, they had been justified to have a right relationship with God.[172] This form of the three verbs, which are all aorist passive, is not used in any sense of chronological order, rather it gives the same instantaneous experience.[173]

---

to Professor F.F. Bruce on His 70*th* Birthday (Exeter: Paternoster, 1980), 250-51.

[169] N. Watson, *The First Epistle to the Corinthians* (London: Epworth, 1992), 57; C.K. Barrett, *The First Epistle to the Corinthians*, BNTC (London: A. & C. Black, 1991), 142.

[170] Some suggest that the word, ἀπελούσασθε infers the baptismal rite (e.g., H. Ridderbos, *Paul: An Outline of His Theology* [Grand Rapids: Eerdmans, 1975], 397; G.R. Beasley-Murray, *Baptism in the New Testament* [Grand Rapids: Eerdmans, 1962, 162-67]). However, in several points, the view of baptism is not meant in the present text: 1) Elsewhere in the Pauline letters, Paul employs the preposition εἰς instead of ἐν in the reference of baptism (cf. 1 Cor. 1:13-15; 12:13; Gal. 3:27); 2) The use of the non-technical word ἀπελούσασθε rather than the more technical word ἐβαπτίσθητε suggests that Paul gives more inward meaning rather than the outward circumstances of the rite; 3) In the light of the overall previous context of the Corinthians' sinful acts, the word ἀπελούσασθε would possibly mean heart and conscience, and spiritual cleansing of their sins. Cf. Menzies, *Development*, 299-300; Barrett, *1 Corinthians*, 141; Fee, *Empowering*, 130-31; Dunn, *Theology*, 454.

[171] Vos, 'Spirit', 110, n. 34.

[172] Turner argues that 1 Cor. 6:11 refers to a pre-Pauline tradition based on Ezek. 36:25-27. *Holy Spirit*, 110-11. However, it does not seem to be the case because the overall context is much more decisive in determining the three verbs than the quotation of a tradition. Paul certainly points out the former life styles (see the list prior to v. 11 concerning the sinful life) of the Corinthians and then their present status as being washed, sanctified, and justified. See Fee, *Empowering*, 129. For a more detailed defence on the Pauline nature of the passage, see Menzies, *Development*, 269-300 (298).

[173] Fung, 'Justification', 250.

Furthermore, they imply a great turning point in the Corinthians' former lives and this fact is hinted at as well by the word ἀλλά: 'once you were, but now you are not'.[174] Thus, there is little question that Paul attributes the two prepositional phrases to all three verbs.

If this is right, the operational role of the Spirit is naturally connected to justification/righteousness[175] along with 'cleansing and sanctification': ἐδικαιώθητε ἐν τῷ πνεύματι τοῦ θεοῦ ἡμῶν. Here the prepositional phrase is best understood in an instrumental sense meaning that the Spirit exists as the 'means' in the believer's present life.[176] God has accomplished the work of δικαιοσύνη through Christ and he has at the same time effected and actualized it through the Spirit. The Corinthian community had experienced salvation by the presence of the Spirit. So Paul elsewhere indicates that the Spirit initiates the salvation process, bringing individuals into the Corinthian community (1 Cor. 12:13). The ministry of the Spirit in the Corinthian community is characterized by his life-giving function (2 Cor. 3:6, '... the Spirit gives life'). In this sense, God's justifying act in the lives of the Corinthians has been effected through the ministry of the life-giving Spirit. In other words, their experience of justification is actualized through the life-giving Spirit (2 Cor. 3:8-9).[177]

The close connection between the Spirit and righteousness also appears in the letter to the Galatians, particularly 3:1-14. Paul here associates God's sending the Spirit with the blessing of Abraham, which refers to the status of being justified by God (cf. Gal. 3:8). This can be seen from a close link between Galatians 3:5 and 3:6, where Abraham's experience of being reckoned righteous by faith is linked to the Galatians' experience of having the Spirit on the basis of faith.[178] The concluding verse (Gal. 3:14) of the whole discussion starting in Galatians 3:1 makes this fact clearer: 'that in Christ Jesus the blessings of Abraham might come upon the Gentiles, that we might receive the promise of the Spirit through faith'. Here, the Galatians' reception of the Spirit is paralleled with God's transaction with Abraham, whom God justified by faith: a correlation is drawn between what God did for Abraham and what the Galatians community has received: faith and its essential subject, the promised Spirit.[179] Thus, the Galatians' new relationship with God, their status of being righteous, is actualized by the work of the Spirit. In this sense, Paul inevitably links justification to the

---

[174] Fee, *Empowering*, 129.

[175] Of course, this does not deny the relationship between the prepositional phrase ἐν τῷ ὀνόματι τοῦ κυρίου Ἰησοῦ Χριστοῦ and justification as seen above.

[176] Fee, *1 Corinthians*, 247; *Empowering*, 129.

[177] Fee, *Empowering*, 308; Bultmann, *Theology*, 1, 271.

[178] Williams, 'Justification', 92-95.

[179] Williams, 'Justification', 91-92; R.Y. Fung, *The Epistle to the Galatians*, NICNT (Grand Rapids: Eerdmans, 1988), 132. Paul, in Gal. 3:1-2, says that the Spirit is granted as a result of faith in Christ. See n. 190 below in detail.

Spirit.[180]

Paul further discusses the correlation between the two in the letter to the Romans. In Romans 8:9, Paul says that if anyone does not possess the Spirit, he/she does not belong to Christ. So, for him, the meaning of the phrases 'in the Spirit' and 'in Christ' is identical. In the subsequent verse (v. 10), Paul says that if Christ is in believers, although human bodies are dead because of sin, the Spirit is alive in them and able to give life διὰ δικαιοσύνην. So the indwelling and life-giving Spirit makes it possible for believers to have a right relationship with God. In Romans 14:17, Paul states the nature of the kingdom: 'the kingdom of God is. . . righteousness, peace, and joy in the Holy Spirit'.[181] Paul connects the presence of the divine rule to the blessings of the kingdom attributed to the Spirit. A life joined to the Spirit produces the blessings so that the kingdom is to be seen as a present reality available in the community.[182] For Paul, the possession of the Spirit guarantees the realization of justification so that he is able to associate righteousness with the Spirit.[183] Thus, for him, life in the Spirit is the presentness of the kingdom of God. On the other hand, with this present aspect of the justification/righteousness attributed to the Spirit, Paul also refers to its eschatological sense in the activity of the Spirit. The most instructive example is Galatians 5:5: 'ἡμεῖς γὰρ πνεύματι ἐκ πίστεως ἐλπίδα δικαιοσύνης ἀπεκδεχόμεθα'. Although some seem to hesitate to think of the future sense of righteousness in Pauline texts (e.g., Rom. 2:13; 3:20, 30; 5:19; 8:33f.; 1 Cor. 4:4),[184] Paul in Galatians 5:5 clearly denotes that there is the final righteousness which is not different from what has already been disclosed. The word, ἀπεκδεχόμεθα is distinctively used by Paul to signify eschatological expectation.[185] The reference δικαιοσύνης, a genitive

---

[180] Note Williams's claim that 'the experience of the Spirit and the status of justification are, for the apostle, inconceivable apart from each other. Each implies the other. Those persons upon whom God bestows the Spirit are justified; the persons whom God reckons righteous have the Spirit poured out upon them'. 'Justification', 97.

[181] Cranfield connects the prepositional phrase 'in the Holy Spirit' only to 'joy'. *Romans*, vol. 2, 718. However, most scholars agree that all three nouns, 'righteousness and peace and joy', belong together and are modified by the prepositional phrase. Fee, *Empowering*, 620, n. 448. Käsemann notes that 'The prepositional phrase relates to all three members, so that Gal. 5:22 is the closest parallel'. Käsemann, *Romans*, 377.

[182] See §3.2.2 above.

[183] Vos, 'Spirit', 110.

[184] E.g., Fung, *Galatians*, 232-35.

[185] W. Grundmann, 'ἀπεκδέχομαι', *TDNT*, II, 56; H.D. Betz, *Galatians*, Hermeneia (Philadelphia: Fortress Press, 1979), 262, n. 82; Lull, *Spirit*, 171; C.H. Cosgrove, *The Cross and the Spirit: A Study in the Argument and Theology of Galatians* (Macon: Mercer University, 1988), 153; J. Dunn, *The Epistle to the Galatians*, BNTC (London: A. & C. Black, 1993), 269. It is not surprising to learn that Paul frequently uses the word in his most eschatological text. E.g., Rom. 8:19, 23, 25; Phil. 3:20; 1

of apposition or objective, is used as an object of ἐλπίδα meaning the 'hope of righteousness'.[186] Hence, the δικαιοσύνης is pointed to as the matter or the content of the ἐλπίδα. The phrase ἡμεῖς πνεύματι ἐκ πίστεως is fairly understood that 'we, who have experienced the Spirit solely by faith' eagerly ἀπεκδεχόμεθα ἐλπίδα δικαιοσύνης.[187] Paul's argument is thus clear that the future righteousness, which is a present reality in the believer,[188] is also characterized as a reality for which the believer has to wait. Furthermore, Paul attributes this eschatological hope for future righteousness to πνεύματι and ἐκ πίστεως.[189] Here, πνεύματι is combined with the instrumental dative, ἐκ πίστεως giving the predicate sense of the Spirit who comes through faith or is obtained by faith.[190] Thus, over against the nomists in Galatia, who observe justification on the basis of the works of the Torah (here circumcision) in Galaltians 5:4, Paul argues in verses 5 and 6 that life in the Spirit comes from faith and stresses that the basis of confident hope for justification depends upon, not circumcision as one of the works of the Torah, but 'faith working through love' which is directed by the Spirit.[191] In this context, Paul sees the Spirit received by faith as a crucial factor in guaranteeing the future righteousness/justification, not the works of the Torah. As Fee asserts, the Spirit effects and fulfills the righteousness found in the Torah. By the Spirit, the Galatians are

---

Cor. 1:7.

[186] Betz, *Galatians*, 262; Hamilton, *Holy Spirit*, 34, n. 2; G. Schrenk, 'δικαιοσύνη', *TDNT*, II, 207; Lull, *Spirit*, 180, n. 23; Ridderbos, *Paul*, 166; Fung, in his *Galatia*, 224-27, instructively explains a variety of possible interpretations based on the appositional or objective genitive and the alternative subjective genitive. In any case, the fundamental meaning of the genitive depends on the interpretation of the 'hope of righteousness'.

[187] Dunn, *Galatians*, 269.

[188] E.g., Gal. 2:16; 3:8, 11.

[189] Fung, dealing with the text, seems to neglect the association between the Spirit and justification in his statement: '. . . no clear inference can be drawn from this verse regarding the place of the Spirit in Justification'. However, just as the eschatological activity of the Spirit is well characterized elsewhere in Pauline concepts such as resurrection (Rom. 8:11, 23), sonship (Rom. 8:14-15) etc., the same eschatological character of the Spirit is also attributed to justification.

[190] Ridderbos, *Paul*, 166. As observed above, for Paul, faith is regarded as the necessary prerequisite for the experience of the Spirit. Paul asks a question of the Galatians in Gal. 3:2, 'Did you receive the Spirit by observing the law, or by believing what you heard?' and continues to ask in a slightly different manner in Gal. 3:5: 'Does God give you his Spirit and work miracles among you because you observe the law, or because you believe what you heard? In these sayings, Paul wants to remind the readers that the Spirit comes as a result of their belief. Cf. Gal. 3:13-14; 5:22, where πίστις is part of the fruit of the Spirit; 1 Cor. 12:3, 9.

[191] Fee, *Empowering*, 418; Cosgrove, *Spirit*, 152.

guaranteed their hope of the final realization of justification.[192]

Accordingly, believers are able to wait in the Spirit in faith for the future righteousness since they have confidence in the presence of the Spirit.

So, Paul closely links δικαιοσύνη to the work of the Spirit. The Spirit not only actualizes δικαιοσύνη in those who believe (1 Cor. 6:11; Rom. 8:10; 14:17; Gal. 3:5-6, 14), but also attests its complete realization as a seal (Gal. 5:5). Thus, for Paul, righteousness/justification and the Spirit cannot be separated from one another.

3.3.4.2. THE KINGDOM AND RIGHTEOUSNESS (Mt. 5:10, cf. Lk. 6:21; Mt. 5:20; Mt. 6:33, cf. Lk. 12:31)

In the Synoptics, the concept of righteousness is relatively rare and is not as broadly used as by Paul.[193] Nonetheless, it still appears in Jesus' teaching basically meaning, conforming to the will of God or the law of God (Mt. 3:15; Mt. 5:6, 10, 20; 6:1, 33; 21:32; Mt. 27:19; Lk. 1:6; 2:25; 23:47, 50; cf. Acts 10:22 etc.). While the study of the concept of righteousness in the Synoptics lies outside the scope of this study,[194] our present concern lies with how the concept is closely connected to the kingdom.

The relationship between the kingdom and righteousness is frequently found in the Sermon on the Mount, notably, in Matthew 5:10 (cf. Lk. 6:21), 5:20, and Matthew 6:33 (cf. Lk. 12:31). In both Matthew 5:10 and 5:20, righteousness is depicted as the entrance requirement to the kingdom of God.[195] Matthew 5:10 reads 'Blessed are those who are persecuted because of righteousness (ἕνεκεν δικαιοσύνης), for theirs is the kingdom of heaven'. Scholarly consensus is that righteousness (with that in Mt. 5:6) here primarily means an ethical indication rather than an eschatological vindication of God.[196] Those who suffer for the sake of righteousness are identical with those who obey the will of God. The promise is that the possession of the kingdom is theirs.

In a similar manner, in Matthew 5:20, the righteousness which is to be expected of Jesus' followers is described as 'a greater righteousness' than

---

[192] *Empowering*, 418-19.

[193] The word 'righteousness' occurs 8 times in the Synoptics: 7 times in Matthew (3:15; 5:6, 10, 20; 6:1, 33; 21:32) and once in Luke (1:75). Mark does not have the noun form of the word, but uses the adjective form only twice (Mk. 2:17; 6:20).

[194] E.g., B. Przybylski, *Righteousness in Matthew and His World of Thought*, SNTSMS 41 (Cambridge: CUP, 1980); J. Reumann, *Righteousness in the New Testament* (Philadelphia: Fortress Press, 1982).

[195] However, as will be noted below, the concept of righteousness in Matthew should not be taken exclusively as conduct, as an entrance requirement of the kingdom. There is also a sense of gift in the term in relation to the kingdom, particularly in Mt. 5:20 and 6:33. See below in this section.

[196] G. Schrenk, 'δικαιοσύνη', 198-200; Hill, *Greek Words*, 128; Przybylski, *Righteousness*, 98; Allison and Davies, *Matthew*, 1, 460; Hagner, *Matthew 1-13*, 94.

the righteousness of the scribes and Pharisees: 'Unless your righteousness surpasses that of the Pharisees and the teachers of the law, you will certainly not enter the kingdom of heaven'. Here again, as in verses 6 and 10, the meaning of righteousness basically indicates a moral standard which conforms to the teachings of Jesus. So those who live in a way qualified by righteousness in Jesus will enter the kingdom of God. However, in addition to the idea of conduct in the meaning of righteousness, the larger context of Matthew 5:20 gives a further meaning in relation to the kingdom.

The central message of Matthew 5:20 lies in the term righteousness which has been argued from Matthew 5:17. In Matthew 5:17-18, the coming of Jesus upholds the law rather than abolishes it. Then, Matthew compares the righteousness of the scribes and Pharisees with some greater righteousness in Matthew 5:20. The whole context in Matthew 5:17-20 clearly relates this greater righteousness to the coming of Jesus. So Jesus' demand for a greater and new righteousness (Mt. 5:20) can be regarded as christological and messianic in nature (Mt. 5:17) which closely links it to the presence of the kingdom.[197] Thus, the presence of Jesus the Messiah, whose person and ministry convey the presence of the kingdom, signals a new stage in God's purpose, bringing a new and greater way of righteousness. This greater righteousness, which is realized in the presence of the kingdom, connotes a new relationship with God (the gift of God) in Jesus' coming and ministry and keeping the will of God (conduct in the concept righteousness) is understood on the basis of this new relationship.[198] So, based on this recognition, Jesus requires of his disciples that their righteousness should surpass what the scribes and Pharisees have required.[199] The following paragraphs in Matthew 5:21-48 show how Jesus interprets righteousness as the real meaning of the law and how this new understanding of righteousness in him is greater than the demand of the law.[200] So, righteousness in Matthew 5:20 is integral to the realization of the kingdom in the coming of Jesus so that both righteousness and the kingdom are inextricably related. Moreover, righteousness here contains the meaning of relationship in addition to the element of conduct.[201] This notion is further confirmed in Matthew 6:33.

The text reads, 'But seek (ζητεῖτε) first his kingdom and his

---

[197] Guelich, *Sermon*, 171. 'This righteousness integral to the coming of the Kingdom in Jesus' ministry stands in stark contrast to the righteousness of the scribes and Pharisees'.

[198] Guelich, *Sermon*, 171.

[199] Hagner, *Matthew 1-13*, 104-10; Guelich, *Sermon*, 171f. Hagner further notes that 'it (a way of righteousness) is a new way that rests upon the true meaning of the Torah now delivered by the Messiah' (109).

[200] It is generally suggested that Mt. 5:20 is an introductory statement to 5:21-48. See Davies and Allison, *Matthew*, 1, 498; Przybylski, *Righteousness*, 80.

[201] Guelich, *Sermon*, 172; Hagner, *Matthew 1-13*, 109.

righteousness (τὴν βασιλείαν καὶ τὴν δικαιοσύνην αὐτοῦ), and all these things will be given to you as well'.[202] Although some regard the reference to the kingdom as in the future,[203] several observations support it rather as a present reality.[204] It has been noticed above that the kingdom is both present and future in the Synoptics and so in Matthew as well (cf. Mt. 12:28). The overall context fits with this view in Matthew 6:25-33: living in response to Jesus' teaching and ministry rather than anxiously pursuing food and clothing is a life under the sovereign rule of God.[205] The present tense, ζητεῖτε (keep seeking) also verifies this.[206]

Of particular importance is the question, what is the meaning of righteousness here and how does the term relate to the kingdom? Gundry argues that God's righteousness in Matthew 6:33 refers to his eschatological vindication or salvation for believers.[207] However, if this interpretation is right, the kingdom in Matthew 6:33 should be viewed in an eschatological sense.[208] But it has been noted that the kingdom here refers to the present reality. Furthermore, Jesus here exhorts his disciples to seek God's righteousness. The idea of human conduct in the concept of righteousness is clearly implied in the text. However, a question remains: does the idea of the righteousness of God here only mean human conduct? Is there any further meaning in the term, namely God's gift? Davies and Allison claim that it is the norm for human righteousness so that it should be understood as 'only God's demand' without the notion of God's gift.[209] However, this claim should be questioned in the following views.

At first glance, if the idea of demand only is implied here, the main discourse of the text emphasizes the human responsibility to be righteous. So, personal righteousness should be understood as a pre-requisite for entrance into the kingdom as in Matthew 5:20. However, as Guelich correctly claims, this interpretation is 'only half correct' since it is not Matthew's intention that 'the former (kingdom) opens the door for the latter

---

[202] There can be no doubt that the addition of righteousness is Matthew's redaction. Luke does not have the term in his gospel (12:31).

[203] E.g., Kümmel, *Promise*, 125-26.

[204] So most, Hagner, *Matthew 1-13*, 165-66; Davies and Allison, *Matthew*, 1, 661; Hill, *Greek Words*, 129; Guelich, *Sermon*, 345.

[205] Guelich, *Sermon*, 345.

[206] Hagner, *Matthew 1-13*, 166.

[207] R.H. Gundry, *Matthew: A Commentary on his Literary and Theological Art* (Grand Rapids: Eerdmans, 1982), 118.

[208] Davies and Allison, *Matthew*, 1, 661.

[209] Davies and Allison, *Matthew*, 1, 661. See also Przybylski, *Righteousness*, 89-91. By way of contrast, Schrenk argues the righteousness of God is to be taken primarily as the pure gift from God. 'δικαιοσύνη', 199. However, as seen above, the idea of human conduct governed by the norm of God's righteousness is obvious in the text.

(righteousness)'.²¹⁰ As noted above, the presence of the kingdom through Jesus, whose ministry reveals God's sovereign rule, is God's gift. In addition, as is the case in Matthew 5:20, righteous conduct is possible from a transformed relationship with God in the new age. So, it is not simply the entrance requirement for the kingdom, but connotes a gift which results in a person's right conduct (righteousness) in a new relationship between God and his people. Thus, 'Both *righteousness* as conduct in keeping God's will and the *Kingdom* as God's sovereign, redemptive rule come as God's offer - his gift - to his own as promised for the age of salvation through Jesus Messiah'.²¹¹ Furthermore, in light of the fact that the audience of Jesus are the recipients of the kingdom, this interpretation (righteousness as a gift of God, i.e., not entirely as the entrance requirement of the kingdom) weighs more. Therefore, it is a mistake to interpret 'to seek righteousness' as one's efforts to make the kingdom available in the present. Rather, the gift of the kingdom makes it possible for its recipients to keep the will of God.²¹² Seeking the kingdom and the righteousness of God cannot be separated and living in the former and living according to the latter go together.

In short, inaugurating the kingdom of God, Jesus encourages his followers to be characterized by the pursuit of righteousness. So remaining in the kingdom means to live in a way of righteousness in character and action.

3.3.4.3. SUMMARY

Paul's understanding of the concept δικαιοσύνη is closely linked to the work of the Spirit. For him, δικαιοσύνη and the Spirit cannot be separated. In a very similar manner, the concept δικαιοσύνη in the Synoptics is intimately linked to the kingdom. For the Synoptics, life in the kingdom and the way of righteousness cannot be separated. If for Paul the Spirit actualizes righteousness in those who believe, the realization of the kingdom results in righteousness in the Synoptics.²¹³ This similarity

---

[210] Guelich, *Sermon*, 347.

[211] Guelich, *Sermon*, 347. Emphasis is original. See also Hagner, *Matthew 1-13*, 166.

[212] Guelich claims that 'Apart from the enabling gift of God's redemptive reign (the presence of the Kingdom), one could not carry out the demand (the right conduct or *righteousness*)'. *Sermon*, 347.

[213] It must be remembered that the concept of righteousness in the Synoptics is not directly associated with the work of the Spirit as in Paul. Although the only case where righteousness is indirectly linked to the reference to the Spirit appears in Mt. 3:15-16 (which reflects Matthew's redactional addition), the meaning of righteousness (to fulfill all righteousness) in v. 15 should be rather understood in connection with the coming of the kingdom in Jesus' messianic task, the establishing of the salvation that God has promised. Through the obedient reception of baptism in the beginning of his ministry, Jesus is ready to accomplish the will of God. (See also the word ἡμῖν in Mt. 3:15 which refers to John as well. Here the role of John is his

between Paul and the Synoptics in terms of righteousness leads us safely to deduce that for Paul kingdom concepts have been expressed in Spirit language. This also indicates that the Spirit in Paul functions as the mediator of the life of the kingdom.

3.3.5. Ethics in Paul and the Synoptics

Scarcely anyone denies that Pauline ethics are based on the Spirit.[214] While this has been widely discussed, its relationship with the issue of ethics in the kingdom of God in the Synoptics has not been emphasized. The Spirit is portrayed as the source of the ethical life of the believer in Paul, but in the Synoptics Jesus broadly speaks of it in relationship to the kingdom of God or life in the kingdom.[215] The concrete and commonly manifested ethical standard in both the Spirit (in Paul) and the kingdom (in the Synoptics) is 'love'. Paul's encouragement to live in love in the Spirit is comparable to Jesus' demand for love in the kingdom.

3.3.5.1. THE SPIRIT AND ETHICS IN PAUL

According to Paul, the believer's present life is eschatologically oriented between the 'already' and the 'not yet'. Although believers live in a new

---

preparation for the promised one, the Messiah [cf. Mt. 21:32]). Hagner, *Matthew 1-13*, 56-57. Furthermore, according to the context, Jesus' saying 'to fulfill all righteousness' in Mt. 3:15 is derived from John's refusal of his baptism so that its meaning is not directly connected to the Spirit (or the righteousness is not portrayed in connection with the presence of the Spirit). It is notable that only Matthew has the word righteousness in the baptismal story in the Synoptics and it is characteristically a Matthean term. As has been seen, the concept of righteousness is an integral part of the kingdom of God elsewhere in Matthew (e.g., Mt. 5:10, 20; 6:33). On the other hand, Luke uses the term 'righteousness' only once in his gospel (1:75; cf. the adjective form: 1:6, 17; 2:25; 14:14; 23:47, 50; Acts 10:22) and three times in Acts (10:35; 13:10; 24:25). Its meaning is basically described as the fulfillment of God's will. Schrenk, 'δικαιοσύνη', 199. However, as in the case of Matthew, the concept of righteousness is not attributed to the work of the Spirit. Simeon is described as a 'righteous' man and this reference is in relation to the Spirit in Lk. 2:25. However, Luke does not indicate that the Spirit makes Simeon righteous, but rather since he is righteous, 'the Holy Spirit was upon him'. Above all, the Spirit is portrayed as the inspirer of prophecy in Lk. 2:25 as will be seen.

[214] E.g., E.J. Schnabel, 'How Paul Developed His Ethics: Motivation, Norms and Criteria of Pauline Ethics', in B. Rosner (ed.), *Understanding Paul's Ethics: Twentieth-Century Approaches* (Grand Rapids: Eerdmans, 1995), 273: 'Paul's ethics is pneumatologically motivated'. Fee, *Empowering*, 'Christian ethics can only be by the Spirit's empowering'. 878.

[215] However, as will be discussed in chapter 4 in detail, it is important to note that the Synoptic writers, particularly Luke, do not directly relate ethical transformation to the Spirit, while Paul entirely connects it to the Spirit.

age, they are not taken out of the old age but remain in the fallen Adamic nature (Rom. 12:1-2; 13:11-14). For this reason, the present life is characterized by the struggles and limitations of a life in the era between two ages. However, life in this eschatological tension is not a life in 'continuing frustration'[216] but a life 'promised' in the future (Rom. 8:23) as well as a 'required' moral earnestness (Rom. 1:13) based on life in the Spirit. Paul thus connects the eschatological ethical life to the Spirit in his theology. Although some question the concrete role of the Spirit in the believer's ethical life,[217] the active role of the Spirit cannot be denied in numerous Pauline letters.

As discussed earlier, Paul maintains that the believer's life is life in the Spirit. For Paul, the believer's life not only begins by means of the Spirit but the whole of his/her life is a matter of the Spirit (Rom. 5:2, 5; 8:14-15, 26, 27; 15:13; 1 Cor. 3:16; 2 Cor. 3:18; 13:13; Phil. 1:19).[218] Moreover, Paul concludes that the successful moral life is only possible in the framework of the Spirit's guidance. Paul himself indicates that the foundation of his instruction derives from his possession of the Spirit (1 Cor. 7:40).

Believers in the new age are described as beings guided and led by the Spirit (Rom. 8:14; Gal. 5:18, πνεύματι ἄγεσθε; cf. Gal. 5:16; 2 Cor. 12:18, πνεύματι περιπατεῖν; Rom. 8:4, κατὰ πνεῦμα περιπατᾶειν; Gal. 5:25,

---

[216] Dunn argues that the believer's present life is characterized as 'continuing frustration' by conflict between the power of the Spirit and that of the flesh. *Jesus and Spirit*, 313; *Theology*, 477-82; cf. 496. However, although there is an internal struggle in the believer's life in the overlap of ages (Rom. 8 and Gal. 5), Dunn goes too far in his description, 'continuing frustration'. The newness of the believer's triumphant life over sin and death based on the christological event (Gal. 2:20; 3:24; 5:24; 6:14; Rom. 6:2; 8:13) and the work of the Spirit (Rom. 6:14; 7:1-6; 8:3, 4, 9, 11; 1 Cor. 15:45; 2 Cor. 3:6; Gal. 1:4; 6:6) should not be simply regarded as 'continuing frustration'. As Wenham rightly points out, 'he (Paul) would not subscribe to the melancholy view that Spirit and flesh are two almost equal contestants in the believer's life'. D. Wenham, 'The Christian Life: A Life of Tension? A Consideration of the Nature of Christian Experience in Paul', in *Pauline Studies*, 89.

[217] E.g., V.P. Furnish, *Theology and Ethics in Paul* (Nashville: Abingdon, 1968), 231-33. Furnish, however, admits the Spirit offers the moral impulse. Nonetheless, Paul points out that the Spirit-possessed person can judge all things in 1 Cor. 2:15: 'The spiritual man judges (ἀνακρίνει) all things. . .' As Barrett notes, the verb ἀνακρίνει does not simply mean to investigate but also gives more by saying that the spiritual man 'is able to consider and appraise all things because he is not only inspired to understand what he sees; he is also furnished with a moral standard by which all things may be measured'. *1 Corinthians*, 77.

[218] Fee, *Empowering*, 876. Fee further points out that 'Life in the Spirit is full and wide-ranging. . . Paul's view of life in Christ is so thoroughly dominated by the Spirit that the Spirit is the one absolutely essential ingredient for that life'. 865-66.

πνεύματι ζῆν, πνεύματι στοιχεῖν). Romans 8:4f. implies that not only do believers experience the power of the Spirit who sets them free from the law of sin and death (Rom. 8:2-3), but they also experience the direction and norm of the Spirit who leads them to specific good conduct.[219] In Galatians 5:16, Paul argues that the believer's life is to live by the Spirit. In the following verses, he further notes that life in the Spirit negates life controlled by the sinful nature (Gal. 5:16-18; cf. 2 Cor. 12:18). The Spirit exists as a sustaining directive in the midst of the believer's moral choice.[220] The Spirit therefore influences the believer's conduct and decision in a specific ethical situation. Accordingly, although for Paul the present life in the flesh still lies in tension, the believer's life attained in the new age has been ethically transformed and empowered by the presence of the Spirit.[221] As Fung notes, 'The new life (with the Spirit as its source) must become evident in the new conduct (under the Spirit's direction)'.[222]

The concept 'love',[223] which is produced by the Spirit in the believer, further confirms how his/her ethical life is closely influenced by the Spirit according to Paul. Paul commands the Galatians to walk by the Spirit.[224] He argues that walking in the Spirit is to be done 'in love' (Gal. 5:6). The first mentioned 'fruit of the Spirit' (Gal. 5:22; cf. Rom. 13:8-10) is love. Paul issues a warning to those who do the works of the flesh rather than produce the fruit of the Spirit in love (Gal. 5:21).[225] Love thus defines what

---

[219] Hamilton, *Holy Spirit*, 30.

[220] Lull, *Spirit*, 123.

[221] Note Hansen's claim based on the Galatian context, that 'the law could only present objective moral standards, but could not produce subjective moral transformation. . . however. . . the Spirit succeeds'. G.W. Hansen, 'Paul's Conversion and His Ethics of Freedom in Galatians', in R. Longenecker (ed.), *The Road from Damascus: The Impact of Paul's Conversion on His Life, Thought, and Ministry* (Grand Rapids: Eerdmans, 1997), 225.

[222] Fung, *Galatians*, 282-83.

[223] The importance of love in the present life of believers virtually assumes the status of an all-encompassing principle in Pauline ethics: love itself reflects the character of God (Gal. 5:13-14; 1 Cor. 8:2-3; 14:4-7; Rom. 13:8-10; cf. Col. 3:14; Eph. 5:2, 25); love is the first-fruit of the Spirit (Gal. 5:22); the ultimate goal of spiritual gifts (1 Cor. 12-14); the demand of the law: 'he who loves his neighbour has fulfilled the law' (Rom. 13:8).

[224] Fee, *Empowering*, 879-80. Fee argues that Paul used the verb, 'walk' as his most metaphor for ethical conduct (17 occurrences).

[225] In contrast to the phrase ἔργα τῆς σαρκός in Gal. 5:19, which denotes conduct done by the flesh, the fruit of the Spirit is characterized as the concrete manifestation of the Spirit's work in believers. These ethical characteristics naturally result from the transformed nature in the believer's new way of life empowered and produced by the Spirit under the new covenant. For a further discussion on the issue of the fruit of the Spirit, see Fung, *Galatians*, 262; W. Russell, 'The Apostle Paul's Redemptive-Historical Argumentation in Galatians 5:13-26', *WTJ* 57 (1995), 353.

it means to be in the Spirit. In Romans 5:5, where the love of God is described as being poured into the believer's life by the Spirit, the role of the Spirit in God's love is mediated in the believer who may lose hope. The nature of God's love provides the ground of hope (1 Cor. 13:8, 13) and the present appearance of hope is the Spirit who can produce the love of God. Life in the Spirit in the present is a life of trusting God with hope for the future, learning to love one another. Paul also profiles love as the essential locus on his argument of spiritual gifts in 1 Corinthians 12-14. Paul especially describes the essence of the believer's walk in the Spirit as a walk in love in 1 Corinthians. 13.

The overall relationship between the Spirit and ethics in Paul can be suitably described as the indicative and the imperative framework in Paul.[226] The presence of the Spirit characterizes the believer's new existence (indicative) and the admonitions and exhortations in the life of the Spirit are based on the ethical imperative. Paul clearly presents this idea, particularly in the letter to the Galatians: 'If we live by the Spirit, let us also walk by the Spirit' (Gal. 5:25).[227] Paul reminds his readers in Galatia that they have already entered a new existence in the Spirit. They are the people of God, who are indwelt by the Spirit (Gal. 3:26; 4:7; 6:1). The antithetical structure in Galatians 6:8 (and Rom. 8:13) shows that believers have an obligation continually to sustain their new status in Christ by the divine gift, the Spirit. Since the Spirit is the source of the new status of the Galatians, they should live by the Spirit and embody their new identity in the community by the Spirit.[228] In this way, for Paul, the Spirit is not only the cause of Christian existence, but he also plays a vital role as the source of the believer's ethical life.

In short, Paul clearly brings the Spirit into his ethical concept. The Spirit ethically transforms believers into a new existence in the new age. This

---

[226] For the overall discussion on the issue of 'indicative and imperative' in Pauline ethics, see W. Dennison, 'Indicative and Imperative: The Basic Structure of Pauline Ethics', *CTJ* 1 (1979), 55-78; A. Verhey, *The Great Reversal: Ethics and the New Testament* (Grand Rapids: Eerdmans, 1984), 104-06; M. Parsons, 'Being Precedes Act: Indicative and Imperative in Paul's Writing', in *Understanding Paul's Ethics*, 217-47.

[227] The chiastic form of the verse clearly emphasizes that one's status and life are dependent upon the Spirit.

εἰ
  A ζῶμεν
    B πνεύματι
    B⁻ πνεύματι καὶ
  A⁻ στοιχῶμεν

Here, the emphasis lies in the Spirit in BB⁻ and accordingly, Paul combines AB (indicative: status) and A⁻ B⁻ (imperative: life). Cf. Betz, *Galatians*, 293.

[228] Parsons, 'Being Precedes Act', 241.

ethical transformation in the Spirit-led believer is a sign of salvation. In addition, the believer's ethical life is portrayed as a product of walking and living in the Spirit.[229] The Spirit furnishes new possibilities for living ethically in the present life for the one who experiences salvation. Paul's ethical principle is love and the Spirit who produces this love within the believer's life is the key to his/her ethical life.[230]

3.3.5.2. THE KINGDOM AND ETHICS IN THE SYNOTICS

If the believer's ethical life is rooted in a life in the Spirit according to Paul, the Synoptic writers generally associate it with the teaching of Jesus, which centres on the kingdom of God and is the foundation of the life of discipleship. However, while this has been often argued, the question of how the ethics in Jesus' teaching are related to the kingdom is debatable.

Recently, Kvalbein has argued that Jesus' ethical teaching cannot be derived from his message of the kingdom of God. Assuming that the kingdom of God in the Synoptics does not have the abstract meaning of God's rule, but indicates the actual realm, Kvalbein concludes that

> It is impossible to deduce an ethical teaching directly from Jesus' message of the βασιλεία τοῦ θεοῦ. The kingdom of God is an eschatological and theocentric expression for the gift of God. The moral demands belong to human life *before* they enter the kingdom. . . The ethical demands can function as entrance requirements for the kingdom of God. In this way the kingdom of God is a motivation for moral responsibility and to live according to the will of God. But to do the will of God is no realization of the kingdom of God.[231]

He reasonably points out that the Synoptic writers have very little to say about God's reign compared with the actual realm or time in the references to the kingdom. He also carefully asks how one derives ethics from the kingdom. However, two questions remain about his conclusions: 1) Is Kvalbein's denial of the characterization of the reign of God in the concept kingdom correct?; 2) In relation to this, is Kvalbein's claim that the ethical demands of Jesus are understood only as entrance requirements for the kingdom of God, so that it is impossible to relate them to the realization of the kingdom, correct?

---

[229] As Fee points out, 'in Pauline ethics there is a *walking* in the Spirit, that is *led by* the Spirit'. *Empowering*, 882. Emphasis is original. Longenecker also argues that being in Christ means 'a new quality of life based in and directed by the Spirit'. R.N. Longenecker, *Galatians*, WBC 41 (Dallas: Word, 1990), 246.

[230] Cf. Russell's comment: 'In a very real sense, ἀγάπη could be called the distinctive of the new-covenant life'. Russell, 'Apostle', 353.

[231] H. Kvalbein, 'The Kingdom of God in the Ethics of Jesus', *CV* 40:3 (1998), 197-227 (214). Emphasis is original. Kvalbein claims that the phrase kingdom of God in the gospels 'does not refer to God's rule or position as a king'. 213.

In regard to the first question, while it has been widely pointed out among NT scholars that the lopsided interpretation of the kingdom of God in the Synoptics as either only the actual realm or only God's actual reign is too narrow, several further points suggest that Kvalbein's view is inadequate. First of all, the term kingdom of God is closely associated with the activity of the Messiah who is by definition God's royal agent in it.[232] Furthermore, as Kvalbein himself admits, if the kingdom of God is not only future but also present, then the latter should involve the reality of God's reign. This concept can be found in the Lord's prayer (cf. also Mt. 12:28/Lk. 11:20; Lk. 17:21), particularly in the Matthean form as seen earlier.[233] 'Thy kingdom come' is parallel with 'Thy will be done' in Matthew 6:10: both of which indicate that the manifestation of God's reign takes place in the present world. So, to understand the phrase only to mean the actual realm in the future would be a mistake.[234] In short, the phrase kingdom of God contains the nuances of 'what is set up by God' and 'God's rule over this realm'.[235]

With regard to the second question, although it is conceivable that the ethics of Jesus may not be deduced from what he says about the kingdom of God, they are nonetheless closely tied to his message of the kingdom of God in light of the following observations.

If it is correct to presume that, as seen above, Jesus announces the present reality of the kingdom of God (which Kvalbein admits but does not seem to develop very much), then the teaching of Jesus should also express how people are to live if they are in the kingdom of God.[236] God has manifested his kingdom - his saving rule - in Jesus and the centre of Jesus' teaching lies in the kingdom of God. In the light of this, the believer's life is essentially based on life in the kingdom.[237] Thus, the believer, whose life is transformed as new, must live by the ethical standards of the manifested

---

[232] See I.H. Marshall, 'The Hope of a New Age: The Kingdom of God in New Testament', *Themelios* 5 (1985), 10-11.

[233] See §3.3.3.2.2 above.

[234] So most scholars, e.g., Marshall, *Luke*, 457; Betz, *Sermon*, 391; Guelich, *Sermon*, 290; Mitton, *Kingdom*, 32. Contra C. Rowland, who argues the kingdom in the Lord's prayer as only future. He claims that the Lord's prayer regarding that the 'kingdom of God may come' is 'an accurate exposition of the essential features of the Jewish (and Jesus') belief concerning the eschatological'. *Christian Origins* (London: SPCK, 1985), 135. For the present aspect of the rule of God in the kingdom, see §3.3.2.2 above.

[235] I personally owe this insight to Prof. I.H. Marshall.

[236] So, as Jeremias notes, the kingdom of God is 'inconceivable without the life of discipleship. For belonging to the reign of God transforms a man's whole life'. J. Jeremias, *New Testament Theology*, 1, *The Proclamation of Jesus* (London: SCM Press, 1971), 204.

[237] B.D. Chilton and J.I.H. McDonald, *Jesus and the Ethics of the Kingdom* (London: SPCK, 1987), 4.

kingdom.[238] In that experience, the believer is called and enabled to live according to right ethics. Certainly the realization of the kingdom supplies the ethical motivation.

Jesus' love command is also to be seen in this way. Kvalbein argues that the commandment of love (e.g., Mt. 22:34-40; Mk. 12:28-34) in Jesus' primary teaching is not seen as a realization of the kingdom but is presented as the entrance requirement to the future kingdom of God.[239] Indeed, Jesus' love command is widely delineated in the Synoptics as the condition for participation in the coming kingdom of God (e.g., Lk. 10:25-37;[240] Mt. 5:43-47; Lk. 6:27-36;[241] Mt. 22:34-40; Mk. 12:28-34[242]). However, while this idea is undoubtedly right, what should be added to this argument is that the love command represented in Jesus' teaching can also be understood as a realization of the kingdom. If one takes the love command as the only entrance requirement (or a condition) for the kingdom, a pre-condition for entrance into it should be 'human effort or responsibility'. However, such an idea is inappropriate,[243] since as Piper rightly states, the fulfillment of the love command 'is *impossible* if one has not in a sense already entered the Kingdom, or better, been entered by the powers of that Kingdom'.[244] This adversely emphasizes that the power of God realized in Jesus enables one to perform the love command. So if one achieves the love command by

---

[238] H. Ridderbos, *The Coming of the Kingdom* (Philadelphia: Presbyterian and Reformed, 1962), 252; Chilton and McDonald, *Ethics of the Kingdom*, 61f.

[239] 'Kingdom of God', 216-18.

[240] The parable of the Good Samaritan is an exemplary explication of 'what disciples' ethics are' by describing that loving God and the neighbour are primary requirements for the kingdom. It is notable that unlike Matthew and Mark who simply say that the second commandment is to love one's neighbour (Mt. 22:34-40; Mk. 12:28-34), Luke details the scope of the neighbour to include an enemy (Lk. 10:30-37). So, for Luke, loving neighbours turns out to be loving enemies.

[241] Loving enemies is represented as a conditional qualification to participating in the kingdom.

[242] Just as in Luke's parable of the merciful Samaritan, love is described as determinative for one's reception of the kingdom of God. Jesus certainly connects the importance of the scribe's ethical insight, particularly in light of the fulfillment of Jesus' love command, to entering the kingdom of God.

[243] Similarly, we have earlier argued that it would be only half correct if one takes the meaning of 'righteousness' in Mt. 6:33 as only God's demand (human conduct) for an entrance requirement for the kingdom. But we have suggested that the righteous conduct is possible from a transformed relationship with God in the new age. See §3.3.4.2 above.

[244] Piper, *Love your Enemies*, 79. (Emphasis is original). Piper further notes that 'if we take seriously both the commands of Jesus and his sober pessimism about man's moral ability, the only conclusion we can come to is that, if a man is to enter the Kingdom of heaven, God must enable him to fulfill the conditions contained in the command'. 78.

the power of God (cf. Mk. 10:27, 'all things are possible with God'), not by human effort, there is a close relationship between the love command and the kingdom of God. The present experience of one who obeys Jesus' love command reflects the realization of the coming kingdom of God.[245] Thus, in the concept of Jesus' love command, two ideas are closely linked: 'how to enter the kingdom of God' (love as an entrance requirement for the kingdom) and 'how to live in the realized kingdom of God' (love as the nature of the kingdom itself).

Jesus' command to love is *implicitly* seen through his own forgiving fellowship with sinners. Jesus' open fellowship at a meal with sinners (Lk. 15:1-2; Mk. 2:15-16) and his unconditional forgiveness of their sins (Lk. 7:36-47; 15:11-32; 19:1-10) indicate the life of the kingdom in which the rule of God is actively manifested in the present.[246] Although there is no explicit connection between Jesus' love command and his work of forgiveness, his unconditional forgiving fellowship with sinners nevertheless implies his loving reception of them.[247] Schlatter states, 'Jesus saw the power of forgiveness to stand a man upright and to heal him in this: forgiveness produces love. And when he was reproached for forgiving he justified with the fact that it brings forth not hardening and new guilt but rather love'.[248]

Jesus' own loving reception of sinners not only indicates the presence of the kingdom, but also is an indirect call for them to offer the same forgiveness in that kingdom life (cf. Mt. 18:23-35; Lk. 17:3-4). Furthermore, the act of love for the poor by sharing possessions (cf. Lk. 12:31-33; Mk. 10:17-31) is not only a requirement for entering the kingdom, but also 'creates a foretaste of the life of the kingdom in anticipation of its final coming'.[249] Above all, as Ireland notes, 'love manifests the kingdom and gives evidence of one's membership in it'.[250]

Therefore, the concluding remark of this discussion forbids the conclusion by Kvalbein that the ethical life in Jesus' teaching is simply portrayed as the entrance requirements for the future kingdom of God. It can be argued that the ethical life issues from the realization of the kingdom in Jesus' teaching. The concept of love, as the heart of the kingdom ethics, supports this notion. It is not only a requirement for entering the kingdom

---

[245] Piper, *Love your Enemies*, 86-87.

[246] Piper, *Love your Enemies*, 80-85, esp. 83; Jeremias, *Theology*, 1, 115.

[247] It should be noted that the forgiveness that Jesus granted is not one that simply eliminates punishment or removes a bad conscience.

[248] Cited by Piper, *Love your Enemies*, 84. See A. Schlatter, *Die Geschichte des Christus* (Stuttgart: Calwer, 1922), 201.

[249] D.J. Ireland, *Stewardship and the Kingdom of God: A Historical, Exegetical, and Contextual Study of the Parable of the Unjust Steward in Luke 16:1-13*, NovTS 70 (New York: Brill, 1992), 213.

[250] Ireland, *Stewardship*, 212.

of God, but also represents a realization of the kingdom. The overall discussion brings the clear conclusion that the ethics of Jesus are in any event related to the kingdom in the Synoptics. As Stein rightly notes, 'In seeking to understand the essence of Jesus' ethical teaching, we must not divorce his ethical teaching from his teaching on the kingdom of God'.[251] The two cannot be separated: 'Jesus' ethics are kingdom ethics and vice versa'.[252]

3.3.5.3. SUMMARY

Paul relates the believer's ethical life to the Spirit while the Synoptics' Jesus speaks of it in connection with the life in the kingdom. Love describes what it means to abide in the kingdom (Synoptics) and to walk in the Spirit (Paul). This enables us to see the common ground in the concept of ethics between life in the Spirit (Paul) and life in the kingdom (Synoptics' Jesus). Once again, this similarity in ethics shows that Paul presents kingdom concepts with his Spirit-language. This also indicates that the Spirit in Paul functions as the arbitrator of the life of the kingdom in its entirety.

3.3.6. Summary

An attempt has been made to find whether Jesus' emphasis on the kingdom may have been communicated by Paul with his doctrine of the Spirit. The outcome is that it is highly probable that Paul uses language of the Spirit to speak of the kingdom of God. This can be seen through the inverse ratio between the term kingdom of God in the Synoptics and the Spirit in Pauline corpus. This can be also seen through the commonality of the eschatological tension between the Spirit in Paul and the kingdom of God in the Synoptics. The similarity between life in the Spirit for Paul and life in the kingdom in the Synoptics further clarifies Paul's choice of the Spirit for the kingdom.

3.4. Conclusion

This chapter has aimed at investigating the close relationship between the Spirit in Paul and the kingdom of God in the Synoptics. For this purpose, Paul's kingdom of God sayings in his letters were first examined in order to show how the phrase is used in a limited way. Paul, in his seven kingdom of God references, maintains Jesus' two-fold time element of the kingdom, but the language is not used as extensively as in the Synoptics. Furthermore,

---

[251] R.H. Stein, *The Method and Message of Jesus' Teachings* (Philadelphia: Westminster Press, 1978), 106.

[252] Wenham, *Paul*, 241. Cf. Hunter's comment, 'To understand Jesus' ethic aright, we have to remember what he taught about the kingdom of God and its coming'. A.M. Hunter, *Design for Life* (London: SCM Press, 1965), 114.

some notable distinctions between Jesus' tradition on the kingdom of God and Paul's kingdom of God sayings have been pointed out.

Then some possible reasons for Paul's infrequent use of the term have been listed. However, whatever the reasons, it should be remembered that in any event Paul did tend to be cautious in his use of the term. So the lack of frequency of the term in Paul raises the question whether it might be replaced by other concepts.

It has thus subsequently been observed that Paul carries on Jesus' preaching of the kingdom in the Synoptics utilizing the alternative concept of the Spirit. The similarity between both the emphasis upon the Spirit in Paul and the kingdom in the Synoptics in their mutual eschatological tension indicates that Paul has used his Spirit language when speaking of the kingdom concepts. The similarity can further be found in the close relationship between 'life in the Spirit' (Paul) and 'life in the kingdom' (Synoptics). For this, the main aspects of the presentness of the kingdom (new life, sonship, resurrection, righteousness, and ethics) which Paul closely attributes to the role of the Spirit have been listed and it has been argued how these aspects are equivalent to the life of the kingdom in the Synoptics. The experience of a new life in the Spirit, according to Paul, conceptually overlaps with entering a new life in the kingdom in the Synoptics. The blessing of sonship in this age and the age to come is attributed to the work of the Spirit by Paul while the Synoptic writers describe it in terms of the life of the kingdom. Both Paul and the Synoptics regard the resurrection as the believer's central hope. While the former attributes it to life in the Spirit, the latter relate it to life in the kingdom. Furthermore, while, for Paul, the presence of the Spirit makes people righteous, righteousness issues from the realization of the kingdom in the Synoptics. Finally, the believer's ethical life is closely linked to the Spirit while the Synoptics' Jesus speaks of it in connection with the life in the kingdom. So, the conceptual commonality appears in the believer's ethical life in the Spirit and the kingdom.

All of these similarities between the Spirit in Paul and the kingdom in the Synoptics plausibly suggest Paul's choice of Spirit-language as a means of speaking about kingdom realities. Paul understands Jesus' central teaching on the kingdom through his own emphasis on the concept 'Spirit'. The continuity between Jesus and Paul is undeniable, but the uniqueness of Paul's language is also evident. Accordingly, for Paul, life in the Spirit becomes his way of speaking about life in the kingdom. The Spirit mediates the entirety of the blessings of the kingdom in Paul and becomes the source of its life. In short, the Spirit embodies the essence of the kingdom of God.

This conclusion presumably offers a foundation for the important corollary that there is a development in Paul's theological understanding by reformulating the concept of the kingdom of God by a new term, the Spirit, in a new and more comprehensive way. How can this judgment be more convincingly proven? If it is right that the Pauline pneumatological perspective is generally unparalleled in intertestamental literature as seen in the previous chapter, the next line of inquiry to be pursued is whether this concept of Paul's understanding of the Spirit was similarly understood in the early non-Pauline church.

CHAPTER 4

The Spirit and the Blessings of the Kingdom of God in Luke-Acts

4.1. Introduction

In the previous chapter (ch. 3), we have argued that what Jesus sees as the blessings brought about when God inaugurates His kingdom (Synoptics), Paul describes as the effects of the working of the Spirit. So, by attributing all the blessings of the kingdom to the Spirit, Paul presents the Spirit as the life of the kingdom. However, when we turn to Luke-Acts,[1] it becomes much more complicated so that one must be careful not simply to assume that the Spirit represents the existence and life of the kingdom. Nonetheless, a close systematic connection between Lukan and Pauline pneumatology has been recognized among scholars, particularly by Dunn and Turner as seen in the introductory review of scholarship (ch. 1). The most recent argument of this school of thought has been updated by Turner.[2]

According to Turner, as in the ideas of intertestamental literature, the Spirit in Luke-Acts functions as the giver of life-giving wisdom. This conclusion clearly implies that the Spirit in Luke-Acts should be seen to be like the Spirit in Paul, i.e., the Spirit as the source of the kingdom blessings. If Turner's argument is right, some qualification is naturally called for in regard to this issue and it should be addressed more precisely. Although I have already argued (ch. 2) that the Spirit is not usually understood as the giver of life-giving wisdom in intertestamental literature, it is necessary to

---

[1] Although Matthew and Mark contain reference to pneumatology, I will focus on the Lukan writings since pneumatology is so prominent in Luke-Acts so that the two pneumatologies of Paul and Luke may be easily compared. For the relationship between the third gospel and Acts, see n. 1 in chapter 1. Moreover, my study of Lukan pneumatology will be undertaken by 'redaction criticism', which is the corresponding hermeneutical device of most recent pneumatological scholars, on the basis of the two-document hypothesis (Mark and Q).

[2] *Holy Spirit*, 150-68; *Power*, 439-55.

look for clear evidence of the corresponding view in Luke-Acts.[3] The purpose of the present chapter is therefore to answer the question: whilst it is true that the Spirit functions as the source of the blessings of the kingdom according to Paul, is it also true that Luke associates the Spirit with these blessings?

Since a whole discussion about the Spirit in Luke-Acts such as miracle-working power or prophecy is beyond the scope of this study, the material to be discussed will be related to the present concern, i.e., whether the Spirit is the source of the blessings of the kingdom (or as the source of life-giving wisdom). In order to demonstrate whether there is a different pneumatological perspective between Luke and Paul, in this chapter, I will categorize these kingdom blessings of sonship, ethical transformation, resurrection and conversional experience (new life) as in chapter 3. Since the lack of a relationship between the Spirit and justification is unquestionable in Luke-Acts as seen above,[4] it will be omitted in this discussion. The texts to be discussed will not be structurally in the order outlined in Luke-Acts. In addition, since, in the subsequent chapter, we will discuss the distinctive characteristic of the Spirit in relation to the kingdom of God in Luke-Acts, discussion of its relative material will not be offered here.

4.2. The Spirit and Sonship (The Sense of Abba): The Experience of Jesus' Pneumatic Anointing (Lk. 3:21-22; cf. Lk. 11:2; 22:42): A Spirit-given Sonship?

Scholars have debated the controversial question of whether Jesus' baptism at the Jordan represents the divine approval of the Son of God. This account of Jesus' baptism is a possible case which supports the idea that for Luke the Spirit is the source of sonship since in the account the Spirit and Jesus' sonship are connected with each other (e.g., Dunn and Büchsel). However, a careful reading of the account leads rather in the opposite direction. The purpose of this section is to ask, can one accurately say, according to Luke, that at the Jordan the Spirit attributes sonship to Jesus? The answer to this question will be an exemplary case for comparing this matter with Paul's clear notion that the Spirit is a crucial source of the sense of sonship of believers as a kingdom blessing.

---

[3] The Jewish background of Lukan pneumatology has been generally argued by most scholars. E.g., Büchsel, *Geist Gottes*, 252-53; Schweizer, 'πνεῦμα', 407; Hill, *Greek Words*, 254, 261-65.

[4] See §3.3.4.3, esp. n. 213 in chapter 3.

4.2.1. Lukan Redactional Features

In comparison to Mark's report 1:9-11 (and Mt. 3:13-17), Luke's version in general has several unique characteristics. Luke seems to down-play Jesus' baptism as a general baptism of all the people without mentioning John the Baptist. Uniquely, Luke shifts the focus from the baptism to Jesus' prayer just before the descent of τὸ πνεῦμα τὸ ἅγιον. This is probably because, as is well-known, for Luke, prayer is a crucial theme and Luke particularly draws special attention to Jesus' practice of prayer (5:16; 6:12; 9:18; 11:1; 22:32 etc.). In contrast to Mark and Matthew, Luke uses the term τὸ πνεῦμα τὸ ἅγιον while Mark uses τὸ πνεῦμα and Matthew employs τὸ πνεῦμα τοῦ θεοῦ. Luke emphasizes the physical manifestation of the Spirit with the phrase σωματικῷ εἴδει. Although there is an underlying significance in the form of a dove-like appearance, this debate has failed to generate a consensus among scholars.[5] Along with these unique Lukan features,[6] a more significant issue in the story of Jesus' baptism is his encounter at the Jordan with the heavenly voice and its connoted meaning.

4.2.2. The Messianic Figure of the Heavenly Proclamation and Its Pneumatological Concern

The account of Jesus' baptism at the Jordan plays an important role in establishing the messianic figure of Jesus. Luke 3:22 reads '... σὺ εἶ ὁ υἱός μου ὁ ἀγαπητός, ἐν σοὶ εὐδόκησα'. Most scholars concede that the tradition of this heavenly declaration is directed by two OT citations, Psalm 2:7 and Isaiah 42:1.[7] The former implies a royal-Messiah who will rule over the nations; the latter refers to the servant-herald who will perform God's justice among the nations. Since the status of Jesus as 'Son' was already applied to him in the infancy narrative (Lk. 1:35; 2:49) as will be

---

[5] The precise interpretation of the dove has been discussed with no consensus. For instance, Turner holds that a bodily descent of the Spirit is no more literal than the descent of a sheet full of animals to Peter in Acts 10:11. *Holy Spirit*, 28-29. Penney on the other hand argues that Luke clearly intends an objectification and 'that some form of material representation of the descent took place is confirmed by the testimony of John the Baptist in John's Gospel (Jn. 1:32-34)'. *Missionary*, 37. Whatever options are taken, it is clear that one can see the dove 'as a sign of the presence of the Spirit to Jesus'. So J.A. Fitzmyer, *The Gospel According to Luke I-IX*, AB 28 (New York: Doubleday, 1981), 484. For a general survey of the dove interpretation, see L.E. Keck, 'The Spirit and the Dove', *NTS* 17 (1970), 41-68; S. Gero, 'The Spirit as a Dove at the Baptism of Jesus', *NovT* 18 (1976), 17-35.

[6] The general accounts of Jesus' baptism of Mark and Matthew are juxtaposed in comparison to that of Luke.

[7] Dunn, *Baptism*, 27; Marshall, *Luke*, 154-57; Turner, *Power*, 191, 197-98; Contra Jeremias, *Theology*, I, 53-55; 'παῖς θεοῦ', *TDNT*, V, 701-02, who argues that the heavenly declaration is reminiscent of only Isa. 42:1.

seen, the main factor in applying the title of 'Son' to Jesus in Luke 3:22 is to represent Jesus as the Messiah.[8]

On the other hand, one may emphasize that the dominant stress in this passage conveys christological uniqueness.[9] Nonetheless, within the view that the tasks of both the servant of Isaiah 42:1 and the Davidic Messiah of Psalms 2:7 are enabled by the Spirit in Isaiah 11:1-2, the pneumatological significance of the account should not be minimized. Whereas the identification of Jesus as the Messiah-king is a recognized feature in this passage, Luke's reference to the Spirit reflects his crucial concern to present a picture of Jesus as a man of the Spirit. In other words, Luke's pneumatological significance is interconnected with his christology.

4.2.3. The Spirit: The Inauguration of Jesus' Sense of Sonship or of the Messianic Task?

As noted in the introductory survey, Dunn, following Büchsel,[10] argues that the Jordan event is depicted primarily in terms of new age and covenant, or Jesus' paradigmatic experience of the Spirit in eschatological sonship.[11] He argues that it is only at the moment of Jesus' anointing with the Spirit that he may suitably be called Messiah and only then that the messianic age has been inaugurated.[12] Although Jesus had an awareness of his divine sonship and messianic self-awareness before Jordan (Lk. 1:35, 43, 76; 2:1, 26, 49), the ultimate sense of Jesus' sonship is only made by the descent of the Spirit at the Jordan.[13] So for Luke, according to Dunn, the Spirit given at the Jordan is a reason for Jesus' sense of real sonship. However, Dunn's adoptionistic reading of Jesus' baptismal experience is not convincing for the following reasons.

First of all, the status of Jesus' sonship is explicitly illustrated before Jordan.[14] The Lukan infancy narrative clearly shows Jesus' sonship both in terms of the line of Davidic heredity and the title of 'Son' given to Jesus together with his self-conscious statement. As to the former, the sonship of Jesus in the infancy narrative is particularly established on the basis of Davidic heredity. In Luke 1:27, Luke reports that Jesus, who will be born

---

[8] I.H. Marshall, 'The Divine Sonship of Jesus', in *Jesus the Saviour: Studies in New Testament Theology* (London: SPCK, 1990), 143; *Luke*, 155. See below in detail in this section.

[9] Penney, *Missionary*, 41.

[10] Büchsel argued that Jesus' sonship was perfected at Jordan through the experience of the Spirit. *Geist Gottes*, 161-67.

[11] Dunn, *Baptism*, 23-37.

[12] Dunn, *Baptism*, 27.

[13] Dunn, *Baptism*, 28-29. '. . . there is also a sense in which he only becomes Messiah and Son at Jordan' (28).

[14] Turner, *Power*, 199; Menzies, *Development*, 153.

by Mary, became the son of David through Joseph who, as a legal father of Jesus, was in the line of David (Lk. 3:23).[15] More directly, the angel Gabriel in Luke 2:32b foretells the status of Jesus in terms of his accession to the throne of David his father.[16] Furthermore, Jesus, as a descendant of David, is born in Bethlehem, the city of David, and will be a Saviour, Christ the Lord. These all show that Jesus' birth and royal sonship as David's heir have already featured in the story of his birth. Thus, the concept of sonship, particularly quoted from Psalms 2:7 at Jordan simply confirms what is already promised and announced about the son of David before Jordan. At this point, Luke's proclamation in the form of the heavenly voice about Jesus' sonship is retrospective.[17]

On the latter (the title of Jesus), the status of Jesus' sonship is also clear in his titles. Luke in the angel Gabriel's announcement informs that Jesus is to be called 'υἱὸς ὑψίστου' (Lk. 1:32) and 'υἱὸς θεοῦ' (Lk. 1:35), which indicate 'the true being of the person so called'.[18] The title υἱός in Luke 1:35 is parallel with Luke 1:32[19] and may be understood as ruling activity of David.[20] Moreover, Jesus' own understanding of his unique and close relationship with God in Luke 2:49-50 further confirms his divine sonship. Jesus himself, in his first recorded statement, appears to fully understand that he is the Son of God in the expression of the phrase 'ἐν τοῖς τοῦ πατρός μου' (Lk. 2:49). Jesus' ability to speak of God as 'my Father' is 'not simply the "official" position of the Messiah, but a personal consciousness of God'.[21]

Second, the overall contextual consideration in relation to the voice from heaven does not support Jesus' baptism in an adoptionistic sense. Two notable alterations in Mark's redaction from Psalms 2:7 (LXX) provide for this notion: 1) The alteration of the word order from 'Υἱός μου εἶ σύ' (LXX) to 'σὺ εἶ ὁ υἱός μου' may suggest the identification of Jesus as the υἱός of God as he was.[22] 2) But, more convincingly, Mark's reason for the partial quotation of Psalms 2:7 (με υἱός μου εἶ συ) omitting the following clause (ἐγὼ σήμερον γεγέννηκά σε) adequately explains that at least to Mark and the other evangelists Jesus was in an already adoptive

---

[15] Marshall, *Luke*, 64.
[16] Marshall, *Luke*, 68.
[17] R. Stronstad, *The Prophethood of All Believers: A Study of Luke's Charismatic Theology*, JPTS 16 (Sheffield: SAP, 1999), 43.
[18] Marshall, *Luke*, 67.
[19] J.A. Fitzmyer, 'The Contribution of Qumran Aramaic to the Study of the New Testament', *NTS* 20 (1974), 391.
[20] F. Hahn, *The Titles of Jesus in Christology: Their History in Early Christianity* (New York: World Publishing, 1969), 296.
[21] Marshall, *Luke*, 129.
[22] E. Lohmeyer, *Das Evangelium des Markus* (Göttingen: Vandenhoeck & Ruprecht, 1963), 23; Guelich, *Mark 1-8:26*, 33-34.

relationship rather than its beginning at Jordan. The matter is well summed up by Witherington:

> It is more probable to conclude that Jesus believed that in his vision these words had been spoken to him and that the church later felt it had to pass on the words from this sacred occasion in spite of their possible adoptionist implications, than to deduce that the early church without any precedent would have chosen an adoptionist text to express its theology. None of the evangelists interpret the text in adoptionist fashion.[23]

Hence, the several lines of evidence mentioned above suggest that Dunn's assertion that Jesus' sonship is only accomplished by the Spirit-anointing at Jordan needs to be modified.

Most scholars argue that Jesus' anointing at the Jordan does indicate the inauguration of his messianic ministry.[24] The role of the Spirit coming upon Jesus at the Jordan is mainly for the purpose of empowerment for ministry. This is particularly based upon the quotation from Isaiah 42:1 where the immediate public messianic task of Jesus is introduced with him as a servant figure and an anointed prophet. The fact that Jesus' subsequent task has been depicted as performed by a suffering-servant figure throughout Luke-Acts further confirms how the anointing event of Jordan is important for Jesus' future specific task. At this point, the quotation from Isaiah 42:1 which implies the nature of the servant's calling and function is prospective.[25] As Squires argues, 'The appearance of the Holy Spirit at the baptism of Jesus (Lk. 3:22) conveys God's commissioning and proleptic approval of Jesus' ministry'.[26] The overall conclusion therefore prevents us from asserting that the connection between the Spirit and sonship in Luke should be understood to be in the same degree as Paul's clear notion.

This notion becomes clearer from the weakness of Dunn's conclusion about the discussion of the 'Abba' cry. According to Dunn, Jesus' use of 'Abba Father' in his prayer is not simply a formal convention but expresses a sense of sonship which is fundamentally derived from the work of the Spirit. Dunn concludes that 'the early Christians' experience of sonship (as indicated in Rom. 8:15 and Gal. 4:6) was understood as an echo and

---

[23] B. Witherington, *Christology of Jesus* (Minneapolis: Fortress Press, 1990), 151. It is also notable that all three evangelists again make a point of focusing on Jesus' unique existing sonship in the transfiguration narrative and exhort the disciples to listen to him. In Lk. 9:35, '. . . Οὗτός ἐστιν ὁ υἱός μου ὁ ἐκλελεγμένος, αὐτοῦ ἀκούετε', See also Mk. 9:7; Mt. 17:5.

[24] M.D. Goulder, *Luke: A New Paradigm*, JSNTS 20 (Sheffield: JSOT Press, 1989), 282; Marshall, 'Divine Sonship', 134-49; Menzies, *Development*, 153-54; J.T. Squires, *The Plan of God in Luke-Acts*, SNTSMS 76 (Cambridge: CUP, 1993), 113; Turner, *Power*, 199; Tannehill, *Luke*, 84; Stronstad, *Prophethood*, 41-43.

[25] Stronstad, *Prophethood*, 43.

[26] Squires, *Plan of God*, 113.

reproduction of Jesus' own experience'.[27] In this manner, there is a close connection between Luke (Jesus) and Paul. For both of them the Spirit is the source of the eschatological sonship. However, as noted above, while the Abba-prayer was undoubtedly in currency in the Jesus tradition and the early church, it would be a mistake to look at this common ground in terms of a unity between both Luke's and Paul's pneumatologies. For Luke never suggests that the source of Jesus' (and his disciples') conscious ability to call God 'Father' in his (and their) prayers is the Spirit (Lk. 11:2; 22:42; cf. Mk. 14:36).[28] On the contrary, for Paul, as already seen, the Spirit makes sonship real to the believer through calling this concrete expression, 'Abba' (Rom. 8:15-16 and Gal. 4:6).[29]

To sum up, the proclamation from heaven in the story of Jesus' baptism is retrospective to the infancy narrative while it is also prospective to his immediate messianic task. The fact that the Spirit is not related to Jesus' declared sonship at baptism is an example of the suggestion that the Spirit should not be understood as the source of sonship in Luke, whereas Paul links them so clearly together.

4.3. The Spirit and Ethics

Previously, we have argued that Jesus in Luke and the other Synoptic writers speak of ethical transformation in relation to the kingdom of God. By contrast, we have also observed that Paul frequently and clearly presents the Spirit as the source of ethical transformation rather than the kingdom of God. In this manner, there is an important distinction between the way in which Luke and the other Synoptic writers relate the kingdom of God to ethics and the way in which Paul relates the Spirit to ethics. If this conclusion is right, the next question which needs to be reasonably asked is how far does Luke associate the Spirit with this ethical dimension? The purpose of this section is therefore to look at whether the Spirit in Luke-Acts is clearly portrayed as the source of the ethical transformation of

---

[27] *Jesus and Spirit*, 22. See also *Christology*, 22-29; *Baptism*, 24. Although Dunn does not discuss and compare the relationship between the Spirit and sonship (of Luke and Paul) in detail, it is clear that in view of Dunn's argument on the continuity between Luke and Paul, the Spirit certainly conveys a sense of sonship in both Luke (Jesus) and Paul. Cf. Dunn's claim 'At the Jordan he becomes the uniquely anointed Man of the Spirit, the *first fruits* (to use a Pauline expression) of the new age and covenant (3:22; 4:18; Acts 10:38)'. *Pneumatology*, 138 (cf. p. 136). Emphasis is original.

[28] Wenham also attributes Jesus' ability to call 'Abba Father' in the Gethsemane story to the Spirit: 'Jesus prays intensely to his "Abba" by the Spirit, as Paul might well say'. *Paul*, 279, n. 160. However, this is based on Pauline interpretation and nothing in the passages in the Synoptics connects the work of the Spirit to Jesus' sense of sonship in calling on God as Father.

[29] See §3.3.3.2.1 in chapter 3.

individuals and communities or not. The outcome of the following survey will clarify the difference between the two pneumatologies (Luke's and Paul's) in terms of ethical relationship.[30]

4.3.1. The Role of the Spirit-endowed Mighty One: John the Baptist's Prophecy (Lk. 3:16-17)

In his description of the role of the 'mightier One', who is to come after him, John, putting himself in a lower status, distinguishes his role from that of the coming One: his baptism is with water, but the stronger One 'ὑμᾶς βαπτίσει ἐν πνεύματι ἁγίῳ καὶ πυρί·'.[31] Most commentators concede that the baptism with the Spirit and fire indicates one baptism event since the single preposition ἐν embraces both the terms.[32] So the performance of the coming One's baptism encompasses the two different aspects in a single action and all would probably experience this baptism, i.e., some would be redemptive while others would be destructive.

The interpretation of this text in terms of pneumatology has long been controversial among scholars. Probably the most debatable area is whether the Spirit in this text functions as the source of moral transformation (cleansing of the individual) or not. Although the argument of Dunn, who interprets the role of the Spirit as the purification of repentant individuals and accordingly as a source of 'the blessings of the messianic kingdom', has become popular,[33] Dunn's view has been significantly challenged by some.[34] More recently, a similar view to Dunn's has been expressed by Turner.[35] According to him, the messianic role in the future Spirit baptism is closely associated with cleansing of the repentant. Turner argues that 'If John's words are, as we have suggested, an allusion to traditional Jewish views of the Davidic messiah - and if his point is that the messiah will be empowered to cleanse and so restore Israel through the mighty Spirit with

---

[30] Although Wenk recently argues the overall relationship between the Spirit and the ethical dimension in Luke-Acts, I will respond mostly to Turner in this section since Wenk's view is an expansion of that of Turner. See n. 3 in chapter 1 for a full reference of Wenk's book.

[31] Mark omits the phrase καὶ πυρί. Most agree that Luke's wording, which is identical to Matthew (3:11-12) is originally derived from Q. Dunn, *Baptism*, 8-10; *Pneumatology*, 95; Marshall, *Luke*, 144-48; Menzies, *Development*, 135-36; Turner, *Power*, 172-74.

[32] Dunn, *Baptism*, 11-13; Marshall, *Luke*, 146-47. Contra, R.L. Webb, *John the Baptizer and Prophet: A Socio-Historical Study*, JSNTS 62 (Sheffield: SAP, 1991), 289-95.

[33] Dunn, *Baptism*, 8-22.

[34] E.g., Menzies, *Development*, 137-41; B. Charette, *Restoring Presence: The Spirit in Matthew's Gospel*, JPTS 18 (Sheffield: SAP, 2000), 44, n. 34.

[35] *Power*, 170-87; *Holy Spirit*, 25-27.

which he is (to be) endowed - then, for the Baptist at least, *the Spirit is clearly in some sense "soteriologically necessary"*.[36]

While Luke does not clearly elucidate the Baptist's intention in his prophecy as Turner himself admits, this claim is particularly supported by his analysis of the description of the winnowing process in Luke 3:17. Hence, Turner further claims that

> From the Baptist's perspective, the task of the coming one is not to sift the wheat from the chaff in Israel, nor is the instrument in his hand a threshing fork (as is usually maintained). John understood himself largely already to have accomplished the sifting process through his preaching and baptismal ministry. From this point of view what remains is for the Coming One to '*cleanse the threshing floor*' (17b), and deal with the already-separated wheat and chaff: so, appropriately, he comes with a *spade* (ptuon) in hand.[37]

While Turner rightly points out the significance of the Jewish background in understanding John's prophecy, his reading of the Spirit in the text as a soteriological agent or an agent for moral transformation, particularly in the interpretation of the winnowing process,[38] is unlikely for several reasons.

a. Turner's employment of Webb's interpretation of the word πτύον as a spade rather than a winnowing fork in the metaphor should be reconsidered. According to Webb's interpretation, the activity described by John's metaphorical illustration does not indicate the actual winnowing process but the threshing floor after the winnowing. This thesis is possible because of the word πτύον being construed as a winnowing shovel rather than winnowing fork.[39] However, Menzies rightly points out its improbability in that: 'the significance of Webb's contention that the term *ptuon* refers to a spade rather than a winnowing fork should not be overestimated. I suspect this is a classic example of over-exegesis'.[40] The general picture of the metaphor is, as the text suggests, that the role of the instrument in the hand of the coming One is to separate the wheat from the chaff so that the former will be gathered in the granary while the latter will be destroyed.[41] Although Luke does not strictly refer to the role of the instrument in the winnowing process, yet, whether the instrument is a spade

---

[36] Turner, *Power*, 186. Emphasis is original.
[37] Turner, *Holy Spirit*, 26. Emphasis is original. *Power*, 171, 181
[38] What is to be asked in the present text in order to understand the role of the Messiah bestowed by the Spirit lies mainly in the interpretation of the winnowing process in v. 17 as Turner does.
[39] R.L. Webb, 'The Activity of John the Baptist's Expected Figure at the Threshing Floor (Matthew 3:12=Luke 3:17)', *JSNT* 43 (1991), 103-11.
[40] Menzies, *Spirit and Power*, 95.
[41] This is most common interpretation among commentators. E.g., Marshall, *Luke*, 148; Fitzmyer, *Luke I-IX*, 474; Hagner, *Matthew 1-13*, 52.

or a fork, does not affect the coming One's sifting role, i.e., a separation of the wheat from the chaff.[42] In this manner, the prophecy of John refers to the cleansing of Israel by the removal of the wicked.

b. In connection with the first point, if it is not impossible for the Baptist to interpret the concept of winnowing in terms of the wind (cf. v. 16), then the general imagery of the winnowing process suggests sifting rather than simply the cleansing (of the repentant individual).[43] The grain and chaff were tossed into the air with a winnowing fork or a shovel and as the wind blows it takes away the chaff. This double role of the wind is clearly represented in the Hebrew scripture by the double meaning of רוּחַ/wind.[44] Jeremiah 4:11-12 reads: 'At that time this people and Jerusalem will be told, "A scorching wind (רוּחַ) from the barren heights in the desert blows toward my people, but not to winnow or cleanse; a wind (רוּחַ) too strong for that comes from me. Now I pronounce my judgements against them"'. Isaiah 41:15 uses a similar imagery of winnowing as a role of the wind.[45] In short, the overall contextual attention in the winnowing metaphor (Lk. 3:16-17), particularly in the role of the wind as the characterization of the Spirit might interpret the Baptist's prophecy in terms of the coming One's sifting work.

c. Turner's argument that 'John understood himself largely already to have accomplished the sifting process through preaching and baptismal ministry' misleads the whole context of Luke-Acts. This view is beyond doubt one encouraged by Webb's earlier claim that 'it is John's own ministry which has effectively separated the wheat from the chaff, the repentant from the unrepentant... Thus, it is John's ministry which creates this division between these two groups'.[46] This assumption basically contains the meaning that John's ministry (his baptism and preaching) separates Israelites: those who positively respond to his ministry are wheat while those who refuse it are chaff and the expected one's role is only to cleanse the threshing floor. However, this overlooks some points.

First of all, Luke does not clearly describe the scope of John's separating ministry in Israel in the overall context of Luke 3:1-20 and the infancy narrative. Although the nature of John's baptism is represented in the

---

[42] Menzies further claims that 'it is unreasonable to assume that when Luke's audience read the term "spade" rather than "fork" they would have immediately understood the entire metaphor (Luke 3:17) to refer simply to the cleansing of the threshing floor and not sifting as well'. *Spirit and Power*, 95.

[43] Charette, *Spirit*, 45; Marshall, *Luke*, 148. Cf. C.K. Barrett, *The Holy Spirit and the Gospel Tradition* (London: SPCK, 1966), 125-26; E. Best, 'Spirit-Baptism', *NovT* 4 (1960), 240.

[44] J. Nolland, *Luke 1-9:20*, WBC 35a (Dallas: Word, 1989), 153.

[45] 'You will winnow them, the wind (רוּחַ) will pick them up, and a gale will blow them away. But you will rejoice in the LORD and glory in the Holy One of Israel'.

[46] Webb, 'Threshing Floor', 109.

description, 'a baptism of repentance for the forgiveness of sins' (Lk. 3:3), this can hardly be descriptive of John's eschatological separating role for all of Israel. As will be seen, if John's ministry is mainly preparatory to the coming One, Luke fails to specify the means John the Baptist will prepare and use for his people. 'What is already plain is that the scope of John's ministry is limited to Israel'.[47] Luke 3:1-20 is possibly understood as the fulfillment of the earlier prophecy in Luke 1:13-17, 76-79 in which John's ministry is anticipated. The emphasis on John's future function in both prophetic oracles is depicted as forerunner and preparer before and for the Lord. In other words, John's specific role does not lie in the vicissitudes of many in Israel but in preparation for the one who will perform it.[48] Although Luke's Jesus considers the Baptist as a prophetic figure with the highest regard for him (Lk. 7:26-28; cf. 1:76), it does not mean that he sees John (or that John sees himself) as the certain messianic performer. Rather 'the one who pronounced John's greatness could yet turn out to be the Messiah John had foretold'.[49]

Accordingly, secondly, the eschatological judgement of Israel is to be performed not by someone like John the Baptist, but by the Messiah, Jesus.[50] In Luke 2:34, when Simeon prophesies about the child Jesus, he 'is thinking of Jesus' own ministry' by proclaiming that 'this child is set for the fall and rising of many in Israel ('Ἰδοὺ οὗτος κεῖται εἰς πτῶσιν καὶ ἀνάστασιν πολλῶν ἐν τῷ 'Ἰσραὴλ)'.[51] It is *Jesus* (and his mission) who will

---

[47] J.A. Darr, *On Character Building: The Reader and the Rhetoric of Characterization in Luke-Acts* (Louisville: Westminster/John Knox Press, 1992), 69.

[48] The motive of preparing the way in John's ministry is echoed in Mal. 3:1 where the messenger will prepare the way before the Lord. Cf. Darr, *Building*, 63-65. It is generally argued that there is a certain parallelism between Jesus and John in Lk. 1-2 including the annunciation episodes (Lk. 1:8-23, 26-38), the accounts of birth-circumcision (Lk. 1:57-66; 2:16-17), and the prophetic oracles (1:67-79; 2:22-38). While many emphasize the parallelism, (e.g., S. Farris, *The Hymns of Luke's Infancy Narratives: Their Origin, Meaning and Significance*, JSNTS 9 [Sheffield: JSOT Press, 1985], 99-107), Darr importantly compares and contrasts the two, particularly in terms of their specific future ministries. See *Building*, 66-69. However, whereas Darr rightly distinguishes the nature of their ministries by emphasizing John's restriction of his work to Israel, he fails to illustrate the importance of the prophecy of Simeon upon the child Jesus in Lk. 2:34 in his survey. See below in this section for further illustration.

[49] J.C. O'Neill, *Messiah, Six Lectures on the Ministry of Jesus* (Cambridge: Cochrane, 1980), 1-12 (12, 3-4). This further draws attention to the light of the tradition which emphasizes John's role as a witness to Jesus: 'the Son of God' and 'the Lamb of God' in the fourth gospel (Jn. 1). The several simple inferior expressions (e.g., the metaphor of untying the sandal etc.) claimed by John the Baptist in v. 16 indicate his own lower status than the coming One.

[50] Menzies, *Spirit and Power*, 95.

[51] Marshall, *Luke*, 122.

bring the eschatological judgement and redemption by dividing men into two groups, i.e. a separation role (Lk. 12:49-53; cf. 5:32). The fact that the metaphorical usage of the term βαπτίζω in Luke 12:50 means 'overwhelming by deluge', further confirms the future eschatological tribulation to be performed by Jesus.[52]

Furthermore, Luke certainly understands that the fulfillment of the sifting work is accomplished by the Spirit-inspired proclamation of the disciples on the day of Pentecost (Acts 1:5, 8; 11:16) although the final judgement remains still in the future.[53] Thus, the overall descriptions of the role of the coming One before and after Luke 3:17 prevent us proposing that Jesus deals with 'the already-separated piles of grain and chaff'.[54]

d. As already argued in the previous chapter (ch. 2), the first-century Jewish readers did not understand the messianic endowment of the gift of the Spirit as cleansing or purifying the individuals. A variety of Jewish texts show an understanding that the role of the Messiah empowered by the Spirit with a special wisdom and power is closely related to the sifting work of eliminating all the wicked from the nation rather than to a transforming work in individuals (Isa. 4:3-4; *1 En.* 62:2; *Pss. Sol.* 17:26-37; 1 QSb 5:24-25). This tendency is obvious in *Psalms of Solomon* 17. The Messiah, who is powerful in the divine Spirit,

> will gather a holy people whom he will lead in righteousness; and he will judge the tribes of the people that have been made holy by the Lord their God. . . And he himself (will be) free from sin, (in order) to rule a great people. He will expose

---

[52] Turner, altering his old view in his earlier article, 'Spirit Endowment in Luke-Acts: Some Linguistic Considerations', *VoxEv* 12 (1981), 43-63 (50-53), argues that the term βαπτίζω in Lk. 3:16 does not mean 'the catastrophic apocalyptic deluge', but rather connotes to 'wash' or 'cleanse'. See Turner, *Power*, 180-84 (181, 183) for detail of his revised argument. However, if John's prophecy about the eschatological baptism is taken up in Lk. 12:49-50 as Dunn rightly suggests (*Baptism*, 43), Turner's interpretation has a great difficulty since a baptism in Lk. 12:50 clearly means 'the metaphorical sense of being overwhelmed by catastrophe'. See Marshall, *Luke*, 547; 'The Meaning of the Verb "to Baptize"', *EvQ* 45 (1973), 130-40; Nolland, *Luke 1-9:20*, 152-53; Penney, *Missionary*, 35-36.

[53] Menzies, *Development*, 144; Penney, *Missionary*, 20; Marshall, *Luke*, 146.

[54] Cf. Turner's further claim: 'John viewed himself as having in large measure *effected the eschatological sifting of Israel*' (Emphasis is original). However, if John is such a sifting performer, Turner's case is difficult to reconcile with the question of John in Lk. 7:19-20. When John faces a quandary, he, in the passage, expects the coming One as 'a judging figure' (which echoes Lk. 3:16) who will release him from the wicked. If John regarded himself as such a great eschatological performer, why did he expect the eschatological coming One when the time of his imprisonment was getting longer in Lk. 7:19-20 if John's doubt was produced by the delay of Jesus' judgement on Israel? Cf. Witherington, *Jesus*, 42-44. Thus it is unreasonable to attribute such an expectation to John and his ministry.

officials and drive out sinners by the strength of his word (vv. 26 and 36).

The whole chapter of *1 Enoch* 62 depicts the future destiny of the ruling class (the wicked and the sinners) and the righteous ones on the day of judging by the Elect One; the sinners will be frantic while the righteous and elect ones will rejoice over the sinners.[55] Above all, the role of the Spirit in the Messiah's final judgement lies with the sifting and cleansing of Israel, according to Jewish background.

To sum up, the overall picture of the prophecy of John the Baptist, as gathering the righteous (grain) and burning up the wicked (chaff), does not suggest the role of the Spirit as a soteriological necessity in cleansing the repentant individual as Turner argues. It rather suggests that the role of the Spirit in the advent of the messianic eschaton lies in causing a great separation between the righteous (the repentant) and the wicked (the unrepentant) by sifting Israel.[56] From this perspective, it is difficult to understand the Spirit here in John's prophecy as the source of cleansing the individual by transforming the heart.

4.3.2. *The Temptations of Jesus (Lk. 4:1-13)*

The temptation narrative contains numerous significant themes including christology, pneumatology, demonology, several quotations from Deuteronomy etc. and they are intermingled together in the narrative. However, the primary concern for the present study lies in the question of how far the Spirit functions in Jesus' temptation by the evil one. In other words, to what extent does the Spirit function ethically in this narrative?

4.3.2.1. A SYNOPTIC STUDY OF THE TEMPTATION NARRATIVE

All three Synoptic writers record the temptation narrative. Mark's version (Mk. 1:12-13) is brief and gives little explicit information about Jesus' three-fold temptation, while both Matthew and Luke (Mt. 4:1-11; Lk. 4:1-13) have a longer form with the details of the accounts.[57] However, the

---

[55] In *1 En.* 62, the messianic epithets are described as both the Elect one (v. 1) and the Son of Man (vv. 5, 7, 9). But this is a different way of expression indicating the same character so that it does not influence his general messianic role. Vanderkam, 'Biblical Interpretation', 116.

[56] It is notable that the verb συνάγω in the LXX is frequently used 'in contexts describing the eschatological restoration of Israel'. This is particularly prevalent in the texts of Isaiah such as 27:12; 34:16; 3:10. For example, Isa. 34:16 reads: 'They passed by in *full* number, and not one of them perished: they sought not one another; for the Lord commanded them, and his Spirit gathered them' (καὶ τὸ πνεῦμα αὐτοῦ συνήγαγεν αὐτάς). Charette, *Spirit*, 45, n. 36.

[57] Although there is little overlap in substance with Mark's brief account, it is generally assumed that the Lukan (Matthew) temptation narrative is explained as a Mark-Q

order of the temptations is shifted in Matthew and Luke: both of them put the first temptation (turning stones into loaves of bread) in the first place, but while Matthew takes Jesus' leading to the pinnacle of the Temple in the second place and to a high mountain as the third, Luke's version has these two in reverse order. Most scholars agree that Matthew's order is originally maintained in Q.[58] Luke's reason for putting the Temple in the third and last position can be theologically explained, i.e., in the light of his view of salvation history, Jerusalem (where there is the Temple) plays a central role.[59]

The account of Jesus' temptation is situated after his baptism and prior to his public mission in all three Synoptics. But it is only Luke who inserts the genealogy (Lk. 3:23-38) before the temptation narrative. Beyond these differences, what is notable in relation to our present discussion is Luke's unique redaction of the opening verse of the narrative.

4.3.2.2. LUKAN DISTINCTIVE REDACTION IN THE OPENING VERSE

While the three Evangelists basically agree that Jesus was led by the Spirit into the wilderness, Luke's account has some unique alterations with the double reference to the Spirit.

Mt. 4:1. Τότε ὁ Ἰησοῦς ἀνήχθη εἰς τὴν ἔρημον ὑπὸ τοῦ πνεύματος.	Mk. 1:12. Καὶ εὐθὺς τὸ πνεῦμα αὐτὸν ἐκβάλλει εἰς τὴν ἔρημον.	Lk. 4:1. Ἰησοῦς δὲ πλήρης πνεύματος ἁγίου ὑπέστρεψεν ἀπὸ τοῦ Ἰορδάνου καὶ ἤγετο ἐν τῷ πνεύματι ἐν τῇ ἐρήμῳ.

There are some notable redactional alterations of Luke which differ from Mark and Matthew: 1) Luke adds the phrase 'πλήρης πνεύματος ἁγίου'; 2) Luke uses ἄγω instead of ἀνάγω (Matthew) and ἐκβάλλω (Mark); 3) Luke employs the prepositional phrase ἐν τῷ πνεύματι instead of ὑπὸ τοῦ πνεύματος (Matthew) and τὸ πνεῦμα (Mark); 4) Luke uses the preposition evn in the phrase 'in the desert' instead of εἰς (Mark and Matthew). With

---

overlap. C.M. Tuckett, 'The Temptation Narrative in Q', in F. van Segbroeck (ed.), *The Four Gospels* (Leuven: LUP, 1992), 479.

[58] E.g., Fitzmyer, *Luke 1-IX*, 165. The reason is usually suggested as follows: 1) Matthew's order keeps a progression from desert to Temple and then to high mountain; 2) Matthew's quotation from Deuteronomy is a tidy reverse order (Deut. 8:3; 6:16, 13); 3) Matthew's maintenance of the theme of Jesus' sonship in the first two temptations. Cf. Marshall, *Luke*, 166-68.

[59] W.R. Stegner, 'The Use of Scripture in Two Narratives of Early Jewish Christianity (Matthew 4:1-11; Mark 9:2-8)', in C.A. Evans and J.A. Sanders (eds.) *Early Christian Interpretation of the Scriptures of Israel: Investigations and Proposals*, JSNTS 148 (Sheffield: SAP, 1997), 99.

these Lukan redactional changes, it is generally argued that the Spirit functions as the main agent in Jesus' success over Satan so that the Spirit is understood as the source of Jesus' moral determination. Those who argue for this depend entirely on the importance of Lukan redaction in this opening verse. While this is not impossible, there is also a high probability of not interpreting it in this way in the light of both examinations of Lukan redaction and particularly the whole context of the narrative.

a. A syntactical analysis of Lukan redaction in the opening verse should be firstly sought for our purpose. As seen above, there is primarily one Lukan redactional addition (πλήρης πνεύματος ἁγίου) and three Lukan modifications in one phrase, 'ἤγετο ἐν τῷ πνεύματι ἐν τῇ ἐρήμῳ'. On the basis of the former, Turner argues that since the phrase denotes a 'long-term state of affairs' and characterizes an endowment of some duration, which is in contrast with 'filled (πίμπλημι) with the Spirit' which defines rather a definite event of short duration, Jesus while in the wilderness is said to be led by the Spirit and this indicates that the Spirit functions as a helper of Jesus.[60] However, it should be pointed out that Turner's attempt to distinguish between the two expressions is not fully supported in Luke. The phrase 'full of the Holy Spirit' is not uniquely used of Jesus in the narrative, but is also used several times in his second volume (Acts 6:3, 5; 7:55; 11:24). Note that Luke uses the phrase three times of Stephen. This indicates that the phrase rather connotes his special and sudden state of inspiration, which is more or less temporary and passes away when its purpose has been accomplished. This is particularly clear in Acts 7:55 ('But Stephan, full of the Holy Spirit [πλήρης πνεύματος ἁγίου] looked up to heaven and saw the glory of God, and Jesus standing at the right hand of God') in which Stephen's visionary experience denotes a transitory state of inspiration.[61] All this suggests that to make a sharp contrast between the two phrases requires some caution.

A better understanding of the phrase seems rather to refer to the moment of Jesus' highest elevated spiritual status referring to his baptismal anointing at Jordan.[62] Unlike Matthew and Mark, Luke specifies the general locale, Jordan, where he was filled with the Spirit and might possibly describe the spiritual status of Jesus in his subsequent narrative having this crucial event in mind. Having been anointed by the Spirit at Jordan, Jesus experiences the fullness of the Spirit as the unique bearer of the Spirit.[63]

b. In regard to Luke's alteration of the phrase ἤγετο ἐν τῷ πνεύματι ἐν

---

[60] Turner, *Power*, 165-69, 202.
[61] There is also a crucial exception to Turner's suggestion on 'filled with the Spirit', as a definite event of short duration. This is in Lk. 1:15 where the phrase is used in future reference implying almost a permanent state.
[62] Menzies, *Development*, 157.
[63] Stronstad, *Prophethood*, 43.

τῇ ἐρήμῳ, there is little significance in the passive verb ἤγετο compared with Matthew and Mark in terms of the Spirit's role. One different connotation from Mark's version is, as usually suggested, that Luke's use of the verb ἄγω softens Mark's ἐκβάλλω but 'the difference is trivial and mostly stylistic'.[64] The simple stylistic difference may be particularly compared with Matthew's passive verb ἀνήχθη and as Bock comments, 'each uses different terminology to express the same idea'.[65] In regard to the phrase ἐν τῷ πνεύματι, Turner argues that Luke's modifying phrase ἐν τῷ πνεύματι rather than ὑπὸ τοῦ πνεύματος qualifies Jesus' direct subordination to the Spirit by indicating him (the Spirit) as an agent.[66] But there seems little reason to distinguish the two phrases except for the idea of Jesus' subordination to the Spirit in leading him to the desert. The two phrases are elsewhere used in Luke as functional equivalents. For example, in Luke 2:26-27, Simeon was informed by the Spirit (ὑπὸ τοῦ πνεύματος) concerning his encounter with Christ before his death and immediately he entered into the temple by the Spirit (ἐν τῷ πνεύματι). This example suggests that the syntactical difference between the two is not as clear as Turner argues. Also with the case of Luke's alteration of the verb (ἄγω), this modification is involved with Luke's stylistic reasons simply to indicate that Jesus' trial was originated by divine guidance.[67] Finally, the difference between the two prepositional phrases, Luke's 'in (ἐν) the desert' and Matthew's and Mark's 'into (εἰς) the desert' is minor in view of the importance of the theme of the prior phrase, ἤγετο ἐν τῷ πνεύματι, being led *there* under divine direction.[68]

In short, it seems that the outcome of a syntactical analysis of Lukan redaction does not signal any theological weight. It rather simply gives us the idea that Jesus is led by the Spirit with his spiritual status (full of the Holy Spirit) and after that Luke does not specify whether the role of the Spirit has been clearly presented in Jesus' triumph over the evil. The general context of the narrative confirms this notion.

4.3.2.3. THE AGENT OF JESUS' MORAL DETERMINATION: SPIRIT?

More decisively, when taking into account the overall context of the narrative, the agent of Jesus' success over the temptation is rather his use of

---

[64] Penney, *Missionary*, 41. The overemphasis of Schweizer's claim, i.e., the Lukan emphasis on Jesus as the Lord of the Spirit, has been widely criticized by others. Cf. Marshall, *Luke*, 168; Turner, *Power*, 203; Menzies, *Development*, 155-57.

[65] D.L. Bock, *Luke 1:1-9:50*, BECNT 3 (Grand Rapids: Baker, 1994), 369; F. Bovon, *Das Evangelium nach Lukas*: *Lk 1:1-9:50* (Zürich: Benziger Verlag, 1989), 194.

[66] Turner, *Power*, 203.

[67] Menzies, *Development*, 156-57.

[68] Gibson, following Swete and Klostermann, argues that Mark's Jesus is already in the wilderness like Luke's reading, 'in the wilderness'. See J.B. Gibson, 'Jesus' Wilderness Temptation according to Mark', *JSNT* 53 (1994), 16, n. 47.

Scripture than the Spirit. Jesus turns aside the three-fold temptation with use of quotations from Deuteronomy (Lk. 4:4, 8, 12). Jesus' fidelity to Scripture in the third temptation against the evil one's misuse of it further confirms that the main agent in this match is 'Scripture'.[69] Furthermore, the importance of Jesus' use of Scripture in this unique situation is that this narrative is the only case where the OT is explicitly quoted in Luke (Q) except Luke (Q) 7:27.[70] The whole narrative further shows that the Lukan Jesus is not simply portrayed as the one who cites Scripture but as being faithful and obedient to it.[71]

As many agree, the temptation narrative shows the interplay between the activity of Jesus and that of the people of Israel. References to 'the wilderness', 'testing' and a period of 'forty days' link up together in the two episodes and support this.[72] But the typology between these two is unique: while the people of Israel were disobedient and failed the test, Jesus was obedient and remained faithful to God. In this respect, the relationship between the two is 'a special kind of typology in which one serves as an anti-type to the other'.[73] The focus that Luke wants to make throughout the whole narrative is thus to distinguish between Jesus' triumph over the tempter and Israel's failure (and to encourage the church through this story). However, what should be remembered in this typological comparison is the manifestation of the Spirit in both situations. The presence of the Spirit is clearly described in Israel's desert wandering as an agent of providential leading for the people according to Nehemiah 9:20 (cf. Isa. 63:14).[74] However, the unfaithful Israelites' stiff-necks resisted the gracious offer of God and they had failed his test by *grieving the Spirit* according to Isa. 63:10. In a strikingly similar situation, Jesus, the new representative of Israel, successfully passed the test by being faithful to Scripture. Clearly,

---

[69] F. Bovon, 'The Role of the Scriptures in the Composition of the Gospel Accounts: The Temptations of Jesus (Lk. 4:1-13 par.) and the Multiplication of the Loaves (Lk. 9:10-17 par.)', in G. O'Collins and G. Marconi (eds.), *Luke and Acts* (New York/Manwah: Paulist Press, 1993), 30.

[70] Cf. Tuckett, 'Temptation Narrative', 481.

[71] Tuckett, 'Temptation Narrative', 487. Cf. also Bovon's claim that 'In the episode of the temptations the scriptures do not provide the form of the story. . . but they do serve as an explicitly cited norm for the decisions and actions of Jesus, who is presented as hero of faith and obedience'. Bovon, 'Role of the Scriptures', 26-27.

[72] Stegner, 'Use of Scripture', 103-05; Gibson, 'Temptation', 15-16; D.L. Bock, 'Proclamation from Prophecy and Pattern: Luke's Use of the Old Testament for Christology and Mission', in C.A. Evans and W.R. Stegner (eds.), *The Gospels and the Scriptures of Israel*, JSNTS 104 (Sheffield: SAP, 1994), 289; Bovon, 'Role of the Scriptures', 31.

[73] Stegner, 'Use of Scripture', 105.

[74] Neh. 9:20 reads 'You (God) gave the good Spirit to instruct them'. The presence of the Holy Spirit upon Israel in the wilderness is also indicated in rabbinic tradition. See *Exod. R.* 23:2.

the issue of faithfulness or fidelity to the word of God is the core of both of the tests.[75]

This judgement requires a degree of caution when comparing Jesus' temptation with that of Israel in the desert. Indeed, many scholars rightly draw a parallelism between the two in terms of the outcomes of both tests, but unfortunately ignore the 'causes' of each outcome particularly in terms of pneumatology. For instance, Wenk, following Turner, argues that;

> As Israel was led by God while in the desert, Jesus is led by God through the Spirit during the 40 days of testing in a way that made the Spirit's help manifest. This suggests that Luke thought that just as Yahweh led Israel through the desert experience and provided for the people, so the Spirit was the continuous help and guide for the anointed messiah and led him through his time of testing in the wilderness.[76]

While Wenk rightly points out the divine initiative in terms of 'leading' to the desert in both oracles, his statement however ignores two important factors: 1) The Spirit was also given to Israel to *instruct* her people while they were in the desert (Neh. 9:20) like Jesus; 2) The outcome of the test is entirely different. Jesus returns in triumph, ἐν τῇ δυνάμει τοῦ πνεύματος (Lk. 4:14)[77] while Israel, with failure, grieved the Spirit (Isa. 63:10). What is evidently implied in the two is that the Spirit of God is present in both cases but the victory is given only to the faithful one, Jesus. The logic is clear: Israel's failure is due to her unfaithfulness in spite of the leading and instruction of the Spirit of God, but Jesus' success is entirely due to his own fidelity. In other words, Jesus is worthy to be the bearer of the Spirit while the unfaithful Israel causes the Spirit to be grieved and depart.[78]

---

[75] Bock, *Luke 1:1-9:50*, 383; Gibson, 'Temptation', 15. Gibson further points out that there is 'a strong correlation between the concept denoted by the phrase ἡ ἔρημος and that of "testing" of obedience, . . . In Mark's time, then, to say that one was *in* the ἔρημος (i.e. the "wilderness" of the exodus) was a kind of shorthand way of saying that one's faithfulness was being "put to the test"' (16).

[76] Wenk, *Community*, 199.

[77] One may argue that since the Spirit enabled Jesus to overcome the temptation (cause), Jesus returned to Galilee in the power of the Spirit (outcome). But in light of Israel's example, Luke's point is the other way. Since Jesus remained faithful (cause), he (and his very faithfulness) is worthy to be a *Pneumatiker* by filling with the Spirit, not grieving the Spirit. Rabbinic perspective in several relevant references is strikingly similar with Luke and supports this (*b. Sot.* 48b; *b. Sanh.* 11a; *t. Sot.* 13:4, *MHG* Gen. 140). For instance, *t. Sot.* 13:4 reads: 'There is among you a man who is worthy to receive the Holy Spirit, but the generation is unworthy of such an honor'. ET by J. Neusner, *The Tosefta*, III, *Nashim (The Order of Women)* (New York: KTAV, 1979), 102.

[78] Menzies similarly observes this fact by re-reading Turner's statement about the parallelism between the two: 'Turner himself notes that "the final temptations echo

This argument goes back to the question about the source of Jesus' moral determination in the temptation narrative. The larger context supports Jesus' faithfulness to God and Scripture as the main agent in triumphing over the temptation rather than any other aspects. Of course, there is little reason to deny the Lukan emphasis on the Spirit in the opening verse but this emphasis should not be understood in terms of the direct role or agent of Jesus' moral determination. This is because, as argued above, Jesus' main triumphal agent in the face of a moral defilement is his remaining faithful to God (and his Word). This does not mean that the Spirit makes Jesus worthy. Rather the Spirit comes and rests on Jesus because he is worthy. Therefore, it is important to consider Luke's point as follows: Jesus' faithfulness is not so much derived from the Spirit's empowerment but that because Jesus is faithful, he can be the bearer of the Spirit. As Marsh argues: 'the Spirit is not a power at the disposal of Jesus, an agent he can put to work; rather Jesus is the agent directed by the Spirit'.[79]

4.3.3. Summaries of Community Life (Acts 2:42-47; 4:32-37; cf. 5:12-16)

The summaries of community life are generally recognized in the book of Acts as being 2:42-47; 4:32-35 and 5:12-16. They show the inner as well as the outer life of the early church in Jerusalem from a basically positive point of view.[80] But the negative aspect within the community exists in the panoramic scene of Acts 5:1-11 and 6:1-6, and it is often argued that it should not be underestimated in the study of the summaries of the community life. The major discussion relating to the summaries has frequently been with the questions of 'a primitive communism', 'primitive Christian social welfare' or 'the realization of Hellenistic friendship in the community'.[81] In regard to the Lukan pneumatological perspective, the

---

Israel's in the wilderness, but while they rebelled and grieved his Holy Spirit there (Isa 63:10), the new representative of Israel remains faithful and overcomes the tempter". The point is clear: unlike Israel of old, Jesus demonstrates that he is worthy to be the bearer of the Spirit'. *Spirit and Power*, 96.

[79] T. Marsh, 'Holy Spirit in Early Christian Teaching', in W. Harrington (ed.), *Witness to the Spirit: Essays on Revelation, Spirit, Redemption* (Manchester: Koinonia, 1979), 63. See also K. Warrington, *Jesus the Healer: Paradigm or Unique Phenomenon?* (Carlisle: Paternoster, 2000), 156.

[80] Treating the summaries of the community life in Acts, most commentators often ignore the outer life of the community while they over-emphasize the inner life. However, the outer life of witness evidently dominates the summaries: witness by works of power (Acts 2:43; 4:33a; 5:12, 15-16); witness by words of power (2:47; 4:33b). See Stronstad, *Prophethood*, 77-84 (80-84).

[81] M. Hengel, *Property and Riches in the Early Church: Aspects of a Social History of Christianity* (Philadelphia: Fortress Press, 1974), 31-34; E. Haenchen, *The Acts of the Apostles: A Commentary* (Oxford: Blackwell, 1971), 233-35; D.P. Seccombe, *Possessions and the Poor in Luke-Acts* (Linz: SNTU, 1982), 119-214 (202-07);

interpretation of these passages has been debated as to whether or not the Spirit functions as the source of the ethical life of the community.

4.3.3.1. THE AGENT OF THE COMMUNITY'S MORAL LIFE: SPIRIT?

Gunkel's influential interpretation on the passages which says that there is no indication that 'the ideal state of community described derives from the Spirit' is still supported by contemporary scholars, while Büchsel's interpretation that the love and sacrifice presented in the earliest church (Acts 2:42-47; 4:32-37) is prompted by the Spirit is at the same time influential.[82] In particular, the latter's view has been recently developed by some scholars. For instance, Turner argues that the Spirit, as the source of the ethical life, is the direct cause of the community life summarized in Acts 2:42-47 and 4:32-37. He argues that these passages are such as to naturally follow the diffusion of the Spirit although there is literally 'not a syllable' to indicate the function of the Spirit in the life of the community. Turner goes on to assert that;

> Acts 2:42-47 follows so immediately (with 2:41) upon Peter's promise, that the reader naturally assumes the state of affairs described there is a measure of the impact of the promised Spirit on the community. The lack of any specific comment about the Spirit in 2:42-47, to earth the tense expectation built up from 2:1-11 through to 2:38-39, serves only to strengthen the reader's assumption.[83]

However, at first sight, there is a certain overstatement made by Turner in the above. As Menzies points out, the 'tense expectation' that Turner assumes 'would not have been felt by Luke's first-century readers' (including Theophilus) but 'is generated by his (Turner's) own theological presupposition'.[84] An absence of any mention of the Spirit in the passage simply indicates this fact.[85] Additionally, some textual and contextual

---

A.C. Mitchell, 'The Social Function of Friendship in Acts 2:44-47 and 4:32-37', *JBL* 111 (1992), 255-72; B. Capper, 'The Palestinian Cultural Context of Earliest Christian Community of Goods', in B.W. Winter (ed.), *The Book of Acts in Its First Century Setting*, 4 (Grand Rapids: Eerdmans, 1995), 323-56.

[82] Gunkel, *Influential*, 16; Büchsel, *Geist Gottes*, 254.

[83] *Power*, 414; *Holy Spirit*, 49.

[84] Menzies, *Spirit and Power*, 96-97.

[85] Schweizer, 'πνεῦμα', 412. This sort of unwarranted assumption is often practised by some scholars in other instances such as the descriptions of the life of the Samaritan community in Acts 8:5-13. For instance, according to Oulton, although there is no mention about the Spirit, it is possible for the Samaritans to possess the Spirit before the coming of the apostles in the light of the similarity with the community life in Jerusalem. J.E.L. Oulton, 'The Holy Spirit, Baptism, and Laying on of Hands in Acts', *ExpT* 66 (1955), 236-40 (238). But clearly, Luke depicts the baptized believers who have not yet received the Spirit in Acts 8:16 and declines to identify the Spirit as the source of the ethical life of the Samaritan community like that of Jerusalem.

observations in the passages lead to a different conclusion from that of Turner.

4.3.3.1.1. A Textual Consideration

The power of the Spirit, with little doubt, may directly or indirectly function in the making of the new community. Nonetheless, in the light of Scripture, it is unlikely to associate the Spirit with the moral life of the community. The clear scriptural basis for the motivation and source of their moral activities rather supports human response to God's saving acts. In Acts 4:33, Luke announces that 'great grace (χάρις τε μεγάλη) was upon them all'[86] (cf. 2:47: ἔχοντες χάριν πρὸς ὅλον τὸν λαόν). Here the phrase 'great grace' means that it operated among the congregation in response to God's salvation. The word χάρις is Lukan (and Pauline) in comparison with the other evangelists and is frequently associated with the message of salvation (Lk. 4:22; Acts 14:3; 20:24, 32).[87] The state of χάρις of the community results from this salvific message through the witness of the apostles (Acts 4:33). Luke (in Peter's expression) elsewhere proclaims that this grace is the only means of salvation for all (Acts 15:11). Luke also testifies that the overruling of χάρις encourages the church to remain faithful to the Lord (Acts 11:23). In Acts 4:34f., Luke then states the immediate outcome of its overruling among the Christian community in terms of the interests of others, i.e., sharing possessions. In a later chapter of Acts, Luke offers a similar story. Apollos, by his grace (διὰ τῆς χάριτος),[88] greatly helped the believers in Achaia (18:27). This all suggests that a possible source of the communal generosity within the community is the human response rather than the gift of the Spirit.[89] Without any unnecessary assumption, a clearly *mentioned* source of the community's standard life is God's grace experienced through the words of grace. As Marshall points out, 'The activity of God's grace was seen not merely in the preaching, but also in the way in which the members of the church were freed from material need'.[90]

---

[86] The terms 'them all' refer to the whole congregation and link with v. 34 rather than refer to only to the apostles. Haenchen, *Acts*, 231; I.H. Marshall, *The Acts of the Apostles*, TNTC 5 (Grand Rapids: Eerdmans, 1992), 109; B. Witherington, *The Acts of the Apostles: A Socio-Rhetorical Commentary* (Grand Rapids: Eerdmans, 1998), 207.

[87] H. Conzelmann, 'χάρις', *TDNT*, IX, 392.

[88] Witherington renders the phrase διὰ τῆς χάριτος with those who had become believers. *Acts*, 568. But a more plausible reading is suggested by others as the way of our present interpretation. See Marshall, *Acts*, 304; Conzelmann, 'χάρις', 393.

[89] One may argue that the Spirit is the supplier of the grace. But, the present text does not indicate such a notion, but rather shows the immanence of God.

[90] Marshall, *Acts*, 109.

4.3.3.1.2. Contextual Considerations: The Conflicts in the Community (Acts 5:1-11; Acts 6:1)

It is crucial to look at the function of the summaries of the community life within the overall context of the early church rather than as isolated individual passages. Witherington states that 'it is wrong to take these summary passages *in isolation* from the source material they link together. Studying the summaries alone leads to distortion and false impressions'.[91] Agreeing with the statement in terms of pneumatology, it should be noted that Luke, in the summaries of the community life, has not merely idealized the inner life of the community.[92] This can be seen in some darker examples such as 'the story of Ananias and Sapphira' (Acts 5:1-11) and 'the problem of the lack of support for the Hellenistic widows' (Acts 6:1) which Luke frankly presents.[93] Two opposing expressions, 'one heart and soul' (Acts 4:32, cf. v. 34) and 'complaining' (Acts 6:1) concerning one community simply show this fact. Therefore, if it is right that Luke has not intended to describe an over-favourable picture of the community,[94] it is difficult to simply match the work of the Spirit with the various negative features of the community.

a. Concerning the story of Ananias and Sapphira, it may be possible to assume that the moral characteristic of the Spirit monitors the lie of Ananias and Sapphira.[95] However, Luke intends to draw a picture not simply to give an idea of the Spirit of holiness, but more probably to show how the prophetic nature of the Spirit works in Peter with special insight to see their deception, which is offensive to the Spirit and brings a disastrous judgement upon them.[96] Undoubtedly, the whole story leans towards 'the lie' of the couple, which threatens the unity of the community, but Luke's pneumatological perspective gives more weight to the prophetic insight and ability of Peter in whom the Spirit is operating.[97] The similar prophetic

---

[91] Witherington, *Acts*, 157. Emphasis is original.

[92] R.C. Tannehill, *The Narrative Unity of Luke-Acts: A Literary Interpretation*, II. *The Acts of the Apostles* (Philadelphia: Fortress Press, 1990), 80-81.

[93] Apart from the Jerusalem church, Luke also presents a record of problems in the early Christian communities as appearing in Acts 8:18-24; 9:26-28; 11:1-18; 15:1-35; and 21:20-36.

[94] Seccombe argues that the story of Ananias and Sapphira is to be seen 'within the framework of the "summaries" of the life of the early church'. *Possessions*, 199, 209, n. 60. Witherington further argues that the story presented in Acts 6:1-7 (along with Acts 5) is an example of friction in the earliest Christian community. These are clear evidence that it is not Luke's intention to simply gloss over the problems in the community. *Acts*, 247.

[95] Turner, *Power*, 403.

[96] Menzies, *Development*, 224, n. 2.

[97] It is possible to say that lying to the community is also lying to the Spirit in Acts 5:3 so that the Spirit can impact the ethical life of the community. But more careful

action of the Spirit appears in the ministry of Paul in Acts 13:8-11. Paul, whose status looks to be prophetic, filled with the Spirit (v. 9), looks *intently* at Elymas, a morally defiled person, with extraordinary insight and strikes him with blindness. The actions of the Spirit in both Peter and Paul are understood in a prophetic sense in their ongoing prophetic lineage.

b. Moreover, when breakdown happens in the community in the context of the continuing growth of the church (Acts 6:1) and accordingly when better organization is required for the community, the disciples choose seven qualified men who should be good and *full of the Spirit and wisdom*. The condition for becoming the new administrators for the community includes the 'fullness of the Spirit'. This indicates that *not all* the members of the community have been spiritually qualified although their moral life may reach a good standard. In other words, the members of the community are not all filled and used by the Spirit. The conflict between 'Hellenists' and 'Hebrews' in the church simply shows the different status of the spirituality of the members of the community.[98] This may suggest that it is difficult to attribute the Spirit as being the direct source of the unity and moral life of the church.

On the other hand, concerning Stephen, one of the chosen seven, one may argue that the characterization of Stephen's being 'full of the Spirit' is connected mainly with serving tables as in Acts 6:2-3. However, Luke clearly points out that there is a shift in Stephen's role, i.e., from serving tables to speaking the word of God and performing wonders and signs (Acts 6:8, 10; 7:55) as the apostles have been practising (Acts 2:43; 5:12). In other words, being 'full of the Spirit and wisdom' Stephen was initially appointed as an inner server (human organization), and then he becomes a powerful missionary as a witness (Spirit-working) which is a more dominant feature than the former. A very similar story is also shown in the case of Philip. Like Stephen, as will be seen, the Spirit-filled Philip's dominant ministry is not serving tables, but preaching the word of good news for the Gentiles (Acts 8:1-12).

c. Finally, it is notable that the description of community life is recorded only in the earlier part of Acts (chapters 2, 4 and 5). This generally suggests that Luke intentionally depicts the primordial beginning of the community to his readers.[99] However, one remaining question should be asked in this regard: why does Luke record these summaries only in the earlier part of his book if the Spirit affects their moral life although in what follows there are numerous examples of the outpourings of the Spirit? As a matter of fact,

---

reading of the text shows that the ethical impact of the Spirit *indirectly* effects it *through* the prophetic activity.

[98] Of course, there are some possible reasons behind the conflict such as the difference in language and culture.

[99] L.T. Johnson, *Sharing Possessions: Mandate and Symbol of Faith* (London: SCM Press, 1981), 128.

after Acts 5, Luke frequently describes the outpourings of the Spirit both on communities (Acts 8:17; 10:44; 10:6; 19:6) and individuals (Acts 6:8; 7:55; 8:29, 39; 9:17; 10:19; 11:12, 28; 13:2, 4, 9; 16:6-7), but without any detailed descriptions of their internal life. Rather they are almost always related to the outward witness: prophetic activities such as speaking in tongues, miraculous works, or prophecy and missionary activities. From the outpouring of the Spirit at Pentecost comes a similar impact upon the community: missiological power (Acts 1:8), miraculous language (Acts 2:4-13) and prophetic inspiration (Acts 2:4-11). What then is Luke's general concern about the outpouring of the Spirit throughout the book of Acts from this perspective? We may suggest that it is not Luke's general view that the outpouring of the Spirit is responsible for the community's moral life. As Tannehill rightly argues, Luke is much more concerned with the outward witness and its effects rather than the inner life of the Christian communities.[100]

To sum up, the various lines of evidence suggest that one is not necessarily forced to read the ethical conduct of the community life primarily in terms of its pneumatological origin. Rather the activities of the community are understood in terms of human response to God's saving acts (χάρις). On a scriptural basis, there is only a subtle and indirect (i.e., the Spirit produces prophecy which impacts ethical behaviour) link between the Spirit and the summaries of the moral life of the community.

4.3.4. Summary

Luke's association of the Spirit with an ethical dimension in the relevant texts is rare and not clear. Although Luke relates the Spirit to ethical transformation in the summaries of the community life, it is only presented in an indirect way, i.e., through the impact of prophetic speech. Luke's way of presentation is significantly distinct from Paul. For him, without any doubt, the Spirit liberates the people of God from the power of sin and enables them to live righteously. Certainly, from an ethical viewpoint, there exists a contraposition in their pneumatologies.[101]

4.4. The Spirit and Resurrection

In chapter 3, we have observed that Paul clearly attributes the resurrection to the activity of the Spirit so that there is no doubt that for Paul the Spirit functions as the source of kingdom blessings. However, when turning to the

---

[100] Tannehill, *Narrative*, II, 80-82.
[101] However, this does not mean that the perspectives of Luke and Paul are incompatible even if they are different. This is simply a reflection of Paul's fuller and more developed pneumatology. This can also be seen from Paul's closer association of the work of the Spirit with new life, sonship, resurrection, and righteousness.

issue of the Lukan material, it is not difficult to find that the connection between the resurrection and the Spirit is remarkably absent.[102]

Nevertheless, some interpreters attempt to associate the Spirit with the resurrection in Luke-Acts. But it appears that they usually fail to properly explain the relationship between the two. For instance, Lodahl argues that the Spirit is the main agent of Jesus' and the believers' resurrection in both Paul and Luke. But he simply quotes Acts 2:24, 32-33 in supporting the Lukan notion on the issue without any supporting exegetical illustration whilst supporting the notion primarily from Pauline material.[103] In a similar manner, Hawthorne, who also regards the Spirit as the agent of Jesus' resurrection, quotes numerous passages concerning Jesus' resurrection from Acts, but explains its agent, the Spirit, from Pauline material such as Romans 1:3-4.[104] This merely warns us that any discussion of Luke's connection between the Spirit and the resurrection through Pauline spectacles is unsafe.

To a lesser degree than the scholars mentioned above, as discussed earlier, Horn has argued that the recognition of the resurrection of Jesus as the work of the Spirit is the foundation of the early tradition. Against Horn's claim, we have pointed out two reasons for rejecting it,[105] one of which is that the attribution of the resurrection to the Spirit is remarkably absent apart from the Pauline epistles, particularly in Luke (and the other Synoptics) and Acts. However, we have not yet discussed the notion in Luke-Acts in detail for a structural reason. In this section, it is naturally necessary to investigate how far the Spirit is related to the resurrection in Luke-Acts.[106]

As seen above, in Luke's gospel (and the other evangelists), Jesus, who seems to follow the line of Pharisaic tradition rather than that of the Sadducees[107] speaks of his *belief* in the resurrection. He, not only believes in it, but also *performs* miracles of resuscitation (Lk. 7:11-17; 8:40-42, 49-56). Furthermore, Jesus *teaches* his followers about the future resurrection,

---

[102] Likewise, in chapter 2 (§2.5), we observed that the association between the Spirit and resurrection is virtually absent from the intertestamental literature.

[103] M.E. Lodahl, *Shekhinah, Spirit: Divine Presence in Jewish and Christian Religion* (New York: Paulist Press, 1992), 183-88.

[104] G.F. Hawthorne, 'Holy Spirit', *DLNTD*, 491-92. A similar exegetical failure to illustrate the relationship between the Spirit and resurrection in Luke is also seen in some articles. E.g., D.J. Davies, 'Rebouncing Vitality: Resurrection and Spirit in Luke-Acts', in M.D. Carroll, D. Clines, and P. Davies (eds.), *The Bible in Human Society: Essays in Honour of John Rogerson*, JSOTS 200 (Sheffield: SAP, 1995), 205-24.

[105] See n. 144 in chapter 3.

[106] Since the other evangelists have the same view in this regard, I will only discuss Luke's gospel and Acts, which is the scope of this study.

[107] Lk. 20:27-38 (cf. Mk. 12:18-27; Mt. 22:23-33).

eternal life in the kingdom of God (Lk. 18:18-30).[108] Is it then not surprising to know that in this threefold account concerning resurrection, i.e., 'belief in resurrection', 'its performance' and 'teaching about it', Luke's (and the other evangelists') Jesus never attributes it to the activity of the Spirit? In addition, Luke presents Jesus' own resurrection in detail (Lk. 24) but without reference to the Spirit.

One would expect a connection between the Spirit and the resurrection in the context of the exaltation of the risen Lord and the outpouring of the Spirit, and in the post-resurrection community in the book of Acts. Indeed there are plenty of references to the resurrection in Acts. However, it is generally known that Luke does not introduce a new doctrine of the resurrection in Acts, but rather mainly views it as the apostolic announcement that Jesus is Lord.[109] Nonetheless, Luke fails to connect the Spirit to the resurrection in Acts as in his gospel. While the reference to the general resurrection of believers is notably rare in Acts,[110] Jesus' resurrection is widely and rhetorically represented in the testimonies of Peter, Stephen, and Paul (Acts 2:24, 32; 3:15; 4:10; 5:30; 7:37; 10:40; 13:30, 33, 34, 37; 17:31; cf. 24:21; 26:8, 23). Luke, in this persistent refrain of Jesus' resurrection, clearly portrays *God* as the agent who raises the crucified Jesus. One possible link between the Spirit and resurrection appears in Acts 2:32-33 as Lodahl attempts to connect them. But, as the passage suggests, God is depicted as the agent rather than the Spirit.[111]

4.4.1. The Spirit and the Proclamation of the Resurrection

If it is so, how does Luke show the relationship between these two? Is there any point in him connecting them? As observed above, Luke in Acts presents the resurrection (of Jesus) in the core proclamations and announcements of the apostles. In many cases, surprisingly, there is Spirit-inspired speech behind the announcements of the resurrection by the apostles. Peter, in 'a Spirit-filled state', announced that God raised Jesus (Acts 2:33; 3:15; 4:10, 20; 10:40-43; cf. 4:8). 'The Spirit-filled apostles' preached the 'resurrection of the dead' (Acts 4:2, 33). Paul, 'filled with the

---

[108] Cf. Mt. 19:16-30; Mk. 10:17-31.

[109] E.g., C.F. Evans, *Resurrection and the New Testament* (London: SCM Press, 1970), 132-35.

[110] But, Luke records the general resurrection in Acts 4:2; 26:8; cf. 24:15. Although Luke (in the apostles' proclamations) depicts the resurrection of believers by reference to the case of Jesus, it does not have the Pauline implication that the resurrection of Jesus, as the first-fruits, initiates and guarantees the future resurrection of believers. Evans, *Resurrection*, 134.

[111] By contrast, as observed earlier, Paul clearly links the Spirit with the resurrection of both Jesus and the believer (Rom. 1:3-4; 6:4; 8:11; 1 Cor. 6:14; 15:44-46; 2 Cor. 13:4 etc.).

Spirit', proclaimed the resurrection of Jesus (Acts 13:30-34, 37). Although the role of the Spirit is generally and broadly understood as proclamation in Luke, his association of the Spirit-inspired speech with the resurrection which is treated as the core of apostolic announcement is also worth remembering.[112] Luke's idea is clear: the Spirit is not presented as the agent of the resurrection, but Luke portrays the work of the Spirit as an empowering force which enables the apostles to proclaim the resurrection.

In short, there is no doubt that Luke (and the other evangelists) never portrays the Spirit as the agent of the resurrection of Jesus (and that of the believer) while Paul in his letters widely does so.

4.5. Salvific or Conversional Experience and the Gift of the Spirit[113]

The final section to be dealt with concerns the question of how far Luke relates the Spirit to the experience of conversion. Prior to embarking on a discussion of the matter, it is necessary to refer briefly to the general notion of Luke's pneumatology, particularly focusing on the infancy narratives.

4.5.1. The Spirit in Luke-Acts (Infancy Narratives): Prophetic or Soteriological?

There can be no doubt that the portrayal of the Spirit in Luke-Acts is most often presented in a prophetic character or inspired speech.[114] Luke's emphasis on this idea is prevalent and self-evident beginning from the infancy narrative through to Paul's prophetic ministry throughout his two volume-work.[115] Nonetheless, it is hardly deniable that Luke somehow associates the Spirit of prophecy with the matter of salvation. One notable instance is the story of the miraculous conception of Jesus in relation to the creative role of the Spirit in Luke 1:35.[116] According to the story of Mary's

---

[112] Unfortunately, this crucial point has received little attention among pneumatological scholars.

[113] Since this topic is closely related to the present study in terms of the relationship between the Spirit and the authentic believer's existence (i.e., initiation into the kingdom life and blessing), it is critical to deal with it as this is the final matter for our discussion in the present chapter.

[114] So, most scholars, e.g., P.S. Minear, *To Heal and to Reveal: Prophetic Vocation According to Luke* (New York: Seabury, 1976); D. Hill, *New Testament Prophecy* (London: Marshall, Morgan, & Scott, 1979); C. Keener, *The Spirit in the Gospels and Acts: Divine Purity and Power* (Peabody: Hendrickson, 1997), ch. 5; Turner, *Power*; Stronstad, *Prophethood*; and Menzies, *Development*.

[115] E.g., Lk. 1:15-17, 41-42, 46-55, 67-79; 2:29-32; 4:16-30; 12:12; Acts 1:2, 8; 2:4, 17; 4:31; 5:32; 6:10; 7:51; 11:28; 13:2, 4, 9; 20:23; 21:4, 11 etc.

[116] For the general view of the story of Jesus' birth, see R.E. Brown, *The Birth of the Messiah: A Commentary on the Infancy Narratives in Matthew and Luke* (London:

conception, by responding to Mary's question in Luke 1:34, the angel Gabriel says that 'The Holy Spirit will come upon (ἐπελεύσεται)[117] you, and the power of the Most High (ὑψίστου)[118] will overshadow (ἐπισκιάσει)[119] you' (Lk. 1:35).[120] In this way, Luke, following the traditional account, attributes Jesus' miraculous conception to the creative work of the Spirit.[121] Then, how does one understand the role of the Spirit with this creative function? Two facts need to be noted.

a. This creative role of the Spirit according to Luke cannot be compared with Paul's broad understanding of the Spirit.[122] The former is understood as the source of physical life[123] while the latter is understood as the source of spiritual life given to those who already have physical life. In other words, the function of the Spirit in Luke 1:35 is depicted as creative power, but *not* the power which initiates the believer's new status (Rom. 8:2; 2 Cor. 3:6; Rom. 8:14-15, 23; Gal. 4:6), operates justification, cleansing and regeneration in sinners (1 Cor. 6:11), works to realize what is God's will (and accordingly a life which pleases God) through the guidance of the Spirit (Rom. 8:4-8; Gal. 5:25), and guides the believer's moral life (Gal. 5:16-26). Plainly it is not difficult to distinguish between these two. In this way, the miraculous work of the Spirit in Luke 1:35 should be distinguished

---

Doubleday, 1993); E.D. Freed, *The Stories of Jesus' Birth: A Critical Introduction*, BS 72 (Sheffield: SAP, 2001). On the other hand, the unique picture that the Spirit is the source of the conception of the Messiah has no Jewish antecedent. See Brown, *Birth*, 302. But unlike the biblical illustrations in which both Rebecca (a wife of Isaac) in Gen. 25:21 (LXX) and Zipporah (a wife of Moses) in Exod. 2:21-22 (LXX) became pregnant in the usual way, Philo's Rebecca and Zipporah were conceived by the special power of God, but not the Spirit. See Philo, *Cher.* 13:47.

[117] The word 'ἐπέρχομαι' is characteristic of Luke in comparison to the other Synoptic writers (Acts 1:8, cf. 2:25).

[118] The word 'ὕψιστος' is Lukan (Lk. 1:32, 35, 76; 6:35; Acts 7:48; 16:17) while Matthew does not use it at all but Mark uses it only once in 5:7.

[119] Luke's word 'ἐπισκιάζω' probably means the power of God's presence (cf. Exod. 40:35) as well as his protection (cf. Ps. 91:4; 140:7).

[120] In comparison with Luke's account, Matthew's 'Spirit' is directly and solely responsible for the conception of Jesus in 1:18f. and '. . . the child conceived in her is of the Holy Spirit' (v. 20).

[121] Most pneumatological scholars concede the soteriological function of the Spirit in Luke's story of Jesus' conception. E.g., Turner, *Power*, 140-65 (153-60); Penney, *Missionary*, 27-35; Shelton, *Mighty*, 16-17; R. Stronstad, *The Charismatic Theology of St. Luke* (Peabody: Hendrickson, 1984), 36-39; Menzies, 'A Reply to James Dunn', 126-27; *Development*, 127. Although Menzies minimizes Mary's miraculous conception of Jesus by the Spirit but rather attributes it to 'the power (δύναμις) of the Most High', he still admits the Spirit's creative role in the conception of Jesus.

[122] Menzies, 'A Reply to James Dunn', 127.

[123] We have already seen that Philo describes the Spirit in this way: e.g., *Leg. All.* 4:123; *Op. Mund.* 134-135, 144; *Plant.* 18; *Der. Pot. Ins.* 83.

from the Spirit's work as the source of spiritual life. In any event, Luke does not describe the Spirit as the agent of spiritual life as Paul clearly does.

b. Although Luke 1:35 has a link between the Spirit and the soteriological aspect, this relationship should be understood in terms of Luke's broad understanding of salvation-history. Stronstad gives a plausible illustration of this idea when he states that 'Since Luke-Acts is the story of the origin and spread of the gospel, it is historically and theologically impossible for there not to be a close relationship between salvation and the gift of the Spirit'.[124] Although Stronstad presents his statement in an overview of Luke-Acts including some ambiguous texts such as Acts 2:38-39 and 11:15-17, it is precisely applicable to the story of Jesus' conception which functions as an overture to salvation-history. Nevertheless it is not legitimate to think of the single pneumatological context as typical or representative of Luke's pneumatology since Luke's link between the Spirit and salvation is extremely rare throughout Luke-Acts, as will be discussed.[125] As noted above, Luke's general perspective of his pneumatology is of the prophetic dimension, following the traditional understanding of intertestamental Judaism.

This prophetic character of Luke's pneumatology is made very clear in the experiences of the other characters (the unborn John, Elizabeth, Zechariah, Simeon, and even Mary) in the infancy narratives. In particular, this prophetic role of the Spirit is largely represented as bearing witness to Jesus and his future messianic mission in the form of prophetically inspired speech/praise rather than alluding to personal salvation. For example, the Spirit-inspired unborn John (Lk. 1:15: 'even before his birth he πνεύματος ἁγίου πλησθήσεται')[126] is depicted as bearing witness to the unborn Messiah by the action of leaping for joy in his mother's womb (Lk. 1:41, 44).[127] At the same moment, when Elizabeth, the unborn John's mother, is greeted by Mary, she is filled with the Holy Spirit (ἐπλήσθη πνεύματος ἁγίου) in Luke 1:41 and testifies of Mary as the 'mother of my Lord' (Lk. 1:43). Thus in both the case of Elizabeth and her unborn son, the Spirit is portrayed as a source of inspired-speech in witnessing to the unborn Jesus.

---

[124] Stronstand, *Prophethood*, 122.

[125] Contra Turner, *Power*, 161-62. Hence, Stronstad's subsequent statement is justifiable: 'in spite of the close relationship between salvation and the gift of the Spirit, for Luke-Acts the function of the gift of the Spirit is not soteriological but prophetic. To confuse the close relationship between the two as meaning an identity of function is a serious methodological error and leads to a gross distortion of Luke's very clear and explicit pneumatology'. *Prophethood*, 122.

[126] The phrase 'filled with the Holy Spirit' is peculiar to Luke, particularly in the infancy narratives (Lk. 1:41, 67. See also Acts 2:4; 4:8, 31; 9:17; 13:9).

[127] John's unique reception of the Spirit is linked to his prophetic status (Lk. 7:26, 28: he is more than a prophet) and special task (Lk. 1:17: he will go before him [the Lord]). Menzies, *Development*, 119.

This characterization of the Spirit is more explicit in Zechariah's Spirit-filled prophecy in Luke 1:67-79: he was filled with the Holy Spirit (ἐπλήσθη πνεύματος ἁγίου) and prophesied (ἐπροφήτευσεν) (v. 67), concerning John's future mission as the forerunner-witness to the coming One. Undoubtedly, Simeon's oracle upon the baby Jesus is a further clear instance of prophetic influence. Luke depicts Simeon's prophetic status in the three following interruptions of the prophetic Spirit: the Holy Spirit rested upon him (πνεῦμα ἦν ἅγιον ἐπ' αὐτόν) in Luke 2:25; the Holy Spirit revealed (κεχρηματισμένον ὑπὸ τοῦ πνεύματος τοῦ ἁγίου) that he would not see death before he had seen the Lord's Christ in Luke 2:26; and Simeon was guided by the Spirit (ἦλθεν ἐν τῷ πνεύματι) in verse 27. Again, by the inspiration of the Spirit, Simeon bears witness to Jesus and his future messianic role (vv. 29-32, 34-35).

Contrary to Dunn, who argues that the characterization of the Spirit in relation to Mary is only of a soteriological function in the miraculous conception,[128] the influence of Mary's prophetic speech/praise, the *Magnificat* (Lk. 1:46-55) is also derived from the inspiration of the Spirit (Lk. 1:35). Although this prophetic announcement follows some time after her experience of the Spirit in her impregnation, the flow of the immediate context in her meeting with Elizabeth explicitly supports this idea. Furthermore, in view of the other homogenous prophetic speeches in the infancy narrative which we have seen above, it is reasonable to attribute Mary's prophetic announcement of Luke 1:35 to the inspiration of the Spirit.[129] By the inspiration of the Spirit, Mary is able to anticipate the nature of Jesus' messianic mission[130] and in this way the Spirit is indirectly depicted as bearing witness to Jesus and his mission.

Thus, the characterization of the Spirit in the witness of the various prophetic characters in the infancy narratives is not explicitly portrayed as a cause of salvation, but rather is unquestionably described as an inspired

---

[128] Dunn, *Pneumatology*, 229. The title of the article in the collection, *Pneumatology* is 'Baptism in the Spirit: A Response to Pentecostal Scholarship on Luke-Acts', *JPT* 3 (1993), 3-27.

[129] So Shepherd argues that 'Luke's statement that the Spirit will "come upon" and "overshadow" Mary (v. 35, cf. Acts 1:8) cannot be limited to the conception of Jesus, but also functions to assure the reader of the reliability of Mary's proclamation'. *Narrative Function*, 121-22 (22). See also the similar statement of B.R. Gaventa, *Mary: Glimpses of the Mother of Jesus* (Edinburgh: T. & T. Clark, 1999), 58; Menzies, *Development*, 127; Turner, *Power*, 143-44, n. 13.

[130] Although the aorist verbs in this section (vv. 51-54) have been generally interpreted as referring to the past redemptive activities of God in Israel, they can also refer to the future events in the salvation of God which are partly realized at the time of the hymn. See Marshall, *Luke*, 83-84; Bock, *Luke 1:1-9:50*, 155; cf. M. Coleridge, *The Birth of the Lukan Narrative: Narrative as Christology in Luke 1-2*, JSNTS 88 (Sheffield: JSOT Press, 1993), 92.

prophetic witness to the unborn Jesus and the baby Jesus. God's salvation is pointedly referred to in each canticle (the *Magnificat* 1:47; the *Benedictus* 1:69, 71, 77; and the *Nunc Dimittis* 2:30-32, cf. 2:11); but this good news is proclaimed through each Spirit-inspired prophetic speech. In other words, the Spirit is not described as the source of salvation, but rather as that of its proclamation.[131] Although the Spirit is linked to Jesus' birth in terms of a creative role, as will be seen in what follows, other texts in Luke-Acts never clearly and purposely represent the Spirit as the source of salvation (or conversion) like both the Johannine and Pauline pneumatologies.

4.5.2. Conversion and the Reception of the Spirit

As observed earlier, there can be no doubt that the Spirit functions crucially in conversion experience according to Paul.[132] However, when reading Luke-Acts, the connection between the Spirit and conversional experience in Acts becomes one of the difficult issues, but nonetheless, it is crucial since it is directly related to the question of whether Luke attributes a soteriological function to the Spirit or not. Generally speaking, the difficulty is probably that there are some controversial texts such as Acts 2:38-39; 11:15-17; 19:1-7 etc. where the chronology of the two events (baptism and reception of the Spirit) is somewhat ambiguously linked. The reason is also because many have traditionally read Luke in the light of Paul concerning the issue. So some interpret Luke's ambiguous texts to mean exactly the same as Paul's clear view. Having the reasons for the difficulty in mind, what is to be asked is, does Luke explicitly state that the Spirit is the source of the soteriological dimension (the initiation of the kingdom)? The purpose of this section is to explore how Luke himself understands the Spirit's relation to conversional experience. The first and most critical passage for this argument is Peter's preaching at Pentecost, particularly in Acts 2:38-39 where the soteriological dimension and reception of the Spirit are interconnected. Based on the exegetical enquiry into the passage, other relevant texts will be discussed.

4.5.2.1. ACTS 2:38-39: A PARADIGM?

In his recent article, against Quesnel, who argues that there is no consistent norm in Acts concerning the issue of the Spirit and conversion, Turner argues that there is a norm in it. Against Stronstad, Mainville, and Menzies, Turner asserts that the norm is not that the gift of the Spirit is given subsequent to conversion and salvation, but it is 'a conversion-initiation

---

[131] Similarly, as will be discussed in the next chapter, Luke understands the Spirit as the source of the proclamation of the kingdom.

[132] E.g., 1 Thess. 1:4-6; 1 Cor. 2:6-3:1; 6:11; 2 Cor. 1:21-22; 3:1-18; 11:4; Gal. 3:1-5; 4:6; 5:5-6; Rom. 5:5; 7:4-6; 8; Phil. 3:3 etc.

pattern in which conversional repentance/faith is crystalised in baptism, and the Spirit is received in connection with the whole process'.[133] Turner depends heavily on the reading of Acts 2:38-39 for his thesis and regards it as 'a paradigm' or 'a norm': '2:38-39 paradigmatically associates the gift of the Spirit with conversion faith and baptism'.[134] In other words, for Turner, all three (conversion, baptism, and the gift of the Spirit) constitute one compound. However, is Turner's conclusion clearly warranted? Can the text be really regarded as an interpretative model for conversion-initiation? There remain some weighty questions to be asked in order to elucidate Turner's thesis. These are: 1) Concerning the textual consideration, what does Luke actually want to express in the text? 2) Related to the first question but being more specific, what is the connoted meaning of the promise in verse 39 in relation to the gift of the Spirit of verse 38 and how should it be understood in the larger context according to Luke? 3) If Turner's thesis is right, does the post-Pentecostal sequence in Acts consistently and unquestionably support Turner's conversion-initiation pattern? Let us examine each of these points in turn.

4.5.2.1.1. Textual Consideration

In the final part of his discourse at Pentecost, Peter declares, 'Repent (Μετανοήσατε), and be baptized (βαπτισθήτω) every one of you, in the name of Jesus Christ for the forgiveness of your sins. And you will receive the gift of the Holy Spirit (τὴν δωρεὰν τοῦ ἁγίου πνεύματος)' (Acts 2:38). Luke evidently regards the three elements (repentance, baptism, and the gift of the Spirit) as important parts of the normal Christian life taking them in the light of his frequent use of them in the immediate texts although at times they are separated.

Turner understands the collocation of repentance, baptism, and the gift of the Spirit in the text as one event so that the reception of the Spirit becomes a necessary element for conversion experience. Is Turner's reading entirely credible? According to the text, two apparent requirements are indicated as a condition for the forgiveness of sins (i.e., conversion experience) in the imperative forms, 'μετανοήσατε and βαπτισθήτω'. But the chronology of the events μετανοήσατε, βαπτισθήτω and reception of τὴν δωρεὰν τοῦ ἁγίου πνεύματος is not so clear as to allow it to be called, as Turner does, a conversion-initiation pattern. Rather, it is undeniably possible to read the text the other way. As the text suggests, repentance and baptism precede the reception of the Spirit so that it is highly possible to argue that the former two are prerequisites for receiving the Spirit.[135] This reading proposes that

---

[133] Turner, 'Spirit of Prophecy', 339-40. Turner substantially follows Dunn's position at this point. See *Baptism*, chs. 4-9.

[134] Turner, 'Spirit of Prophecy', 340. Similarly, Penney argues that 'This (Acts 2:38-39) is surely a paradigm for conversion-initiation in Acts'. *Missionary*, 91.

[135] E.g., Schweizer, 'πνεῦμα', 412; Menzies, *Development*, 246-48; Stronstad,

the gift of the Spirit is to be granted to those who are already converted, forgiven, and baptized. Furthermore, as will be seen, since Luke is not consistently connecting the reception of the Spirit with the baptismal rite (Acts 8:12-17; 10:44-48 etc.), any attempt to forge a link between the bestowal of the Spirit and conversion experience from Acts 2:38 is unwarranted. In short, a textual consideration suggests that it is difficult to permit one (including Turner) to regard the text as a paradigm for a conversion-initiation pattern.

4.5.2.1.2. The Promise of the Gift of the Spirit

In Acts 2:39, Luke states that 'The promise (ἡ ἐπαγγελία) is for you and your children and for all who are far off—for all whom the Lord our God will call'. At first sight, ἡ ἐπαγγελία, which certainly refers to the gift of the Spirit in verse 38 implies a salvific dimension to every believer. However, while this is true, the thorough examination of the term ἐπαγγελία in the larger context of Lukan writings suggests more than this notion.

It is quite striking that only Luke among the Synoptics uses the term ἐπαγγελία. Although the term is used elsewhere on different occasions (Acts 7:17; 13:23, 32; 26:6), the promise with reference to the Spirit is used four times (Lk. 24:49; Acts 1:4; 2:33, 39; cf. 1:8). The content of the promise of the Father in Luke 24:49 (clothed with power from on high) is the power which will be the source of the disciples' prophetic vocation (Lk. 24:48; Acts 1:8). The promise of the Father in Acts 1:4-5 is more specifically expressed as 'a baptism with the Holy Spirit' (Acts 1:5), which connotes the prophecy of John the Baptist and will soon be bestowed upon the disciples in Jerusalem. However, the promise of the Father in both accounts is surely identified with the gift of the Spirit which prepares for what follows at Pentecost.[136] At this point, the promise intimated in Luke 24:49 and Acts 1:4 is prospective: it introduces what is to be accomplished in the gift of the Spirit at Pentecost. There is thus a continuity between the formulated expression 'τὴν ἐπαγγελίαν τοῦ πατρός' in Luke 24:49 and Acts 1:4.[137]

Luke then presents the identical content of the promise in retrospective terms. Luke's Peter not only testifies of the resurrection of Jesus (Acts 2:32), but also of the bestowal of the Spirit, the promise of the Father (Acts 2:33), which had been seen and heard on that day of Pentecost (Acts 2:4). The promise in Acts 2:33 refers to the coming of the Spirit at Pentecost. Thus 'τὴν ἐπαγγελίαν τοῦ πατρός' in Luke 24:49, Acts 1:4 and 2:33 all indicate one event, the coming of the Spirit, initially fulfilled at Pentecost. This promise is however crucially identified with Luke's Joel citation (LXX 3:1-

---

Prophethood, 10-11; S. Brown '"Water-Baptism" and "Spirit-Baptism" in Luke-Acts', *ATR* 59 (1977), 144; Hawthorne, 'Holy Spirit', 493.

[136] Dunn, *Baptism*, 47; Turner, *Power*, 342; Menzies, *Development*, 202.

[137] D.W. Palmer, 'The Literary Background of Acts 1:1-4', *NTS* 33 (1987), 427-38.

5) which obviously represents the promise of the Father.[138]

If so, then in what sense, particularly in the light of Acts 2:17-21 (LXX Joel 3:1-5), is the gift of the Spirit bestowed at Pentecost to be understood? Is it given to the repentant or unrepentant? What is the purpose of the outpouring of the Pentecostal gift? The answer to these questions offers a significant key to understanding 'the promise' in Acts 2:39.

Joel's citation constitutes the climax of Peter's Pentecost speech and represents the core of Luke's pneumatological concern. The quotation comes from the LXX Joel 3:1-5 and forms a link between the Pentecost event and the tradition of the prophetic Spirit. The passive structure of δια in Acts 2:16 'indicates that the Holy Spirit was the real speaker, the prophet but his mouthpiece'.[139] The significance of the role of the Spirit in the citation can be distilled from a basic examination of the Lukan alterations from the LXX which in turn reflect his theological concern. There are six notable alterations: 1) The changing of the LXX μετὰ ταῦτα by ἐν ταῖς ἐσχάταις ἡμέραις in verse 17; 2) The insertion of λέγει ὁ θεός in verse 17; 3) The double insertion of μου after men-servants and maid-servants in verse 18; 4) The addition of καὶ προφητεύσουσιν in verse 18; 5) The addition of ἄνω, σημεῖα and κάτω in verse 19;[140] 6) The omission of Joel 3:5b (for on Mount Zion and in Jerusalem there will be deliverance, as the Lord has said, among the survivors whom the Lord calls). For the present purpose of this study, the alterations of 2, 3, and 4 are to be taken into consideration.[141]

1) The insertion of λέγει ὁ θεός in verse 17

The insertion of λέγει ὁ θεός is often used by NT writers when quoting the OT (e.g., Acts 7:6, 49; Rom. 12:19; 1 Cor. 14:21; 2 Cor. 6:17). Luke's intention in inserting the phrase is to stress that the promise of Joel is to be

---

[138] E. Lohse, 'Die Bedeutung des Pfingstberichtes im Rahmen des lukanischen Geschichtswerkes', in *Die Einheit des Neuen Testament* (Göttingen: Vandenhoeck & Ruprecht, 1973), 178-92 (188). 'Diese göttliche Verheißung ist in den Worten des Propheten Joel verbürgt'. See also Menzies, *Development*, 200-04; Turner, *Power*, 342.

[139] F.F. Bruce, *The Acts of the Apostles: The Greek Text with Introduction and Commentary* (London: Tyndale, 1952), 89.

[140] The importance of these three insertions appears when we consult the broader context of Luke-Acts. The inclusion of the three terms is echoed in the subsequent verse (22) and the verse refers to God who works signs and wonders through Jesus in his ministry. More widely, Luke elsewhere associates the miraculous events (signs and wonders) with the disciples (Acts 2:19, 22, 43; 4:30; 5:12; 6:8; 7:36; 14:3; 15:12). Cf. Menzies, *Development*, 221-23.

[141] For the comprehensive observation of the alterations in Acts 2:17-21, see D.L. Bock, *Proclamation from Prophecy and Pattern: Lucan Old Testament Christology*, JSNTS 12 (Sheffield: JOST Press, 1987), 156-69; Menzies, *Development*, 213-23; Turner, *Power*, 268-70.

attributed to God himself. It is the promise of the Pentecostal gift of the Spirit which is that of the Father.[142] Thus Luke is able to describe the single word, 'the promise' as the full description 'the promise of the Father' in all three references (Lk. 24:49; Acts 1:4; 2:33).

2) The double insertion of μου after men-servants and maid-servants in verse 18

This double addition of μου to the LXX in verse 18 emphasizes the Lukan intention to address them as the servants of God and that the gift belongs to them: 'on *my* menservants and *my* maidservants in those days I will pour out my Spirit'. What is characteristically implied in the genitive μου is that the outpouring of the Spirit is bestowed only on those who have become the members of the salvific community.[143] There is certainly a servant meaning in a broad understanding of verse 18 as referring to prophetic witnesses, but Luke's purpose in the double addition of the genitive μου should be properly pointed out.[144]

3) The addition of καὶ προφητεύσουσιν in verse 18

There can be little doubt that the insertion of the phrase, καὶ προφητεύσουσιν is theologically intended by Luke.[145] The phrase elucidates that the Pentecostal gift of the Spirit is the Spirit of prophecy. Its insertion does not merely mean that the Spirit-inspired people to speak the word of God, but it also indicates that the utterances are prophetic.[146] This is denoted by the fact that the phrase καὶ προφητεύσουσιν is added to the quotation after 'I will pour out my Spirit' (Acts 2:18). Furthermore, the third person plural pronoun 'they' (shall prophesy) designates the preceding phrase 'τοὺς δούλους μου καὶ τὰς δούλας μου' showing that the recipients of the Spirit are the servants of God, the members of the salvific community. Pentecost involved for the disciples a filling of the Spirit in terms of an equipping for prophetic speech.

These all properly suggest that the initial fulfillment of the promise of the Father (Lk. 24:49; Acts 1:4; 2:33) is identified with the gift of the Spirit in the light of the Joel citation presented at Pentecost. In view of Lukan redaction in Acts 2:18, this gift is granted to those who are the members of

---

[142] Turner, *Power*, 270; Menzies, *Development*, 203, 217; Bock, *Proclamation*, 344, n. 25.

[143] J. Roloff, *Die Apostelgeschichte* (Göttingen: Vandenhoeck & Ruprecht, 1981), 53. 'Der Geist ist speziell den Gliedern der endzeitlichen Heilsgemeinde gegeben'. See also Menzies, *Development*, 219.

[144] Contra Penney, *Missionary*, 86.

[145] Contra Haenchen, *Acts*, 179, who regards the repetition (of v. 17) as a mere scribal error. However, it is Luke's tendency to repeat OT quotations. See Menzies, *Development*, 217.

[146] Bock, *Proclamation*, 162.

the salvific community. This gift is not only as a source of the prophetic inspiration of the disciples (Acts 2:17), but also as that of power for being witnesses (Lk. 24:48-49; Acts 1:8).[147] In short, all three references to the promise of the Father are connected to this Joel citation so emphasizing its prophetic character.

How do we then reconcile these characteristics of the promise of the Father to the promise in Acts 2:39 in which the promised gift of the Spirit has a potentially universal and salvific dimension which also echoes LXX Joel 3:5a (Acts 2:21)? Based on the overall discussion above, Joel's prophecy includes two promises: the promise of the restoration of the Spirit of prophecy and the promise of salvation for those who respond to God's call. In Luke 24:49, Acts 1:4, and 2:33, Luke speaks of the promise of the restoration of the Spirit of prophecy because he is speaking to disciples. In Acts 2:38-39, Luke refers to both promises, the promise of the restoration of the Spirit of prophecy and the promise of salvation, because the audience whom Luke's Peter is addressing includes the crowd who are not believers. This indicates that 'the promise' of Acts 2:39 contains more than the salvific dimension. In view of the prophetic nature of the gift in the three Lukan references to 'the promise of the Father' (Lk. 24:49; Acts 1:4 and 2:33) and its fulfillment of the Joel citation, it is appropriate to assume that the promised gift of the Spirit in Acts 2:39 is granted to the repentant and connects with its prophetic nature, i.e., the Spirit of prophecy in Joel's citation.[148] Thus all four references to the promise are focused on the nature of the promise cited from Joel. In other words, the promised gift of the Spirit in the Joel citation makes explicit what is implicitly promised in Acts 2:39. The point is that the promise with reference to the Spirit is always and clearly defined as the promise of prophetic power. As Menzies states: 'The promise of Acts 2:39, like the promise of Jesus in Acts 1:8, points beyond "the restoration of the preserved of Israel": salvation is offered (Joel 2:32), but the promise includes the renewal of Israel's

---

[147] This prophetic vocation of the promise of the Spirit for witness might be further confirmed in Jesus' pre-ascension promise in Lk. 12:12 and Lk. 21:15 where the Spirit will function as the counsel for the defence before the synagogues and the rulers and authorities. Although the term 'promise' is not referred to in the texts, the content of a promise is constituted and Luke indicates the fulfillment of this promise in two occasions in his second work: one is fulfilled in Peter's fearless and extraordinary defence before the Sanhedrin (Acts 4:8-12) and the other is Stephen's powerful inspired speech which resulted in his opponents not being able to withstand the 'wisdom and Spirit' with which he was speaking. Particularly, the latter echoes Jesus' promise indicated in Lk. 21:15: 'For I will give you words and wisdom that none of your adversaries will be able to resist or contradict'. Cf. I.H. Marshall, 'The Significance of Pentecost', *SJT* 30 (1977), 347-69 (350-51).

[148] Menzies, *Development*, 203; 'Spirit of Prophecy', 65.

prophetic vocation to be a light to the nations' (Joel 2:28).[149]

To sum up, Turner himself rightly observes that 'The nature of the gift of the Spirit promised to Christians in 2:38-39 is clear enough - it is Joel's gift of the Spirit of prophecy'.[150] However, the larger context of Acts 2:38-39 does not seem to support Turner's case that the gift of the Spirit of prophecy is an additional form of a single conversion-initiation pattern as a paradigm. The consideration of the larger context of the term 'τὴν ἐπαγγελίαν τοῦ πατρός' rather supports reading the gift of the Spirit as a prophetic enabling for witness (Lk. 24:48-49; Acts 1:4-8; 2:17-18).

4.5.2.2. RELEVANT TEXTS ON THE SPIRIT-RECEPTION

The final point that needs to be discussed is of texts relevant to the 'reception of the Spirit'. The purpose of this section is to look at how consistently and inextricably linked together are conversional experience (and water baptism) and the reception of the Spirit in other relevant texts if Turner's case is right.[151]

4.5.2.2.1. Samaria (Acts 8:12-17)

The first post-Pentecostal conversion story appears in Acts 8:12-17 and clearly contradicts Turner's normative rule established from Acts 2:38. The outcome of Philip's proclamation forces the Samaritans to believe and to be baptized (Acts 8:12). But Luke does indicate that the gift of the Spirit has not yet been granted to the Samaritan believers, as evidenced in verse 16. Finally, they submit to baptism in the name of Jesus, but surprisingly this rite is not accompanied by the bestowal of the gift of the Spirit. They rather receive this by the laying on of the apostles' hands (Peter and John) (v. 17).[152] Undoubtedly, the conversion narrative of the Samaritans clearly implies a certain period of time between baptism and the reception of the Spirit, therefore the Samaritans have come to believe and be baptized without receiving the gift of the Spirit. This is a clear case which shows that Luke 'did not think that the gift of the Spirit was necessary to salvation'.[153]

In spite of this clear perspective on Luke's pneumatology, some, who maintain a close link between the Spirit and conversion experience, attempt to undermine the evidence that the Samaritan text shows. For instance,

---

[149] Menzies, 'Spirit of Prophecy', 65.

[150] *Power*, 349.

[151] This section is intended to discuss only the relationship between the two (or other relative activities in relation to the Spirit such as laying on of hands) rather than to draw out the entire exegesis of the passages.

[152] There are two other cases of a connection between 'the laying on of hands' and 'the reception of the Spirit' - Acts 9:17 and 19:6. However, in view of Acts 2:38; 6:6; 10:44 and 13:3, the rite is not exclusively conditional for receiving the Spirit.

[153] K. Lake, 'The Twelve and the Apostles', in H.J. Cadbury and K. Lake (eds.), *The Beginnings of Christianity*, V (London: Macmillan, 1933), 53.

Dunn, earlier than Turner, argues that the Samaritans were not authentic Christians prior to the experience of the reception of the Spirit so that their 'initial response and commitment *was* defective'. For Dunn, this deduction comes from his thesis that it is impossible to think of a believer without the Spirit which is based on a Pauline perspective.[154] While Dunn's view has been widely and severely criticized by many scholars,[155] it is worth noting two fundamental problems of Dunn's interpretation as criticized by Turner.[156]

First of all, Turner argues that it is most unlikely that Luke considered Philip's preaching and ministry as either deficient or misunderstood since Luke does not indicate that Peter and John complement, amend or add to any of Philip's preaching and proclamation. Luke's view of Philip is of a successful evangelist who acts and leads in the power of the Spirit. Secondly, since the Samaritans genuinely believed the kerygma they heard, they were adequately prepared for their baptism which was a proper baptism. This becomes clear in the apostles' acceptance of what they heard that 'Samaria had received the Word of God' (8:14) without any suggestion that this was merely a defective report. They accepted it as a fact.

By way of contrast, Turner himself argues that the Samaritans were true believers before their reception of the Spirit by admitting the possibility of being believers without the reception of the Spirit. But Turner regards this episode as an exception to the norm of Luke's pneumatological perspective, believing that this instance is quite distinct from Acts 2:38-39.[157] However, is it fair merely to regard this text as an exception to the rule established by Turner? In opposition to Turner's argument, this exception was usual in some narratives up to this episode. We have already seen a link between repentance, baptism, and the reception of the Spirit, but they are not necessarily simultaneously linked in Acts 2:38: it is highly possible to read that repentance is the pre-requisite to receiving the promised gift of the Spirit. The disciples themselves experienced the endowment of the Spirit on

---

[154] *Baptism*, 63-68 (63). Emphasis is original. Cf. 55.

[155] E.g., E.A. Russell, '"They Believed Philip Preaching" (Acts 8:12)', *IBS* 1 (1979), 169-79; K. Giles, 'Is Luke an Exponent of "Early Protestantism"? Church Order in the Lukan Writings (Part 1)', *EvQ* 54 (1982), 197; H. Ervin, *Conversion-Initiation and the Baptism in the Holy Spirit: A Critique of James D.G. Dunn, Baptism in the Holy Spirit* (Peabody: Hendrickson, 1984), 25-40; Marshall, *Acts*, 156; Stronstad, *Charismatic*, 64-65; F.S. Spencer, *The Portrait of Philip in Acts*, JSNTS 67 (Sheffield: JSOP Press, 1992), 48-53; especially, Menzies, *Development*, 252-57 and Turner, *Power*, 362-67. Because of the massive criticism against this view, Dunn, in his recent response to Pentecostal criticisms, admits the fact that the coming of the Spirit is delayed. See Dunn, *Pneumatology*, 228.

[156] *Power*, 363-67.

[157] This episode is 'a clear break with the "norm" we might expect from Acts 2:38-39'. *Power*, 360; 'Spirit of Prophecy', 338.

Pentecost some time after they had experienced John's water-baptism of repentance (cf. Acts 1:5, 22). They also received another Spirit-bestowal after this when they gathered in prayer in the Jerusalem church (Acts 4:31).[158] In addition, there is little agreement in linking the water rite and the reception of the Spirit elsewhere in Luke's writings, but rather he separates the former from the latter (Lk. 3:21-22; Acts 8:12-17; Acts 9:17-19; 10:44-48).

Furthermore, elsewhere after Acts 8, as will be seen, Luke never *explicitly* indicates that the Spirit is an essential element for new life. Rather, there is an apparent instance in which Luke separates conversion from the gift of the Spirit (Acts 19:1-7). Of course, one may find some ambiguous texts which are currently debated and interpreted differently, i.e., soteriologically, particularly by those who are steeped in Pauline and Johannine pneumatology. However, the debatable texts should not be read as if they are a normative pattern for conversion-initiation since other scholars read those debatable texts in other ways, as will be discussed. Likewise, a clear and unambiguous text such as Acts 8:14-18 (cf. Acts 19:1-7) should not be taken as an exception. One clear fact is that this text undoubtedly shows Luke's understanding of the Spirit as separating the gift of the Spirit from faith (repentance). In view of Luke's evident pneumatological implications in this narrative, it is probably fair to say that this text becomes a real problem (rather than a simple exception) for Turner. Furthermore, the pneumatological perspective in this account is a clear instance of Luke's pneumatology being decidedly different from Paul or John.[159]

4.5.2.2.2. Paul and Ananias (Acts 9:17-18)

At the conclusion of his first account of Paul's encounter with the risen Lord, Luke describes the overall picture after the activity of Ananias' laying on of hands on Paul: 'Brother Saul, the Lord Jesus who appeared to you on the road as you were coming here has sent me so that you may see again and πλησθῇς πνεύματος ἁγίου (9:17)'. The prophecy is then immediately accomplished and subsequently Paul rose and was baptized (9:18).

It is generally agreed that the agency and time of Paul's reception of the Spirit are not clearly specified in Acts 9:17 while the text (and the immediate verse) refers to the relationship of the laying on of hands, the

---

[158] F.S. Spencer, *Acts* (Sheffield: SAP, 1997), 87. Cf. Lk. 11:13.

[159] In the light of some debatable and ambiguous texts elsewhere in Luke, Menzies probably goes too far when he states that this text shows Luke's theological perspective in which Luke separates repentance and water rite from the reception of the Spirit. Nonetheless, in view of this unambiguous instance of Luke's crafted interpretation of the event, Menzies is undoubtedly right when he argues that this perspective is absolutely different from that of Paul and John. Menzies, 'Spirit of Prophecy', 63. See below for a further discussion of this matter.

reception of the Spirit, and baptism (vv. 17-18).[160] Nevertheless, from the statement of Ananias in Acts 9:17 it can possibly be assumed that Paul received the gift of the Spirit at that time.[161] Turner tries to link Paul's reception of the Spirit to the water baptism performed by Ananias since this interpretation fits with 'the paradigm set forth in 2:38'.[162] But the text rather seems to suggest that the falling of the Spirit came before water baptism.[163] Turner might be right to consider the laying on of hands as an act of healing, but it is problematic when he confines it only to Paul's healing. As Bruce argues, it is highly possible to 'connect the laying on of Ananias' hands with Saul's reception of the Holy Spirit'.[164] This interpretation is possible in the light of other cases such as Acts 8:17-19 and Acts 19:6.[165] Furthermore, Turner argues that Paul's conversion experience was finally completed when he was baptized at Ananias' direction in 9:17-18.[166] But others view it that Paul's faith comes first prior to the reception of the Spirit since Ananias 'addresses Saul as ἀδελφέ, recognizing him as a fellow Christian (1:15), though he has not yet been baptized'.[167] Alternatively, Porter safely suggests that 'this passage provides very little

---

[160] The difficulty of determining the role of the Spirit in this narrative is generally argued in the following way. Although Paul's call/conversion story is reported in Acts 22:3-16 and 26:9-18 including 9, Luke does not refer to the Spirit except in Acts 9. However, even though the Spirit is referred to in Acts 9, the actual endowment of the Spirit is not explicitly depicted. See L.T. Johnson, *The Acts of Apostles* (Collegeville: Liturgical, 1992), 165; C.K. Barrett, *A Critical and Exegetical Commentary on the Acts of the Apostles*, I, ICC (Edinburgh: T. & T. Clark, 1994), 457. Assuming that all three Pauline conversion/call accounts are closely supplemented by each other from one source, Menzies argues that the narrative in Acts 9 indicates Paul's missionary calling rather than conversion. But it is to be noted that the other two accounts (Acts 22 and 26) give little help to understanding the relationship between the Spirit and his missionary commission since they have no information concerning the reception of the Spirit. In other words, Paul's missionary commission in relation to the experience of the Spirit should be answered in Acts 9. Cf. S.E. Porter, *The Paul of Acts: Essays in Literary Criticism, Rhetoric, and Theology*, WUNT 115 (Tübingen: Mohr, 1999), 72.

[161] Cf. Menzies, *Development*, 260.

[162] *Power*, 376.

[163] Giles, 'Luke', 194; J.C. O'Neill, 'The Connection between Baptism and the Gift of the Spirit in Acts', *JSNT* 63 (1996), 94; cf. F.F. Bruce, *The Book of the Acts*, NICNT (Grand Rapids: Eerdmans, 1988), 189, n. 42. Although this order cannot be certain according to the narrative, Bruce puts the coming of the Spirit first.

[164] Bruce, *Greek Text*, 202. See also Roloff, *Die Apostelgeschichte*, 162; Stronstad, *Charismatic*, 66; cf. Johnson, *Acts*, 338; Porter, *Paul*, 85.

[165] O'Neill, 'Baptism', 95.

[166] *Power*, 375.

[167] Barrett, *Acts*, 457. See also Bruce, *Greek Text*, 202; W. Neil, *The Acts of the Apostles*, NCB (London: Marshall, Morgan & Scott, 1973), 131; Ervin, *Conversion-Initiation*, 41-49; Giles, 'Luke', 194; Shelton, *Mighty*, 131.

detail regarding *how* and *when* the Spirit worked in Paul at or after his conversion'.[168]

But one should not fail to recognize a certain role for the Spirit in the narrative. It is widely accepted that the primary intention of the narrative may be to stress the significance of Paul's pneumatic experience in terms of Paul's commissioning as a witness.[169] This view is apparently supported by the immediate account of Paul's missionary activity. As a chosen instrument to bear witness to the name of Jesus (Acts 9:15-16), Paul, being filled with the Spirit, proclaims Jesus to be the Son of God (Acts 9:20) and witnesses to him as the Messiah (9:22) in the Damascus synagogue.[170] Luke reports Paul's continuing proclamation in the name of Jesus at Jerusalem (9:27-29) as he did in Damascus. Paul's conversion is reported in relation to the reception of the Spirit, but one needs to look at how the connection between the two is not clear. However, the endowment of the Spirit upon Paul is rather clearly linked to Paul's missionary calling to the Gentiles.

In summary, various scholarly views suggest that the relationship between the Spirit and the conversional experience of Paul (and his water baptism) is not inextricably linked as Turner seeks to argue from Acts 2:38. Scholarly consensus is that the characterization of the Spirit in the narrative is presented as empowering Paul to bear witness to Jesus.

4.5.2.2.3. Cornelius' Household (Acts 10:44-48; cf. 11:14-18; 15:7-9)

The narrative of Cornelius indicates that the gift of the Spirit is granted to Gentiles for the first time in Acts 10:44-48. It contains the collocation of a water rite, the endowment of the Spirit, and the implied event of forgiveness. While Peter, who was commissioned as a prophetic missionary to the Gentiles, is proclaiming the good news, the Spirit falls on Cornelius' household (v. 44). The manifestation of the reception of the gift primarily appears as an audible and visible phenomenon of inspired speech (v. 46, λαλούντων γλώσσαις καὶ μεγαλυνόντων τὸν θεόν). The event causes those circumcised believers to be amazed (vv. 45-46) and subsequently to be baptized (vv. 47-48).

The conversion of Cornelius' household is of great importance to Luke

---

[168] Porter, *Paul*, 72. Emphasis is original. Similarly, Stronstad, *Charismatic*, 66.

[169] Bruce, *Acts*, 188-89; Hill, *Greek Words*, 260; C. Burchard, *Der dreizehnte Zeuge: Traditions-und kompositionsgeschichtliche Untersuchungen zu Lukas' Darstellung der Frühzeit des Paulus*, FRLANT 103 (Göttingen: Vandenhoeck & Ruprecht, 1970), 104; B.R. Gaventa, *From Darkness to Light: Aspects of Conversion in the New Testament* (Philadelphia: Fortress Press, 1986), 90-92; Menzies, *Development*, 260-63; Shelton, *Mighty*, 135; D.S. Huffman, *The Theology of the Acts of the Apostles: Lukan Compositional Markedness as a Guide to Interpreting Acts* (Ann Arbor: Bell and Howell, 1994), 168-75 (esp. n. 121); Penney, *Missionary*, 97.

[170] Burchard claims that 'Der Geist ist die Bedingung der Möglichkeit, daß Paulus predigt, was er alsbald tut (9:19b ff.)'. *Der dreizehnte Zeuge*, 104.

since he recounts it later in his testimonies (Acts 11:14-18; 15:7-9). In addition, while the scope of the role of the Spirit in the Cornelius episode is theologically still disputed, as will be shown, the event of the falling of the Spirit upon the Gentile converts is significant since Luke interprets it as a new experience of the Spirit for them. Luke reiterates the event five times (10:44, 45, 47; 11:15, 17; cf. 11:16).

Two points are to be noted for our purpose. First, as the passage clearly shows, Luke ignores the close linkage between the reception of the Spirit and water baptism: the former is experienced prior to the latter like Paul's baptism in Acts 9:17-18.[171] The second point, which will be mainly discussed in what follows, is that of how far the gift of the Spirit functions in relation to the forgiveness and cleansing of Cornelius and his household. The answer to the second point remains difficult as most agree. Nevertheless, investigations of the question have been discussed among scholars.

Dunn's interpretation of the narrative is well-known: the gift of the Spirit is the essential sign of the conversion of the Cornelius household. The Spirit falls when Peter declares the promise of forgiveness to those who believe (10:43-44). In this manner, the Spirit becomes the bearer of forgiveness.[172] This thesis is further confirmed by similar expressions: 'the gift of the Spirit' in Acts 11:17 and 'the gift of repentance' in Acts 11:18. 'God gave the Spirit means (11:17) that God gave repentance unto life (11:18)'.[173] Similarly, Dunn equates the concept 'giving them the Holy Spirit' in 15:8 with 'cleansing their hearts by faith' in 15:9.[174]

However, Dunn's interpretation is substantially criticized by both Menzies and Turner.[175] Turner argues that there is no reason to equate receiving the Spirit and God's forgiveness. What Cornelius received is the Spirit of prophecy, an element that is 'transparently additional to forgiveness and acceptance'.[176] Turner also argues that the gift of the Spirit should not be equated with the gift of repentance in 11:17-18 since elsewhere the latter is the condition of the former (Acts 2:38-39), 'not the gift itself'.[177] Likewise, it is difficult to equate 'cleansing their hearts by faith' (15:9b) with 'giving them the Holy Spirit' (15:8b) since the structure

---

[171] Barrett, *Acts*, 154; O'Neill, 'Baptism', 93.

[172] Dunn, *Baptism*, 80. In his recent book, Dunn reiterates this statement similarly but cautiously, the Spirit is 'the embodiment or transmitter of forgiveness'. *Pneumatology*, 230.

[173] Dunn, *Pneumatology*, 231.

[174] Dunn, *Pneumatology*, 231-32.

[175] For Menzies' criticism against Dunn, see Menzies, *Spirit and Power*, 80-82.

[176] *Power*, 381-82.

[177] *Power*, 382. In addition, it is notable that Luke is consistent in connecting forgiveness to Jesus, not to the Spirit (e.g., Lk. 1:77; 3:3; 4:18; Acts 2:38; 5:31; 13:38; cf. 26:18). See Menzies, *Spirit and Power*, 80.

of verses 8 and 9 does not prove the parallelism and each phrase has a different role in the overall argument.[178] Nevertheless, at the end of his argument Turner is no different from Dunn when he argues that the gift of the Spirit is associated with the conversional experience of Cornelius' household. Turner once again goes back to his previous assumption: '*we need to. . . have returned to the norm of the gift of the Spirit being immediately associated with conversional repentance and baptism. . .* at Acts 2:38'.[179] Turner supports this in a twofold way: 1) Cornelius and his household were converted when Peter was preaching rather than earlier; and 2) the Gentile Pentecost reminds Peter of the promise of John the Baptist in Jesus' logion (Lk. 3:16-17; Acts 1:5) in which Luke understands that the Messiah cleanses Israel through the power of the Spirit. However, each argument that Turner offers is not conclusive to support his case.

First of all, the text itself does not clearly inform us when or how the conversion of Cornelius' household occurred.[180] This is simply because there is no mention concerning their conversion or repentance in Acts 10 except in verse 43 where forgiveness is referred to in the conclusion of Peter's sermon. This omission opens various assumptions concerning the time of their conversion. Some suggest that Cornelius' household, similarly to the case of Samaria, became Christians through the ministry of some unnamed evangelist before Peter's arrival and preaching.[181] This is due to Luke's positive description of Cornelius (and his friends) as devout, a God-fearer, an ethically sincere prayer, and the one who knows the story of Jesus and his message (Acts 10:2, 4, 22, 31, 33, 36-37). This is a possible illustration in the light of Acts 13:26 where Luke refers to Jews as 'those who fear God among you' which suggests converts or proselytes.[182] Others such as Turner himself suggest that the Gentiles whose status had been semi-proselyte were completely converted while Peter was preaching.[183] In

---

[178] *Power*, 383.

[179] *Power*, 384. Emphasis is original.

[180] Even the way of translating the aorist participle πιστεύσασιν in 11:17, whether it be taken as 'when' or 'after' is not definitive to answer this issue as long as it is used in one's theological presupposition. Penney, following Peterson and NIV, argues that it 'is used circumstantially ("to us who believed", NIV), without any particular time reference intended'. *Missionary*, 104.

[181] F. Arrington, *The Acts of the Apostles: An Introduction and Commentary* (Peabody: Hendrickson, 1988), 114; U. Wilckens, *Die Missionsreden der Apostelgeschichte: Form-und Traditionsgeschichtliche Untersuchungen* (Neukirchen-Vluyn: Neukirchener Verlag, 1974), 46-50, 63-70.

[182] Cf. Barrett, *Acts*, 638. Witherington argues that if we compare the phrase 'those who fear God' in Acts 13:26 to the term 'proselyte', where both phrases refer to Gentiles who attend the synagogue it would appear that both have the same meaning. *Acts*, 343.

[183] *Power*, 385, n. 111.

the light of Acts 15:7 where Peter testifies that he had been led by God to the Gentiles and they would hear and believe the good news from his proclamation (cf. 11:13-14), the latter's view is more probable since the text implies that the Gentiles might become believers from Peter's lips. However, even if the latter's view is acceptable so that the coming of the Spirit accompanies their conversion, a difficulty still remains: Luke does not specify in the text the role of the gift of the Spirit as the essential means for their cleansing and forgiveness. It is thus probably fair to assume that 'Luke does not exactly say when the conversion occurred or what the Holy Spirit's role was in the conversion'.[184]

What is clearly involved in the reception of the Spirit is the Gentile's inspired speech prompted by the Spirit as seen above. This clear audible pneumatic sign, speaking in tongues and magnifying God, shows that the gift can be equally granted to the uncircumcised members in Caesarea. The distinctive Pentecostal pneumatic phenomena among the Jews are also manifested in the Gentiles in whom the same Spirit evidently works. Ultimately, the Spirit in this instance is a legitimate and decisive sign that the Gentiles could be participants in salvation history.[185]

With regard to the logion of Jesus in Acts 11:16 (Turner's second point), Turner assumes that the conceptual background of Acts 15:8-9 is 11:16 ('... John baptized with water, but you shall be baptized with the Holy Spirit') so that he interprets the Spirit as the source of the Gentile's cleansing. However, we have already observed that Turner's understanding of Luke 3:16-17 (John the Baptist's prophecy) is a defective one: the Spirit in John the Baptist's prophecy is not described as the cause of the purging of individuals. If so, then what is Peter's reason for quoting the Jesus logion? It is notable that when Jesus recounted John's prophecy as recorded in Acts 1:5, the promise was applicable to Jews, but now Peter's reiteration of the logion is applicable to the Gentiles. The answer to the above question is simple: Peter now has a new perspective that the promise of the gift of the Spirit is universally available among the Gentiles as he and his fellow Jews had experienced.[186] This becomes clear in the following context. Peter in Acts 11:17 declares that God granted the *same* gift to the Gentiles as they received on the day of Pentecost; the gift of the Spirit in a Gentile house in

---

[184] Shelton, *Mighty*, 132-33. Nonetheless, a possible timetable can be assumed from the text: the Spirit falls while Peter is preaching. Then simultaneously the new converts experience the inspired speech. They are finally baptized. It can be possible to think of the logical distinction between the coming of the Spirit and their cleansing heart by baptismal rite. In his account in Acts 11:17-18, Luke builds the similar logic: the Spirit is granted to the Gentiles and then they are granted repentance unto life and are eligible for the baptismal rite. Menzies, *Spirit and Power*, 81.

[185] Shelton, *Mighty*, 132-33; Menzies, *Spirit and Power*, 81; Tannehill, *Narrative*, II, 143; Penney, *Missionary*, 103.

[186] Tannehill, *Narrative*, II, 144.

Caesarea and in the upper room in Jerusalem is the same. In this way, Peter (Luke) compares two events. What is then the central character of the gift of the Spirit in both cases? Hill correctly answers this question: 'The second Pentecostal endowment, that of the Gentiles... is the same character as the first (Pentecost)... That Luke is so careful to record the same signs of Spirit-possession on these two occasions demonstrates clearly that for him the "prophetic" character of the gift is central: it is the equipment for Gospel proclamation'.[187]

Peter in his quotation in Acts 11:16 does not state that the promise of the Spirit is the means by which the Gentiles are virtually cleansed.[188] Against this premise, as Peter presents in Acts 15:9, it is by *faith* that the hearts of the Gentiles were cleansed. The gift of the Spirit is rather presented as a sign of the reality that their hearts were cleansed by faith.

To sum up, the argument that Turner suggests is left unclear. One apparent point against Turner's paradigm is that there is a gap between the reception of the Spirit and the water rite. The role of the Spirit in the cleansing and forgiveness of Cornelius and his household is not being clearly connected in this instance. But as a sign of the successful Gentile mission, the coming of the Spirit to the Gentiles verifies them as the people of God by creating a remarkable audible and visible phenomenon of inspired speech like that of Pentecost at the beginning.

4.5.2.2.4. Ephesus (Acts 19:1-7)

The final text that links 'faith', 'water rite' and the 'Spirit' is the incident at Ephesus where Paul first visits. This text like that of Cornelius has been widely disputed among scholars regarding the role of the Spirit in connection with conversion, but without any satisfactory conclusions. While various scholarly interpretations of the text have been offered by, among others, Porter,[189] the scope of the present discussion will again be in

---

[187] Hill, *New Testament Prophecy*, 96-97.

[188] It is curious to note that Turner, against Dunn, argues that the function of Acts 15:8 (giving them the Spirit) is to guarantee the fact in Acts 15:9 (cleansing of the Gentiles' hearts by faith): 'God's gift of the "Spirit of prophecy" would readily "bear witness" to the fact they were "clean"'. *Power*, 383. However, ironically, he, agreeing with Dunn, closely connects the Spirit in v. 8 with cleansing in v. 9 as if the former were the source of the latter. He then concludes 'Jesus' baptizing the Cornelius household with the Spirit here is interpreted in terms of his cleansing a people for his name'. *Power*, 387. The two illustrations from one passage seem to conflict.

[189] A good summary of six different scholarly views (J.C. O'Neill, R. Strelan, E. Käsemann, I.H. Marshall, J. Dunn, and R.P. Menzies) regarding the incident at Ephesus is recently offered by Porter. For the details of each interpretation, see *Paul*, 81-85. But Porter does not respond to Turner's view though he briefly mentions Turner.

response to Turner's paradigm, the conversion-initiation pattern.

Once again, Turner does not fail to bring and emphasize the norm of Acts 2:38-39 and argues that the Spirit granted to the Ephesian disciples functions in their conversion. Turner argues that for whatever reason Luke has portrayed them as 'almost' believers until 19:4, they finally become believers when they submit to water baptism and receive the Spirit: 'the Spirit is then granted as usual as part of their (the Ephesians') conversion-initiation package'.[190] Turner maintains that in this episode 'water baptism', the 'laying on of hands', and the 'reception of the Spirit' are one event and assumes that their submission to baptism means their reception of the Spirit identifying their becoming believers. While Turner is right when he connects water baptism and reception of the Spirit in this episode,[191] a fundamental question about the status of the Ephesian disciples is to be asked: are they not Christians at all before their reception of the Spirit? Turner argues that the Ephesians are people baptized by John awaiting the promised Messiah. They are only 'in the process of conversion' and 'their submission to baptism completes their conversion-initiation'.[192] Thus, Turner, following Dunn, argues that the disciples at Ephesus are not believers: 'τινες μαθηταί does not *necessarily* refer to Christians'.[193] Turner has suggested two main reasons to support his case.[194]

---

[190] 'Spirit of Prophecy', 339; *Power*, 391-92.

[191] Turner states 'the very fact that Paul, having ascertained the "disciples" do not know of the gift of the Spirit, immediately asked "Into what, then, were you baptized?" (19:3) suggests a *usual* association between baptism and reception of the Spirit. Once again the norm of Acts 2:38-39 is assumed to hold'. *Power*, 392. Emphasis is original. Nonetheless, as observed earlier, Luke elsewhere does not develop a strong connection between the water rite and the reception of the Spirit.

[192] *Power*, 391.

[193] *Power*, 391. Emphasis is original. Turner even knows the similar phrase in singular form, μαθητής in Acts 9:10 and 16:1 which denote both Ananias (9:10) and Timothy (16:1) as believers. On the other hand, it is pointed out that Dunn uses the term the 'definite article', when he argues the status of the τινας μαθητάς as 'certain disciples' rather than 'true disciples'. *Baptism*, 84. However, as Porter points out, there are not two articles in Greek (definite and indefinite), but only the single article which is different from English usage. 'in Greek the presence or the absence of an article does not determine whether the substantive is particular or non-particular, categorical or individual'. See S.E. Porter, *Idioms of the Greek New Testament* (Sheffield: JSOT Press, 1994), 103-05 (105).

[194] Turner's two points (i.e., the Ephesians' ignorance of the Spirit and their need of re-baptism) are based on the contrasting example of Apollos (Acts 18:24-28). For the response of this thesis, see notes 198 and 215 below. For a detailed discussion of the relationship between Apollos and the Ephesians in Acts 18:24-19:7, see C.K. Barrett, 'Apollos and the Twelve Disciples of Ephesus', in W.C. Weinrich (ed.), *The New Testament Age: Essays in Honor of Bo Reicke*, I (Macon: Mercer University Press, 1984), 29-39; Spencer, *Portrait*, 232-39; Dunn, *Baptism*, 83-89; Menzies,

a. One is concerning the Ephesians' ignorance of the Spirit: they 'have *not* heard of the gift of the Spirit' in Acts 19:2.[195] Somewhat unlike Dunn, who argues that it is inconceivable to think of a Christian without the Spirit,[196] Turner rightly and carefully assumes that one could be a believer without the Spirit. Nonetheless, this first point implies that Turner might associate the hearing about the Spirit with believing.

This is an answer from Paul's question: 'Εἰ πνεῦμα ἅγιον ἐλάβετε πιστεύσαντες;' Witherington states that 'the answer of this question would determine whether they were Christians or not'.[197] This statement clearly implies that the Spirit is the essence of becoming a believer. At first sight, it is actually quite surprising that the disciples at Ephesus had not heard of the Holy Spirit despite the fact that they had experienced John's baptism. But if we properly understand Luke's perspective on the matter, this is not surprising since, as seen above, the relationship between the 'Spirit' and 'believing' is not necessarily co-existent, according to Luke.[198] We have already seen that Acts 8:12-17 is a clear example of Luke's pneumatological perspective, i.e., there are baptized believers who have not yet experienced the gift of the Spirit. For this reason, the answer to Paul's question should not determine whether they were believers or not. The question of whether or not they were believers should be understood from its *context* as will be seen. Hence, the disciples' deficient knowledge of the Spirit should not be connected to their status as unbelievers.

Strelan, who thinks that the Ephesians were indeed believers, argues that they had not heard about the Spirit but only about a gift (holiness for the church) from the Spirit.[199] Thus, Strelan reads Paul's question and the disciple's response in Acts 19:2 as: 'When you became believers (in Jesus)

Development, 268-77; Turner, *Power*, 388-97.

[195] Turner, 'Spirit of Prophecy', 338. Emphasis is original. See also *Power*, 389.

[196] Dunn's inexplicable link between the Spirit and believing in his exegesis of Acts 19:2 in terms of the Pauline perspective (the absolute necessity of possession of the Spirit for being a believer) should be questioned. As will be seen, if it is granted as such, there is no point pursuing Luke's own theological perspective. The whole dialogue issued by the people in this text is undoubtedly constructed and shaped by Luke's own hand. For some substantial criticisms against Dunn's interpretation, see Menzies, *Spirit and Power*, 74-76; Porter, *Paul*, 84; R. Strelan, *Paul, Artemis, and the Jews in Ephesus* (Berlin: de Gruyter, 1996), 238.

[197] *Acts*, 571.

[198] Turner contrasts Apollos' experience of the Spirit (ζέων τῷ πνεύματι, 18:25) with the Ephesians' ignorance of the Spirit and argues that the Ephesians are unbelievers (or not yet fully believers), while Apollos is a Spirit-inspired believer. This assumption is based on a clear connection between receiving the Spirit and becoming a believer: there is no Christian without possessing the Spirit. However, this is inconclusive because Luke does not necessarily link the two realities of the Spirit and faith (e.g., Acts 8:12-17).

[199] Strelan, *Ephesus*, 239.

did you receive a holy spirit which the (Holy) Spirit gives?. . . We did not hear (in our instruction) that there is a gift of the Spirit'. For this interpretation, he invokes and quotes N. Turner: in Luke the use of anarthrous 'ἅγιον πνεῦμα is an unknown power, God's Spirit as opposed to that of men or demons'.[200] However, Porter criticizes Strelan's inadequate linguistic basis by stating that 'the use of anarthrous "holy spirit" in Luke is. . . hardly the gift necessary for Strelan's view'.[201] Luke elsewhere uses the anarthrous πνεῦμα ἅγιον as a clear reference to the Holy Spirit (Acts 8:15). Porter also rightly asks: 'how is it that in receiving the Holy Spirit his gift was not also received?'[202]

In addition to Porter's points, it should also be noted that the general context in this episode does not support Strelan's view. Paul reminds the disciples of that repentance which is associated with John's baptism (John baptized with the baptism of repentance) not the Spirit in Acts 19:4. Then, in verse 6, Luke reports that the evidence of the reception of the Spirit is primarily manifested by the disciples' charismata of 'speaking in tongues and prophecy'.[203] Thus, several lines of evidence suggest that it is difficult to agree with Strelan's thesis. If so, what is it that they did not hear?

Spencer reasonably suggests that the disciples' ignorance of the Spirit is not to be understood in an ontological sense, but rather from an eschatological point of view about the outpouring of the Spirit bestowed by the Messiah after John in the last days.[204] The fact that Paul in his response to the Ephesians' answer does not specify the meaning of the term Spirit supports this. Even the Western reviser clarifies and gives an easier sense in this regard: 'We have not even heard whether people are receiving (λαμβάνουσίν τινες) the Holy Spirit'.[205] While it is clear that the disciples, as believers,[206] have not yet received the Spirit, the evidence suggests that they probably knew of the existence of the Spirit.[207] The following argument will clarify this suggestion.

b. The other reason Turner suggests concerns why they are 'rebaptized'. The justification for this step of (re)baptism is Paul's new information about the 'Messiah' whom they were hoping for in Acts 19:4 and 'faith' in him.[208]

---

[200] Quoted in Strelan, *Ephesus*, 240.

[201] Porter, *Paul*, 81-82.

[202] Porter, *Paul*, 82.

[203] Cf. n. 213 below.

[204] As Spencer points out, 'The sense of this declaration is commonly interpreted as ignorance not of the Spirit's existence but of the Spirit's special outpouring in the last days'. *Portrait*, 236. For the eschatological sense of the coming of the Spirit, see below in this section.

[205] Metzger, *Textual Commentary*, 469.

[206] This will further be clarified in what follows.

[207] Bruce, *Acts*, p. 363; Lake and Cadbury, *Beginnings*, IV, 237.

[208] Turner, 'Spirit and Prophecy', 338-39.

However, although Paul's reminder clearly provides the motive for the disciples' (re)baptism according to the context, in the light of 19:2 where they are considered by Paul as believers (πιστεύσαντες), it is difficult to understand the reference to faith in the Messiah as a disclosure of new information to them.[209] Furthermore, if belief in the Messiah is new information to them so that it is a real motivation to their (re)baptism, one would expect to hear what happened to them, i.e., that they repented and believed.[210] But such a description is not offered by Luke in the following context.[211]

If they believed in the Messiah and experienced John's baptism, what is newly communicated to them is probably the baptismal message which John declared concerning the future coming of the Messiah who will baptize his followers with the Spirit.[212] Although the reference to the Messiah's bestowal of the Spirit is not mentioned in verse 4, the overall context implies this information: Paul's instruction about the role of the Messiah in verse 4 is derived from the Ephesians' answer about their ignorance of the Spirit (in an eschatological sense) in verse 2. The following context clearly shows the result of Paul's instruction: they finally realized that the Messiah would administer the Spirit and were baptized and received the Spirit.[213]

Furthermore, the emphatic use of the phrase 'εἰς τὸν ἐρχόμενον' indicates the eschatological role of the Messiah who will bring the Spirit after John (v. 4). The Ephesians, like the disciples at Pentecost, were an eschatological community of believers in Jesus. Once they were baptized in the name of Jesus and received the same prophetic Spirit, they experienced the miraculous charismatic phenomena and finally became an eschatological prophetic community empowered for their missionary task.[214] This can be seen through the whole picture of Paul's ministry to the disciples and its charismatic outcomes in Acts 19:6. In particular, their

---

[209] Spencer, *Portrait*, 235-36, similarly, Menzies, *Development*, 274. Those who also think of the Ephesians as believers include Lake and Cadbury, *Beginnings*, IV, 237; Lake, 'The Twelve and the Apostles', 57; Haenchen, *Acts*, 556; Bruce, *Acts*, 363; Shelton, *Mighty*, 133-34; Stronstad, *Charismatic*, 68; Strelan, *Ephesus*, 237.

[210] Spencer, *Portrait*, 236.

[211] Elsewhere in Acts when the Christian message is proclaimed to unbelievers so that they accept it, Luke often reports that they believed and were baptized. E.g., Acts 8:12, 13; 18:8; cf. 2:41; 16:14f, 33f. Menzies, *Development*, 275.

[212] Bruce, *Acts*, 363; Spencer, *Portrait*, 236.

[213] The continuity of the saying about the Spirit can be described as follows: 1) The Ephesians' ignorance of the Spirit (v. 2) - - - - - -> 2) The implied information of the Spirit in connection with the Messiah in Paul's instruction (v. 4) - - - - -> 3) The result of the reception of the Spirit (vv. 5-6).

[214] Bruce argues that 'Ephesus was to be a new centre for the Gentile mission. . . and these twelve disciples probably to be the nucleus of the Ephesian church'. *Acts*, 365.

ability to speak in tongues and prophesy gives a signal that they had now become the eschatological people of God with charismatic empowerment. Luke does not report their forgiveness or repentance, but indicates that they had received the promised gift of the Spirit which would enable them to be effective in the task for which they had been commissioned like the disciples at Pentecost. If this is right, the direct motivation for the disciples' re-baptism is not 'believing in the Messiah', but rather 'believing in the Spirit-giving Messiah' in the end time.[215] Paul's point in verse 4 is to remind the Ephesians that John's baptism was simply preparatory for what was to come thereafter.

To sum up, several lines of evidence suggest that the Ephesians were believers before their reception of the Spirit. The motivation of their (re)baptism is that they, as believers, through Paul's instruction recognized the Messiah who would be a bestower of the Spirit in the end-time. It is not related to their new life experience. This all leads us once again to conclude that the gift of the Spirit is not an essential aspect of conversional experience in Luke's view.

4.5.3. Summary

Luke importantly connotes all three experiences, faith, water rite, and the reception of the Spirit as part of the normal believer's life, but he does not consciously put the order as a paradigm or rule. This suggests that any kind of exegesis should not be offered on a given interpreter's prior paradigm or conclusion. Furthermore, there is no reason to agree with any attempt to link the Spirit and conversion in the light of Luke's failure to do so in his writings. Luke's pneumatological perspective does not present the Spirit as the source of conversion or new life whereas Paul clearly connects the two.[216]

---

[215] Cf. Strelan, *Ephesus*, 242. Turner connects and contrasts the Ephesians' reception of re-baptism with Apollos, who did not receive a re-baptism. Turner argues that since the latter was a believer, who possessed the Spirit, he did not need to be re-baptized with water. By way of contrast, since the former were not believers (or not fully believers) without the Spirit, they essentially needed it in order to become fully believers although they knew the baptism of John. *Power*, 390-92. However, if the motivation for the Ephesians' re-baptism is rightly considered as argued above (i.e., their recognition of the Messiah who would bestow the Spirit in the end-time rather than belief in the Messiah), so that it is legitimate to regard them as believers before they received the Spirit, it is difficult to agree with Turner's ready contrast between Apollos and the Ephesians in terms of re-baptism. Furthermore, Turner's thesis is based on a clear connection between the Spirit and the rite of baptism. However, we have seen that Luke does not inevitably link the Spirit with the rite of baptism (e.g., Acts 8:17; 10:44).

[216] This conclusion raises a question regarding a common understanding between Luke

4.6. Conclusion

In response to my initial question in this chapter regarding to what extent Luke relates the Spirit to various aspects of the life of the kingdom, I have argued that Luke does not associate the Spirit with the blessings of the kingdom. For Luke, the Spirit is not understood as the source of sonship and he never suggests the source of Jesus' (and his disciples') conscious ability to call God, Abba, as a work of the Spirit. Luke's association of the Spirit with an ethical dimension in the relevant texts is rare and unclear. Even if there does exist some connection in Acts, particularly in the summaries of the community life, it is only presented in an indirect way, i.e., through the impact of prophetic speech. The Spirit is never presented as the

---

and Paul about reception of the Spirit. This matter has recently been defended by Menzies, who in particular argues against Turner. Turner argues that there is only a one-stage model for reception of the Spirit in the New Testament, particularly demonstrated in Paul's pneumatology which embraces all that really matters including the soteriological and prophetic dimensions of the work of the Spirit so that Luke has nothing to add to this broader pneumatology. Turner further maintains that since Paul does not allude to the two-stage model for reception of the Spirit, we should not speak of a second gift of the Spirit (see *Holy Spirit*, 150-68). Over against this thesis, Menzies points out two matters: 1) Although Paul has a more developed and comprehensive view of pneumatology than Luke, we should not forget the fact that Luke does have something distinctive and important to offer (e.g., the Pentecostal gift, a prophetic empowering rather than the chief element of conversion). 2) There is no reason to suggest that because Paul does not specifically speak of a gateway experience distinct from conversion, neither should we. This is because the Christian canon is rather larger than Paul's epistles. We need to allow the various New Testament authors 'to bring their unique insights which, at times, will help clarify the incomplete views of their biblical colleagues'. So, in Luke's perspective, 'there is a dimension of the Spirit's enabling that one enters by virtue of a baptism in the Spirit distinct from conversion'. Menzies, *Spirit and Power*, 98-102 (101, 102). Menzies raises two further questions: one is a matter concerning the inspiration of Scripture and the other is that Luke traveled with Paul. Menzies makes three points in responding to these two matters: 1) Following Marshall, 'An Evangelical Approach to "Theological Criticism"', *Themelios* 13 (1988), 81, Menzies argues that a high view of Scripture does not demand uniformity and rather suggests that the diversity in Scripture is ultimately harmonious. 2) Although Luke traveled with Paul and spent a considerable amount of time with the apostle, he, in other areas of theology, is not merely a slavish imitator of Paul. If so, why should Luke be so with respect to pneumatology? 3) The speeches in Acts suggest that, while Luke knew Paul's gospel well, he had not wrestled with his soteriological pneumatology. Paul's speeches in Acts accurately reflect Paul's gospel, but they do so without any reference to his distinctive soteriological pneumatology. Menzies, *Empowered*, 240-42. Above all, in view of Menzies' forceful argument, it is highly probable that Luke's view of the reception of the Spirit is distinct from that of Paul. Paul sees that the Spirit is at work in conversion in a soteriological way, but Luke does not clearly allude to this soteriological pneumatology.

source of the resurrection but inspires the apostles to proclaim it. Finally, according to Luke, the Spirit is not portrayed as the agent of conversion experience.

The manner of Luke's dissociation between the Spirit and the kingdom blessings is thus hardly comparable with Paul's wider association between the two as seen above. In any event, for Luke, the Spirit is not portrayed as the life of the kingdom in its totality as in Paul. This leads to an important conclusion that Paul *developed* the role of the Spirit more fully than Luke's (and the early [non-Pauline] church's) pneumatology in terms of the blessings and life of the kingdom: so there is a considerable difference between Paul's pneumatology and that of Luke.[217]

If, for Paul, the Spirit embodies the essence of the kingdom of God, then how does Luke relate the Spirit and the kingdom of God in his writings? The next chapter will therefore address the question of the manner in which Luke associates the Spirit with the kingdom of God.

---

[217] This brings the significant implication that although Paul's epistles were written earlier than Luke (and the other Synoptics) and Acts, which all reflect early material, it should be noted that this does not mean that Paul's ideas were widely influential on the non-Pauline sectors of the early church. In fact, the universal judgement among scholars suggests that Paul's epistles were not collected together and widely known until later, i.e., until after the writing of Luke-Acts. See Kümmel, *Introduction*, 186. They 'were collected toward the end of the first century'. Note Maddox's comments: 'It is today generally recognized that Luke did not know the Pauline letters, and that if he had any personal contact with Paul at all, it was not in such a way that he could get to know his theology in any more than a superficial way'. R. Maddox, *The Purpose of Luke-Acts*, FRLANT 126 (Göttingen: Vandenhoeck & Ruprecht, 1982), 68; J.C. O'Neill, *The Theology of Acts in Its Historical Setting* (London: SPCK, 1970), 134-35: 'Luke has no knowledge of the Pauline epistles' (135). M. Hengel, *Acts and the History of Earliest Christianity* (London: SCM Press, 1979), 66-67: 'Luke presumably did not know Paul's letters. He may have known that Paul sometimes sent letters to his churches, but these were no longer available to him at the time when he wrote, between 80 and 90' (66). See also Conzelmann, *Acts*, xxxiii; Haenchen, *Acts*, 125f. Thus, with reference to pneumatology based on this theory, the Synoptics and Acts in which a less developed pneumatology is reflected, stand as proof that Paul's broader pneumatology had not significantly influenced these sectors of the church, particularly Luke-Acts in that pneumatology which is prominent as seen above. Menzies, *Empowered*, 242.

CHAPTER 5

The Primary Role of the Spirit in Relation to the Kingdom of God in Luke-Acts: Proclamation

5.1. Introduction

In the previous chapter, we have argued that the Spirit has a limited relationship to the life of the kingdom (sonship, ethics, resurrection, new life, righteousness etc.) in Luke-Acts. With this point in view, it can be convincingly demonstrated that for Luke the Spirit is not characterized as the life of the kingdom in its entirety. On the contrary, we have seen that Paul presents the Spirit as the essence of the kingdom. So, the remaining question which needs to be more specifically asked is how the Spirit functions in relation to the kingdom of God in Luke-Acts.

While few would deny that Luke makes a relationship between the Spirit and the kingdom of God, this relationship has not been fully developed among scholars. Nevertheless, an attempt to correlate the two in Luke's writings has been explored by both Dunn and Smalley. They have argued that Luke views the Spirit as the manifestation of the kingdom. Jesus experiences the kingdom of God through the presence of the Spirit in his earthly ministry. Likewise, the disciples do not taste the kingdom during Jesus' ministry but experience it at Pentecost through the gift of the Spirit. This leads both of them to conclude that there is 'some form of equation between Spirit and kingdom'[1] and 'Luke's theological understanding, moreover, is such that he also views the activity of the Spirit among men and the arrival of the kingdom of God as aligned if not synonymous. Where the Spirit is, there is the kingdom'.[2] However, the nature of the relationship between the two should be carefully questioned as follows: 1) Does the Spirit mediate the presence of the kingdom in Luke as Dunn (and Smalley) argues? and 2) If the activity of the Spirit is closely connected to the

---

[1] *Pneumatology*, 138. Dunn further comments that 'It is not so much a case of Where *Jesus* is there is the kingdom of God, as Where the *Spirit* is there is the kingdom'. Emphasis is original.

[2] S. Smalley, 'Spirit, Kingdom and Prayer in Luke-Acts', *NovT* 15 (1973), 59-71 (64).

The Primary Role of the Spirit 163

kingdom as Smalley maintains, what is Luke's account of the specific or primary role (or activity) of the Spirit, (which Smalley has failed to explain the significance of, as will be shown), in bringing the kingdom? The purpose of this chapter is to answer these two questions, particularly focusing on the latter.

The procedure for the pursuit of this purpose will unfold as follows: in section 1, it will be noted that Spirit and kingdom are not equated according to Luke, in contrast to what Dunn argues. Then in section 2, the emphasis on the activity of the Spirit in relation to the kingdom will be offered: Luke sees the Spirit as an empowering to inspire people to proclaim the kingdom which gives others an opportunity to enter into it. What is the principal role of the Spirit upon Jesus the Messiah in his bringing the kingdom? Can the same role of the Spirit in relation to the kingdom be applicable to the disciples and the church after Pentecost?[3]

5.2. The Spirit as the Presence of the Kingdom of God?

As mentioned above, Dunn argues that Spirit-reception is the manifestation of the kingdom. Dunn supports his thesis primarily from Luke 11:2; Luke 12:31-32 (in relation to Lk. 11:13); and Acts 1:3-8. We will examine each of these texts in turn, particularly focusing on 12:31-32 (and Lk. 11:13).[4] In addition to these texts, I will discuss Luke 11:20 since it refers directly to the coming of the kingdom with the reference to the finger of God.[5]

5.2.1. Luke 11:2

Dunn, while he admits its weak attestation, prefers the Lukan variant 'let thy Holy Spirit come upon us and cleanse us' (ἐλθέτω τὸ πνεῦμα σου τὸ

---

[3] Since we have already discussed some important pneumatological texts in Luke-Acts in the earlier chapter, the texts to be discussed in this chapter will be confined to the narratives in which the Spirit is connected to the kingdom of God. For the study of the kingdom of God in Luke-Acts, see O. Merk, 'Das Reich Gottes in den lukanischen Schriften', in E.E. Ellis & E. Grässer (eds.), *Jesus und Paulus* (Göttingen: Vandenhoeck & Ruprecht, 1975), 201-20; O'Toole, 'The Kingdom of God', 147-62; A. Weiser, '"Reich Gottes", in der Apostelgeschichte', in C. Bussmann & W. Radl (eds.), *Der Treue Gottes trauen* (Freiburg: Herder, 1992), 127-35; M. Wolter, '"Reich Gottes" bei Lukas', *NTS* 41 (1995), 541-63; A. Prieur, *Die Verkündigung der Gottesherrschaft: Exegetische Studien zum lukanischen Verständnis von βασιλεία τοῦ θεοῦ*, WUNT 2.89 (Tübingen: Mohr, 1996).

[4] However, a comprehensive discussion of Acts 1:3-8 will be offered in the following section.

[5] Although Dunn does not directly discuss Lk. 11:20 in supporting his thesis, nonetheless, he argues elsewhere that the phrase 'finger of God' is equivalent to 'the Spirit of God'. This conclusion certainly supports Dunn's argument to equate the Spirit with the kingdom. *Jesus and Spirit*, 46-49.

ἅγιον ἐφ' ἡμᾶς καὶ καθαρισάτω ἡμᾶς) to 'Let thy kingdom come' (ἐλθέτω ἡ βασιλεία σου) as the possible original reading. Dunn, based on this reading, further argues that 'the petition concerning the Spirit was an appropriate substitution for the petition concerning the kingdom, or vice-versa'.[6]

However, two considerations undermine Dunn's argument: 1) The manuscript evidence for the variant is decisively weak: it is conserved in 700 and 162, is supported by some Fathers such as Gregory-Nyssa and Maximus of Turin, and is mentioned by Tertullian. The two late minuscule manuscripts (700 [11th century] and 162 [12th century]) cannot be enough to overturn the whole of the unanimous witness of the Greek manuscripts.[7] 2) As Metzger argues, in the light of the fact that the variant represents a liturgical adaptation of the original form of the Lord's prayer, 'one cannot understand why, if it were original in the prayer, it should have been supplanted in the overwhelming majority of the witnesses by a concept originally much more Jewish in its piety'.[8] These two arguments cast considerable doubt upon Dunn's assertion that the variant could be original and, for this reason, Dunn's attempt to equate the Spirit and the kingdom in Luke 11:2 cannot be accepted.[9]

5.2.2. Luke 12:31-32 (cf. Luke 11:13)

According to Dunn, Jesus in Luke 12:31-32 declares that the kingdom of God is the highest good that the disciples can seek and that it is God's pleasure to give it to them. In a similar manner, Dunn understands the gift of the Holy Spirit in Luke 11:13 as the highest good promised to those who ask (the disciples). Dunn then concludes that both the Spirit and the kingdom are represented as the highest good promised to the disciples: 'the kingdom and the Spirit are alternative ways of speaking about the disciples' highest good'.[10] Thus, as the highest good in each text, the two are constituted as an equation. However, it is highly questionable whether Luke has such an intention in mind to equate the Spirit and the kingdom by connecting these two texts. Some points need to be considered.

a. With regard to Luke 11:13, the first point that needs to be made is Dunn's view that the Spirit is pictured as the disciples' highest good. The point to note in Luke 11:13 is that whereas Matthew's parallel has 'ἀγαθά' (Mt. 7:11), Luke describes the gift as the 'πνεῦμα ἅγιον'. Matthew's reading is regarded by most commentators as originating from Q.[11] This

---

[6] *Pneumatology*, 138.
[7] Marshall, *Luke*, 458.
[8] *Textual Commentary*, 156.
[9] See also Betz, *Sermon*, 392: this petition (the coming of the Holy Spirit) appears to be a later substitution'.
[10] Dunn, *Pneumatology*, 137-38.
[11] E.g., E. Ellis, *The Gospel of Luke*, NCB (London: Marshall, Morgan & Scott, 1974),

argument, particularly in the light of pneumatology, is confirmed by the fact that 'Matthew keeps close to his sources (Mark or Q) and *never* in the passages examined *adds* references to the Holy Spirit. On the other hand Luke both adds such references, *and deletes them'*.[12]

Based on the probability that Luke's 'πνεῦμα ἅγιον' is redactional, one may say that this is Luke's emphasis on the reference to the Spirit. However, while this is true[13] and Luke is more specific than Matthew about what the 'good things' are, this does not mean that Luke understood the gift of the Spirit to be the 'highest good'. Luke does not say or connote this in the text. It would be reasonable to understand it as Luke's interpretation of one aspect of the 'good gifts' the Father delights to give. As Luke widely states elsewhere, the Spirit is clearly characterized as the promised gift from God (Lk. 24:49; Acts 1:4, 5, 8; 2:38; 8:20; 10:45; 11:17; 15:8), but it does not necessarily connote the highest good. Luke in 11:13 highlights this one aspect of the 'good gifts' of which Jesus spoke, particularly designating the gift that would be bestowed at Pentecost.[14]

A further point needs to be made in regard to Luke 11:13: if Dunn's overall thesis, 'the presence of the Spirit means the presence of the kingdom', is right, the gift promised to the disciples in Luke 11:13 should

---

164; Fitzmyer, *Luke X-XXIV*, 915-16; C.F. Evans, *Saint Luke* (London: SCM Press, 1990), 487; Nolland, *Luke 9:21-18:34*, 361; Menzies, *Development*, 181.

[12] C.S. Rodd, 'Spirit and Finger', *ExpT* 72 (1961), 157-58 (158). Emphasis is original. See below in this section for a further discussion on this matter.

[13] The term 'Holy Spirit' occurs a total of 26 times in Luke-Acts: 8 times in Luke's gospel and 18 times in Acts compared with 3 times in Matthew's gospel and only once in Mark's gospel.

[14] Based on Lk. 11:13 (cf. 9:1-10:22), Turner argues that the Spirit is depicted as a present availability to some of Jesus' followers (i.e., before Pentecost) so that 'they could experience this beneficent "Spirit" from God in answer to prayer'. *Power*, 340. However, in view of the fact that Luke generally depicts the disciples as those who fail to pray in spite of their request to learn to pray (e.g., Lk. 9:28, 32; 22:39, 45-46; cf. Lk. 11:1), it is difficult to argue that they have experienced the Spirit in response to their prayers *before* Pentecost. Hur, *Dynamic Reading*, 216-17, n. 116. By way of contrast, Luke in his second work positively describes the disciples' prayer in relation to the reception of the gift of the Spirit (e.g., 1:14; 4:31; cf. 2:42; 3:1. For the prayer activities of the early church, cf. 7:55-60; 8:15, 17; 9:11; 10:9, 19; 13:1-2). Particularly, in 4:31, Luke reports that the disciples, as a consequence of their prayer, 'were all filled with the Holy Spirit, and began to speak the word of God with boldness'. Hence, as most scholars agree, the gift of the Spirit in Lk. 11:13 refers to the future experience of the church rather than to the time of Jesus' ministry. E.g., Rodd, 'Spirit or Finger', 158; Tannehill, *Narrative*, I, 239; J. Lieu, *The Gospel of Luke* (Peterborough: Epworth, 1997), 91; Shelton, *Mighty*, 96; Stronstad, *Charismatic*, 46; E. Franklin, *Luke: Interpreter of Paul, Critic of Matthew*, JSNTS 92 (Sheffield: JSOP Press, 1994), 300, particularly for the critique of Turner's argument, see Menzies, *Development*, 182, n. 3.

be understood as an initiatory or soteriological gift. However, in view of the fact that the promise is made to those who have already experienced the kingdom, i.e., the disciples (cf. Lk. 11:2, Father), Dunn's thesis is hard to sustain.[15]

b. With regard to Luke 12:31-32, Dunn is right when he argues that the kingdom is the thing that the disciples should seek first as their highest good. However, although similar expressions can be found in the concepts of 'asking/seeking', and 'being given from the Father' in each text, Dunn's connection of this text with Luke 11:13 seems to be mistaken. For, as noted above, the gift of the Spirit in Luke 11:13 does not indicate the disciples' highest good.[16]

A substantial reason for rejecting Dunn's view (his equating the Spirit and the kingdom) should now be considered. Indeed, Dunn has a faulty assumption when he argues elsewhere that the kingdom of God is only a future reality to the disciples.[17] In other words, as noticed in our introduction, Dunn argues that the disciples do not participate in the kingdom of God during Jesus' ministry and they only experience it at Pentecost due to their experience of the Spirit.[18] The corollary of Dunn's sayings would clearly appear to be that the Spirit is the essential reason for the disciples' experience of the kingdom of God. However, while Dunn rightly notes that the disciples initially experience the Spirit at Pentecost, it is difficult to agree with his identifying the manifestation of the Spirit at Pentecost with the disciples' inaugural experience of the kingdom of God since the promise of the kingdom in Luke 12:31-32 is not directly related to Pentecost.[19] As Turner rightly suggests, the promise in Luke 12:31-32 'does not constitute a specific promise that "the kingdom of God" would be "given to them" at Pentecost (or at any other time)'.[20] The following observation will clarify this.

In fact, there is abundant evidence that the disciples (and Jesus' followers) have experienced the kingdom, regardless of their lack of experience of the Spirit, during Jesus' ministry as shown in Luke's gospel.[21]

---

[15] Menzies, *Development*, 184, n. 3.
[16] Turner, *Power*, 332, n. 39.
[17] Dunn, *Baptism*, 38-54 (41-43); *Pneumatology*, 140.
[18] Likewise, according to Dunn, as noted earlier, Jesus experiences the kingdom of God at Jordan because of the Spirit.
[19] For the tense and the meaning of the kingdom in Lk. 12:31, see below in this section.
[20] Turner, *Power*, 332, n. 39.
[21] As noted earlier, there is a considerable consensus among scholars that the kingdom of God is a present reality, particularly in the person of Jesus and his ministry. The evidence of this notion is sufficiently depicted by Luke in that those who have responded to and committed themselves to the kingdom of God in the present ministry of Jesus have foretasted the benefits of the future rule of God. Lk. 5:1-11; 7:36-50; 8:1-3, 48; 9:21-27, 60; 10:1-20; 11:2, 14-22; 12:31-32; 13:10-17; 14:15-24;

This is made clear by the fact that Luke characterizes the tasks of the disciples as both 'kingdom-proclamation' and 'kingdom-ministry' by Jesus sharing his task with them. Luke in 9:2 says that 'He (Jesus) sent them out to preach the kingdom of God' (Lk. 9:2, 6; cf. Lk. 10:9, 11). This sending formulation is quite similar to that of Jesus himself as in Luke 4:18; 43-44; 8:1. So the disciples' proclamation of the kingdom is an extension of Jesus' proclamation of it.[22] In 9:1 (cf. v. 6), Luke further shows that they are called to manifest the benefits of the kingdom through the power and authority displayed by Jesus: 'When Jesus had called the twelve together, he gave them power and authority to drive out all demons and to cure diseases' (cf. 10:17-19). Hence, Jesus' exorcisms are not only a manifestation of God's ruling power, but also indicate the availability of its benefits to the hearers (Lk. 11:20).[23] Jesus' ministry makes the kingdom accessible to all who respond to and accept the message of its bringer.[24] Jesus' ministry is partly passed on to the disciples and the kingdom is proclaimed by them, who are *already* the tasters of the kingdom, so that it comes near and is subsequently available to the hearers who respond to the kingdom-message.[25] This two-fold ministry, preaching the kingdom and performing the signs of the reign of God, in Luke 9:1-2 is analogous to that of Jesus (Lk. 9:11):[26] '. . . He welcomed them and spoke to them about the kingdom of God, and healed those who needed healing'. The disciples are certainly co-workers with Jesus (or members of the kingdom) both in the proclamation of the kingdom of God and in the establishment of God's sovereign reign.

Furthermore, returning to Luke 12:31-32, the expression, 'your Father' spoken by Jesus in verse 32 indicates the disciples' new relationship of sonship to God. As seen earlier, in his teaching on prayer, Jesus teaches the disciples to call God Father using the intimate form (Lk. 11:2). The use of this intimate form encourages the disciples 'into the same close relationship with the Father that he (Jesus) enjoyed'.[27] Hence, seeking the kingdom of their Father[28] is a privilege enjoyed by the disciples (as his children) in a

---

15:1-32; 17:21; 19:1-10; 22:29 etc. See Merk, 'Reich Gottes', 216, 219; Turner, *Power*, 319-33; Marshall, *Historian*, 128-44.

[22] Tannehill, *Narrative*, I, 215.

[23] As Dunn himself, based on Lk. 11:20, notes that 'the exercise of this power *was evidence that the longed-for kingdom of God had already come upon his hearers*: his exorcisms demonstrated that the last days were already present'. *Jesus and Spirit*, 47. Emphasis is original. See below in this section for the discussion on Lk. 11:20.

[24] Turner, *Power*, 320.

[25] Marshall, *Historian*, 134.

[26] Marshall, *Luke*, 352.

[27] Marshall, *Luke*, 456.

[28] Bock argues that the present tense, ζητεῖτε denotes the disciples' habit, that is, 'keep seeking his kingdom'. *Luke 9:51-24:53*, 1164; Nolland, *Luke 9:21-18:34*, 693. See

new relationship, though not of all humanity. The description that 'giving the kingdom' is the Father's *pleasure* further denotes that the kingdom, while it will be consummated in the future, is available to the disciples at present by their seeking and pursuing it. The promise of the kingdom can be presently realized in an intimate and secure relationship with God.[29] This all suggests that the kingdom of God is not simply a future entity which the disciples may experience only at Pentecost.

To sum up, the texts that Dunn shows do not appropriately support his assertion that the Spirit is the presence of the kingdom of God. The promise of the gift of the Spirit in Luke 11:13 is not concerned with the disciples' 'highest good'. The kingdom of God in Luke 12:31-32 as the highest good should not be connected with the saying of Jesus in Luke 11:13 and should not be confused with the gift of the Spirit at Pentecost.

5.2.3. Luke 11:20

Luke 11:20 reads: 'But if it is by the finger of God (δακτύλῳ θεοῦ) that I cast out demons, then the kingdom of God has come upon you (ἄρα ἔφθασεν ἐφ' ὑμᾶς[30] ἡ βασιλεία τοῦ θεοῦ)'. This text contains the reference to the kingdom of God and an ambiguous phrase 'the finger of God'.

It is often argued that since the phrase 'finger of God' in Luke 11:20 designates the 'Spirit' as the divine agent in Jesus, it can be said that the manifestation of the kingdom in Jesus' ministry means the presence of the Spirit. Indeed, there is a considerable debate among scholars about the meaning of the phrase 'δακτύλῳ θεοῦ'.[31] Matthew's version (12:28)[32] is almost identical to that of Luke except that Matthew's 'πνεύματι θεοῦ' is substituted for Luke's 'δακτύλῳ θεοῦ'.[33] So, the question as to which version is the original of Q has been often debated. However, in relation to this question, a more important question that needs to be considered for the present study is that if Matthew preserves the original reading (see below), what is Luke's reason for altering his source in spite of his interest in the Spirit (cf. Lk. 11:13)? The following discussion will focus on this question.

While a number of observations support Luke's version as being original,[34] a more recent view lends weight to the view that Matthew's

---

also §3.3.4.2.

[29] Bock, *Luke 9:51-24:53*, 1165.
[30] For the meaning of ἔφθασεν ἐφ' ὑμᾶς, see §3.3.2.2.
[31] For the overall study of Lk. 11:20, see Woods, *Finger*.
[32] 'But if it is by the Spirit of God that I cast out demons, then the kingdom of God has come upon you'.
[33] As Marshall notes, since there is a close verbal agreement between the two verses, one must be a substitution for the other from his source. *Luke*, 475.
[34] Notably, 1) Since the πνεῦμα is Luke's favourite term, there is no reason to alter what already existed in his source; 2) It is argued that Matthew's alteration of the original

version is original. Nolland claims that 'all the more recent studies that have focused attention on this matter conclude that Luke is the one who has altered the text'.[35] The evidence is substantiated by the following.

a. Matthew in 12:28 appears to be following his source without changing the phrase 'kingdom of God' while he regularly alters it to 'kingdom of heaven', which is his favourite expression (e.g., Mt. 4:17; 5:3; 8:11; 10:7; 11:11f.; 13:11, 31, 33; 19:14, 23, but with the exception of 19:24).[36]

b. Luke's redactional freedom can be applied in this case. As seen above, while Matthew usually follows his source with the reference from either Mark and/or Q, Luke not only inserts the term Spirit to his source (e.g., Lk. 4:1, 14; 10:21; 11:13), but also deletes it (e.g., Lk. 21:15=Mk. 13:11; Lk. 20:42=Mk. 12:36).[37]

c. Luke never uses the phrase 'Spirit of God' in his works, and Matthew is the only evangelist to use it (e.g., 3:16; 12:28).[38]

d. In view of Matthew's interest in comparing Jesus and Moses rather than the Spirit, there is little reason for Matthew to alter the 'finger of God' to the 'Spirit of God'.[39]

e. Luke has changed the original word (Spirit of God) to the 'finger of God' in order to avoid attributing the miracles and exorcisms to the Spirit.[40]

f. Finally, while the above considerations seem to strongly support the

---

source is to avoid an anthropomorphism. E.g., T.W. Manson, *The Teaching of Jesus* (Cambridge: CUP, 1951), 82-83; Barrett, *Gospel Tradition*, 62-63; Ellis, *Luke*, 165; Bock, *Luke 9:51-24:53*, 1079, n. 21. For the critique of the above views, see J.E. Yates, *The Spirit and the Kingdom* (London: SPCK, 1963), 90-94; R.G. Hamerton-Kelly, 'A Note on Matthew XII. 28 Par. Luke XI. 20', *NTS* 11 (1965), 167-69.

[35] *Luke 9:21-18:34*, 639.
[36] Dunn, *Jesus and Spirit*, 45.
[37] Rodd, 'Spirit and Finger', 157-58; Menzies, *Development*, 186.
[38] Rodd, 'Spirit and Finger', 158; Woods, *Finger*, 152, 158.
[39] Dunn, *Jesus and Spirit*, 45; Turner, *Power*, 257.
[40] Franklin, *Luke*, 300; Menzies, *Spirit and Power*, 149; Schweizer, 'πνεῦμα', 407-08. Evans, while he is not sure which version is originally from Q, argues that Luke's use of the phrase, 'finger of God', which goes back to Exod. 8:19 and Deut. 9:10, is to be seen by the fact that Luke in his writings tends to use OT terms such as the 'power of the Lord' (Lk. 5:17; 6:19) or the 'hand of the Lord' (Acts 4:28-30; 13:11) in attributing healing or exorcism rather than the Spirit. Evans, *Luke*, 492. On the other hand, on the basis of the closely related anthropomorphism the 'hand of God' with the Spirit in *Targum Ezekiel*, Turner identifies the 'finger of God' with the Spirit of God in attributing miracles of healing and exorcism. *Power*, 258. However, this cannot be convincing since the phrase 'hand of the Lord' used in each text of *Targum Ezekiel* (1:3; 3:14, 22; 8:1-3; 33:22; 37:1; 40:1) indicates 'an overpowering experience of prophetic transportation, empowering, and divine revelation. Each of these ultimately relates to the prophetic task of *proclamation*' rather than to miracles performed on others. Woods, *Finger*, 256. Emphasis is original. Turner's identification of the two is also weakened by Evans' argument discussed above.

view that Matthew preserves the original version,[41] an important implication can be made from this change, particularly in relation to the present study. That is, Luke 11:20 shows that for Luke the work of the Spirit is not described as the presence of the kingdom of God. Of course, it may be difficult to argue that Luke consciously alters his source from 'Spirit' to 'finger' for this reason. Nevertheless, the question may be asked, if the Lukan alteration is correct and even if the Spirit is Luke's favourite term, why does Luke alter his source? In addition, in relation to this question, we may consider the fact that when Luke refers to the kingdom of God along with the reference to the Spirit in the various contexts, he never substitutes the latter for any other expressions *except* Luke 11:20 (e.g., Lk. 4:16f.; Acts 1:3-8; 8:12-15, 29-40; 19:1-8; 20:22-25; 28:23-31; cf. Lk. 1:32-35; 11:1-13). Furthermore, the texts which link the Spirit to the reference to the kingdom in Luke-Acts (see references above) do not present the work (or presence) of the Spirit as the manifestation of the kingdom. Rather, as will be seen in detail in what follows, Luke's connection between the two is carefully depicted: the role of the Spirit is primarily characterized as the means by which the kingdom is *proclaimed*, i.e., the Spirit inspires Jesus and his witness and thereby provides the context, i.e., the proclamation of the good news of the kingdom of God, for people to hear and enter into the kingdom. Luke 11:20 perhaps highlights that for Luke, proclamation is the primary manifestation of the Spirit's inspiration.

If it is right that Luke's redaction is motivated by his pneumatological concern, Luke 11:20 is a significant indication that for Luke the Spirit is related to the kingdom of God in a very narrow and specific way. Unlike Paul, Luke does not present the work of the Spirit as the manifestation of the kingdom of God. This is confirmed by the fact that, as seen above, the various aspects of the manifestation of the kingdom are not generally attributed to the work of the Spirit by Luke. Luke 11:20 most likely emphasizes this fact through the alteration of by the 'Spirit of God' to by the 'finger of God'. However, above all, although the overall context of Luke 11:20 is clearly related to Lukan pneumatology in view of his redaction, it ultimately shows that the realization of the kingdom of God is essentially linked with the person of Jesus and his event rather than the work of the Spirit.[42]

---

[41] For further support for this view, see Yates, *The Spirit and the Kingdom*, 90-94; Hamerton-Kelly, 'A Note', 167-69; R.W. Wall, '"The Finger of God": Deuteronomy 9:10 and Luke 11:20', *NTS* 33 (1987), 144-50; Nolland, *Luke 9:21-18:34*, 639-40; Turner, *Power*, 257-58.

[42] Note Prieur's critique about both Dunn and Smalley's statement, '"it is not so much a case of Where *Jesus* is there is the Kingdom, as Where the *Spirit* is there is the Kingdom"; eine These, die exegetisch nicht zu überzeugen vermag'. *Verkündigung*, 176, n. 41. Note also Agua's comment: 'Where he (Jesus) arrives, arrives the Basileia'. A.D. Agua, 'The Lukan Narrative of the "Evangelization of the Kingdom

5.2.4. Summary

Dunn's intentional correspondence of the Spirit and the kingdom from Luke 11:2; 11:13; 12:31-32; and Acts 1:3-8 (which will be seen) has certainly oversimplified the nature of the relationship. His attempt to equate the Spirit and the kingdom presents rather the view of Paul as seen above (chapter 3). For Luke, the Spirit is not presented as the manifestation of the kingdom. Luke 11:20 underscores this fact. As Acts 1:3-8 will show, the nature of the relationship is something like the following: the presence of the Spirit is represented as the divine power that lies behind the proclamation of the kingdom of God.

5.3. The Spirit and the Proclamation of the Kingdom of God

While the theme of the kingdom of God is a vast subject in Luke-Acts, one of the distinctive uses of the kingdom of God terminology in Luke is in the description 'to proclaim the kingdom of God' (expressed with its various verbs).[43] These expressions are used only by Luke among the other New Testament writers and occupy up to one quarter of the total references to the kingdom of God in Luke-Acts.[44] Its proclamation by Jesus and the disciples is the means by which the kingdom of God becomes a present reality. However, although this is widely pointed out in scholarly circles, the nature of the activity of the Spirit behind the proclamation of the kingdom in Luke-Acts has not been fully discussed. Thus, returning to Smalley's thesis cited in our introduction, the primary role of the Spirit in relation to the kingdom should be dealt with in this section.

5.3.1. The Spirit and Jesus' Proclamation of the Kingdom of God (Lk. 4:16-30, 42-44)

NT scholars have taken increasing notice of this passage in the past few decades. For instance, Barrett regards this passage as an anticipation of Jesus' whole ministry.[45] Danker views the passage as highlighting Jesus' ultimate fate.[46] Marshall sees within this passage a programmatic significance, and that it contains many of the important themes of Luke-

---

of God": A Contribution to the Unity of Luke-Acts', in J. Verheyden (ed.), *The Unity of Luke-Acts* (Louvain: LUP, 1999), 653; Völkel, *Reich Gottes*, 63; Franklin, *Luke*, 300.

[43] E.g., with εὐαγγελίζεσθαι (Lk. 4:43; 8:1; 16:16; Acts 8:12); with κηρύσσειν (Lk. 8:1; 9:2; Acts 20:25; 28:31); with διαγγέλλειν (Lk. 9:60); with λέγειν (Acts 1:3); with λαλεῖν (Lk. 9:11). Weiser observes that 'Er verwendet als einziger neutestamentlicher Schriftsteller den Ausdruck "das Reich Gottes verkünden"'. 'Reich Gottes', 127.

[44] Merk, 'Reich Gottes', 204-11 (204); Weiser, 'Reich Gottes', 127.

[45] C.K. Barrett, *Luke the Historian in Recent Study* (London: Epworth, 1961), 64.

[46] F.W. Danker, *Jesus and the New Age* (Philadelphia: Fortress Press, 1988), 106.

Acts.[47] According to de Jonge, this passage, especially Luke 4:18, confirms the fact that Jesus is the Christ and explains why he could be so called. Of the Synoptics, it is only Luke who gives such an explanation in the earliest period.[48] Furthermore, it has been stated by some that there is a Lukan emphasis on the role of the Spirit associated with Jesus' ministry, particularly in the quotation of Isaiah 61:1-2 in Luke 4:18-19.[49] Amidst these views the fact should not be missed that in the narrative there is a close connection between the Spirit and the kingdom of God, a matter which has been given little attention by scholars. So, in what sense does the Spirit function and relate to the kingdom of God in the Nazareth pericope?

5.3.1.1. THE FIGURE OF JESUS: THE HERALD-PROPHET OF THE KINGDOM OF GOD

Jesus puts himself within the prophetic tradition by declaring the words of Isaiah 61:1f., 'the Spirit of the Lord is on me because he has anointed me. . .'. Along with Jesus' return from the wilderness 'in the power of the Spirit' in Luke 4:14 (also 4:1), the reference to Jesus' anointing here 'continues the thread running back to the descent of the Spirit on Jesus in 3:22'.[50] The passage of Isaiah 61:1-2, the anointing by God and possession of the Spirit of the Lord, identifies the orator of the passage as Jesus who has been baptized not so long ago.[51]

Although it is not easy to decide whether the anointing of Jesus here is essentially royal-Davidic or prophetic-Mosaic as Tiede suggests,[52] there is no doubt that one clear representation of Jesus is intended here. That is, Jesus is described as the eschatological prophet in terms of OT fulfillment and he himself is regarded as the fulfillment[53] of the prophecy.[54] For Luke, 'the fairly considerable use of the category of a prophet to interpret the person of Jesus in Luke affords some presumption that the idea is present in

---

[47] Marshall, *Luke*, 177-78.

[48] M. de Jonge, *Christology in Context: The Earliest Christian Response to Jesus* (Philadelphia: Westminster Press, 1988), 100.

[49] Menzies, *Development*, 161-77; Turner, *Power*, 213-66.

[50] Penney, *Missionary*, 41-42. See also Bock, 'Proclamation from Prophecy', 290.

[51] Lieu, *Luke*, 32.

[52] D.L. Tiede, *Prophecy and History in Luke-Acts* (Philadelphia: Fortress Press, 1980), 42.

[53] It is noteworthy that Luke depicts the prophetic image of Jesus' identity by his claiming that 'this scripture is now fulfilled'. This proclamation is meant as a counter claim against the Nazarenes' prejudice that Jesus was just Joseph's son. Hence Luke attaches a prophetic image to Jesus' identity as the Spirit-filled Messiah according to the Isaiah passage. R. Brawley, *Luke-Acts and the Jews: Conflict, Apology, and Conciliation* (Atlanta: Scholars Press, 1987), 16.

[54] Marshall, *Historian*, 118-28. (esp. 125-28).

this passage'.⁵⁵ On the other hand, Fitzmyer argues that there is no messianic anointing here, but maintains that Jesus is presented as a prophetic figure.⁵⁶ But to confine this only to a prophetic anointing 'would isolate the text from the preceding references to Jesus as Davidic Messiah and Son of God'.⁵⁷ The anointing indicates that Jesus will act out of divine motivation in a Davidic rule to fulfill God's promise to Abraham. Jesus is the Messiah who reflects a messianic servant figure. The messianic servant is markedly a prophet because the functions of the eschatological prophet and the Messiah are represented as identical to the other as indicated in Luke 7:19-22.⁵⁸ Thus it is not difficult to understand Jesus in Luke 4:18f. as both prophet and Messiah.

More significantly, Luke portrays Jesus as the herald-prophet of the kingdom of God. As will be seen in what follows, the primary purpose of Jesus' task indicated in Luke 4:18-19 consists of the proclamation of the kingdom of God. Jesus has been sent 'to preach good news to the poor, captives, blind' and 'to proclaim the year of the Lord's favour'. The purpose of this task is emphatically indicated in Jesus' own statement of his heralding of the kingdom of God in Luke 4:43 for which Jesus has been sent (the divine passive: ἐπὶ τοῦτο ἀπεστάλην⁵⁹) 'to preach the good news of the kingdom of God' (εὐαγγελίσασθάι με δεῖ τὴν βασιλείαν τοῦ θεοῦ).⁶⁰ Furthermore, Jesus declares 'Today this scripture has been fulfilled in your hearing' (Lk. 4:21). In this saying, reflecting his self-consciousness, Jesus indicates himself as a prophetic figure, the Messiah anointed by the Spirit

---

⁵⁵ Marshall, *Historian*, 125. For instance, Lk. 7:16, 'A great prophet has arisen among us'; Lk. 13:33, 'for it cannot be that a prophet should perish away from Jerusalem'; Lk. 24:19, 'Concerning Jesus of Nazareth, who was a prophet mighty in deed and word before God and all the people'. Jesus also regards himself as a prophet as the first person in the passage and he describes his fate as that of a prophet in Lk. 4:24, '. . . no prophet is acceptable in his hometown'.

⁵⁶ Fitzmyer, *Luke I-IX*, 529-30, 532.

⁵⁷ Tannehill, *Narrative*, I, 63.

⁵⁸ Marshall, *Historian*, 127.

⁵⁹ In Jesus' sending formula for his task, Mark in 1:38 simply says 'for that is why I came out' (ἐξῆλθον), but Luke apparently describes this sending in terms of divine mandate (ἀπεστάλην). This alteration is also closely linked to Luke's emphasis on the proclamation of the good news for which Jesus was sent (Lk. 4:18). Cf. Prieur, *Verkündigung*, 169.

⁶⁰ In comparison with Mark's account in 1:35-39, esp. v. 38 where the content of Jesus' proclamation is not referred to ('I may preach [κηρύσσω] there also'), Luke here clearly mentions its object, the kingdom of God. Prieur, *Verkündigung*, 171. Furthermore, in 4:44 ('And he was preaching in the synagogues of Judea'), Luke also omits the reference to Jesus' exorcism indicated in Mark's account (4:39) in order to emphasize the importance of proclaiming the good news of the kingdom of God. See Marshall, *Luke*, 198. For the overall discussion of Luke's alteration in Lk. 4:42-44 from Mk. 1:35-39, see Prieur, *Verkündigung*, 167-74.

and the herald of the kingdom of God.⁶¹ Thus, as will be shown in detail, the endowment of the Spirit functions as evidence that Jesus has been sent by God to fulfill his prophetic mission by proclaiming the kingdom of God.

In short, at the beginning of his public ministry in Nazareth, Jesus proclaims himself as the herald-prophet of the kingdom of God to show how central and crucial this task is to his future mission.

5.3.1.2. THE SPIRIT AND THE TASK OF THE MESSIAH

5.3.1.2.1. Luke's Unique Emphasis on the Spirit in the First Public Announcement of Jesus (Kingdom of God)

Jesus' first public announcement is recorded in all the Synoptic gospels, but it is only Luke who refers to the Spirit in connection with Jesus' ministry.

Mt. 4:12-17	Mk. 1:14-15	Lk. 4:14-19
When Jesus heard that John had been put in prison, he returned to Galilee... From that time on Jesus began to preach, 'Repent, for the kingdom of heaven is near' (Μετανοεῖτε· ἤγγικεν γὰρ ἡ βασιλεία τῶν οὐρανῶν).	After John was put in prison, Jesus went into Galilee, proclaiming the good news of God. 'The time has come', he said. The kingdom of God is near. Repent and believe the good news' (ἤγγικεν ἡ βασιλεία τοῦ θεοῦ· μετανοεῖτε καὶ πιστεύετε ἐν τῷ εὐαγγελίῳ).	Jesus returned to Galilee in the power of the Spirit (ἐν τῇ δυνάμει τοῦ πνεύματος) ... 'The Spirit of the Lord is on me (Πνεῦμα κυρίου ἐπ' ἐμέ), because he has anointed me to preach good news (ἔχρισέν με εὐαγγελίσασθαι) to the poor. He has sent me to proclaim (ἀπέσταλκέν με κηρύξαι) freedom for the prisoners and recovery of sight for the blind, to release the opressed, to proclaim the year of the Lord's favor (κηρύξαι ἐνιαυτὸν κυρίου δεκτόν)'.

There appear to be several notable differences between Matthew, Mark, and Luke in relation to our present concern. 1) All three gospels contain the reference to the kingdom of God in Jesus' first public word,⁶² but while both Matthew and Mark emphasize the nearness of the kingdom of God, Luke is more concerned with what the kingdom of God consists of and he focuses on its proclamation.⁶³ 2) Only Luke presents the liturgical setting

---

⁶¹ Agua, 'Kingdom of God', 639-61 (650).
⁶² For the discussion of the kingdom of God in Lk. 4:18-19 (cf. 43), see below in what follows.
⁶³ Cf. Agua, 'Kingdom of God', 650.

for Jesus' initial proclamation of the kingdom of God.[64] 3) While both Matthew and Mark emphasize 'repentance' as the condition of experiencing the kingdom of God, Luke does not mention it. 4) Most importantly, as mentioned above, only Luke introduces the Spirit in the beginning of Jesus' public ministry in connection with the inaugural preaching at Nazareth. After Luke's Jesus returned to Galilee in the power of the Spirit (4:14), he announces that 'the Spirit of the Lord is upon me' (4:18). Just as Luke characterizes Jesus' anointing at his baptism in terms of his messianic task (Lk. 3:22),[65] here he also refers to the Spirit in Jesus' own first public recorded words to emphasize his task. Thus, there is Luke's unique concern about the role of the Spirit associated with Jesus' proclamation of the kingdom of God. What is then the nature of the relationship between the Spirit and the kingdom of God in this passage?

5.3.1.2.2. Jesus' Anointing by the Spirit and the Kingdom of God

It is generally accepted that the Nazareth pericope reflects a pre-Lukan tradition rather than his redaction of Mark 6:1-6 (cf. Mt. 13:53-58).[66] However, irrespective of whatever sources Luke follows, the more important issue at stake is Luke's underlying motivation or theological purpose behind the passage, particularly in the Lukan alterations from Isaiah 61:1-2 (LXX) indicated in Luke 4:18-19.[67] While a comprehensive examination of the Lukan alterations has been made elsewhere,[68] the critical issue for our concern is Luke's emphasis on a primarily verbal proclamation of the kingdom of God in connection with the Spirit. There appear three specific injunctions in an infinitival form as a result of the anointing of the Spirit in Luke 4:18-19.

---

[64] A. Finkel, 'Jesus' Preaching in the Synagogue on the Sabbath (Luke 4:16-28)', in *The Gospels and the Scriptures of Israel*, 334. Finkel further argues that Luke continues to account for missionary preaching in the synagogue by the apostles in his second book. E.g., Acts 2:14-37; 13:14-41 (334-35).

[65] See §4.2.3.

[66] Turner, *Power*, 215-20; Menzies, *Development*, 162-63. In comparison with the accounts of Matthew and Mark, Luke has some notable figures. He places this passage near the beginning of his gospel while Matthew and Mark put it at the end of Jesus' Galilean ministry. It is noted that Luke's intention to place it at the beginning of Jesus' ministry is for its programmatic importance.

[67] As Shelton points out, 'Recent research which reveals the pre-Lucan tradition behind our passage does not obscure Luke's redactional emphasis'. *Mighty*, 65.

[68] See particularly, Menzies, *Development*, 166-74; Turner, *Power*, 220-26; cf. M. Prior, *Jesus: The Liberator: Nazareth Liberation Theology (Luke 4:16-30)*, BS 26 (Sheffield: SAP, 1995), 149-62. There appear four crucial alterations which bear upon the reshaping of the passage: 1) The omission of the phrase ἰάσασθαι τοὺς συντετριμμένους τῇ καρδίᾳ; 2) The insertion of the phrase ἀποστεῖλαι τεθραυσμένους ἐν ἀφέσει which is Isa. 58:6 (LXX); 3) The replacement of καλέσαι (LXX) with κηρύξαι; and 4) The omission of καὶ ἡμέραν ἀνταποδόσεως (LXX).

a. To preach good news to the poor (εὐαγγελίσασθαι πτωχοῖς) (v. 18)
b. To proclaim release to captives and recovering of sight to the blind (κηρύξαι αἰχμαλώτοις ἄφεσιν καὶ τυφλοῖς ἀνάβλεψιν) (v. 18)
c. To proclaim the acceptable year of the Lord (κηρύξαι ἐνιαυτὸν κυρίου δεκτόν) (v. 19)

There is the repetition of two key verbs (εὐαγγελίσασθαι and κηρύξαι) from the quotation in 4:18 and the replacement of καλέσαι (Isa. 61:2 [LXX]) with κηρύξαι in 4:19. While the first two verbs clearly indicate the importance of a verbal proclamation as they stand, Luke's alteration of the latter verb (from καλέσαι to κηρύξαι) is worthy of note. This replacement not only helps to substantiate the parallel with the verb εὐαγγελίσασθαι, but it also has an obvious link with the verb κηρύξαι in verse 18.[69] The alteration of καλέσαι to κηρύξαι indicates Luke's deliberate intention to highlight the aspect of powerful proclamation inspired by the Spirit followed by the identical word κηρύξαι in verse 18.[70] This constitutes a clear case of Luke's emphasis on proclamation since Luke never uses καλέω in reference to preaching.[71] This fits a Lukan pattern of the duplication of words in citations from the Old Testament.[72] Hence, as the three infinitival phrases clearly suggest, there is a Lukan emphasis on proclamation in Luke 4:18-19. If so, what is the content of Jesus' proclamation in this passage, particularly in the two terms εὐαγγελίζομαι and κηρύσσω?

It is notable that, throughout his writings, Luke has frequently used the phrase 'kingdom of God' to convey a present reality reflected by expressions like 'to preach good news or the kingdom of God'.[73] For Luke, the terms εὐαγγελίζομαι (Lk. 4:18, 43; 8:1; 9:6; 16:16; Acts 8:12; 11:20) and κηρύσσω (Lk. 3:3; 4:18, 19, 44; 8:1, 39; 24:47; Acts 8:5; 9:20; 10:37, 42; 15:21; 19:13; 20:25; 28:31) are closely linked with both the kingdom of God and the person of Jesus as the object of witness.[74] Likewise, the terms εὐαγγελίζομαι and κηρύσσω are connected to the kingdom of God in Luke 4:18-19: here the good news that Jesus proclaims is none other than his message of the kingdom of God.[75] Moreover, this good news is identical

---

[69] Woods, *Finger*, 221. For the meaning of the verbs εὐαγγελίζομαι and κηρύσσω, see below in this section.

[70] So M. Rese, *Alttestamentliche Motive in der Christologie des Lukas* (Gütersloh: Mohn, 1969), 145; Menzies, *Development*, 173.

[71] As will be seen below, while εὐαγγελίζομαι and κηρύσσω are used interchangeably by Luke in connection with the proclamation of the gospel, the kingdom of God, or Jesus, Luke uses καλέω to indicate naming (Lk. 1:32, 76; 2:23; 6:46) or inviting people (Lk. 7:39 etc.).

[72] Menzies, *Development*, 173.

[73] Merk, 'Reich Gottes', 204; Franklin, *Luke*, 268. Maddox notes that for Luke '"to proclaim the kingdom" means to announce its presence'. *Purpose*, 133.

[74] Merk, 'Riech Gottes', 204.

[75] Maddox, *Purpose*, 133.

with 'the proclamation of the acceptable year of the Lord, that is, the coming of the kingdom'.[76] As Spencer correctly observes the concept of the kingdom of God in Luke 4:18-19, 'In Luke's eyes, apparently, bringing good news to the poor, proclaiming release to the captives, and so on elucidates what it means to preach the kingdom of God'.[77] This is evident in the recapitulation of Jesus' ministry in Luke 4:43-44 where 'the words εὐαγγελίσασθαι (to preach good news) and κηρύσσω (to proclaim) give the kingdom its most important interpretation in the light of the *same* combination of words used in the Nazareth sermon at Luke 4:18-19'.[78] Furthermore, the word καί ('also', Lk. 4:43) in the words of Jesus' description of his divine mission ('I must proclaim the good news of the kingdom of God to the other cities *also*') depicts Jesus' primary task in the cities of Nazareth and Capernaum (Lk. 4:16-41) as characterized by proclaiming the kingdom of God.[79]

From this observation, there can be found a clear connection between the Spirit and the kingdom of God: the anointing of the Spirit is *primarily* related to the proclamation of the good news, i.e., the kingdom of God.[80] The Spirit inspires Jesus to proclaim 'good news' to the poor, the captives, the blind, and the oppressed by announcing the kingdom of God. The connection between the Spirit and the kingdom of God is clear: according to the Nazareth pericope, the former is the means by which the latter is proclaimed.

---

[76] R. Denova, *The Things Accomplished Among Us: Prophetic Tradition in the Scriptural Pattern of Luke-Acts*, JSNTS 141 (Sheffield: SAP, 1997), 134. See also Maddox, *Purpose*, 133. Cf. Tannehill, *Narrative*, I, 63 where he argues that the Lord's acceptable year is closely linked to the reign of God.

[77] Spencer, *Portrait*, 39.

[78] Woods, *Finger*, 221. Emphasis is original. See also Maddox, *Purpose*, 133; Prieur, *Verkündigung*, 172, 176. 'in Kontext das εὐαγγελίζεσθαι von 4:43 auf das Jesajazitat in 4:18f. verweist' (172).

[79] Spencer, *Portrait*, 39; cf. Prieur, *Verkündigung*, 169. Indeed, Luke, in his gospel, continues to single out the proclamation of the kingdom of God as the major characteristic of Jesus' ministry (e.g., Lk. 8:1; 9:6, 11; 20:1 etc.).

[80] It might be argued that since the work of the Spirit (implied in Jesus' ministry) includes liberation, and healings in the light of the whole context in Lk. 4 (e.g., 4:18 [ἀποστεῖλαι τεθραυσμένους ἐν ἀφέσει], 38-41), the Spirit mediates the realization of the kingdom of God. However, the important question to note is that what is the *primary* role of the Spirit, in connection with the kingdom of God in particular, in this text? Here, as seen above, Luke views the work of the Spirit as the empowering force which enables Jesus to proclaim the kingdom of God. This proclamation then provides for people to enter into and experience the realization of the kingdom (e.g., liberation or healings etc.). The logic is as follows: 'Jesus proclaims the kingdom of God by the anointing of the Spirit. *As a result*, the kingdom of God is realized and available to people'. For this reason, I am particularly emphasizing the word, 'primarily'.

5.3.2. The Spirit and the Church's Proclamation of the Kingdom of God

As applied to Jesus and his disciples in his first work, Luke in his second work continues to bring the message of the kingdom of God as the focal point of the post-Easter church's preaching. It is often noted that Luke emphasizes the kingdom-preaching mission in the prologue and end of the book of Acts. In the first (Acts 1:3-8), the risen Jesus continues to teach the kingdom and just before his ascension commissions the disciples to proclaim it.[81] In the second (Acts 28:31), which is the summary of Paul's Gentile mission in the heart of Rome, Paul teaches and proclaims the kingdom of God.[82] In the body of the book, the title 'kingdom of God' further appears as a summary of the church's proclamation (8:12; 19:8; 20:25; 28:23). This means that for Luke the concept 'kingdom of God' is theologically still significant in Acts as in his gospel, particularly in the light of the church's Gentile mission. There is thus a continuity between Luke-Acts concerning this central theme. However, in each case where it is proclaimed in Acts, Luke does not fail to connect the theme to the Spirit. So the church's proclamation of the kingdom of God is directly or indirectly governed by the agency of the Spirit. The following discussion will support this statement.

5.3.2.1. THE SPIRIT AND THE DICSIPLES' COMMISSION TO ROCLAIM THE KINGDOM OF GOD (Acts 1:3-8)

This passage is among the most important in Luke-Acts, especially in terms of its function as the transition between the third gospel and Acts. It not only reports what happened before the ascension of Jesus (cf. Lk. 24:47-49) but also records that Jesus commissions his disciples to go and proclaim what they have learned from him. Jesus, as he himself announced earlier, has instructed the disciples on the things concerning the kingdom of God (Acts 1:3) which are to be proclaimed by them (Acts 1:8). So the subject of the kingdom of God in Acts 1:3-8 appears as the main content of both Jesus' and the disciples' proclamation. Furthermore, the reference to the Spirit appears in the text in connection with the kingdom of God (Acts 1:4, 5, 8). The risen Jesus tells the disciples that they are soon to be baptized with the Holy Spirit, the promise of the Father (vv. 4, 5). In verse 8, the Spirit is again depicted as the power for witness to Christ Jesus, and his kingdom.[83] There is thus a certain connection between the Spirit and the

---

[81] Prieur argues that the kingdom of God in Acts 1:3-8 is the theme of Acts. *Verkündigung*, 115-17.

[82] Stanton argues that the emphasis on the proclamation of the kingdom of God in the end of Acts is almost as important for Luke's theology as the closing part of Matthew is for Matthean theology. G.N. Stanton, *Jesus of Nazareth in New Testament Preaching*, SNTSMS 27 (Cambridge: CUP, 1974), 17.

[83] For the concept 'kingdom of God' in Acts 1:8, see §5.3.2.1.2.

kingdom in the passage. However, the question to be taken into account is how the connection appears. As partly discussed in the earlier section, is the Spirit equated with the kingdom of God in this text as Dunn argues? The overall discussion of the text will show how this assertion inaccurately reflects Luke's perspective.

5.3.2.1.1. The Restoration of the Kingdom to Israel

The leading question of the disciples in Acts 1:6 has both a retrospective and prospective function in the prologue. In the former sense, the question is possibly derived from Jesus' previous teaching concerning the kingdom of God,[84] while in the latter sense, it 'sets the context for Luke's narration of the last words which the risen Jesus speaks on earth'.[85] In Acts 1:6, the disciples ask the risen Jesus concerning the timing of the restoration of the kingdom to Israel. Jesus' reply divides the question into two parts: 1) The knowledge of the timing of its completion belongs to the authority of God's time-chart (Acts 1:7); 2) The restoration is closely related to the outpouring of the Spirit with the universal mission of witness (Acts 1:8). Without these points, Jesus' brief response has little information about the nature (or the scope) of the restoration of the kingdom to Israel.

For this reason, the understanding of the phrase 'restoration of the kingdom to Israel' in verse 6 has been variously interpreted among scholars. For instance, Stott argues that the disciples' question concerning the kingdom for Israel should be understood in the sense of a spiritual kingdom. He argues that the kingdom of God is not a spatial concept but rather it is 'spiritual in its character... (which) cannot figure on any map. Yet this is what the apostles were still envisaging by confusing the kingdom of God with the kingdom of Israel'.[86] The difficulty with this interpretation is first of all that, as we have already argued, the kingdom of God in Luke-Acts refers both to God's sovereign activity and to the territory over which God rules so that a one-sided interpretation is too narrow. Furthermore, in light of the fact that this audience comprises the eleven disciples,[87] and Jesus recently instructed them about the kingdom during forty days (v. 3), it is difficult to understand why the disciples were confused about it. What they were confused about was not the nature of the kingdom of God but only

---

[84] Tannehill, *Narrative*, II, 14.

[85] D. Tiede, 'The Exaltation of Jesus and the Restoration of Israel in Acts 1', *HTR* 79 (1986), 278.

[86] J.R.W. Stott, *The Message of Acts: To the ends of the earth* (Leicester: IVP, 1990), 40-41 (41).

[87] Neil argues that the question is asked by 'others who had not heard the Lord's words on the subject' rather than the eleven disciples. Neil, *Acts*, 65-66 (65). But the immediate context, especially in Acts 1:13, clearly regards the audience as only the eleven. See J.A. McLean, 'Did Jesus Correct the Disciples' View of the Kingdom?', *BibSac* 151 (1994), 215.

'when' it would be restored to Israel.[88]

Moreover, the fact that the disciples appear to have thought of the kingdom as something that belongs to Israel as reflected in Luke's writings suggests the kingdom was conceived not simply as a spiritual kingdom.[89] For example, in Luke 24:21, the hope of the disciples on the road to Emmaus was to redeem Israel by Jesus (cf. Lk. 1:68; 2:38). In Peter's language in his sermon (Acts 3:19-21), Luke alludes to the kingdom being restored to Israel. In Acts 3:21, Peter refers to 'the time for restoration (χρόνων ἀποκαταστάσεως) of all that God spoke by the mouth of his holy prophets from ancient time'. In a similar expression in Acts 1:6, Luke employs the verb 'restore' (ἀποκαθίστημι) and the word 'time' (χρόνοι). There is a possible analogous theme in this parallel language between the two passages: the hope of the restoration of the kingdom to Israel in Acts 1:6 and the expression of 'the time for restoration of all that God spoke' through the prophets, in Acts 3:21. The latter concept does conceivably 'include the restoration of the reign to Israel through its messianic king'.[90] This is supported by the following fact. The conditional promise in Peter's sermon is that this fulfillment is accomplished by the restoration of their (Jews') life through repentance and the forgiveness. Hence Peter's sermon shows that the restoration of the Israelites' life is integral to Israel's restoration. Therefore, in view of Luke 24:21 and Acts 3:19-21 which clearly allude to the earthly restoration of Israel, it is unlikely that they meant it simply as a spiritual kingdom.

By way of contrast, McLean argues that since Jesus did not in Acts 1:7-8 correct the disciples' question, their concept of a kingdom is identified with one that is purely nationalistic in nature. He writes, '. . . then the disciples

---

[88] J. Jervell, *The Theology of the Acts of the Apostles*, NTT (Cambridge: CUP, 1996), 110.

[89] At this point, it is difficult to simply regard the disciples' question as a nationalistic misunderstanding. See Jervell, *Theology*, 110; Tannehill, *Narrative*, II, 16-17. Contra Bruce, *Acts*, 35-36. Spencer argues that due to the disciples' misunderstanding of the kingdom implied in Acts 1:6, they are not depicted as the preachers of the kingdom of God in Acts. *Portrait*, 40. But this seems to be an overstatement. Although reference to the kingdom of God in the rest of Acts is restricted to the ministry of Philip (8:12) and Paul (19:8; 20:25; 28:23, 31), it is reasonable to think that Jesus' commission to the disciples to be witnesses to the kingdom and himself indicated in v. 8 is continued in their mission work to the ends of the earth, if we rightly assume v. 8 as the programme and framework of the book of Acts. For the programmatic role of v. 8 in Acts, see Witherington, *Acts*, 110-11. On the other hand, Conzelmann interprets 'the ends of the earth' as Rome. H. Conzelmann, *The Acts of the Apostles*, Hermeneia (Philadelphia: Fortress Press, 1987), 7. But in view of Isa. 49:6 which is the background of Acts 1:8, the phrase designates all nations and ethnic groups including both Jew and Gentile. See Tannehill, *Narrative*, II, 17; Witherington, *Acts*, 111; Prieur, *Verkündigung*, 114.

[90] Tannehill, *Narrative*, II, 15-16.

were thinking in terms of the reestablishment of some kingdom for national Israel'.[91] However, although the hope of the restoration of the kingdom to Israel cannot be denied, as discussed above, in view of the overall context of the text, it is difficult to deduce an entirely nationalistic understanding from the question of the disciples. McLean's exegetical problem is that he does not support his argument from the context of the prologue, particularly from the conversation between the disciples and Jesus, but only discusses verse 6 by drawing his evidence mainly from other texts in Luke-Acts (e.g., Peter's sermon in Acts 3).

However, the concept of the kingdom and its restoration to Israel in Acts 1:3-8 should be primarily understood in its overall context rather than treating only verse 6 since as Polhill correctly points out, verses 6-8 'are closely tied together. . . (and) verse 8 places the disciples' question in proper perspective'.[92] Furthermore, in view of this, if Jesus did not correct the disciples' question, as McLean himself suggests, then we can safely assume that Jesus' answer about the timing of the kingdom in verse 7 and worldwide mission to witness in verse 8 show his understanding to be correct, so it would be difficult to view the kingdom in their question as an entirely nationalistic entity. While it is true that Jesus does not reject the concept of the restoration of Israel, Jesus' answer clearly alludes to an indirect denial that the kingdom would be given *only* to Israel but rather it would encompass all nations to the ends of the earth.[93] The restoration of the kingdom to Israel is just a part of God's universal salvific plan for all nations.[94] Undoubtedly, as will be seen below, the Isaianic background, particularly Isaiah 49:6 indicated in Jesus' saying in Acts 1:8, views 'the eschatological restoration of Israel as cosmic in scope, finding fulfillment in a new creation'.[95]

If this Isaianic background is an important allusion to help interpret Luke's concept of the restoration of Israel in Acts 1:8, as most agree,[96] its fuller discussion will help to understand it. The background of the concept, 'my witnesses' is possibly from the servant Psalms in Isaiah 43:10 (cf.

---

[91] McLean, 'Disciples' View', 215-27 (220, see esp. 221-22, 227).
[92] J.B. Polhill, *Acts* (Nashville: Broadman, 1992), 84, 85. See also Witherington, *Acts*, 110.
[93] Maddox, *Purpose*, 106-08. Maddox argues that 'it is a kingdom where the Gentiles, too, have their rightful place, and is not Israel's private prerogative'. 107-08. See also Prieur, *Verkündigung*, 105.
[94] Cf. Prieur, *Verkündigung*, 107, 114-15.
[95] Penney, *Missionary*, 70. See also Tannehill, *Narrative*, II, 17; Tiede, 'Exaltation', 285.
[96] E.g., D. Schneider, *Die Apostelgeschichte*, I (Freiburg: Herder, 1980), 203, 225-27; Prieur, *Verkündigung*, 113-14; Polhill, *Acts*, 85; Witherington, *Acts*, 111; Tiede, 'Exaltation', 285; Turner, *Power*, 300-01; Menzies, *Development*, 199-200; Penney, *Missionary*, 70.

43:12; 44:8) where God commissioned his servant, i.e., a restored Israel, to be a witness.[97] This task is now given to the disciples who are 'to be the true "restored" Israel' to fulfill the task of being a light to the Gentiles.[98] The conceptual and scriptural background of bearing witness to Jesus 'to the end of the earth' is Isaiah 49:6:[99] 'It is too small a thing for you to be my servant to restore the tribes of Jacob and bring back those of Israel I have kept. I will also make you a light for the Gentiles, that you may bring my salvation to the ends of the earth'. By recognizing the vocation of Israel to be a light to the nations bringing the gift of God's salvation to all the nations, the disciples become the restored Israel as anticipated in Old Testament prophecy. A balanced view is advanced by Tiede: 'the promise of God's reign is not simply the restoration of the preserved of Israel, but the renewal of the vocation of Israel to be a light to the nations to the end of the earth'.[100]

In summary, the context of Acts 1:6-8 does not seem to fit the concept of the restoration of Israel as either a spiritual kingdom or a purely ethnic one. The context rather views it as the renewal or calling of Israel's servant vocation representing the disciples as the restored Israel. The question of how the disciples' task is accomplished will be answered in the next part.

5.3.2.1.2. The Promise of God to the Disciples and the Kingdom of God

The relevant passages about the nature of the promise of the Father have been introduced in the previous chapter (ch. 4). It has been noted that the promise of the Father in Luke 24:49 and Acts 1:4-5, 8 clearly indicates the gift of the Spirit which will be the source of the disciples' vocation and which prepares for what follows after Pentecost. It has been also pointed out that the promise of the Spirit in Acts 2:33 indicates the coming of the Spirit at Pentecost. The phrase 'τὴν ἐπαγγελίαν τοῦ πατρός' in Luke 24:49; Acts 1:4 and 2:33 all indicate one event, the coming of the Spirit, which is fulfilled at Pentecost. This brief summary reassures one that the promise of the Father in the ending of Luke and the prologue of Acts is identical with the gift of the Spirit. If so, what is the nature of the relationship between the promise of the Spirit and the kingdom of God in Acts 1:3-8?

As briefly discussed above, the relationship between the promise of God and the kingdom of God is undoubtedly linked in Acts 1:3-8. As the kingdom has been the main theme of his teaching and proclamation during his earthly life, the principal theme in the risen Jesus' instruction during forty days is the kingdom of God in verse 3. Here, the phrase 'concerning the kingdom of God' (περὶ τῆς βασιλείας τοῦ θεοῦ) in Acts 1:3 is parallel

---

[97] Penney, *Missionary*, 58; Turner, *Power*, 300; Franklin, *Luke*, 234, 266.
[98] Polhill, *Acts*, 85; Bruce, *Acts*, 36.
[99] Turner, *Power*, 300-01; Menzies, *Development*, 199-200; Tannehill, *Narrative*, II, 17.
[100] Tiede, 'Exaltation', 286. See also Turner, *Power*, 300-02; Menzies, *Development*, 199-200.

with 'concerning Jesus of Nazareth' (περὶ Ἰησοῦ τοῦ Ναζαρηνοῦ) in Luke 24:19 by showing the thread of the two stages of the story.[101] This explains that the meaning of 'the things concerning the kingdom of God' in verse 3 has a christological theme including Jesus' own role as the rejected and exalted Messiah expressed in Luke 24.[102] The christological event is now linked to the main subject (the kingdom) of the universal mission of the church. In verses 4-5, it is certainly not by chance that Jesus at the same time gives instruction about waiting for the promise of the Father (v. 4) by specifying the promise as the Spirit anticipated by the Baptist (v. 5). Jesus' instructions on both the kingdom of God and the gift of the Spirit naturally explain the importance of the latter to the disciples in the new stage of the further extension of the reign of God which Jesus had initially taught and proclaimed in the earlier stage.[103] So, there appears a pattern, i.e., kingdom and Spirit expressed in verses 3 and 4-5.

There is a further connection between the two in verses 4-5 and 6: Jesus' instruction about the coming of the Spirit in verses 4-5 gives rise to the disciples' question about the coming of the kingdom in verse 6. As generally recognized, both the coming of the Spirit and the restoration of the kingdom is of an eschatological character not only in this context, but also in the circles of Judaism.[104] This seemingly lies at the background of the disciples' question about the time of the restoration of the kingdom after Jesus' instruction of the coming of the Spirit in verses 4-8. The disciples would have possibly understood the outpouring of the Spirit as an eschatological sign that the consummation of the kingdom was at hand.[105] Then, before his ascension the whole conversation concludes in Jesus' final sayings encompassing all the themes about the forthcoming descent of the Spirit and the concept of the kingdom in verse 8.

Although the phrase 'kingdom of God' is not explicitly referred to in this text (Acts 1:8), its theme is clearly implied by the following facts: a) If we rightly take verses 7-8 as the answer to the question of verse 6, the theme 'kingdom of God' continues in verses 7-8 issuing from verse 6. In verse 7, the concept of kingdom in Jesus' answer connotes the time of its consummation, implying the concept 'already and not yet'. So, rather than the 'when' of the kingdom of God, Jesus, in verse 8, continues to answer

---

[101] Agua, 'Kingdom of God', 655. Agua argues that there is continuity between the third gospel and the book of Acts with respect to the kingdom.

[102] Tannehill, *Narrative*, II, 13.

[103] Cf. Turner, *Power*, 295.

[104] As Longenecker argues, 'In Jewish expectations, the restoration of Israel's fortunes would be marked by the revived activity of God's Spirit, which had been withheld since the last of the prophets'. R.N. Longenecker, *The Acts of the Apostles*, EBC 9 (Grand Rapids: Zondervan, 1981), 256.

[105] Haenchen, *Acts*, 143.

about 'what' of the kingdom.¹⁰⁶ b) As seen above, in the view of the larger contexts of Acts, the proclamation of the kingdom of God and Jesus (and the christological theme) are intimately connected. For instance, as will be seen, Philip's proclamation of the kingdom of God is along with his witness to Jesus' name (8:12). Paul's preaching of the kingdom also conjoins with that of the Lord Jesus Christ (28:31). A particular connection between the kingdom and the christological theme appears in Acts 1:8 and 28:23. The meaning of 'being witness to Jesus' in Acts 1:8 is identical with 'testifying (διαμαρτυρόμενος) to the kingdom of God' in Acts 28:23. As Agua argues, 'This meaning of the verb διαμαρτύρεσθαι, "to bear witness" in favour of Jesus Christ in the light of the Scriptures, corresponds in Acts with μάρτυς, which has Jesus as its object in 1:8. Thus, the command of Acts 1:8 (ἔσεσθέ μου μάρτυρες) corresponds to the fulfillment in Acts 28:23 (διαμαρτυρόμενος τὴν βασιλείαν τοῦ θεοῦ)'.[107]

For Luke, to be a witness of Jesus means to bear witness to the kingdom of God. c) Finally, there is a possible parallelism between Acts 1:3-8 and Luke 4:16ff. Just as Jesus is empowered by the Spirit so that he becomes a proclaimer of the kingdom of God, the disciples in Acts 1:3-8, by the power of the Spirit, become the witness to the kingdom of God and Jesus.[108]

All these lines of evidence safely suggest that the object of the disciples' proclamation in their witness in Acts 1:8 is the kingdom of God and (or about) Jesus. Hence, the connection between the kingdom of God and the promise of the Father in Acts 1:8 is an intrinsic one.

While this cannot be doubted, the nature of this connection should be asked: does it have some form of equation? Dunn attempts to build the parallelism between verses 3-4 (and vv. 6-8) by saying that 'verse 4 (about Jesus' teaching on the Spirit) sums up Jesus' teaching of the forty days from a different angle' than his teaching about the kingdom.[109] He then concludes that 'At all events (including that of Acts 1:3-8), we are left with some form of equation between Spirit and Kingdom'.[110] However, at first sight, if the eschatological entity of the Spirit forms an equation with that of the kingdom, the teaching of Jesus would have faced a contradiction. For while Jesus said that the time of the kingdom remained outside the disciples' knowledge, he gave an idea of the time limit of the Spirit' coming

---

[106] Cf. Dunn, *Pneumatology*, 137.

[107] Agua, 'Kingdom of God', 657. (Cf. Acts 8:12; 28:31).

[108] Prieur, *Verkündigung*, 112, n. 119.

[109] *Pneumatology*, 137.

[110] *Pneumatology*, 138. Furthermore, as noted above, Dunn's connection between the two also depends on his argument that the disciples will experience the kingdom at Pentecost for the first time through the gift of the Spirit. However, it has been noted that this view is inappropriate in the light of the fact that they have already experienced the benefits of the kingdom of God which were present in Jesus and his ministry.

as said in verse 5, 'not many days from now'.[111] If the disciples' question is rightly prompted by Jesus' teaching about the coming of the Spirit in verses 4-5, there is no reason why Jesus would have contradicted himself about the timing of the two entities.

Luke's point is rather that the promise of the Spirit in the prologue of Acts is represented as the source of prophetic empowerment for witness. This clearly appears in the summary of their conversation in Acts 1:8. Here the disciples' question about the restoration of the kingdom to Israel is redirected to a world-wide mission by the power of the Spirit, and not restricted to Israel. The endowment of the Spirit is the prelude to the disciples' task which involves preaching the gospel to the ends of the earth. Hence the disciples, as Isaiah's Spirit-empowered witnesses, will preach the gospel about Jesus and the kingdom of God by the power of the Spirit. They not only need to acknowledge the content of what they will proclaim, but also need to be empowered by the Spirit. This is the reason why Jesus gives them a special charge to wait in Jerusalem for the promise of the Spirit (vv. 4, 5, 8). The nature of the relationship is now clear: the Spirit, the promise of the Father, is not constituted as an equality with or complement of the kingdom, but rather as the power by which the disciples will proclaim the kingdom. In other words, the task that remained for the disciples was to receive the gift of the Spirit as a prophetic empowering to preach the gospel of the kingdom not only to Israel, but also beyond her borders (Acts 8:12; 14:22; 19:8; 20:25; 28:3, 31).

To sum up, just as Jesus' Spirit-inspired ministry was related to the kingdom of God primarily by proclaiming the kingdom in the land of Israel, when the Spirit came and empowered the disciples, the kingdom of God would be extended throughout the world by the disciples' proclamation of it. Here once again, the Spirit is clearly represented as the means by which the kingdom is preached and witnessed.

5.3.2.2. THE SPIRIT AND PHILIP'S PROCLAMATION OF THE KINGDOM OF GOD (Acts 8:4-12, 26-40; cf. 6:5)

In the previous chapter (ch. 3), we have noted that there has been a shift in Philip's role: Luke indicates that the Spirit-filled Philip's *dominant* ministry is not simply serving tables, but preaching the word of good news for the Gentiles.[112] This ministry is widely described in Acts 8, particularly focusing on proclamation of the kingdom of God and the name of Jesus Christ.

---

[111] McLean, 'Disciples' View', 216.
[112] The primary portrait of Philip's ministry is obviously depicted as an evangelist in Acts 21:8, 'Philip *the evangelist*, one of the seven'.

5.3.2.2.1. Philip's Ministry in Acts 8: Proclamation

In Acts 8, when turning to the story of Philip, Luke mainly presents him as an evangelist. This can be known not only from Philip's performance of miracle-working activity (vv. 6, 7, 13), but also from his ministry of proclamation (vv. 4, 5, 12, 35, 40). The result of the evangelist's twofold ministry of 'word and deed' in Samaria is favourable (v. 8, 'πολλὴ χαρὰ ἐν τῇ πόλει'). The crowds pay close attention to what he said (v. 6) and accept the Christian message and baptism (v. 12). In comparison, the combination of Philip's 'word and deed' ministry is well matched with the ministries carried out by Jesus (Lk. 4:22-27, 31-37; 5:15, 17) and his disciples (Lk. 9:1-6; Acts 4:29-30; 13:4-12; 14:3, 7-10; 19:10-12; 20:7-12). This suggests that for Luke performance in word and deed is a crucial element of evangelism by both Jesus and his followers including Philip.

While wonder-working activity is a critical component of Philip's mission service, his ministry is extensively characterized as proclaiming the gospel and this idea is widely displayed throughout Acts 8:[113] Philip 'proclaimed' (ἐκήρυσσεν) to them the Christ (v. 5); Philip 'preached' (εὐαγγελιζομένῳ) good news about the kingdom of God and the name of Jesus Christ (v. 12); he 'preached' (εὐηγγελίσατο) the good news of Jesus (v. 35); and 'preached' (εὐηγγελίζετο) the gospel to all the towns (v. 40). Here, as the references show, the words Luke employs to describe Philip's acts of preaching are κηρύσσω (v. 5) and εὐαγγελίζομαι (vv. 4, 12, 35, 40, cf. v. 25) and, it is worthy of note that these were previously used by him in the mission of Jesus and the disciples (Lk. 4:18, 19, 43, 44; 8:1; 9:2, 6; Acts 5:42).[114] As Tannehill rightly notes, 'Philip is performing the same kind of preaching mission as Jesus and the apostles. The mission begun by Jesus is continuing through a new instrument of God'.[115] It is notable that Luke uses the word εὐαγγελίζομαι five times in the story of Philip and this is the heaviest concentration in Acts.[116] This shows that for Luke the nature of Philip's ministry is dominantly related to preaching.

On the other hand, the content of Philip's preaching is variously described: the christological theme (vv. 5, 12),[117] the gospel (vv. 35, 40)[118] and the kingdom of God (v. 12). However, as Polhill argues, all the content of proclamation basically refers to the same reality.[119] As discussed earlier (and will be seen later), Luke elsewhere regularly combines the kingdom of

---

[113] It is notable that the word 'εὐαγγελίζομαι' is introduced (v. 4) and concluded (v. 40) in Acts 8 as an inclusion attributing Philip's ministry to 'preaching'. Cf. Prieur, *Verkündigung*, 154.

[114] Tannehill, *Narrative*, II, 103.

[115] Tannehill, *Narrative*, II, 104.

[116] Spencer, *Portrait*, 37.

[117] 'Christ (v. 5) and 'the name of Jesus Christ' (v. 12).

[118] 'the good news of Jesus' (v. 35) and 'the good news' (v. 40).

[119] Polhill, *Acts*, 216-17.

God with the christological theme, for example, in Paul's proclamation (Acts 28:23, 31). In Acts 8:12, Philip 'preached (εὐαγγελιζομένῳ) good news about the kingdom of God (βασιλείας τοῦ θεοῦ) and the name of Jesus Christ (ὀνόματος Ἰησοῦ Χριστοῦ)'. The sentence contains the two objects served by the same verb and this indicates that the kingdom of God proclaimed by Philip is inextricably linked with his witness to the name of Jesus Christ.[120] As Schmidt notes, 'The name and message of Jesus Christ, or Jesus Christ himself, are thus equated with the kingdom of God'.[121] In short, Philip's main ministry portrayed in Acts 8 is proclamation and its object is the kingdom of God (and Jesus Christ).

5.3.2.2.2. The Spirit and the Kingdom of God in the Preaching of Philip

The formulation of words 'εὐαγγελιζομένῳ περὶ τῆς βασιλείας τοῦ θεοῦ'[122] in verse 12 recalls Jesus' earlier proclamation of it in Luke 4:43; 8:1; and 16:16 so there is a continuity in its proclamation by Philip.[123] Here the kingdom of God is for the first time explicitly proclaimed in Samaria by Philip after Jesus' prediction in Acts 1:8. In Acts 1:8, the geographical places are referred to in detail by Jesus including a specific reference to Samaria. The kingdom of God as the content of the post-resurrection kerygma is now proclaimed in non-Israelite territory as the fulfillment of Acts 1:8.

Just as in the cases of Jesus and his disciples, Philip's proclamation of the kingdom of God is also closely related to the empowerment of the Spirit. Although there is no explicit reference to the Spirit in relation to Philip's proclamation of the kingdom, it can for the following reasons be safely assumed that Philip, in Samaria, is under the direction of the Spirit.

First of all, the fact that Philip's ministry in Samaria is primarily described in prophetic terms is a clear sign that Philip (and his ministry) is empowered by the Spirit.[124] Along with his preaching ministry as observed above, Philip's ministry is characterized by the performance of signs and great miracles ('σημεῖα καὶ δυνάμεις μεγάλας', Acts 8:13). He exorcises

---

[120] Agua, 'Kingdom of God', 656; cf. Prieur, *Verkündigung*, 158.

[121] K.L. Schmidt, 'βασιλεία', *TDNT*, I, 579-90 (589). See also Stanton's similar claim in his *Jesus*, 17-18; O'Toole, 'Kingdom of God', 151.

[122] Haenchen argues that the kingdom of God proclaimed in 8:12 has a futuristic sense as in 14:22. *Acts*, 723. However, although a possible future-oriented exhortation to 'enter the kingdom of God' in Acts 14:22 (cf. 1:6) is intended, there is nothing in Acts 8:12 or other references that would suggest an eschatological meaning. This is attested by the Lukan understanding of the kingdom of God as a synonym for other preaching topics of the believers (Acts 8:12; 19:8; 20:24; 28: 23, 31). The primary emphasis of the announced kingdom of God in these references including Acts 8:12 should be taken as a present reality. Spencer, *Portrait*, 41.

[123] Prieur, *Verkündigung*, 157.

[124] Shepherd, *Narrative Function*, 179-80; Stronstad, *Prophethood*, 91-92.

'unclean spirits' and heals the 'paralyzed' (Acts 8:7). Philip's triumph in his 'word and deed' ministry over Simon the magician in Acts 8:9-13 shows that Philip is a true prophet.[125] Here, the power (δύναμις) that Philip performs is a 'clear sign of the work of the Spirit'.[126] This twofold prophetic ministry not only recalls Jesus' Spirit-filled prophetic ministry in terms of his performance of signs and wonders (Lk. 4:1, 14, 18, 33-39; Acts 2:22) and his verbal proclamation of the kingdom of God (Lk. 4:18-19, 43-44; cf. 8:1 and 16:16), but also those of the Spirit-inspired Stephen (Acts 6:8-15) and the apostles (Acts 2:43; 4:31; 5:12). Thus Philip, in the narrative, is represented as a true prophet who is empowered by the Spirit and this suggests that the direct cause behind Philip's proclamation of the kingdom of God is the power of the Spirit.[127]

Second, in view of Philip's preaching mission to an Ethiopian in Acts 8:26-40, it is highly conceivable that the Spirit is the direct source of his preaching mission. From the narrative point of view, Philip's preaching mission to him is introduced and concluded by references to the Spirit (vv. 29, 39).[128] Having been led by the Spirit in Acts 8:29 (cf. v. 26), Philip discusses a scripture from the prophet Isaiah with the eunuch and then he preaches the good news of Jesus to him (εὐηγγελίσατο αὐτῷ τὸν Ἰησοῦν) (v. 35).[129] Again in Acts 8:39-40, it is reported that the direct result of the Spirit's bringing of Philip to Azotus is his preaching the gospel (of the kingdom of God) to all the towns. Philip's proclamation of the gospel of Jesus to an Ethiopian would be characterized as a fulfillment of Jesus' prophecy (Acts 1:8) just as his proclamation of the kingdom of God in Samaria.[130] If the Spirit is clearly represented as the source of Philip's proclamation of the gospel to an Ethiopian, it is highly possible to conclude that none other than the Spirit is a direct author of Philip's proclamation of the kingdom of God in Samaria.[131]

To sum up, Philip's proclamation of the kingdom of God in Samaria is the same kind of preaching mission as that of Jesus and the disciples. As with the cases of Jesus (Lk. 4:18-19, 43) and the disciples (Acts 1:3-8), the

---

[125] Shepherd, *Narrative Function*, 180. 'The human conflict between the disciple (Philip) and the magician is indicative of the underlying cosmic conflict between the Spirit which empowers Philip and the demonic forces at work in magic' (181).

[126] Shepherd, *Narrative Function*, 180-81; Tannehill, *Narrative*, II, 104.

[127] It is notable that Philip's mission here in Acts 8 is first narrated in Acts after his introduction in chapter 6 as being 'full of the Spirit and wisdom' (Acts 6:3).

[128] Stronstad, *Prophethood*, 93.

[129] The content that Philip preached to the eunuch in Acts 8:35 is not different from that of his preaching in Samaria (Acts 8:12), i.e., the kingdom of God and Jesus Christ. See Prieur, *Verkündigung*, 158.

[130] Shepherd, *Narrative Function*, 185.

[131] Cf. Shepherd, *Narrative Function*, 181-82, n. 92.

Spirit is the main source of Philip's proclamation of the kingdom of God.[132] The Spirit inspires and empowers him to proclaim the kingdom in Samaria and in this way this ministry of the Spirit ultimately makes it possible for Samaritans to taste and enter the kingdom of God.

5.3.2.3. THE SPIRIT AND PAUL'S PROCLAMATION OF THE KINGDOM OF GOD (Acts 20:22-28; 19:8, cf. vv. 1-7; 28:23-31)[133]

5.3.2.3.1. The Kingdom of God Proclaimed by Paul

According to the Acts record, five references to the kingdom of God out of eight are connected to Paul's testimony regarding it (Acts 14:22; 19:8; 20:25; 28:23, 31). Surprisingly, except for 14:22, all references to the kingdom of God are presented in the context of Paul's preaching ministry.[134]

In Acts 19:8, Luke tells us that Paul begins his Ephesian mission by announcing the kingdom of God. When Paul was forced by Jewish opposition to move to the hall of Tyrannus where he conducted daily discussions for two years, the gospel spreads throughout Asia so that all the

---

[132] Cf. V.C. Pfitzner, '"Pneumatic" Apostleship? Apostle and Spirit in the Acts of the Apostle', in W. Haubeck and M. Bachmann (eds.), *Wort in der Zeit: Festgabe für Karl Heinrich Rengstorf* (Leiden: Brill, 1980), 219.

[133] Although Luke does not demonstrate the role of the Spirit in Paul's proclamation of the kingdom of God as clearly as the cases of Jesus, the disciples, and Philip as has been discussed, he nonetheless seems to be consistent, though indirectly, in linking the two.

[134] There are some notable distinctions between Luke's portrayal of Paul's message with the kingdom of God in Acts and the way of Paul's own use of the reference in his epistles. As observed above, Paul rarely uses kingdom language in his epistles (only 7 times in his [undisputed] epistles: Rom. 14:17; 1 Cor. 4:20; 6:9-10 [x2]; 15:50; Gal. 5:21; 1 Thess. 2:12), but Luke's Paul widely uses the reference (5 times out of 8) in Acts. Furthermore, Luke's Paul uses the kingdom of God as the main theme of his preaching in the context of his preaching ministry, but Paul himself does not use the reference in such a manner in his epistles. The latter point indicates that there is a certain Lukan motive in attributing the kingdom of God to preaching in connection with Paul. This suggests that although it may be argued that Luke seems to be familiar with Paul's kerygma about the kingdom, particularly in view of Acts 14:22 ('we must enter the kingdom of God', i.e., the kingdom as the eschatological goal of believers. Cf. 1 Cor. 6:9-10; 15:50; Gal. 5:21), Paul's message of the kingdom in Acts reflects Luke's own editorial decision. This presumption is further confirmed by Luke's unique and consistent emphasis on 'proclamation' in relation to the theme 'kingdom of God', in his writings as noted above (cf. Lk. 4:18-19, 43; 8:1; 9:2, 11, 60; 16:16; Acts 1:3; 8:12; 19:8; 20:25; 28:23, 31). For the overall discussion of the kingdom of God in Paul's preaching in Acts, see Shogren, 'Kingdom of God', 269-86. For the historical relationship between Luke-Acts and Paul's epistles, see n. 217 in chapter 4.

residents of Asia, both Jews and Greeks, are able to hear the word of the Lord (19:9-10). Here the general label 'the word of the Lord' in 19:10 is possibly paralleled with the message of the kingdom of God which he preached in 19:8.[135] The evangelization of the whole province has been successfully continued by Paul's kingdom-proclamation among the Jews for three months and for two years particularly among the Gentiles. Later in Acts 20:25, Luke reiterates Paul's overall task to both Jews and Greeks in Ephesus as 'preaching the kingdom'. This explains that the main theme of Paul's preaching ministry in Ephesus is his testimony regarding the kingdom of God.

In the concluding chapter of the book of Acts, Luke once again depicts Paul's theme of proclamation in Rome as the kingdom of God. In Acts 28:23, it is reported that Paul spent an entire day testifying to the kingdom of God: '. . . From morning till evening he explained and declared to them the kingdom of God (διαμαρτυρόμενος τὴν βασιλείαν τοῦ θεοῦ) and tried to convince them about Jesus...'. As this text shows, the direct object of his preaching (διαμαρτυρόμενος) is the kingdom of God alongside his witness to Jesus.[136] However, the result of Paul's preaching brings a double reaction from the Jews: 'some were convinced by what he said, while others disbelieved' (v. 24). After warning the Jews of the dangers of disbelief (vv. 26-27, quoting Isa. 6:9-10) and announcing that the 'salvation of God has been sent to the Gentiles' (v. 28), Paul then broadens his kingdom-preaching to include all visitors to his place over a two-year period (vv. 30-31). So in Acts 28:30-31, when Luke recapitulates the activity of Paul's two-year ministry in Rome, he emphasizes it as the preaching of the kingdom of God (and Jesus Christ), particularly focusing his attention on the Gentiles. Hence, although Paul's audience has changed, this final picture in Luke's summary shows that what has been proclaimed by Paul in Rome is the kingdom of God which he had proclaimed in his earlier period there.[137]

5.3.2.3.2. The Spirit and Paul's Proclamation of the Kingdom of God

It is undeniable that throughout Acts Paul is remarkably depicted as a Spirit-filled prophet. We know this from Luke's abundant reports about Paul's experience of being filled with the Spirit (Acts 9:17; 13:9, 52) and being led by the Spirit (Acts 13:2, 4; 16:6-10; 19:21; 20:22; 21:4, 11). These are the essential foundations for Paul's 'word and deed' mission. While Paul's Spirit-filled works are plainly reported in Acts,[138] it is notable that the result of his being filled with the Spirit is greatly linked with his

---

[135] Shogren, 'Kingdom of God', 275.
[136] Agua, 'Kingdom of God', 656.
[137] Prieur, *Verkündigung*, 76.
[138] Cf. Acts 13:9-11; 14:3, 8-10; 19:11-12; 20:9 etc.

inspired proclamation of the word as it was in the case of Philip (Acts 8). As pointed out earlier, Paul's inaugural Spirit-filled ministry is related to his proclamation about Jesus, the Son of God, and the Christ (Acts 9:20, 22, 27). His preaching in the synagogue at Pisidian Antioch is a prophetic exhortation under the Spirit's inspiration (Acts 13:9, 15-41).[139] The manner of Paul's (and Barnabas') Spirit-filled ministry is described as 'speaking boldly' (Acts 14:3; cf. Acts 13:47) along with their performance of signs and wonders.

Having in mind the fact that Paul's Spirit-inspired ministry is mainly related to his preaching-mission, it is notable that his proclamation of the kingdom of God is also (indirectly) related to the Spirit. The connection can be found in Acts 20:22-28; 19:1-8; and 28:23-31.

a) Acts 20:22-28

The section in Acts 20:22-28 records Paul's final words to the Ephesian elders summarizing his entire ministry in Ephesus. There are three references to the Spirit in this section and they are all from his own mouth (vv. 22, 23, 28).[140] Paul says that he is going 'compelled by the Spirit' (or 'bound in the Spirit': 'δεδεμένος τῷ πνεύματι')[141] to Jerusalem (v. 22) and has been warned by the same Spirit of forthcoming trials and tribulations (v. 23). With this personal experience of the Spirit, Paul demonstrates his succeeding ministry as 'testifying to the good news of God's grace' (v. 24) and in the immediate context he reiterates his Ephesian ministry as 'preaching the kingdom' (v. 25).[142]

Lake and Cadbury attempt to make a distinction between 'preaching the good news of God's grace' and 'preaching the kingdom'. They argue that the expression 'the good news of God's grace' is the Hellenized summary of the Christian message which 'almost obliterates the Jewish nature of the original preaching of the Kingdom, Judgement, and Repentance'.[143] However, it is not Luke's (or Paul's) intention to distinguish between what

---

[139] Stronstad, *Prophethood*, 106, 110.

[140] With those of Acts 19:1-6, this is the largest number of references to the Spirit related to Pauline material in Acts. See Porter, *Paul*, 87.

[141] While it is arguable whether the phrase 'τῷ πνεύματι' refers to the human spirit or divine Spirit, most scholars take the latter as the meaning of the text in the light of the similar expression in Acts 19:21. The fact that the word 'being bound or compelled' (δεδεμένος) denotes divine guidance further supports this. See Porter, *Paul*, 86; Shepherd, *Narrative Function*, 233; Marshall, *Acts*, 331; Tannehill, *Narrative*, II, 254; Polhill, *Acts*, 425; Bruce, *Acts*, 390, n. 47.

[142] In Acts 20:17-38, Paul's ministry is dominantly portrayed as speech (vv. 20, 21, 24, 25, 27) and the major content of his announcement is the 'good news of God's grace' (Acts 20:24) and the 'kingdom' (v. 25). M.L. Soards, *The Speeches in Acts: Their Content, Context, and Concern* (Louisville: Westminster Press, 1994), 107.

[143] Lake and Cadbury, *Beginnings*, IV, 261.

is a Hellenistic expression and what is a Jewish expression in his proclamation. Although the exact expression of 'τὸ εὐαγγέλιον τῆς χάριτος τοῦ θεοῦ' in Acts 20:24 never appears elsewhere in Acts or in Paul's epistles, it is likely that the central content of Paul's proclamation is the good news about God's merciful action in redeeming people (cf. Acts 13:43). Likewise, the overall theme of his preaching in Ephesus is described as the good news about the present salvific rule of God in Christ (Acts 19:8, 25). Certainly, Luke does not make any specific distinction between these two subjects in Paul's proclamation and they are synonymous in Luke's mind.[144] Thus, there is no foundation for arguing that the idea of proclaiming God's grace obliterates proclaiming the kingdom.

Although the text itself does not directly describe the Spirit as the agent of Paul's preaching ministry, it can be understood that his proclamation is by the empowerment of the Spirit. Here the general role of the Spirit is characterized as personal guidance. The purpose of this guidance ultimately is missiological in the process of expanding the church, particularly here in Ephesus in Paul's third missionary journey.[145] That Paul is described as 'compelled by the Spirit' (v. 22) to go to Jerusalem indicates the Spirit's direction of mission. Indeed, in an earlier mission stage in Ephesus, it is said that Paul is to be led by the compulsion of the Spirit to Jerusalem, the next mission place (Acts 19:21, 'Paul purposed in the Spirit to go to Jerusalem'). Furthermore, the warnings of the Spirit[146] are not merely of an informative character, but assure Paul that there will be divine guidance and protection in the trials and tribulations he is about to face.[147] So if the Spirit clearly initiates Paul's mission through his definite guidance (Acts 20:22), then his guidance runs throughout Paul's missionary activities including Jerusalem, and this role of the Spirit should be understood in the continuation of his missionary context. If this is so, then the source of Paul's proclamation of the 'good news of God's grace', which refers to the kingdom, can also be the work of the Spirit.[148] This claim can be further

---

[144] Strelan, *Ephesus*, 268. See Bruce's comments: 'It is a fruitless task to try to make a distinction between "proclaiming the kingdom" and "proclaiming the good news of God's grace"'. *Acts*, 391.

[145] Paul's extensive missionary activity is introduced in Acts 13:1-21:16 and the Spirit is represented as Paul's main agent for each of his mission plans: his mission is initiated by the Spirit (Acts 13:1-9); his mission plan is re-directed by the Spirit with a complementary vision and revelation (Acts 16:6-10); and as seen above, his mission is directly guided by the Spirit (19:2; 20:22-23). See Stronstad, *Prophethood*, 104-09; Penney, *Missionary*, 115-16.

[146] Penney argues that the warnings of the Spirit concerning Paul's suffering are examples of conventional prophecy and recall that of Jesus, the suffering servant as demonstrated in Luke's gospel. *Missionary*, 116.

[147] Polhill, *Acts*, 425.

[148] Cf. Shepherd, *Narrative Function*, 234.

confirmed by Luke's portrayal of Paul throughout the book of Acts as a Spirit-filled and equipped man (9:17; 13:2, 4; 16:6-10; 19:21; 20:22; 21:4, 11) whose ministry is widely linked to his proclamation of the word (9:20, 22, 27; 13:9, 15-41; 14:3; cf. 13:47).

b) Acts 19:1-8

As observed above, Luke, when recapitulating Paul's Ephesian ministry, describes his overall task as proclaiming the kingdom (Acts 20:25). This statement clearly includes Luke's earlier statement in Acts 19:8 about Paul's early ministry of proclaiming the kingdom of God in Ephesus. But before narrating Paul's preaching ministry in the synagogue, Luke relates the story about the coming of the Spirit at Ephesus. From Luke's theological point of view, it is interesting to note why he reports Paul's approach to the Ephesian disciples with the theme of the Spirit before his preaching of the kingdom of God. While it is debatable as to whether Paul experiences the charismatic signs of the Spirit along with the Ephesian disciples (Acts 19:1-7), it is clearly possible to assume that Paul is to a great degree empowered by the Spirit from his clear involvement in bestowing the Spirit on them through the imposition of his hands.[149] Thus, it seems no accident that Paul's preaching of the kingdom in Acts 19:8 is closely connected with his experience of the Spirit along with the disciples' reception of the Spirit.[150] Directed and empowered by the Spirit, Paul is able to proclaim the kingdom of God.

c) Acts 28:23-31

This final section of Acts (28:23-31) contains two kingdom references (vv. 23, 31) and one reference to the Spirit (v. 25). While the former is described as the main subject of Paul's preaching ministry in Rome, the latter is portrayed as the source of Isaiah's prophetic message. Although the Spirit and the proclamation of the kingdom can be observed in the passage, each subject is referred to in a different context. For this reason, it would be an oversimplification for one to argue that the Spirit is the agent of Paul's proclamation of the kingdom of God from this one passage. The Spirit is here simply delineated as a prophetic character in inspiring the word of God.[151]

But how does one discover the role of the Spirit in relation to Paul's kingdom-proclamation in Rome? From a narrative point of view, the scene

---

[149] Note Johnson's comments, 'This (Acts 19:1-7) is by far the most extended treatment of Paul's "prophetic" powers to bestow the Spirit'. Johnson, *Acts*, 343.

[150] Pfitzner, '"Pneumatic" Apostleship?', 219.

[151] Shepherd, *Narrative Function*, 242-43. Nonetheless, it is worth noting that this last mention of the kingdom of God is associated with the last mention of the Spirit just like the first mention of the former is introduced with the first mention of the latter at the very beginning of Acts.

of Paul's visit to Rome functions to reveal the accomplishment of the church's universal mission commanded from Jesus (Acts 1:8). Not surprisingly, Luke reports that the fulfillment of this mission has been guided by the Spirit. According to Acts 19:21, which sets the stage for the rest of Acts, Paul's decision to visit Macedonia (cf. 20:1), Achaia (cf. 20:2-3), Jerusalem (cf. 20:22-24; 21:4, 11-17), and Rome (28:14) was directed by the Spirit (ἔθετο ὁ Παῦλος ἐν τῷ πνεύματι). In particular, Luke depicts Paul's visit to Rome and his bearing witness to the gospel there as God's plan and purpose: 'I must (δεῖ) also see Rome' (Acts 19:21). By describing this essential ministry, Luke depicts the Spirit as causing Paul to visit Rome for his kingdom-preaching ministry. This implies that Paul's preaching ministry in Rome is still caused by the direction and empowerment of the Spirit.[152] Furthermore, as has been discussed, in the light of a similar feature indicated in the preceding displays of the Spirit's role in kingdom-preaching, the source of Paul's power to proclaim the kingdom of God in Rome is at least implicitly 'the Spirit' as in the case of his Ephesian ministry. At this point, Pfitzner's comments are worth recalling: 'it is clear that the Spirit is with Paul and at work through him right to the end. The last verse of the book pictures the apostle "preaching the kingdom of God... quite openly and unhindered" in Rome (28:31). Where the kingdom is being proclaimed there the Spirit is still at work'.[153]

In summary, Luke portrays Paul as a kingdom-preacher and describes the universal proclamation of the kingdom of God as being extensively carried out in the process of Paul's Gentile mission. Luke also consistently, but indirectly, brings the Spirit in relation to Paul's kingdom-preaching ministry. In any event, the two subjects are closely connected in Paul, but one could hardly explain the relationship better than to say that the Spirit functions as the vital agent of Paul's preaching of the kingdom. As Penney argues, the role of Paul's prophetic ministry in the power of the Spirit lies with 'the preaching of good news'.[154]

5.4. Conclusion

The intention of this chapter has been to demonstrate how Luke reflects the relationship between the Spirit and the kingdom of God. For this purpose, first of all, over against Dunn (and Smalley), it has been noted that according to Luke the Spirit is not simply presented as the manifestation of the kingdom of God. To equate the Spirit with the kingdom has apparently oversimplified the true relationship between the two and does not exactly

---

[152] See Hur, *Dynamic Reading*, 267-68.

[153] Pfitzner, '"Pneumatic" Apostleship?', 219; similarly, Woods, *Finger*, 152.

[154] Penney, *Missionary*, 116. See also Bruce, *Acts*, 390. 'Paul's main concern was... preaching in the Spirit's power the good news of God's free grace in Christ'.

echo Luke's perspective. Rather, the Spirit should be seen as the divine agent that lies behind the proclamation of the kingdom of God.

In this thesis, it has been argued that Jesus, in the Nazareth pericope, is depicted as the herald-prophet of the kingdom of God indicating how central and crucial this task is in his future messianic mission. The anointing of the Spirit upon Jesus is *primarily* linked to his carrying out this messianic commission in terms of the proclamation of the good news of the kingdom of God.

Similarly, one of the main themes of the church's proclamation in Acts is consistently presented as the kingdom of God. Luke makes it obvious that the kingdom of God is also available to all people beyond the boundaries of Judaism. Furthermore, just as the Spirit is the main source of power for Jesus' kingdom proclamation, the Spirit is still at work in the church's proclaiming of the kingdom. The disciples' mission to witness to Jesus and the kingdom is accomplished by their Spirit-empowerment so extending the kingdom beyond Israel. The universal evangelization of the kingdom of God is realized in Philip's Spirit-inspired proclamation of the kingdom of God in Samaria as the evidence promised in Acts 1:8. The same evangelization of the kingdom is continually carried out in Paul's Spirit-inspired wide proclamation in the process of his Gentile (and Jewish) mission in Ephesus and in Rome.

From this, it can be concluded that for Luke the primary role of the Spirit in relation to the kingdom of God is presented in qualified terms: principally as the power for the proclamation of the kingdom. The Spirit as an empowering force inspires people to proclaim the kingdom so that others have an opportunity to enter into it. This can be compared with the Pauline perspective which understands the Spirit as the source of the life of the kingdom in its entirety. Thus, Luke's portrayal of the nature of the relationship between the Spirit and the kingdom is consistent with my contention: the former is characterized as the cause by which the latter is proclaimed.

CHAPTER 6

Conclusion

This study has sought to establish the distinctive differences between Luke and Paul's understanding of the Spirit in specific relationship to the kingdom of God.

For this purpose, we have questioned why the central message of Jesus (the kingdom of God) has been so sporadically used by the apostle Paul on the one hand, and why he has used the Spirit language in his writings so often on the other. By way of answering these questions, it has been argued that Paul's use of language about the Spirit is an alternative expression for the kingdom of God in the Synoptics: Paul relates Jesus' central teaching on the kingdom through his own emphasis on the concept 'Spirit'. This can be deduced from the similarity of the eschatological framework between the Spirit in Paul and the kingdom of God in the Synoptics. More convincingly, this can be further deduced from the logical thrust that the various aspects of kingdom-life (new life, sonship, righteousness/justification, resurrection, ethical power), which are closely linked to the Spirit in Paul, are also conceptually related to the kingdom of God in the Synoptics. In other words, life in the Spirit in Paul is conceptually close to life in the kingdom of God in the Synoptics. In this way, for Paul, life in the Spirit becomes his way of speaking about life in the kingdom. The Spirit for him embodies the essence of the kingdom of God.

This line of pneumatology found in Paul has not been fully encountered in the literature of intertestamental Judaism. The literature generally understands the Spirit in a prophetic character, but in these writings the life-giving function of the Spirit is reasonably limited. Although soteriological pneumatology is presented at Qumran, particularly in 1 QH (and Wisdom), it should not be regarded as a major or dominant strand within Judaism; rather, it should be seen simply as the viewpoint of one minor strand, a small Jewish group. A much larger and more dominant traditional perspective generally represents the Spirit in a non-soteriological way, i.e., the source of extraordinary wisdom and prophecy.

Luke, whose pneumatology similarly reflects the dominant Jewish pneumatological perception, has not clearly indicated a line of pneumatology to the extent we can discover in Paul. Compared with the Jewish outlook on pneumatology indicated above, Luke does not portray the Spirit as the source of life-giving wisdom or as the life of the kingdom in its totality as in Paul. Luke fails to associate the blessings of the kingdom (new life, sonship, righteousness/justification, resurrection, ethical power) with the Spirit in its wider implications like Paul. We have seen that these blessings are rather closely integral to the kingdom of God in the Synoptics (Luke). Luke's dissociation of the Spirit from the kingdom blessings is thus in sharp contrast to Paul's clear association of the two ideas.

Finally, we have observed the nature of the relationship between the Spirit and the kingdom in Luke-Acts. Unlike Paul, who views the Spirit as the essence of the kingdom of God, Luke's understanding of the Spirit in relation to the kingdom is not depicted in this manner. For Luke, the Spirit primarily functions as the source of the inspired preaching of the kingdom which provides the occasion for people to enter the kingdom. The Spirit inspires Jesus to proclaim the kingdom to Israel, the disciples to proclaim it beyond Israel, Philip to proclaim it in Samaria, and Paul to proclaim it to the wider Gentile community. For Luke, where the Spirit is at work there the kingdom is being proclaimed.

All these observations have led to the important implication that Paul reformulates the kingdom of God by a new concept, primarily by speaking of the Spirit in a new and more comprehensive way. While the continuity between Jesus and Paul cannot be denied, there can also be found a development in the theological understanding of the early church through Paul's unique language. Paul developed the role of the Spirit more fully than the early (non-Pauline) church's pneumatology in understanding the blessings of the kingdom. In this way, Paul makes a key and original contribution with his understanding that the Spirit becomes the source of life in the kingdom in its entirety, mediating all of the blessings of the kingdom.

These observations have also led to the conclusion that there is a major difference between the pneumatologies of Luke and Paul in their respective understandings of the Spirit's relation to the kingdom. Luke's connection of the Spirit to the kingdom is represented in a specific or restricted manner: the Spirit is depicted as the source by which the kingdom of God is proclaimed. Paul's understanding of the connection is more fully developed by expressing the concept of the kingdom in terms of the Spirit. The Spirit becomes a vehicle by which the benefits of the kingdom-life are wholly operative in believers' hearts. Therefore, it is concluded that, for Luke, the presence of the Spirit is not essentially the same as the presence of the kingdom of God as is clearly the case for Paul. This conclusion contains a further implication that it cannot be simply argued that Paul's understanding of the Spirit is analogous with that of the early (non-Pauline) church.

Bibliography

Agua, A.D., 'The Lukan Narrative of the "Evangelization of the Kingdom of God": A Contribution to the Unity of Luke-Acts', 639-61 in J. Verheyden (ed.), *The Unity of Luke-Acts* (Louvain: LUP, 1999).

Alexander, P.S., 'Rabbinic Judaism and the New Testament', *Zeitschrift für die neutestamentliche Wissenschaft* 74, 237-46 (1983).

Allison, D.C., *The End of the Ages Has Come: An Early Interpretation of the Passion and Resurrection of Jesus* (Philadelphia: Fortress Press, 1987).

Allison D.C., and W.D. Davies, *The Gospel according to Saint Matthew*, I, International Critical Commentary (Edinburgh: T. & T. Clark, 1988).

Anderson, H., '4 Maccabees', 531-64 in J.H. Charlesworth (ed.), *Old Testament Pseudepigrapha*, 2 (New York: Doubleday, 1985).

Arrington, F., *The Acts of the Apostles: An Introduction and Commentary* (Peabody: Hendrickson, 1988).

Baer, H. von, *Der Heilige Geist in den Lukasschriften* (Stuttgart: Kohlhammer, 1926).

Barclay, J.M.G., 'Jesus and Paul', 492-503 in G.F. Hawthorne, R.P. Martin, and D.G. Reid (eds.), *Dictionary of Paul and His Letters* (Leicester/Downers Grove: IVP, 1993).

Barrett, C.K., *Luke the Historian in Recent Study* (London: Epworth, 1961).

_ *The Holy Spirit and the Gospel Tradition* (London: SPCK, 1966).

_ 'Apollos and the Twelve Disciples of Ephesus', 29-39 in W.C. Weinrich (ed.), *The New Testament Age: Essays in Honor of Bo Reicke*, I (Macon: Mercer University Press, 1984).

_ *The Epistle to the Romans*, Harper's New Testament Commentary (Peabody: Hendrickson, 1987).

_ *The First Epistle to the Corinthians*, Black's New Testament Commentary (London: A. & C. Black, 1991).

_ *A Critical and Exegetical Commentary on the Acts of the Apostles*, 2 vols.; International Critical Commentary (Edinburgh: T. & T. Clark, 1994-).

Bayer, O., 'Sprachbewegung und Weltveränderung, Ein systematischer Versuch als Auslegung von Mt 5:43-48', *Evangelische Theologie* 35 (1975), 309-21.

Beasley-Murray, G.R., *Jesus and the Kingdom of God* (Grand Rapids: Eerdmans, 1986).

_ *Baptism in the New Testament* (Grand Rapids: Eerdmans, 1962).

Becker, J., *Jesus of Nazareth* (Berlin: Walter De Gruyter, 1998).

Bertone, J.A., 'The Function of the Spirit in the Dialectic between God's Soteriological Plan Enacted but Not Yet Culminated: Rom 8:1-27', *Journal of Pentecostal Theology* 15 (1999), 75-97.

Best, E., 'Spirit-Baptism', *Novum Testamentum* 4 (1960), 236-43.

Betz, H.D., *Galatians*, Hermeneia (Philadelphia: Fortress Press, 1979).

_ *The Sermon on the Mount*, Hermeneia (Minneapolis: Fortress Press, 1995).

Bieder, W., 'πνεῦμα', 368-75 in G. Kittel and G. Friedrich (eds.), *Theological Dictionary of the New Testament*, vol. 6 (Grand Rapids: Eerdmans, 1975).

Black, M., *The Book of Enoch* (Leiden: Brill, 1985).

_ *Romans*, New Century Bible (London: Oliphants, 1973).

Blomberg, C.L., *Matthew*, The New American Commentary 22 (Nashville: Broadman, 1992).
Bock, D., *Proclamation from Prophecy and Pattern: Lukan Old Testament Christology*, Journal for the Study of the New Testament, Supplement Series 12 (Sheffield: JOST Press, 1987).
_ 'Proclamation from Prophecy and Pattern: Luke's Use of the Old Testament for Christology and Mission', 280-307 in C.A. Evans and W.R. Stegner (eds.), *The Gospels and the Scriptures of Israel*, Journal for the Study of the New Testament, Supplement Series 104 (Sheffield: Sheffield Academic Press, 1994).
_ *Luke*, 2 vols.; Baker Exegetical Commentary on the New Testament 3 (Grand Rapids: Baker, 1994-96).
Bornkamm, G., *Paul* (New York: Harper and Row, 1971).
Bovon, F., *Luke the Theologian: Thirty Three Years of Research* (1950-1983) (Allison Park: Pickwick, 1987).
_ *Das Evangelium nach Lukas*: *Lk 1:1-9:50* (Zürich: Benziger Verlag, 1989).
_ 'The Role of the Scriptures in the Composition of the Gospel Accounts: The Temptations of Jesus (Lk. 4:1-13 par.) and the Multiplication of the Loaves (Lk. 9:10-17 par.)', 26-31 in G. O'Collins and G. Marconi (eds.), *Luke and Acts* (New York/Manwah: Paulist Press, 1993).
Braude, W.G., *The Midrash on Psalms*, 2 vols. (New Haven: Yale University, 1959).
Brawley, R., *Luke-Acts and the Jews: Conflict, Apology, and Conciliation* (Atlanta: Scholars Press, 1987).
Brown, R.E., *The Birth of the Messiah: A Commentary on the Infancy Narratives in Matthew and Luke* (London: Doubleday, 1993).
Brown, S., *Apostasy and Perseverance in the Theology of Luke* (Rome: Pontifical Biblical Institute, 1969).
_ '"Water-Baptism" and "Spirit-Baptism" in Luke-Acts', *Anglican Theological Review* 59 (1977), 135-51.
Bruce, F.F., *The Acts of the Apostles: The Greek Text with Introduction and Commentary* (London: Tyndale, 1952).
_ *1&2 Thessalonians*, Word Biblical Commentary 45 (Waco: Word, 1982).
_ *I & II Corinthians*, New Century Bible (Grand Rapids: Eerdmans, 1982).
_ *The Book of the Acts*, The New International Commentary on the New Testament (Grand Rapids: Eerdmans, 1988).
Bruner, F., *A Theology of the Holy Spirit: The Pentecostal Experience and the New Testament Witness* (Grand Rapids: Eerdmans, 1970).
Bultmann, R., 'ζάω', 832-72 in G. Kittel and G. Friedrich (eds.), *Theological Dictionary of the New Testament*, vol. 2 (Grand Rapids: Eerdmans, 1974).
_ *Theology of the New Testament*, I (London: SCM Press, 1952).
_ 'The Significance of the Historical Jesus for the Theology of Paul', 220-46 in *Faith and Understanding: Collected Essays* (London: SCM Press, 1969).
Burchard, C., *Der dreizehnte Zeuge: Traditions-und kompositionsgeschichtliche Untersuchungen zu Lukas' Darstellung der Frühzeit des Paulus*, Forschungen zur Religion und Literature des Alten und Neuen Testaments 103 (Göttingen: Vandenhoeck & Ruprecht, 1970).
Büchsel, F., *Der Geist Gottes im Neuen Testament* (Gütersloh: C. Bertelsmann, 1926).
_ 'ἀπολύτρωσις', 351-56 in G. Kittel and G. Friedrich (eds.), *Theological Dictionary of the New Testament*, vol. 4 (Grand Rapids: Eerdmans, 1977).
Capper, B., 'The Palestinian Cultural Context of Earliest Christian Community of

Goods', 323-56 in B.W. Winter (ed.), *The Book of Acts in Its First Century Setting*, 4 (Grand Rapids: Eerdmans, 1995).

Caragounis, C.C., 'Kingdom of God, Son of Man and Jesus' self-understanding', *Tyndale Bulletin* 40 (1989), 3-23, 223-38.

_ 'Kingdom of God/Heaven', 417-30 in J.B. Green, S. McKnight, and I.H. Marshall (eds.), *Dintionary of Jesus and Gospels* (Leicester/Downer Grove: IVP, 1992).

Charette, B., *Restoring Presence: The Spirit in Matthew's Gospel*, Journal of Pentecostal Theology, Supplement Series 18 (Sheffield: Sheffield Academic Press, 2000).

Charles, R.H., *The Book of Enoch or 1 Enoch* (Oxford: Clarendon, 1912).

Chilton, B.D. and J.I.H. McDonald, *Jesus and the Ethics of the Kingdom* (London: SPCK, 1987).

Coleridge, M., *The Birth of the Lukan Narrative: Narrative as Christology in Luke 1-2*, Journal for the Study of the New Testament, Supplement Series 88 (Sheffield: JSOT Press, 1993).

Collins, A.Y., 'Aristobulus', 831-42 in J.H. Charlesworth (ed.), *Old Testament Pseudepigrapha*, vol. 2 (New York: Doubleday, 1985).

Conzelmann, H., 'χάρις', 372-402 in G. Kittel and G. Friedrich (eds.), *Theological Dictionary of the New Testament*, vol. 9 (Grand Rapids: Eerdmans, 1982).

_ *1 Corinthians*, Hermeneia (Philadelphia: Fortress Press, 1975).

_ *The Acts of the Apostles*, Hermeneia (Philadelphia: Fortress Press, 1987).

Cosgrove, C.H., *The Cross and the Spirit: A Study in the Argument and Theology of Galatians* (Macon: Mercer University Press, 1988).

Cranfield, C.E.B., *A Critical and Exegetical Commentary on the Epistle to the Romans*, 2 vols.; International Critical Commentary (Edinburgh: T. & T. Clark, 1975-79).

Cullmann, O., *The Christology of the New Testament* (London: SCM Press, 1963).

Dalman, G., *The Words of Jesus* (Edinburgh: T. & T. Clark, 1902).

Danker, F.W., *Jesus and the New Age* (Philadelphia: Fortress Press, 1988).

Darr, J.A., *On Character Building: The Reader and the Rhetoric of Characterization in Luke-Acts* (Louisville: Westminster/John Knox Press, 1992).

Davies, D.J., 'Rebouncing Vitality: Resurrection and Spirit in Luke-Acts', 205-24 in M.D. Carroll, D. Clines, and P. Davies (eds.), *The Bible in Human Society: Essays in Honour of John Rogerson*, Journal for the Study of the Old Testament, Supplement Series 200 (Sheffield: Sheffield Academic Press, 1995).

Davis, J.A., *Wisdom and Spirit: An Investigation of 1 Corinthians 1.18-3.20 against the Background of Jewish Sapiential Tradition in the Greco-Roman Period* (Lanham: University Press of America, 1984).

Dennison, W., 'Indicative and Imperative: The Basic Structure of Pauline Ethics', *Canadian Journal of Theology* 1 (1979), 55-78.

Denova, R., *The Things Accomplished Among Us: Prophetic Tradition in the Scriptural Pattern of Luke-Acts*, Journal for the Study of the New Testament, Supplement Series 141 (Sheffield: Sheffield Academic Press, 1997).

de Silva, D.A., *4 Maccabees* (Sheffield: Sheffield Academic Press, 1998).

Dodd, C.H., *The Parables of the Kingdom* (London: Collins, 1961).

Dunn, J.D.G., *Baptism in the Holy Spirit: A Re-examination of the New Testament Teaching on the Gift of the Spirit in Relation to Pentecostalism Today* (London: SCM Press, 1970).

_ 'Spirit and Kingdom', *Expository Times* 82 (1970), 37-40.

_ *Jesus and the Spirit* (Philadelphia: Westminster Press, 1975).

_ *Unity and Diversity in the New Testament* (London: SCM Press, 1977).

_ *Christology in the Making* (Philadelphia: Westminster Press, 1980).
_ *Romans*, 2 vols.; Word Biblical Commentary 38 (Dallas: Word, 1988).
_ 'Baptism in the Spirit: A Response to Pentecostal Scholarship on Luke-Acts', *Journal of Pentecostal Theology* 3 (1993), 3-27.
_ *The Epistle to the Galatians*, Black's New Testament Commentary (London: A. & C. Black, 1993).
_ 'Jesus Tradition in Paul', in B. Chilton and C.A. Evans (eds.), *Studying the Historical Jesus* (New York: Brill, 1994).
_ *The Christ and the Spirit*, 2 vols. (Grand Rapids: Eerdmans, 1998).
_ *The Theology of Paul the Apostle* (Grand Rapids: Eerdmans, 1998).
Ellis, E., 'Christ Crucified', 69-75 in R. Banks (ed.), *Reconciliation and Hope* (Grand Rapids: Eerdmans, 1974).
_ *The Gospel of Luke*, New Century Bible (London: Marshall, Morgan & Scott, 1974).
Engel, H., *Die Susanna-Erzählung: Einleitung, Übersetzung und Kommentar zum Septuaginta-Text und zur Theodotion-Bearbeitung* (Göttingen: Vandenhoeck & Ruprecht, 1985).
Ervin, H., *Conversion-Initiation and the Baptism in the Holy Spirit: A Critique of James D.G. Dunn, Baptism in the Holy Spirit* (Peabody: Hendrickson, 1984).
Evans, C.A., 'From Anointed Prophet to Anointed King: Probing Aspects of Jesus' Self-Understanding', in *Jesus and His Contemporaries* (Leiden: Brill, 1995), 437-56.
Evans, C.F., *Resurrection and the New Testament* (London: SCM Press, 1970).
_ *Saint Luke* (London: SCM Press, 1990).
Farris, S., *The Hymns of Luke's Infancy Narratives: Their Origin, Meaning and Significance*, Journal for the Study of the New Testament, Supplement Series 9 (Sheffield: JSOT Press, 1985).
Fee, G., *The First Epistle to the Corinthians*, The New International Commentary on the New Testament (Grand Rapids: Eerdmans, 1987).
_ *God's Empowering Presence: The Holy Spirit in the Letters of Paul* (Peabody: Hendrickson, 1994).
Finkel, A., 'Jesus' Preaching in the Synagogue on the Sabbath (Luke 4:16-28)', 325-41 in C.A. Evans and W.R. Stegner (eds.), *The Gospels and the Scriptures of Israel*, Journal for the Study of the New Testament, Supplement Series 104 (Sheffield: Sheffield   Academic Press, 1994).
Fitzmyer, J.A., *The Gospel According to Luk*, 2 vols.; Anchor Bible 28 (New York: Doubleday, 1981-85).
_ 'The Contribution of Qumran Aramaic to the Study of the New Testament', *New Testament Studies* 20 (1974), 382-407.
Foakes-Jackson, F.J., and K. Lake (eds.), *The Beginnings of Christianity*, 5 vols. (London: Macmillan, 1920-33).
Franklin, E., *Luke: Interpreter of Paul, Critic of Matthew*, Journal for the Study of the New Testament, Supplement Series 92 (Sheffield: JSOP Press, 1994).
Freed, E.D., *The Stories of Jesus' Birth: A Critical Introduction*, The Biblical Seminar 72 (Sheffield: Sheffield Academic Press, 2001).
Fuller, R.H., *The Mission and Achievement of Jesus*, Studies in Biblical Theology 12 (Naperville; Allemson, 1954).
Fung, R.Y., 'Justification by Faith in 1&2 Corinthians', 246-61 in D.A. Hagner & M.J. Harris (eds.), *Pauline Studies: Essays Presented to Professor F.F. Bruce on His 70th Birthday* (Exeter: Paternoster, 1980).
_ *The Epistle to the Galatians*, The New International Commentary on the New

Testament (Grand Rapids: Eerdmans, 1988).
Furnish, V.P., *Theology and Ethics in Paul* (Nashville: Abingdon, 1968).
_ *II Corinthians* (New York: Doubleday, 1984).
Gaffin, R.B., Jr., *The Centrality of the Resurrection* (Grand Rapids: Baker, 1978).
Gaventa, B.R., *From Darkness to Light: Aspects of Conversion in the New Testament* (Philadelphia: Fortress Press, 1986).
_ *Mary: Glimpses of the Mother of Jesus* (Edinburgh: T. & T. Clark, 1999).
Gero, S., 'The Spirit as a Dove at the Baptism of Jesus', *Novum Testamentum* 18 (1976), 17-35.
Gibson, J.B., 'Jesus' Wilderness Temptation according to Mark', *Journal for the Study of the New Testament* 53 (1994), 3-34.
Giles, K., 'Is Luke an Exponent of "Early Protestantism"? Church Order in the Lukan Writings (Part 1)', *Evangelical Quarterly* 54 (1982), 193-205.
Goldberg, A., 'Form-Analysis of Midrashic Literature as a Method of Description', *Journal of Jewish Studies* 36 (1985), 159-74.
Goulder, M.D., *Luke: A New Paradigm*, Journal for the Study of the New Testament, Supplement Series 20 (Sheffield: JSOT Press, 1989).
Grundmann, W., 'ἀπεκδέχομαι', 55-59 in G. Kittel and G. Friedrich (eds.), *Theological Dictionary of the New Testament*, vol. 2 (Grand Rapids: Eerdmans, 1974).
Guelich, R.A., *The Sermon on the Mount: A Foundation for Understanding* (Waco: Word, 1982).
_ *Mark 1-8:26*, Word Biblical Commentary 34a (Dallas: Word, 1989).
Gundry, R.H., *Matthew: A Commentary on his Literary and Theological Art* (Grand Rapids: Eerdmans, 1982).
Gunkel, H., *Die Wirkungen des heiligen Geistes nach der populären Anschauung der apostolischen Zeit und nach der Lehre des Apostels Paulus* (Göttingen: Vandenhoeck & Ruprecht, 1888), ET, *The Influence of the Holy Spirit: The Popular View of the Apostolic Age and the Teaching of the Apostle Paul* (Philadelphia: Fortress Press, 1979).
Haenchen, E., *The Acts of the Apostles: A Commentary* (Oxford: Blackwell, 1971).
Hafemann, S., *Paul, Moses, and the History of Israel: The Letter/Spirit Contrast and the Argument from Scripture in 2 Corinthians 3*, Wissenschaftliche Untersuchungen zum Neuen Testament 81 (Tübingen: Mohr, 1995).
Hagner, D.A., *Matthew*, 2 vols.; Word Biblical Commentary 33 (Dallas: Word, 1993-95).
Hahn, F., *The Titles of Jesus in Christology: Their History in Early Christianity* (New York: World Publishing, 1969).
Hamerton-Kelly, R.G., 'A Note on Matthew XII. 28 Par. Luke XI. 20', *New Testament Studies* 11 (1965), 167-69.
Hamilton, N.Q., *The Holy Spirit and Eschatology in Paul*, SJT Occasional Papers 6 (Edinburgh: Oliver & Boyd, 1957).
Hansen, G.W., 'Paul's Conversion and His Ethics of Freedom in Galatians', 213-37 in R. Longenecker (ed.), *The Road from Damascus: The Impact of Paul's Conversion on His Life, Thought, and Ministry* (Grand Rapids: Eerdmans, 1997).
Harrington, D.J., 'Pseudo-Philo', 297-377 in J.H. Charlesworth (ed.), *Old Testament Pseudepigrapha*, 2 (New York: Doubleday, 1985).
Harris, M.J., *Raised Immortal: The Relation between Resurrection and Immortality in New Testament Teaching* (London: Marshall, Morgan & Scott, 1983).
Haufe, G., 'Reich Gottes bei Paulus und in der Jesustradition', *New Testament Studies* 31 (1985), 467-72.

Hawthorne, G.F., 'Holy Spirit', 489-99 in R. P. Martin and P. H. Davids (eds.), *Dictionary of the Later New Testament and Its Developments* (Leicester/Downers Grove: IVP, 1997).

Haya-Prats, G., *L'Esprit force de l'église: Sa nature et son activité d'après les Actes des Apôtres* (Paris: Cerf, 1975).

Hengel, M., *Property and Riches in the Early Church: Aspects of a Social History of Christianity* (Philadelphia: Fortress Press, 1974).

_ *Acts and the History of Earliest Christianity* (London: SCM Press, 1979).

_ *Judaism and Hellenism: Studies in their Encounter in Palestine during the Early Hellenistic Period*, 2 vols. (Minneapolis: Fortress Press, 1981).

Hill, D., *Greek Words and Hebrew Meanings: Studies in the Semantics of Soteriological Terms*, Society for New Testament Studies Monograph Series 5 (Cambridge: Cambridge University Press, 1967).

_ *New Testament Prophecy* (London: Marshall, Morgan, & Scott, 1979).

Holladay, C.R., *Fragments from Hellenistic Jewish Authors: Aristobulus* (Atlanta: Scholars Press, 1995).

Hooker, M.D., 'David Wenham's *Paul: Follower of Jesus or Founder of Christianity?*: A Review Article', *Journal of Biblical Literature* 115 (1996), 756-58.

Horn, F.W., 'Holy Spirit', 260-80 in D.N. Freedman (ed.), *Anchor Bible Dictionary*, 3 (New York: Doubleday, 1992).

_ *Das Angeld des Geistes: Studien zur paulinischen Pneumatologie* (Göttingen: Vandenhoeck & Ruprecht, 1992).

Huffman, D.S., *The Theology of the Acts of the Apostles: Lukan Compositional Markedness as a Guide to Interpreting Acts* (Ann Arbor: Bell and Howell, 1994).

Hull, J.H.E., *The Holy Spirit in the Acts of the Apostles* (London: Lutterworth, 1967).

Hunter, A.M., *Design for Life* (London: SCM Press, 1965).

Hur, J., *A Dynamic Reading of the Holy Spirit in Luke-Acts*, Journal for the Study of the New Testament, Supplement Series 211 (Sheffield: Sheffield Academic Press, 2001).

Hübner, H., *Law in Paul's Thought* (Edinburgh: T. & T. Clark, 1984).

Ireland, D.J., *Stewardship and the Kingdom of God: A Historical, Exegetical, and Contextual Study of the Parable of the Unjust Steward in Luke 16:1-13* Novum Testamentum, Supplements 70 (New York: Brill, 1992).

Isaac, E., '1 (Ethiopic Apocalypse of) Enoch', 5-89 in J.H. Charlesworth (ed.), *Old Testament Pseudepigrapha*, 1 (New York: Doubleday, 1983).

Isaacs, M.E., *The Concept of the Spirit: A Study of Pneuma in Hellenistic Judaism and its Bearing on the New Testament* (London: Heythrop College, 1976).

Jeremias, J., 'παῖς θεοῦ', 654-717 in G. Kittel and G. Friedrich (eds.), *Theological Dictionary of the New Testament*, vol. 5 (Grand Rapids: Eerdmans, 1977).

_ 'Flesh and Blood cannot Inherit the Kingdom of God', *New Testament Studies* 2 (1955-56), 151-59.

_ *The Parables of Jesus* (London: SCM Press, 1963).

_ *The Prayers of Jesus* (Naperville: Allenson, 1967).

_ *New Testament Theology*, I: *The Proclamation of Jesus* (London: SCM Press, 1971).

Jervell, J., *The Theology of the Acts of the Apostles*, New Testament Theology (Cambridge: Cambridge University Press, 1996).

Johnson, L.T., *Sharing Possessions: Mandate and Symbol of Faith* (London: SCM Press, 1981).

_ *The Acts of Apostles* (Collegeville: Liturgical, 1992).

Johnston, G., 'Kingdom of God Sayings in Paul's Letters', 143-56 in P. Richardson and J.C. Hurd (eds.), *From Jesus to Paul* (Ontario: Wilfred Laurier University, 1984).
Jonge, M. de., *The Testaments of the Twelve Patriarchs: A Study of their Text, Composition and Origin* (Manchester: Assen, 1953).
_ *Christology in Context: The Earliest Christian Response to Jesus* (Philadelphia: Westminster Press, 1988).
_ 'The Main Issues in the Study of the Testaments of the Twelve Patriarchs', in *Jewish Eschatology, Early Christian Christology and the Testaments of the Twelve Patriarchs* (Leiden: Brill, 1991), 147-63.
_ 'The Testaments of the Twelve Patriarchs: Christian and Jewish', in *Jewish Eschatology*, 233-43.
_ 'Levi in Aramaic Levi and in the Testament of Levi', 71-89 in E.G. Chazon and M.E. Stone (eds.), *Pseudepigraphic Perspectives: the Apocrypha and Pseudepigrapha in light of the Dead Sea Scrolls. Proceedings of the International Symposium of the Orion Center for the Study of the Dead Sea Scrolls and Associated Literature, 12-14 January, 1997* (Leiden / Boston/ Köln: Brill, 1999).
Jüngel, E., *Paulus und Jesus: eine Untersuchung zur Präzisierung der Frage nach dem Ursprung der Christologie* (Tübingen: Mohr, 1964).
Kaiser, O., *Isaiah 1-12* (Philadelphia: Westminster Press, 1974).
Käsemann, E., *Commentary on Romans* (Grand Rapids: Eerdmans, 1980).
Keck, L.E., 'The Spirit and the Dove', *New Testament Studies* 17 (1970), 41-68.
Kee, H.C., 'Approaching the History of God's People: A Survey of Interpretations of the History of Israel in the Pseudepigrapha, Apocrypha and the New Testament', 44-64 in J.H. Charlesworth and C.A. Evans (eds.), *The Pseudepigrapha and Early Biblical Interpretation*, Journal for the Study of Pseudepigrapha, Supplement Series 14 (Sheffield: JSOT Press, 1993).
Keener, C., *The Spirit in the Gospels and Acts: Divine Purity and Power* (Peabody: Hendrickson, 1997).
Kennedy, H.A.A., *Paul's Conception of the Last Things* (London: Hodder and Stoughton, 1904).
Kim, H.S., *Die Geisttaufe des Messias: Eine kompositionsgeschichtliche Untersuchung zu einem Leitmotiv des lukanischen Doppelwerks. Ein Beitrag zur Theologie und Intention des Lukas* (Bern: Peter Lang, 1993).
Kittel, G., 'δόξα', 247-51 in G. Kittel and D. Friedrich (eds.), *Theological Dictionary of the New Testament*, vol. 2 (Grand Rapids: Eerdmans, 1974).
Klein, M.L., *The Fragment-Targums of the Pentateuch according to their Extant Sources* (Rome: Biblical Institute, 1980).
Klijn, A.F.J., '2 (Syriac Apocalypse of) Baruch', 615-52 in J.H. Charlesworth (ed.), *Old Testament Pseudepigrapha*, 1 (New York: Doubleday, 1983).
Knibb, M.A., 'Martyrdom and Ascension of Isaiah', 143-76 in J.H. Charlesworth (ed.), *Old Testament Pseudepigrapha*, 2 (New York: Doubleday, 1985).
Koch, R., *Geist und Messias* (Wien: Herder, 1950).
Kraemer, R., *When Aseneth Met Joseph: A Late Antique Tale of the Biblical Patriarch and His Egyptian Wife, Reconsidered* (New York/Oxford: OUP, 1998).
Kraft, R., 'The Pseudepigrapha in Christianity', 55-86 in J.C. Reeves (ed.), *Tracing the Threads: Studies in the Vitality of Jewish Pseudepigrapha* (Atlanta: Scholars Press, 1994).
Kreitzer, L.J., *Jesus and God in Paul's Eschatology*, Journal for the Study of the New

Testament, Supplement Series 37 (Sheffield: JSOT Press, 1987).
Kremer, J., *Pfingstbericht und Pfingstgeschehen: Eine exegetische Untersuchung zu Apg 2,1-13*, Stuttgarter Bibel-Studien 63-64 (Stuttgart: KBW, 1973).
Kümmel, W.G., *Promise and Fulfillment* (London: SCM Press, 1957).
__*Introduction to the New Testament* (Nashville: Abingdon, 1975).
Kvalbein, H., 'The Kingdom of God in the Ethics of Jesus', *Communio Viatorum* 40:3 (1998), 197-227.
Ladd, G.E., *I Believe in the Resurrection of Jesus* (Grand Rapids: Eerdmans, 1975).
Lampe, G.W.H., 'The Holy Spirit in the Writings of St. Luke', 159-200 in D.E. Nineham (ed.), *Studies in the Gospels* (Oxford: Blackwell, 1957).
_ *The Bampton Lectures, 1976* (Oxford: Clarendon, 1977).
Levison, J.R., 'Inspiration and the Divine Spirit in the Writings of Philo Judaeus', *Journal for the Study of Judaism in the Persian, Hellenistic and Roman Period* 25 (1995), 271-323.
_ *The Spirit in First Century Judaism* (Leiden: Brill, 1997).
Lewis, J.P., 'The Kingdom of God... is Righteousness Peace and Joy in the Holy Spirit (Rom 14:17): A Survey of Interpretation', *Restoration Quarterly* 40 (1998), 53-68.
Lieu, J., *The Gospel of Luke* (Peterborough: Epworth, 1997).
Lodahl, M.E., *Shekhinah, Spirit: Divine Presence in Jewish and Christian Religion* (New York: Paulist Press, 1992).
Lohmeyer, E., *Das Evangelium des Markus* (Göttingen: Vandenhoeck & Ruprecht, 1963).
Lohse, E., 'ὁ νόμος τοῦ πνεύματος τῆς ζωῆς: Exegetische Anmerkungen zu Röm 8:2', 279-87 in H.D. Betz & L. Schotroff (eds.), *Neuen Testament und christliche Existenz* (Tübingen: Mohr, 1973).
_ 'Die Bedeutung des Pfingstberichtes im Rahmen des lukanischen Geschichtswerkes', in *Die Einheit des Neuen Testament* (Göttingen: Vandenhoeck & Ruprecht, 1973), 178-92.
Longenecker, R.N., *The Acts of the Apostles*, The Expositor's Bible Commentary 9 (Grand Rapids: Zondervan, 1981).
_ *Galatians*, Word Biblical Commentary 41 (Dallas: Word, 1990).
Lull, D.J., *The Spirit in Galatia: Paul's Interpretation of Pneuma as Divine Power*, Society of Biblical Literature 49 (Chico: Scholars Press, 1980).
Lührmann, D., 'Liebet eure Feinde (Lk 6, 27-36/Mt 5, 39-48)', *Zeitschrift für Theologie und Kirche* 69 (1972), 412-38.
Maddox, R., *The Purpose of Luke-Acts*, Forschungen zur Religion und Literatur des Alten und Neuen Testaments 126 (Göttingen: Vandenhoeck & Ruprecht, 1982).
Manson, T.W., *The Teaching of Jesus* (Cambridge: Cambridge University Press, 1951).
Marsh, T., 'Holy Spirit in Early Christian Teaching', 60-78 in W. Harrington (ed.), *Witness to the Spirit: Essays on Revelation, Spirit, Redemption* (Manchester: Koinonia, 1979).
Marshall, I.H., *Luke: Historian and Theologian* (Grand Rapids: Zondervan, 1970).
_ 'The Meaning of the Verb "to Baptize"', *Evangelical Quarterly* 45 (1973), 130-40.
_ 'The Significance of Pentecost', *Scottish Journal of Theology* 30 (1977), 347-69.
_ *The Gospel of Luke*, The New International Greek Testament Commentary (Grand Rapids: Eerdmans, 1978).
_ *The Acts of the Apostles*, Tyndale New Testament Commentaries 5 (Grand Rapids: Eerdmans, 1992).
_ *1 and 2 Thessalonians*, New Century Bible (Grand Rapids: Eerdmans, 1983).

_ 'The Hope of a New Age: The Kingdom of God in the New Testament', *Themelios* 5 (1985), 5-15.
_ 'An Evangelical Approach to "Theological Criticism"', *Themelios* 13 (1988), 79-85.
_ 'The Divine Sonship of Jesus', in *Jesus the Saviour: Studies in the New Testament Theology* (London: SPCK, 1990), 134-49.
Martínez, F.G. and E.J.C. Tigchelaar, *The Dead Sea Scrolls* (Grand Rapids: Eerdmans, 2000).
McLean, J.A., 'Did Jesus Correct the Disciples' View of the Kingdom?', *Bibliotheca Sacra* 151 (1994), 215-27.
McNamara, M., *Palestinian Judaism and the New Testament*, Good News Studies 4 (Wilmington: Michael Glazier, 1983).
Menzies, R.P., *The Development of Early Christian Pneumatology with Special Reference to Luke-Acts*, Journal for the Study of the New Testament, Supplement Series 54 (Sheffield: JSOT Press, 1991).
_ 'The Distinctive Character of Luke's Pneumatology', *Paraclete* 25 (1991), 17-30.
_ 'Spirit and Power in Luke and Acts: A Response to Max Turner', *Journal for the Study of the New Testament* 49 (1993), 11-20.
_ 'Luke and the Spirit: A Reply to James Dunn', *Journal of Pentecostal Theology* 4 (1994), 115-38.
_ *Empowered for Witness: The Spirit in Luke-Acts*, Journal of Pentecostal Theology, Supplement Series 6 (Sheffield: Sheffield Academic Press, 1994).
_ 'The Spirit of Prophecy, Luke-Acts and Pentecostal Theology: A Response to Max Turner', *Journal of Pentecostal Theology* 15 (1999), 49-74.
_ *Spirit and Power: Foundations of Pentecostal Experience* (Grand Rapids: Zondervan, 2000).
Merk, O., 'Das Reich Gottes in den lukanischen Schriften', 201-20 in E. Ellis and E. Grässer (eds.), *Jesus and Paulus* (Göttingen: Vandenhoeck & Ruprecht, 1973).
Metzger, B.M., 'The Fourth Book of Ezra', 517-59 in J.H. Charlesworth (ed.), *Old Testament Pseudepigrapha*, 1 (New York: Doubleday, 1983).
_ *A Textual Commentary of the Greek New Testament* (London: UBS, 1975).
Minear, P.S., *To Heal and to Reveal: Prophetic Vocation According to Luke* (New York: Seabury, 1976).
Mitchell, A.C., 'The Social Function of Friendship in Acts 2:44-47 and 4:32-37', *Journal of Biblical Literature* 111 (1992), 255-72.
Mitton, C., *Your Kingdom Come* (London and Oxford: Mowbrays, 1978).
Montague, G., *The Holy Spirit: Growth of a Biblical Tradition* (New York: Paulist Press, 1976).
Moo, D., *Romans 1-8*, Wycliffe Exegetical Commentary (Chicago: Moody Press, 1991).
Morris, L., *The Epistle to the Romans* (Grand Rapids: Eerdmans, 1988).
Müller, D., 'Geisterfahrung und Totenauferweckung: Untersuchungen zur Totenauferweckung bei Paulus und in den ihm vorgegebenen Überlieferungen' (PhD Dissertation; Christian-Albrecht-Universität, Kiel, 1980).
Neil, W., *The Acts of the Apostles*, New Century Bible (London: Marshall, Morgan & Scott, 1973).
Neusner, J., *The Tosefta*, III: *Nashim (The Order of Women): Translated from the Hebrew* (New York: KTAV, 1979).
Nickelsburg, G.W.E., *Resurrection, Immortality, and Eternal Life in Intertestamental Judaism*, Harvard Theological Studies 26 (Cambridge: Harvard University Press, 1972).

Nolland, J., *Luke*, 3 vols.; Word Biblical Commentary 35 (Dallas: Word, 1989-93).
O' Neill, J.C., *The Theology of Acts in Its Historical Setting* (London: SPCK, 1970).
_ *Messiah, Six Lectures on the Ministry of Jesus* (Cambridge: Cochrane, 1980).
_ 'The Kingdom of God', *Novum Testamentum* 35 (1992), 130-41.
_ 'The Connection between Baptism and the Gift of the Spirit in Acts', *Journal for the Study of the New Testament* 63 (1996), 96-102.
Orton, D.E., *The Understanding Scribe: Matthew and the Apocalyptic Ideal*, Journal for the Study of the New Testament, Supplement Series 25 (Sheffield: JSOP Press, 1989).
O'Toole, R.F., 'The Kingdom of God in Luke-Acts', 147-62 in W. Willis (ed.), *The Kingdom of God in Twentieth-Century Interpretation* (Peabody: Hendrickson, 1987).
Oulton, J.E.L., 'The Holy Spirit, Baptism, and Laying on of Hands in Acts', *Expository Times* 66 (1955), 236-40.
Palmer, D.W., 'The Literary Background of Acts 1:1-14', *New Testament Studies* 33 (1987), 427-38.
Parsons, M., 'Being Precedes Act: Indicative and Imperative in Paul's Writing', 217-47 in B. Rosner (ed.), *Understanding Paul's Ethics: Twentieth-Century Approaches* (Grand Rapids: Eerdmans, 1995).
Penney, J.M., *The Missionary Emphasis of Lukan Pneumatology*, Journal of Pentecostal Theology, Supplement Series 12 (Sheffield: Sheffield Academic Press, 1997).
Perkins, P., *Resurrection: New Testament Witness and Contemporary Reflection* (London: Geoffrey Chapman, 1985).
Pfitzner, V.C., '"Pneumatic" Apostleship? Apostle and Spirit in the Acts of the Apostles', 210-35 in W. Haubeck and M. Bachmann (eds.), *Wort in der Zeit: Festgabe Für Karl Heinrich Rengstorf* (Leiden: Brill, 1980).
Piper, J., *Love your Enemies: Jesus' Love Command in the Synoptic Gospels and in the Early Christian Paraenesis*, Society for New Testament Studies Monograph Series 38 (Cambridge: Cambridge University Press, 1979).
Polhill, J.B., *Acts* (Nashville: Broadman, 1992).
Pomykala, K.E., *The Davidic Dynasty Tradition in Early Judaism: Its History and Significance for Messianism*, Society of Biblical Literature 7 (Atlanta: Scholars Press, 1995).
Porter, S.E., *Idioms of the Greek New Testament* (Sheffield: JSOT Press, 1994).
_ *The Paul of Acts: Essays in Literary Criticism, Rhetoric, and Theology*, Wissenschaftliche Untersuchungen zum Neuen Testament 115 (Tübingen: Mohr, 1999).
Powell, M.A., 'Salvation in Luke-Acts', *Word and World* 12:1 (1992), 5-10.
Prieur, A., *Die Verkündigung der Gottesherrschaft: Exegetische Studien zum lukanischen Verständnis von βασιλεία τοῦ θεοῦ* Wissenschaftliche Untersuchungen zum Neuen Testament 2.89 (Tübingen: Mohr, 1996).
Prior, M., *Jesus: The Liberator: Nazareth Liberation Theology (Luke 4:16-30)*, The Biblical Seminar 26 (Sheffield: Sheffield Academic Press, 1995).
Przybylski, B., *Righteousness in Matthew and His World of Thought*, Society for New Testament Studies Monograph Series 41 (Cambridge: Cambridge University Press, 1980).
Rahlfs, A., *Septuaginta* (Stuttgart: Deutsche Bibelgesellschaft, 1979).
Räisänen, H., *Jesus, Paul and Torah*, Journal for the Study of the New Testament, Supplement Series 43 (Sheffield: Sheffield Academic Press, 1992).
Redditt, P.L., 'The Concept of *Nomos* in Fourth Maccabees', *Catholic Biblical Quarterly* 45 (1983), 249-70.

Reider, J., *The Book of Wisdom* (New York: Harper & Row, 1957).
Rese, M., *Alttestamentliche Motive in der Christologie des Lukas* (Gütersloh: Mohn, 1969).
Reumann, J., *Righteousness in the New Testament* (Philadelphia: Fortress Press, 1982).
Richardson, P., 'Spirit and Letter: A Foundation for Hermeneutics', *Evangelical Quarterly* 45 (1973), 214-18.
Ridderbos, H., *The Coming of the Kingdom* (Philadelphia: Presbyterian and Reformed, 1962).
_ *Paul: An Outline of His Theology* (Grand Rapids: Eerdmans, 1975).
Rodd, C.S., 'Spirit and Finger', *Expository Times* 72 (1961), 157-58.
Roloff, J., *Die Apostelgeschichte* (Göttingen: Vandenhoeck & Ruprecht, 1981).
Rowland, C., *Christian Origins* (London: SPCK, 1985).
Russell, D.S., *The Method and Message of Jewish Apocalyptic* (London: SCM Press, 1964).
Russell, E.A., '"They Believed Philip Preaching" (Acts 8:12)', *Irish Biblical Studies* 1 (1979), 169-79.
Russell, W., 'The Apostle Paul's Redemptive-Historical Argumentation in Galatians 5:13-26', *Westminister Theological Journal* 57 (1995), 333-57.
Schäfer, P., 'Die termini "Heiliger Geist" und "Geist der Prophetie" in den Targumim und das Verhältnis der Targumim Zueinander', *Vetus Testamentum* 20 (1970), 304-14.
Schlatter, A., *Die Geschichte des Christus* (Stuttgart: Calwer, 1922).
Schmidt, K.L., 'βασιλεία', 579-90 in G. Kittel and G. Friedrich (eds.), *Theological Dictionary of the New Testament*, vol. 1 (Grand Rapids: Eerdmans, 1976).
Schnabel, E., *Law and Wisdom from Ben Sira to Paul: A Tradition Historical Enquiry into the Relation of Law, Wisdom, and Ethics*, Wissenschaftliche Untersuchungen zum Neuen Testament 2.16 (Tübingen: Mohr, 1985).
_ 'How Paul Developed His Ethics: Motivation, Norms and Criteria of Pauline Ethics', 267-97 in B. Rosner (ed.), *Understanding Paul's Ethics: Twentieth-Century Approaches* (Grand Rapids: Eerdmans, 1995).
Schneider, D., *Die Apostelgeschichte*, I (Freiburg: Herder, 1980).
Schneider, G., 'ἔρχομαι', 666-75 in G. Kittel and G. Friedrich (eds.), *Theological Dictionary of the New Testament*, vol. 2 (Grand Rapids: Eerdmans, 1974).
Schreiner, T.R., *The Law and its Fulfillment: A Pauline Theology of Law* (Grand Rapids: Baker, 1993).
Schrenk, G., 'δικαιοσύνη', 192-210 in G. Kittel and G. Friedrich (eds.), *Theological Dictionary of the New Testament*, vol. 2 (Grand Rapids: Eerdmans, 1974).
_ 'πατήρ', 945-1014 G. Kittel and G. Friedrich (eds.), *Theological Dictionary of the New Testament*, vol. 5 (Grand Rapids: Eerdmans, 1977).
Schürer, E., *The History of the Jewish People in the Age of Jesus Christ*, 3 vols.; rev. and ed. G. Vermes, F. Miller, and M. Black (Edinburgh: T. & T. Clark, 1973-1986).
Schweizer, E., 'πνεῦμα', 389-455 in G. Kittel and G. Friedrich (eds.), *Theological Dictionary of New Testament*, vol. 6 (Grand Rapids: Eerdmans, 1975).
Scott, J.M., *Adoption as Sons of God: An Exegetical Investigation into the Background of ΥΙΟΘΕΣΙΑ in the Corpus Paulinum*, Wissenschaftliche Untersuchungen zum Neuen Testament 2.48 (Tübingen: Mohr, 1992).
Scroggs, R., 'Paul: ΣΟΦΟΣ and ΠΝΕΥΜΑΤΙΚΟΣ', *New Testament Studies* 14 (1967), 33-55.
Seccombe, D.P., *Possessions and the Poor in Luke-Acts* (Linz: SNTU, 1982).
Shelton, J.B., *Mighty in Word and Deed: The Role of the Holy Spirit in Luke-Acts*

(Peabody: Hendrickson, 1991).
Shepherd, W.H., *The Narrative Function of the Holy Spirit as a Character in Luke-Acts* (Atlanta: Scholars Press, 1994).
Shogren, G.R., 'The Pauline Proclamation of the Kingdom of God and the Kingdom of Christ within Its New Testament Setting' (PhD Dissertation; Aberdeen University, 1986).
Smalley, S., 'Spirit, Kingdom and Prayer in Luke-Acts', *Novum Testamentum* 15 (1973), 59-71.
Sneed, R.J., 'The Kingdom of God within You (Lk 17:21)', *Catholic Biblical Quarterly* 24 (1962), 363-82.
Soards, M.L., *The Speeches in Acts: Their Content, Context, and Concern* (Louisville: Westminster Press, 1994).
Spencer, F.S., *The Portrait of Philip in Acts*, Journal for the Study of the New Testament, Supplement Series 67 (Sheffield: JSOP Press, 1992).
_ *Acts* (Sheffield: Sheffield Academic Press, 1997).
Squires, J.T., *The Plan of God in Luke-Acts*, Society for the New Testament Studies Monograph Series 76 (Cambridge: Cambridge University Press, 1993).
Stanton, G.N., *Jesus of Nazareth in New Testament Preaching*, Society for the New Testament Studies Monograph Series 27 (Cambridge: Cambridge University Press, 1974).
Stählin, G., 'νῦν', 1106-23 in G. Kittel and G. Friedrich (eds.), *Theological Dictionary of the New Testament*, vol. 4 (Grand Rapids: Eerdmans, 1977).
Stegner, W.R., 'The Use of Scripture in Two Narratives of Early Jewish Christianity (Matthew 4:1-11; Mark 9:2-8)', 98-120 in C.A. Evans and J.A. Sanders (eds.), *Early Christian Interpretation of the Scriptures of Israel: Investigations and Proposals*, Journal for the Study of the New Testament, Supplement Series 148 (Sheffield: Sheffield Academic Press, 1997).
Stein, R.H., *The Method and Message of Jesus' Teachings* (Philadelphia: Westminster Press, 1978).
Stott, J.R.W., *The Message of Acts: To the ends of the earth* (Leicester: Inter Varsity Press, 1990).
Strack, H.L. and G. Stemberger, *Introduction to the Talmud and Midrash* (Edinburgh: T. & T. Clark, 1991).
Strelan, R., *Paul, Artemis, and the Jews in Ephesus* (Berlin: de Gruyter, 1996).
Stronstad, R., *The Charismatic Theology of St. Luke* (Peabody: Hendrickson, 1984).
_ *The Prophethood of All Believers: A Study of Luke's Charismatic Theology*, Journal of Pentecostal Theology, Supplement Series 16 (Sheffield: Sheffield Academic Press, 1999).
Talbert, C.H., *Literary Patterns and Theological Themes, and the Genre of Luke-Acts*, Society of Biblical Literature Monograph Series 20 (Missoula: SBL and Scholars Press, 1974).
Tannehill, R.C., *The Narrative Unity of Luke-Acts: A Literary Interpretation*, 2 vols. (Philadelphia: Fortress Press, 1986-1990).
_ *Luke*, Abingdon New Testament Commentaries (Nashville: Abingdon, 1996).
Thiselton, A., 'Realized Eschatology at Corinth', *New Testament Studies* 24 (1976/77), 510-26.
Tiede, D.L., *Prophecy and History in Luke-Acts* (Philadelphia: Fortress Press, 1980).
_ 'The Exaltation of Jesus and the Restoration of Israel in Acts 1', *Harvard Theological Review* 79 (1986), 278-86.

Treves, M., 'The Two Spirits of the Rule of the Community', *Revue de Qumran* 3 (1961), 449-52.
Tuckett, C.M., 'The Temptation Narrative in Q', 479-507 in F. van Segbroeck (ed.), *The Four Gospels* (Leuven: LUP, 1992).
Turner, M., 'Luke and the Spirit: Studies in the Significance of Receiving the Spirit in Luke-Acts' (PhD Dissertation; Cambridge University, 1980).
_ 'Jesus and the Spirit in Lukan Perspective', *Tyndale Bulletin* 32 (1981), 3-42.
_ 'The Significance of Receiving the Spirit in Luke-Acts: A Survey of Modern Scholarship', *Trinity Journal* 2 (1981), 131-58.
_ 'Spirit Endowment in Luke-Acts: Some Linguistic Considerations', *Vox Evangelica* 12 (1981), 43-63.
_ 'Spiritual Gifts: Then and Now', *Vox Evangelica* 15 (1985), 7-64.
_ 'The Spirit and the Power of Jesus' Miracles in the Lukan Conception', *Novum Testamentum* 33 (1991), 124-52.
_ 'The Spirit of Prophecy and the Power of Authoritative Preaching in Luke-Acts: A Question of Origin', *New Testament Studies* 38 (1992), 66-88.
_ 'The Spirit of Prophecy and the Ethical/Religious Life of the Christian Community', 166-90 in M.W. Wilson (ed.), *Spirit and Renewal: Essays in Honour of J. Rodman Williams*, Journal of Pentecostal Theology, Supplement Series 5 (Sheffield: Sheffield Academic Press, 1994).
_ *Power From on High*, Journal of Pentecostal Study, Supplement Series 9 (Sheffield: Sheffield Academic Press, 1996).
_ *The Holy Spirit and Spiritual Gifts: Then and Now* (Carlisle: Paternoster, 1996).
_ 'The "Spirit of Prophecy" as the Power of Israel's Restoration and Witness', 327-48 in I.H. Marshall and D. Peterson (eds.), *Witness to the Gospel: The Theology of Acts* (Grand Rapids: Eerdmans, 1998).
Vanderkam, J.C., 'Biblical Interpretation in 1Enoch and Jubilees', 96-125 in J.H. Charlesworth and C.A. Evans (eds.), *The Pseudepigrapha and Early Biblical Interpretation*, Journal for the Study of the Pseudepigrapha, Supplement Series 14 (Sheffield: JSOP Press, 1993).
Verhey, A., *The Great Reversal: Ethics and the New Testament* (Grand Rapids: Eerdmans, 1984).
Vermes, G., *The Complete Dead Sea Scrolls in English* (Allen Lane: Penguin, 1997).
Vos, G., *The Pauline Eschatology* (Grand Rapids: Baker, 1979).
_ 'The Eschatological Aspect of the Pauline Conception of the Spirit', 91-125 in R.B. Gaffin (ed.), *Redemptive History and Biblical Interpretation* (New Jersey: Presbyterian and Reformed, 1980).
Vos, J., *Traditionsgeschichtliche Untersuchungen zur paulinischen Pneumatologie* (Assen: Van Gorcum, 1973).
Wall, R.W., '"The Finger of God": Deuteronomy 9:10 and Luke 11:20', *New Testament Studies* 33 (1987), 144-50.
Walter, N., 'Paul and the Early Christian Jesus-Tradition', 51-80 in A.J.M. Wedderburn (ed.), *Paul and Jesus: Collected Essays*, Journal for the Study of New Testament, Supplement Series 37 (Sheffield: JSOT Press, 1989).
Warrington, K., *Jesus the Healer: Paradigm or Unique Phenomenon?* (Carlisle: Paternoster, 2000).
Watson, N., *The First Epistle to the Corinthians* (London: Epworth, 1992).
Webb, R.L., *John the Baptizer and Prophet: A Socio-Historical Study*, Journal for the Study of the New Testament, Supplement Series 62 (Sheffield: Sheffield Academic

Press, 1991).
_ 'The Activity of John the Baptist's Expected Figure at the Threshing Floor (Matthew 3:12=Luke 3:17)', *Journal for the Study of the New Testament* 43 (1991), 103-11.
Wedderburn, A.J.M., 'Paul and Jesus: The Problem of Continuity', 99-115 in A.J.M. Wedderburn (ed.), *Paul and Jesus: Collected Essays*, Journal for the Study of the New Testament, Supplement Series 37 (Sheffield: JSOT Press, 1989).
Weiser, A., '"Reich Gottes", in der Apostelgeschichte', 127-35 in C. Bussmann & W. Radl (eds.), *Der Treue Gottes trauen* (Freiburg: Herder, 1992).
Wenham, D., 'The Christian Life: A Life of Tension? A Consideration of the Nature of Christian Experience in Paul', 80-105 in D.A. Hagner and M.J. Harris (eds.), *Pauline Studies* (Exeter: Paternoster, 1980).
_ *Paul: Follower of Jesus or Founder of Christianity?* (Grand Rapids: Eedrmans, 1995).
Wenk, M., *Community-Forming Power: The Socio-Ethical Role of the Spirit in Luke-Acts*, Journal of Pentecostal Theology, Supplement Series 19 (Sheffield: Sheffield Academic Press, 2000).
Westerholm, S., *Israel's Law and the Church's Faith: Paul and His Recent Interpreters* (Grand Rapids: Eerdmans, 1988).
Wilckens, U., *Die Missionsreden der Apostelgeschichte: Form - und Traditionsgeschichtliche Untersuchungen* (Neukirchen-Vluyn: Neukirchener Verlag, 1974).
Williams, S.K., 'Justification and the Spirit in Galatians', *Journal for the Study of the New Testament* 29 (1987), 91-100.
Winston, D., *The Wisdom of Solomon*, Anchor Bible 43 (Garden: Doubleday & Company, 1979).
Wintermute, O.S., 'Jubilees', 35-142 in J.H. Charlesworth (ed.), *Old Testament Pseudepigrapha*, 2 (New York: Doubleday, 1985).
Witherington, B., *Jesus, Paul and the End of the World: A Comparative Study in New Testament Eschatology* (Downers Grove: Westminster Press, 1988).
_ *Christology of Jesus* (Minneapolis: Fortress Press, 1990).
_ *The Acts of the Apostles: A Socio-Rhetorical Commentary* (Grand Rapids: Eerdmans, 1998).
Wood, I.F., *The Spirit of God in Biblical Literature* (London: Hodder and Stoughton, 1904).
Woods, E.J., *The 'Finger of God' and Pneumatology in Luke-Acts*, Journal for the Study of the New Testament, Supplement Series 205 (Sheffield: Sheffield Academic Press, 2001).
Wolter, M., '"Reich Gottes" bei Lukas', *New Testament Studies* 41 (1995), 541-63.
Wright, R.B., 'Psalms of Solomon', 639-70 in J.H. Charlesworth (ed.), *Old Testament Pseudepigrapha*, 2 (New York: Doubleday, 1985).
Yates, J.E., *The Spirit and the Kingdom* (London: SPCK, 1963).

Index of References

Old Testament and Apocrypha

Genesis
1:1-4   50
25:21   137
27:42   41
41:14-45 LXX
             36
41:38 LXX   36, 42

Exodus
2:4   39
2:12   41
2:21-22   137
8:19   169
12:1   39
14:13 LXX   35
16:15 LXX   35
16:23 LXX   36
16:25   35
24:12   36
31:3   26
32:36 LXX   36
40:35   137

Numbers
11:29   43
16:28 LXX   36

Deuteronomy
6:13   123
6:16   123
8:3   123
9:10   169
34:6   26, 32
34:9   26

Nehemiah
9:20   126, 127

Psalms
2:7   112, 113, 114
39:3 LXX   66
41:2   45
57:12   44
91:4   137
103:1 LXX   66
109:22 LXX   66
140:7   137

Isaiah
3:10   122
4:3-4   121
6:9-10   190
11:1-2   113
11:1-4   16, 20, 51
11:2   18, 27
16:11 LXX   66
24-27   49
27:12   122
34:16   122
42:1   112, 113, 115
43:10   181
43:12   181
44:8   182
49:6   180, 181, 182
54:13   44
58:6   175
61   9
61:1-2   172
61:1-2 LXX   175
63:10   126, 127, 128
63:14   126

Jeremiah
4:11-12   119
31:33   6

Lamentations
2:9   47

Ezekiel
36   4, 9, 15, 39, 48
36:25-27   40
36:26   43, 44, 45, 46, 47, 51
36:26-27   46
36:27   6
37:12   48
37:14   48
37   49

Daniel
12:1-3   49
12:2   88
5:8   33
5:14 LXX   33

Joel
2:28   146
2:32   145
3:1   43, 44, 45, 51
3:1f   47, 48
3:1-5   40
3:1-5 LXX   142, 143
3:5a LXX   145

Amos
2:11   47

Wisdom of Solomon
1:6   22
2:12   24
2:23-24   49
3:1-4   49
3:1-9   22
6:12   23
6:18   22
7:7   22
7:22   22
7:26-27   24
8:2   23
8:17   22
8:18   23
8:21   22
9:4   22
9:9-18   4

9:10	22	4:46	19	38:1-2	24
9:13-18	22	14:44	19	44:14	24
9:17	22, 51				
9:17-18	20, 23	*2 Maccabees*		*Ben Sirach*	
10:4	22	7:8	49	1:26	26
14:4-5	22	7:13-14	49	6:37	26
15:3	22	7:23	49	14:20-27	26
16:7	22	7:29	49	21:11	26
16:11	22	14:46	49	39:1-5	26
18:4	24			39:6-11	26
18:5	22	*Baruch*		38:24-39:11	27
		3:9-14	24	39:1-5	28
1 Maccabees		4:1-4	24	39:1-5	27
3:19	59	15:5	24	39:6	27, 28

New Testament

Matthew		7:11	81	19:23	169
3:11-12	117	7:12a	59	19:23-24	57
3:12	118	7:21	57, 81, 82	19:35	81
3:13-17	112	8:11	169	20:21	65
3:15	95, 99	8:11-12	65, 75	20:23	81
3:15-16	88	10:7	59, 169	21:32	95, 99
3:16	169	10:13	59	22:23-33	87, 89, 134
4:1	123	10:20	81		
4:1-11	122, 123	10:29	81	22:34-40	105
4:12-17	174	11:11f	169	24:31-33	75
4:17	169	11:12	65	25:34	57, 81
5:3	79, 169	11:27	81	25:46	59
5:5	57	11:28	65, 67, 97, 104	26:29	65, 81
5:6	95			26:42	81, 82
5:9	79, 80	12:28	168, 169	26:53	81
5:20	57, 95, 96, 97, 98, 99	12:35	59	27:19	95
		13:11	169		
		13:31	169	*Mark*	
5:21-48	96	13:33	169	1:9-11	112
5:43-47	105	13:44	59	1:12	123
5:45	79, 81	13:53-58	175	1:12-13	122
5:48	81	13:47-50	65	1:14-15	174
6:1	81, 95	15:13	81	1:15	54, 65, 72
6:4	81	16:17	81	2:17	95
6:9-10	79, 81, 83	16:28	65	3:4	73
6:10	65, 82, 104	17:5	115	4:39	173
		17:25	79	5:34	73
6:14	81	18:3	57, 65	6:1-6	175
6:15	81	18:10	81	6:20	95
6:25-33	59, 97	18:13	59	8:38	81
6:26	81	18:19	81	9:2-8	123
6:32	81	18:23-25	106	9:7	115
6:33	95, 96, 97, 99, 105	19:14	169	9:43-48	57
		19:16-28	72, 74		
		19:16-30	87, 135		

Index of References 215

10:17-31	72, 74, 87, 106, 135	2:11	73	4:19	176, 186
		2:16-17	120	4:21	173
		2:22-38	120	4:22-27	186
10:19	59	2:23	176	4:24	173
10:23	57	2:25	95, 99, 139	4:31	165
10:24-25	57			4:42-44	171, 173
10:27	106	2:26	113, 139	4:43	73, 173, 176, 186, 187, 189
10:52	73	2:26-27	125		
11:25	81	2:27	139		
12:18-27	87, 89, 134	2:29-32	136, 139	4:43-44	167, 177
		2:32	114	4:44	176, 186
12:28-34	105	2:24	120	5:1-11	166
12:36	169	2:34-35	139	5:15	186
13:11	169	2:38	75, 180	5:16	112
13:27-29	75	2:42	165	5:17	169, 186
14:25	65	2:49	81, 112, 113	5:32	121
14:26	82			6:9	73
14:36	81, 116	2:49-50	114	6:12	112
		3:1	165	6:19	169
Luke		3:1-20	119, 120	6:20-23	59
1:6	95, 99	3:3	120, 142, 176	6:21	95
1:8-23	120			6:27-36	80, 105
1:13-17	120	3:16	121	6:31	59
1:14	165	3:16-17	117, 119, 152	6:35	79, 137
1:15	124, 138			6:36	81
1:15-17	136	3:17	118, 121	6:46	57, 176
1:17	99, 138	3:21-22	3, 111	6:54a	59
1:26-38	120	3:22	112, 113, 115, 116, 175	7:11-17	87, 134
1:27	113			7:16	173
1:32	114, 136, 137, 176	3:23	114	7:19-20	121
		3:23-28	123	7:19-22	173
1:32-35	170	4:1	123, 169, 172	7:26	138
1:34	137			7:26-28	120
1:35	112, 113, 114, 136, 137, 138, 139	4:1-13	122, 126	7:27	126
		4:4	126	7:28	138
		4:8	126	7:36-47	106
		4:12	126	7:36-50	166
1:41	138	4:14	127, 169, 172, 175	7:48-50	72, 73
1:41-42	136			7:55-60	165
1:43	113, 138			8:1	73, 176, 177, 186, 187, 189
1:44	138	4:14-19	174		
1:46-55	136, 139	4:16f	170, 184		
1:57-66	120	4:16-28	175		
1:67-79	120, 136, 139	4:16-30	9, 136, 171	8:1-3	166
				8:15	165
		4:16-41	177	8:17	165
1:68	75, 180	4:18	116, 172, 173, 175, 173, 186	8:36	73
1:75	95, 99			8:39	176
1:76	113, 120, 137, 151, 176			8:40-42	87, 134
				8:48	73, 166
		4:18-19	172, 173, 176, 177, 189	8:49-56	87, 134
1:76-79	120			8:50	73
2:1	113			9:1	167

9:1-6	186	12:32	81	23:47	95, 99
9:1-10	9	12:49-53	121	23:50	95, 99
9:2	167, 186, 189	13:10-17	166	24:4-8	183
		13:23-29	75	24:19	173, 183
9:6	167, 176, 177, 186	13:24-30	57	24:21	75, 180
		13:29	65	24:40	142
9:10-17	126	13:33	173	24:47	176
9:11	73, 165, 167, 189	14:14	87, 89, 199	24:47-49	177
				24:48-49	145, 146
9:18	112	14:15-24	166	24:49	46, 81, 166
9:21-27	166	15:1-2	106		
9:22	9	15:1-32	167		
9:28	165	15:6	59	*John*	
9:32	165	15:9	59	1:32-34	112
9:60	166, 189	15:11-32	72, 73, 106	1:37	112
10:1-20	166			3:3	54
10:5-6f	59	15:20-24	73	3:5	54
10:9	65, 165, 167	15:24	59, 74	11:1-46	87
		15:32	59	18:36	54
10:9-11	73	16:16	176, 187, 189		
11:9-13	9			*Acts*	
10:11	167	16:17-31	87, 89	1:1-3	142
10:21	169	17:3-4	106	1:2	136
10:22	81	17:19	73	1:3	189
10:25	57	17:21	65, 66, 67, 73, 104, 167	1:3-8	7, 163, 170, 171, 178, 181, 182, 184, 189
10:25-37	105				
10:30-37	105				
11:1	112	17:24	66		
11:1-13	170	18:15-17	88	1:4	142
11:2	7, 79, 81, 83, 111, 116, 163, 164, 166, 167, 171	18:17	65	1:4-5	185
		18:18	88	1:4-8	146
		18:18-30	72, 74, 87, 135	1:5	121, 142, 148, 152
		18:24	75		
11:13	7, 164, 165, 166, 167, 169, 171	18:24-25	57	1:6	179, 180
		18:25	75	1:6-8	182
		18:26	74	1:7	179
		18:29	75	1:7-8	180
11:14-22	166	18:30	88	1:8	121, 132, 136, 137, 139, 142, 179, 183, 184, 185, 187, 188, 194, 195
11:20	65, 67, 73, 104, 163, 167, 168, 170, 171, 177	18:42	73		
		19:1-10	106, 167		
		19:10	74		
		20:27-38	134		
		20:27-40	87, 89		
		20:42	169		
12:12	136, 145	21:15	145, 169	1:13	179
12:22-23	59	21:28	75	1:22	148
12:30	81	21:31	75	2:1-11	129
12:31	7, 95	22:29	81	2:4	136, 138, 142
12:31-32	163, 164, 166, 167, 168, 171	22:32	112		
		22:42	111	2:4-13	133
12:31-33	106	23:42-43	75	2:14-37	175

2:16	143	6:1	131, 132	9:22	150, 191, 193
2:17	136, 145	6:1-7	131		
2:17-18	146	6:1-16	128	9:26-28	131
2:17-21	143	6:2-3	132	9:27	191, 193
2:18	145	6:3	134, 188	9:27-29	150
2:19	143	6:5	124, 185	10:2	152
2:21	145	6:8	132, 133, 143	10:4	152
2:22	143			10:6	133
2:24	134, 135	6:8-15	188	10:11	112
2:25	137	6:10	136	10:19	133
2:32	135, 142	7:6	143	10:22	95, 99, 152
2:33	142, 145, 183	7:17	142		
		7:36	143	10:28-29	112
2:38	142, 145, 150, 152	7:48	137	10:31	152
		7:49	143	10:33	152
2:38-39	9, 129, 138, 141, 145, 151, 155	7:51	136	10:35	99
		7:55	124, 132, 133	10:36-37	149
				10:38	116
		8:4	186	10:42	176
2:39	142, 143, 146	8:4-12	185	10:44	133, 151, 159
		8:5	176, 186		
2:41	159	8:5-13	129	10:45	151
2:42-47	128, 129	8:6	186	11:1-18	131
2:43	132, 143, 188	8:7	186, 188	11:12	133
		8:9-13	188	11:13-14	153
2:47	130	8:12	158, 176, 178, 184, 185, 186, 187, 189	11:14-18	150, 151
3:15	135			11:15-17	138
3:19-21	180			11:16	121, 154
4:8	138			11:16-17	153
4:8-12	145	8:12-15	170	11:20	176
4:9	73	8:12-17	142, 146, 148, 155	11:23	130
4:10	135			11:24	124
4:22	130	8:13	158, 187	11:28	133, 136
4:28-30	169	8:14-18	148	13:1-9	189
4:29-30	186	8:16	129	13:2	133, 136, 190, 193
4:30	143	8:17	133, 159		
4:31	136, 138, 188	8:18-24	131	13:4	133, 136, 190, 193
		8:26-40	185, 188		
4:32-37	128, 129	8:29	133	13:4-12	186
4:33	130	8:29-40	170	13:8-11	132
4:34f	130	8:35	186	13:9	133, 136, 138, 190, 191, 193
5:1-11	128, 131	8:39	133		
5:12	132, 143, 188	8:40	186		
		9:15-16	150	13:9-11	190
5:12-16	128	9:17	133, 138, 149, 190, 193	13:10	99
5:30	135			13:11	169
5:31	151			13:14-41	175
5:32	136	9:17-19	148	13:15-41	191, 193
5:33	135	9:18-19	151	13:32	142
5:34	135	9:20	150, 176, 191, 193	13:23	142
5:37	135			13:30-34	136
5:42	186			13:37	136

13:38	151	20:22	190, 192, 193	3:21-26	90
13:43	192			3:24	70
13:47	191, 193	20:22-23	192	3:26-27	69
13:52	190	20:22-24	194	3:30	93
14:3	130, 143, 186, 190, 191, 193	20:22-25	170	4:2	90
		20:22-28	189, 191	4:17	58
		20:23	136	4:18	90
14:7-10	186	20:24	130, 189, 192	4:25	90
14:8-10	190			5:1	90
14:9	73	20:25	176, 178, 185, 189, 190, 193	5:1-5	84
14:22	185, 187, 189			5:2	100
				5:5	63, 100, 102, 140
15:1-35	131	20:32	130		
15:2	143	21:4	136, 190, 193, 194	5:8	84
15:7	153			5:9	69, 90
15:7-9	150, 151	21:8	185	5:11	69
15:8	154	21:11	136, 190, 193	5:14	53
15:8-9	153			5:17	53
15:9	154	21:11-17	194	5:19	93
15:11	130	21:20-36	131	5:21	53
15:21	176	22:3-16	149	6:2	100
16:6-7	133	23:6-8	49	6:4	83, 84, 86, 135
16:6-10	190, 192, 193	24:21	135		
		24:25	99	6:12	53
16:14f	158	26:6	142	6:14	100
16:17	1437	26:8	49, 135	6:19	69
16:33f	158	26:9-18	149	6:21	69
17:31	135	26:23	135	7:1-6	100
18:8	158	28:3	185	7:4-6	140
19:1-6	191	28:14	194	7:6	63, 68, 69, 70, 71
19:1-7	148, 154, 190	28:23	178, 184, 187, 188, 190	7:17	69
				7:24	78
19:1-8	170, 191, 193	28:23-31	170, 189, 191, 193	8:1-11	64
19:2	156, 192			8:1-17	63
19:6	133, 158	28:30-31	190	8:2	68, 69, 70, 71, 72, 77, 84, 86, 101, 137
19:8	178, 185, 187, 189 192	28:31	176, 178, 185, 187, 189, 194		
19:9-10	190				
19:10-12	186	*Romans*		8:3	69, 70, 100, 101
19:11-12	190	1:3-4	83, 131, 132		
19:13	176			8:4	60, 100, 101
19:21	191, 192, 193, 194	1:3f	84		
		1:4	63	8:4-8	137
19:25	192	1:11	63	8:5	70
20:1	194	1:13	100	8:5-8	64
20:2-3	194	1:17	93	8:6	70, 84, 86
20:7-12	186	2:13	96	8:9	64, 70, 85, 93, 100
20:9	190	2:28-29	71		
20:17-38	191	2:29	63		
		3:20	96		

Index of References

8:10	70, 86, 90, 93, 95	15:50	58	15:3-11	53
8:11	83, 84, 85, 86, 87, 94, 100, 135	16:26	69	15:12	54, 84
				15:20-28	85
		1 Corinthians		15:22	83
		1:7	94	15:24-25	53
		1:13-15	91	15:42f	58, 60
8:13	70, 78, 86, 100, 102	2:4	58	15:44-46	63, 83, 135
		2:4-26	63	15:45	84, 100
		2:6-16	4	15:50	53, 56, 57, 189
8:14	64, 70, 100	2:6-3:1	140		
		2:15	100	*2 Corinthians*	
8:14-15	76, 94, 100, 137	3:16	63, 100	1:21-22	140
		3:22-23	90	1:22	63
8:15	70, 77, 78, 79, 83, 115	4:4	93	2:12	58
		4:8	53, 54	3:1-18	63, 140
		4:14-17	90	3:3-6	68
		4:20	7, 53, 58, 59, 60, 189	3:6	70, 71, 72, 92, 100, 137
8:15-16	6, 116				
8:15-17	64				
8:16	70	5:1-8	90		
8:18	69	6:1-6	90	3:7-11	71
8:19	93	6:9f	60	3:8-9	90, 92
8:22	69	6:9-10	53, 56, 57, 90, 189	3:14	71
8:23	63, 64, 70, 76, 79, 83, 85, 93, 94, 100, 137			3:17-18	69, 71
				3:17	68
		6:9-11	7, 58	3:18	100
		6:11	63, 90, 91, 95, 137, 140	4:13	63
8:23-27	63			5:5	63
8:25	93			5:17	68
8:26-27	100	6:14	83, 84, 86, 135	6:17	143
8:27	70			11:4	140
8:33f	93	6:17	63	12:18	100, 101
11:5	69	6:19	63, 64	13:4	84, 135
11:30	69	6:20	90	13:13	63, 100
11:31	69	7:40	63, 100		
12:1	64	8:2-3	101	*Galatians*	
12:1-2	100	9:11	63	1:4	100
12:19	143	9:12-14	63	2:13	90
13:8-10	101	10:13	90	2:16	94
13:11	69	11:32	90	2:20	100
13:11-14	100	12:3	94	3:1	92
14:16-17	59	12:4-5	68	3:1-5	63
14:17	7, 11, 53, 60, 63, 90, 93, 95, 189	12:4-11	64	3:1-14	64, 90, 92
		12:9	94	3:2	94
		12:13	91, 92	3:5-6	92, 94, 95
		12:18-20	69	3:6	92
15:13	63, 84, 100	13:8	102	3:8	92, 94
		13:13	102	3:11	94
15:16	63	14:4-7	101	3:13-14	76, 94
15:19	58, 63	14:6	69	3:14	63, 95
15:27	63	14:21	135	3:24	100
15:30	63	15:3-4	68	3:26	102

3:27	91	5:22	93, 94, 101	*1 Thessalonians*	
4:29	63			1:4-6	140
4:4-5	63, 76	5:24	100	1:10	56
4:4-6	4	5:25	64, 100, 102, 137	2:12	53, 55, 56, 189
4:6	6, 63, 64, 76, 77, 78, 79, 83, 115, 116, 137	6:1	102	2:12-13	7
		6:1-8	63	2:19-20	56
		6:6	100	3:13	56
		6:8	64, 87, 102	4:1f	64
4:7	102			4:6	56
5:1	69	6:14	100	4:8	64
5:4	94			5:1-11	56
5:5	63, 64, 90, 93, 94, 95	*Ephesians*		5:23-24	56
		1:14	63		
		5:2	101	*2 Thessalonians*	
5:6	94	5:5	53, 58	1:5	53
5:13-14	101	5:25	101		
5:13-26	63, 64	6:12	58	*1 Timothy*	
5:16	58, 60, 64, 100			2:12	53
		Philippians		3:16	84
5:16-18	101	1:19	63, 100		
5:16-23	7	2:1	63	*2 Timothy*	
5:16-26	137	3:3	63, 140	4:1	53
5:18	100	3:20	9	4:14	53
5:19	101			4:18	53
5:21	52, 56, 57, 101, 189	*Colossians*			
		1:13	53	*1 Peter*	
		3:14	101	3:18-22	84
		4:11	53		

Pseudepigrapha

1 Enoch		92:3-5	49	8:7-13	23
5:8-9	23	104:2	49	9:22	49
42:1-3	23	104:4	49	14:5f	49
48:1	23			14:9f	30
48:6	17	*2 Baruch*		14:21-22	30
49:1-3	23	21:4	49	14:25	30
49:2-4	18	23:5	49	14:40	30
49:2-4	17	85:3	19	14:45	30
49:3	29			16:13	49
52:4	17	*4 Ezra*		17:12	49
52:6	17	4:26	50		
53:6	17	4:41	50	*4 Maccabee*	
62:1	17, 23	4:41-43	50	1:1	24
62:1-2	16	5:9-11	23	1:15	25
61:1-13	23	6:39-41	49	1:16-19	25
62:2	18, 29	7:3	49	1:17	23
62:5	17	7:32	50	1:18-19	25
62:7	17	7:32-38	49	1:20-21	25
91:1	29	7:70-74	23	5:16	24
91:10	23, 43	7:88-99	23	5:35	24, 25

6:17-19	24	4:8-13	23	3:573-600	23
7:7-8	24, 25	13:9-11	48	3:669-697	23
9:2	24	14:1-12	23	4:176-182	49
9:5-7	24	14:10	48		
9:6-9	24	15:12-15	48	*Susanna*	
9:16	24	16:7-8	23	45	37
17:18	24	17:37	18, 19	44-45 LXX	37
17:19	24	18:7-8	19		
18:1	24	*Pseudo Philo*		*T. Ben.*	
18:18	24	3:10	48	8:1-3	28
18:23	24	9:10	31	8:3	28
19:20	25	18:10	31	9:3	28
Jubilees		19:12	48		
25:14	30	20:2-3	32	*T. Jud.*	
31:12	30	25:7	48	20:1f	28
40:5	30	27:9-10	32, 33	24:1-2	28
		28:6	31	24:2	28
Letter of Aristeas		28:10	31	24:2-3	28
27	23	31:9	31		
31	23	32:14	31	*T. Lev.*	
139	23	36:2	32	2:3	28
144	23	51:5	50	18:7	28
161	23	60:1	31	18:11	28
168	23	62:2	31		
169	23	64:7	48	*T. Sim.*	
				4:4	28
Psalms of Solomon		*Sibylline Oracle*			
3:11-16	48	3:219-220	23		

Targums and Talmuds

Targums		35:31	41	35:31	41
Frag. Targ. Gen.					
2:12	42	*Targ. Onq. Num.*		*Targ. Ps-J. on Num.*	
27:1	42	11:25	41	11:17	41
42:1	42	11:26	41	11:25	41
		11:29	41	11:26	41
Frag. Targ. Num.		24:2	41	11:28	41
11:26	42	27:18	41	11:29	41
				24:2	41
Neof. on Gen.		*Targ. Ps-J. on Gen.*		27:18	41
31:21	41	7:5	41		
42:1	41	30:25	41	*Targ. Ps-J. on Deut.*	
		31:25	41	5:21	41
Neof on Exod.		35:22	41	18:15	41
2:12	41	37:33	41	18:18	41
		43:14	41	28:59	41
Neof. on Num.		45:27	41	32:26	41
11:28	41				
		Targ. Ps-J. on Exod.		*Targ. 2 Sam.*	
Targ. Onq. Exod.		31:3	41	23:1-2	42
31:3	41	33:16	41		

Targ. 2 Kings				3:4	48
2:9	42	*b. Ber.*		*m. Soṭ.*	
5:26	42	31b	46	9:15	48, 49
Targ. Job		*b. Meg.*			
32:8	42	14a	41	*t. Pes.*	
Targ. Isa.				2:15	41
11:1-2	16	*b. Sahn.*			
		11a	127	*t. Soṭ.*	
Targ. Ezek.				6:2	19
1:3	42, 169	*b. Soṭ.*		13:2	39
3:14	42, 169	11b	41	13:4	127
3:22	42, 169	48b	127		
8:1-3	42, 169			*y. Šeb.*	
33:2	169	*b. Suk.*		9:1	41
37:1	42, 169	52a	46		
40:1	42, 169			*y. Soṭ.*	
		b. Yom.		1:4	41
Talmuds		73b	41		
b. 'Ahod. Zar.					
20b	48	*j. Sheq.*			

Midrashim

ARN. A.		44:6	39	37:7	41
34	39	96:5	48	84:12	41
				84:19	41
ARN B.		*Lam. R.*		84:97	41
37	39	2:8	47		
		4:14	47	*Midr. R. Exod.*	
Cant. R.				1:28	41
1.1.9	48	*Lev. R.*			
1.2.4	46	35:5	45	*Midr. Lev.*	
3:4	39			1:3	41
6.11.1	46	*Mek. Pisha*		14:2	41
		1	39	21:8	41
Deut. R.		13	41	32:4	41
6:14	40, 43,	*Mek. Shir.*			
	44, 45,	7	41	*Midr. R. Num.*	
	47, 48	10	39	9:20	41
Ecc. R.				14:5	41
1:16	46	*MHG Gen.*		19:3	41
9.15.8	45	135	19	21:9	41
		139-140	19		
Exod. R.		140	47	*Midr. R. Ruth*	
15:6	45	242	39	2:1	41
41:7	45				
48:4	48	*Midr. R. Gen.*		*Midr. Ps.*	
		75:8	40	10:6	41
Gen. R.		91:6	40	14:6	40, 43,
14:8	48	92:7	41		44, 46, 47
34:15	46	93:12	41	73:4	46

85:3	48	1.1.8-9	41	*Per. R.*	
105:5	41			3:4	41
138:2	47	*Num. R.*			
		9:49	46	*Pes. R.*	
Midr. R. Ecc.		14:4	45	1:6	48
3.21.1	41	15:16	46	*Yalq. Isa.*	
		15:25	47	503	48
Midr. R. Cant.					

Other Ancient Writings

Aristobulus		24	35	1:264-265	33
Pr. Ev.		27	34	1:274	33
8.10.3	38	55	34	1:277	34
8.10.4	38			2:187	35
		Jos.		2:188	34, 35
Herodotus		110-116	34, 37	2:191	34, 35
Hist.				2:246-257	35
7.100.3	67	*Leg. All.*		2:259	35
		4:123	34, 137	2:264-265	376
Josephus				2:269	36
Ant.		*Mig.*		2:272	36
1:27	32	34-35	34, 37	2:275-287	36
4:108	32				
4:118	32	*Op. Mund.*		Qummran	
4:119-120	32	134-135	34, 137,	*1 QH*	
4:165	32		141	7:6-7	21
5:285	32	144	34	9:32	21
6:166	32			12:11-13	21
6:222	32	*Plant.*		13:18-19	21
6:223	32	18	33, 137	14:12b-13	21
8:9	49			14:25	21
8:295	32	*Quaest. In Gen.*		16:6-7	21
8:408	32	3:9	34	16:9	21
9:10	32			16:11b-12	21
9:168	32	*Rev. Div. Her.*		17:25-26	21
10:235-236	32	57	34		
10:239	32, 33	249	34	*1QSb*	
18:14	48	265	34	5:24-25	19
Philo		*Som.*		*1QS*	
Abr.		2:252	34	3-4	20
35	37			3:13-4:26	28
		Spec. Leg.		3:26	28
Cher.		1:65	34		
27-29	34, 37	3:1-6	33	Xenophon	
		4:49	34, 37	*Anab.*	
Der. Pot. Ins.				1.10.3	67
83	34, 137	*Virt.*			
		217-218	37	*Hell.*	
Gig.				2.3	67
23-27	37	*Vit. Mos.*		2.19	67

Index of Authors

Agua, A.D. 170, 174, 183, 184, 187, 190
Alexander, P.S. 40
Allison D.C. 97
Anderson, H. 24, 25
Arrington, F. 152
Bachmann, M. 189
Baer, H. von 5, 8, 11
Banks, R. 54
Barrett, C.K. 70, 77, 91, 100, 119, 149, 152, 155, 169, 171
Bayer, O. 80
Beare, F.W. 54
Beasley-Murray, G.R. 69, 72, 73, 74, 82, 88, 91
Becker, J. 72, 73, 74,
Berton, J.A. 69, 78
Best, E. 119
Betz, H.D. 69, 81, 93, 94, 102, 104, 164
Bock, D.L. 65, 88, 89, 125, 127, 139, 143, 144, 167, 168, 172
Bornkamm, G. 63
Bovon, F. 125, 126
Braude, W.G. 43
Brawley, R. 172
Brown, R.E. 136, 137
Brown, S. 142
Bruce, F.F. 55, 56, 91, 143, 149, 150, 157, 158, 180, 191, 192, 194
Bruner, F. 5
Buchard, C. 150
Büchsel, F. 5, 11, 75, 111, 113, 129
Bultmann, R. 60, 61, 88, 90, 92
Cadbury, H.J. 146, 191
Capper, B. 129
Caragounis, C.C. 65, 66
Charette, B. 117, 119, 122
Charles, R.H. 18, 28
Charlesworth, J.C. 17
Chazon, E.G. 28
Chilton, B.D. 104, 105
Cohen, A. 45, 47

Coleridge, M. 139
Collins, A.Y. 38
Colson, F.H. 34
Conzelmann, H. 58, 130, 161, 180
Cosgrove, C.H. 93, 94
Cranfield, 69, 70, 71, 77, 78, 86, 93
Dalman, G. 66
Danker, F.W. 171
Darr, J.A. 120
Davies, W.D. 82, 93, 95, 96, 97
Davis, D.J. 134
Davis, J.A. 26, 27
Dennison, W. 102
Denova, R. 177
Dunn, J.D.G. 1, 2, 3, 5, 6, 7, 8, 9, 11, 12, 61, 85, 100, 110, 111, 112, 113, 115, 116, 117, 121, 137, 139, 141, 142, 147, 152, 154, 155, 156, 162, 163, 164, 166, 167, 168, 169, 170, 171, 179, 184, 194
Ellis, E.E. 54, 163, 164, 169
Engel, H. 38
Ervin, H. 147, 150
Evans, C. A. 16, 17, 123
Evans, C. F. 135, 165, 169
Farris, S. 120
Fee, G.D. 2, 58, 63, 70, 71, 72, 76, 77, 78, 79, 83, 84, 86, 90, 91, 92, 93, 94, 100, 101, 103
Finkel, A. 175
Fitzmyer, J.A. 112, 114, 118, 123, 165, 173
Franklin, E. 165, 169, 182
Freed, E.D. 137
Freedman, H. 45
Fuller, R.H. 65
Fung, R.Y. 90, 91, 92, 93, 94, 101
Furnish, V.P. 70, 71, 100
Gaffin, R.B. 63, 86
Gaventa, B.R. 139, 150
Gero, S. 112
Gibson, J.B. 125, 127
Giles, K. 147, 149

Goldberg, A. 44
Goulder, M.D. 115
Grundmann, W. 93
Guelich, R.A. 72, 80, 81, 82, 83, 96, 97, 98, 103, 114
Gunkel, G. 2, 129
Gutbrod, W. 69
Hafemann, S. 72
Hagner, D.A. 82, 90, 95, 96, 97, 98, 99, 118
Hahn, F. 114
Hamilton, N.Q. 60, 62, 64, 67, 77, 78, 90, 94, 101
Hansen, G.W. 101
Harmerton-Kelly, R.G. 169, 170
Harrington, D.J. 31, 128
Harris, M.J. 86, 87, 89, 90
Haubeck, W. 189
Haufe, G. 53, 55, 57, 59
Hawthorne, G.F. 142
Haya-Prats, G. 8
Hengel, M. 32, 128, 161
Hill, D. 2, 14, 111, 136, 150, 154
Holladay, C.R. 38
Hollander, H.W. 28
Hooker, M.D. 55
Horn, F.W. 2, 49, 52, 84, 134
Hübner, H. 69
Huffman, D.S. 150
Hull, J.H.E. 5, 161
Hur, J. 2, 165, 194
Hurd, J.C. 54
Ireland, D.J. 106
Isaac, E. 17, 18, 29
Isaacs, M.E. 32, 34
Jeremias, J. 57, 73, 74, 81, 104, 106, 112
Jervell, J. 180
Johnson, L.T. 132, 149, 193
Johnston, G. 54, 55, 56, 57, 58, 59
Jongde, M. de. 28, 29, 172
Jüngel, E. 61
Kaiser, O. 17
Käsemann, E. 69, 93, 154
Keck, L.E. 112
Kee, H.C. 22, 26, 30
Keener, C. 136
Kennedy, H.A.A. 53
Kim, H.S. 2
Kittel, G. 56
Klein, M.L. 42
Klijin, A.F.J. 50

Knibb, M.A. 29
Koch, R. 17
Kraemer, R. 49
Kraft, R. 16
Kreitzer, L.J. 53
Kremer, J. 11
Kümmel, G. 67, 84, 97, 161
Kvalbein, H. 103, 104, 105, 106
Ladd, G.E. 48
Lake, K. 143, 155, 188
Lampe, G.W.H. 8, 11
Lehrman, S.M. 45
Levison, J.R. 18, 29, 30, 32, 33, 35, 37
Lewis, J.P. 59
Lieu, J. 172
Lodahl, M.E. 134
Lohmeyer, E. 114
Lohse, E. 143
Longenecker, R.N. 101, 103, 183
Lührmann, D. 80
Lull, D.J. 87, 93, 94, 101
Maddox, R. 161, 176, 177, 181
Mangan, C. 42
Manson, T.W. 169
Marcus, R. 33
Marsh, T. 128
Marshall, I.H. 56, 62, 65, 66, 67, 73, 75, 104, 112, 113, 114, 117, 118, 119, 120, 123, 125, 127, 130, 139, 145, 147, 154, 159, 160, 164, 167, 168, 171, 172, 173, 191
Martínez, F.G. 19
McDonald, J.I.H. 104, 105
McLean, J.A. 179, 180, 181, 185
Menzies, R.P. 1, 2, 3, 4, 8, 9, 10, 11, 15, 20, 23, 26, 28, 32, 33, 44, 46, 48, 50, 115, 117, 118, 119, 120, 121, 124, 127, 129, 131, 137, 138, 139, 140, 141, 142, 143, 144, 145, 146, 147, 148, 149, 150, 154, 155, 158, 159, 160, 161, 165, 166, 169, 172, 175, 176, 181, 182
Merk, O. 163, 167, 171, 176
Metzger, B.M. 30, 56, 157, 163
Millar, F. 40
Minear, P.S. 136
Mitchell, A.C. 129
Mitton, C. 74, 104
Montague, G. 17, 26
Moo, D. 70
Morris, L. 70
Müller, D. 50

Neil, W. 149, 179
Neusner, J. 127
Nickelsburg, G.W.E. 49
Nineham, D.E. 14
Nolland, J. 66, 88, 119, 121, 165, 167, 169, 170
O' Neill, J.C. 65, 120, 149, 154, 161
O' Toole, R.F. 75, 163, 187
Orton, D.E. 27
Palmer, D.W. 142
Parsons, M. 102
Penney, J.M. 2, 112, 113, 121, 125, 141, 143, 144, 150, 172, 181, 182, 192, 194
Perkins, P. 87, 89
Pfitzner, V.C. 189, 193, 194
Piper, J. 80, 105, 106
Polhill, J.B. 181, 182, 186, 191, 192
Pomykala, K.E. 18
Porter, S.E. 149, 150, 155, 157, 191
Prieur, A. 163, 173, 175, 177, 178, 180, 181, 184, 187, 188, 190
Przybylski, B. 95, 96, 97
Rabinowitz, J. 43
Rahlfs, A. 22, 25, 37, 49
Räisänen, H. 70
Redditt, P.L. 24
Reeves, J.C. 15
Reider, J. 23
Rese, M. 176
Reumann, J. 95
Richardson, P. 54, 71
Ridderbos, H. 91, 94, 105
Rodd, C.S. 163, 165
Roloff, J. 144
Rosner, B. 99
Rowland, C. 104
Russell, D.S. 49
Russell, E.A. 147
Russell, W. 101, 103
Saldarini, A.J. 42
Sanders, J.A. 123
Schäfer, P. 39
Schlatter, A. 106
Schmidt, K.L. 187
Schnabel, E. 23, 25, 99
Schneider, D. 181
Schneider, G. 75
Schotroff, L. 69
Schreiner, T.R. 71
Schrenk, G. 81, 82, 94, 95, 97, 99
Schürer, E. 40

Schweizer, E. 2, 8, 10, 14, 86, 111, 125, 129, 141
Scott, J.M. 76
Scroggs, R. 22
Seccombe, D.P. 128, 131
Shelton, J.B. 2, 137, 258, 165, 175
Shepherd, W.H. 139, 153, 187, 188, 191, 192, 193
Shogren, G.R. 55, 56, 57, 59, 190
Silva D.A. de 25
Simon, M. 45
Slotki, J.J. 45
Slotki, W. 45
Smalley, S. 162, 170, 194
Sneed, R.L. 66
Soards, M.L. 191
Spencer, F.S. 148, 155, 158, 177, 180, 186
Squires, J.T. 115
Stählin, G. 69
Stanton, G.N. 178, 187
Stegner, W.R. 123, 126
Stein, R.H. 107
Stemberger, G. 44
Stone, M.E. 28
Stott, J. 179
Strack, H.L. 44
Strelan, R. 154, 156, 157, 158, 159, 192
Stronstad, R. 114, 115, 124, 128, 136, 137, 138, 140, 147, 150, 158, 187, 188, 192
Stuhlmacher, P. 69
Tannehill, R. 131, 133, 153, 165, 167, 173, 177, 179, 180, 182, 183, 186, 188
Thiselton, A. 55
Tiede, D.L. 172, 179, 181, 182
Tigchelaar, E.J.C. 19
Treves, M. 21
Tuckett, C.M. 123, 126
Turner, M.M.B. 1, 2, 8, 9, 10, 11, 12, 14, 15, 16, 17, 19, 20, 21, 22, 23, 28, 34, 38, 39, 40, 43, 44, 46, 48, 49, 50,
  51, 91, 110, 112, 113, 117, 118, 119, 121, 122, 124, 125, 129, 131, 137, 140, 141, 142, 143, 144, 146, 147, 148, 149, 152, 153, 154, 155, 156, 157, 159, 160, 165, 166, 167, 169, 172, 175, 181, 182, 183
Vanderkam, J.C. 122

Verhey, A. 102
Vermes, G. 21, 40
Vos, G. 91
Vos, J. 5
Wall, R.W. 170
Warrington, K. 128
Watson, N. 91
Webb, R.L. 117, 118, 119
Wedderburn, A.J.M. 56, 57, 64
Weiser, A. 163, 171
Wenham, D. 53, 54, 55, 57, 59, 61, 62, 93, 100, 107, 116
Wenk, M. 2, 117, 127
Westerholm, S. 71
Whitaker, G.H. 34
Walter, N. 53

Wiclkens, U. 152
Williams, S.K. 90, 92, 93
Willis, W. 75
Winston, D. 22
Winter, B.W. 126
Wintermute, O.S. 31
Witherington, B. 63, 67, 85, 115, 121, 130, 131, 156, 180, 181
Wolter, M. 163
Wood, I.F. 18
Woods, E.J. 2, 168, 169, 176, 177
Wright, R.B. 18, 19
Yates, J.E. 169, 170

Paternoster Biblical Monographs

(All titles uniform with this volume)
Dates in bold are of projected publication

Joseph Abraham
Eve: Accused or Acquitted?
A Reconsideration of Feminist Readings of the Creation Narrative Texts in Genesis 1–3

Two contrary views dominate contemporary feminist biblical scholarship. One finds in the Bible an unequivocal equality between the sexes from the very creation of humanity, whilst the other sees the biblical text as irredeemably patriarchal and androcentric. Dr Abraham enters into dialogue with both camps as well as introducing his own method of approach. An invaluable tool for any one who is interested in this contemporary debate.

2002 / 0-85364-971-5 / xxiv + 272pp

Octavian D. Baban
Mimesis and Luke's on the Road Encounters in Luke-Acts
Luke's Theology of the Way and its Literary Representation

The book argues on theological and literary (mimetic) grounds that Luke's on-the-road encounters, especially those belonging to the post-Easter period, are part of his complex theology of the Way. Jesus' teaching and that of the apostles is presented by Luke as a challenging answer to the Hellenistic reader's thirst for adventure, good literature, and existential paradigms.

2005 */ 1-84227-253-5 / approx. 374pp*

Paul Barker
The Triumph of Grace in Deuteronomy

This book is a textual and theological analysis of the interaction between the sin and faithlessness of Israel and the grace of Yahweh in response, looking especially at Deuteronomy chapters 1–3, 8–10 and 29–30. The author argues that the grace of Yahweh is determinative for the ongoing relationship between Yahweh and Israel and that Deuteronomy anticipates and fully expects Israel to be faithless.

2004 / 1-84227-226-8 / xxii + 270pp

Jonathan F. Bayes
The Weakness of the Law
God's Law and the Christian in New Testament Perspective

A study of the four New Testament books which refer to the law as weak (Acts, Romans, Galatians, Hebrews) leads to a defence of the third use in the Reformed debate about the law in the life of the believer.

2000 / 0-85364-957-X / xii + 244pp

July 2005

Mark Bonnington
The Antioch Episode of Galatians 2:11-14 in Historical and Cultural Context

The Galatians 2 'incident' in Antioch over table-fellowship suggests significant disagreement between the leading apostles. This book analyses the background to the disagreement by locating the incident within the dynamics of social interaction between Jews and Gentiles. It proposes a new way of understanding the relationship between the individuals and issues involved.

2005 / 1-84227-050-8 / approx. 350pp

David Bostock
A Portrayal of Trust
The Theme of Faith in the Hezekiah Narratives

This study provides detailed and sensitive readings of the Hezekiah narratives (2 Kings 18–20 and Isaiah 36–39) from a theological perspective. It concentrates on the theme of faith, using narrative criticism as its methodology. Attention is paid especially to setting, plot, point of view and characterization within the narratives. A largely positive portrayal of Hezekiah emerges that underlines the importance and relevance of scripture.

2005 / 1-84227-314-0 / approx. 300pp

Mark Bredin
Jesus, Revolutionary of Peace
A Non-violent Christology in the Book of Revelation

This book aims to demonstrate that the figure of Jesus in the Book of Revelation can best be understood as an active non-violent revolutionary.

2003 / 1-84227-153-9 / xviii + 262pp

Robinson Butarbutar
Paul and Conflict Resolution
An Exegetical Study of Paul's Apostolic Paradigm in 1 Corinthians 9

The author sees the apostolic paradigm in 1 Corinthians 9 as part of Paul's unified arguments in 1 Corinthians 8–10 in which he seeks to mediate in the dispute over the issue of food offered to idols. The book also sees its relevance for dispute-resolution today, taking the conflict within the author's church as an example.

2006 / 1-84227-315-9 / approx. 280pp

Daniel J-S Chae
Paul as Apostle to the Gentiles
His Apostolic Self-awareness and its Influence on the Soteriological Argument in Romans
Opposing 'the post-Holocaust interpretation of Romans', Daniel Chae competently demonstrates that Paul argues for the equality of Jew and Gentile in Romans. Chae's fresh exegetical interpretation is academically outstanding and spiritually encouraging.
1997 / 0-85364-829-8 / xiv + 378pp

Luke L. Cheung
The Genre, Composition and Hermeneutics of the Epistle of James
The present work examines the employment of the wisdom genre with a certain compositional structure and the interpretation of the law through the Jesus tradition of the double love command by the author of the Epistle of James to serve his purpose in promoting perfection and warning against doubleness among the eschatologically renewed people of God in the Diaspora.
2003 / 1-84227-062-1 / xvi + 372pp

Youngmo Cho
Spirit and Kingdom in the Writings of Luke and Paul
The relationship between Spirit and Kingdom is a relatively unexplored area in Lukan and Pauline studies. This book offers a fresh perspective of two biblical writers on the subject. It explores the difference between Luke's and Paul's understanding of the Spirit by examining the specific question of the relationship of the concept of the Spirit to the concept of the Kingdom of God in each writer.
2005 / 1-84227-316-7 / approx. 270pp

Andrew C. Clark
Parallel Lives
The Relation of Paul to the Apostles in the Lucan Perspective
This study of the Peter-Paul parallels in Acts argues that their purpose was to emphasize the themes of continuity in salvation history and the unity of the Jewish and Gentile missions. New light is shed on Luke's literary techniques, partly through a comparison with Plutarch.
2001 / 1-84227-035-4 / xviii + 386pp

Andrew D. Clarke
Secular and Christian Leadership in Corinth
A Socio-Historical and Exegetical Study of 1 Corinthians 1–6

This volume is an investigation into the leadership structures and dynamics of first-century Roman Corinth. These are compared with the practice of leadership in the Corinthian Christian community which are reflected in 1 Corinthians 1–6, and contrasted with Paul's own principles of Christian leadership.

2005 / 1-84227-229-2 / 200pp

Stephen Finamore
God, Order and Chaos
René Girard and the Apocalypse

Readers are often disturbed by the images of destruction in the book of Revelation and unsure why they are unleashed after the exaltation of Jesus. This book examines past approaches to these texts and uses René Girard's theories to revive some old ideas and propose some new ones.

2005 / 1-84227-197-0 / approx. 344pp

David G. Firth
Surrendering Retribution in the Psalms
Responses to Violence in the Individual Complaints

In *Surrendering Retribution in the Psalms*, David Firth examines the ways in which the book of Psalms inculcates a model response to violence through the repetition of standard patterns of prayer. Rather than seeking justification for retributive violence, Psalms encourages not only a surrender of the right of retribution to Yahweh, but also sets limits on the retribution that can be sought in imprecations. Arising initially from the author's experience in South Africa, the possibilities of this model to a particular context of violence is then briefly explored.

2005 / 1-84227-337-X / xviii + 154pp

Scott J. Hafemann
Suffering and Ministry in the Spirit
Paul's Defence of His Ministry in II Corinthians 2:14–3:3

Shedding new light on the way Paul defended his apostleship, the author offers a careful, detailed study of 2 Corinthians 2:14–3:3 linked with other key passages throughout 1 and 2 Corinthians. Demonstrating the unity and coherence of Paul's argument in this passage, the author shows that Paul's suffering served as the vehicle for revealing God's power and glory through the Spirit.

2000 / 0-85364-967-7 / xiv + 262pp

Scott J. Hafemann
Paul, Moses and the History of Israel
The Letter/Spirit Contrast and the Argument from Scripture in 2 Corinthians 3
An exegetical study of the call of Moses, the second giving of the Law (Exodus 32–34), the new covenant, and the prophetic understanding of the history of Israel in 2 Corinthians 3. Hafemann's work demonstrates Paul's contextual use of the Old Testament and the essential unity between the Law and the Gospel within the context of the distinctive ministries of Moses and Paul.
2005 / 1-84227-317-5 / xii + 498pp

Douglas S. McComiskey
Lukan Theology in the Light of the Gospel's Literary Structure
Luke's Gospel was purposefully written with theology embedded in its patterned literary structure. A critical analysis of this cyclical structure provides new windows into Luke's interpretation of the individual pericopes comprising the Gospel and illuminates several of his theological interests.
2004 / 1-84227-148-2 / xviii + 388pp

Stephen Motyer
Your Father the Devil?
A New Approach to John and 'The Jews'
Who are 'the Jews' in John's Gospel? Defending John against the charge of antisemitism, Motyer argues that, far from demonising the Jews, the Gospel seeks to present Jesus as 'Good News for Jews' in a late first century setting.
1997 / 0-85364-832-8 / xiv + 260pp

Esther Ng
Reconstructing Christian Origins?
The Feminist Theology of Elizabeth Schüssler Fiorenza: An Evaluation
In a detailed evaluation, the author challenges Elizabeth Schüssler Fiorenza's reconstruction of early Christian origins and her underlying presuppositions. The author also presents her own views on women's roles both then and now.
2002 / 1-84227-055-9 / xxiv + 468pp

Robin Parry
Old Testament Story and Christian Ethics
The Rape of Dinah as a Case Study

What is the role of story in ethics and, more particularly, what is the role of Old Testament story in Christian ethics? This book, drawing on the work of contemporary philosophers, argues that narrative is crucial in the ethical shaping of people and, drawing on the work of contemporary Old Testament scholars, that story plays a key role in Old Testament ethics. Parry then argues that when situated in canonical context Old Testament stories can be reappropriated by Christian readers in their own ethical formation. The shocking story of the rape of Dinah and the massacre of the Shechemites provides a fascinating case study for exploring the parameters within which Christian ethical appropriations of Old Testament stories can live.

2004 / 1-84227-210-1 / xx + 350pp

Ian Paul
Power to See the World Anew
The Value of Paul Ricoeur's Hermeneutic of Metaphor in Interpreting the Symbolism of Revelation 12 and 13

This book is a study of the hermeneutics of metaphor of Paul Ricoeur, one of the most important writers on hermeneutics and metaphor of the last century. It sets out the key points of his theory, important criticisms of his work, and how his approach, modified in the light of these criticisms, offers a methodological framework for reading apocalyptic texts.

2006 / 1-84227-056-7 / approx. 350pp

Robert L. Plummer
Paul's Understanding of the Church's Mission
Did the Apostle Paul Expect the Early Christian Communities to Evangelize?

This book engages in a careful study of Paul's letters to determine if the apostle expected the communities to which he wrote to engage in missionary activity. It helpfully summarizes the discussion on this debated issue, judiciously handling contested texts, and provides a way forward in addressing this critical question. While admitting that Paul rarely explicitly commands the communities he founded to evangelize, Plummer amasses significant incidental data to provide a convincing case that Paul did indeed expect his churches to engage in mission activity. Throughout the study, Plummer progressively builds a theological basis for the church's mission that is both distinctively Pauline and compelling.

2006 / 1-84227-333-7 / approx. 324pp

David Powys
'Hell': A Hard Look at a Hard Question
The Fate of the Unrighteous in New Testament Thought

This comprehensive treatment seeks to unlock the original meaning of terms and phrases long thought to support the traditional doctrine of hell. It concludes that there is an alternative—one which is more biblical, and which can positively revive the rationale for Christian mission.

1997 / 0-85364-831-X / xxii + 478pp

Sorin Sabou
Between Horror and Hope
Paul's Metaphorical Language of Death in Romans 6.1-11

This book argues that Paul's metaphorical language of death in Romans 6.1-11 conveys two aspects: horror and hope. The 'horror' aspect is conveyed by the 'crucifixion' language, and the 'hope' aspect by 'burial' language. The life of the Christian believer is understood, as relationship with sin is concerned ('death to sin'), between these two realities: horror and hope.

2005 / 1-84227-322-1 / approx. 224pp

Rosalind Selby
The Comical Doctrine
The Epistemology of New Testament Hermeneutics

This book argues that the gospel breaks through postmodernity's critique of truth and the referential possibilities of textuality with its gift of grace. With a rigorous, philosophical challenge to modernist and postmodernist assumptions, Selby offers an alternative epistemology to all who would still read with faith *and* with academic credibility.

2005 / 1-84227-212-8 / approx. 350pp

Kiwoong Son
Zion Symbolism in Hebrews
Hebrews 12.18-24 as a Hermeneutical Key to the Epistle

This book challenges the general tendency of understanding the Epistle to the Hebrews against a Hellenistic background and suggests that the Epistle should be understood in the light of the Jewish apocalyptic tradition. The author especially argues for the importance of the theological symbolism of Sinai and Zion (Heb. 12:18-24) as it provides the Epistle's theological background as well as the rhetorical basis of the superiority motif of Jesus throughout the Epistle.

2005 / 1-84227-368-X / approx. 280pp

July 2005

Kevin Walton
Thou Traveller Unknown
The Presence and Absence of God in the Jacob Narrative
The author offers a fresh reading of the story of Jacob in the book of Genesis through the paradox of divine presence and absence. The work also seeks to make a contribution to Pentateuchal studies by bringing together a close reading of the final text with historical critical insights, doing justice to the text's historical depth, final form and canonical status.
2003 / 1-84227-059-1 / xvi + 238pp

George M. Wieland
The Significance of Salvation
A Study of Salvation Language in the Pastoral Epistles
The language and ideas of salvation pervade the three Pastoral Epistles. This study offers a close examination of their soteriological statements. In all three letters the idea of salvation is found to play a vital paraenetic role, but each also exhibits distinctive soteriological emphases. The results challenge common assumptions about the Pastoral Epistles as a corpus.
2005 / 1-84227-257-8 / approx. 324pp

Alistair Wilson
When Will These Things Happen?
A Study of Jesus as Judge in Matthew 21–25
This study seeks to allow Matthew's carefully constructed presentation of Jesus to be given full weight in the modern evaluation of Jesus' eschatology. Careful analysis of the text of Matthew 21–25 reveals Jesus to be standing firmly in the Jewish prophetic and wisdom traditions as he proclaims and enacts imminent judgement on the Jewish authorities then boldly claims the central role in the final and universal judgement.
2004 / 1-84227-146-6 / xxii + 272pp

Lindsay Wilson
Joseph Wise and Otherwise
The Intersection of Covenant and Wisdom in Genesis 37–50
This book offers a careful literary reading of Genesis 37–50 that argues that the Joseph story contains both strong covenant themes and many wisdom-like elements. The connections between the two helps to explore how covenant and wisdom might intersect in an integrated biblical theology.
2004 / 1-84227-140-7 / xvi + 340pp

Stephen I. Wright
The Voice of Jesus
Studies in the Interpretation of Six Gospel Parables
This literary study considers how the 'voice' of Jesus has been heard in different periods of parable interpretation, and how the categories of figure and trope may help us towards a sensitive reading of the parables today.
2000 / 0-85364-975-8 / xiv + 280pp

Paternoster
9 Holdom Avenue,
Bletchley,
Milton Keynes MK1 1QR,
United Kingdom
Web: www.authenticmedia.co.uk/paternoster

July 2005

www.ingramcontent.com/pod-product-compliance
Lightning Source LLC
Chambersburg PA
CBHW062013220426
43662CB00010B/1319